A History of the Irish Language

A History of the Irish Language

From the Norman Invasion to Independence

AIDAN DOYLE

OXFORD
UNIVERSITY PRESS

OXFORD

UNIVERSITY PRESS

Great Clarendon Street, Oxford, OX2 6DP,
United Kingdom

Oxford University Press is a department of the University of Oxford.
It furthers the University's objective of excellence in research, scholarship,
and education by publishing worldwide. Oxford is a registered trade mark of
Oxford University Press in the UK and in certain other countries

Published in the United States of America by Oxford University Press
198 Madison Avenue, New York, NY 10016, United States of America

British Library Cataloguing in Publication Data

Data available

Library of Congress Cataloging in Publication Data

Data available

ISBN 978-0-19-872476-6

Printed and bound by
CPI Group (UK) Ltd, Croydon, CR0 4YY

The manufacturer's authorised representative in the EU for product safety is Oxford University Press
España S.A. of El Parque Empresarial San Fernando de Henares, Avenida de Castilla, 2 – 28830 Madrid
(www.oup.es/en or product.safety@oup.com). OUP España S.A. also acts as importer into
Spain of products made by the manufacturer.

In memory of my mother, who didn't speak a word of Irish,
but who loved language

Contents

Acknowledgements

This book arose partly as a response to the lack of suitable teaching materials for a course on the history of Irish which I have been teaching for the last five years. For this reason, several groups of students have unwittingly provided me with feedback on various parts of the book which began as lecture material. I would like to acknowledge their collective assistance.

The Research Sabbatical Leave Committee of the College of Arts, Social Sciences, and Celtic Studies, University College Cork, granted me six months' leave to work on this project. I thank Graham Allen in particular for his help.

My colleagues in the School of Irish Learning, UCC, have all helped and encouraged me in this undertaking. Special thanks to Pádraig Ó Macháin for formatting the manuscript images in Chapter 2, and to Kevin Murray for his help with the index. I am also grateful to Seán Ó Coileáin, Caitríona Ó Dochartaigh, Siobhán Ní Dhonghaile, Ciara Ní Churnáin, Daragh O'Connell, Emma MacCarthy, and Jason Harris.

I would like to acknowledge the assistance of Crónán Ó Doibhlin, Mary Lombard, and Sheyeda Allen in Special Collections, Boole Library, UCC. Teresa O'Driscoll in Arts and Humanities helped me with locating and copying material. Thanks to Boole Library also for permission to publish an image from Irish Manuscript 1, and to Irish Script on Screen for making the image available.

A special word of thanks for Michael Murphy, Dept of Geography, UCC, for preparing Figures 1.1, 6.1, 6.2, and 7.1 for me. His aid enhanced the overall appearance of the book considerably.

Virve-Anneli Vihman read Chapter 6 and made many useful comments which greatly improved it.

Michelle O'Riordan prepared Figure 8.1, for which I am extremely grateful.

I would like to acknowledge the help of Arndt Wigger, who spent hours tracking down a single reference for me.

Thanks to Routledge for permission to reproduce Figures 3.1 and 4.1, taken from Diarmait Mac Giolla Chríost (2005) *The Irish language in Ireland* (London/New York: Routledge).

Figure 6.1 is based on two sources: Figure 4.3 in Diarmait Mac Giolla Chríost (2005), *The Irish language in Ireland* (London/New York: Routledge); and Map 2 in Garret Fitzgerald (1984), 'Estimates for baronies of minimum level of Irish-speaking amongst successive decennial cohorts: 1771–1781 to

1861–1871', *Proceedings of the Royal Irish Academy* C, 117–55. Thanks to Routledge and the Royal Irish Academy for permission to use these sources.

Material based on this book was presented at a conference at the University of Bristol and at a seminar at the University of Glasgow. I would like to thank the participants for their remarks.

The two anonymous reviewers chosen by OUP to referee this work have influenced the final product significantly. One was a linguist, the other a historian. While it is invidious to single out one of them, I am obliged to mention the contribution of the historian reviewer. This person went through the work with a fine comb, drawing to my attention countless errors and suggesting many substantial additions to the references; they also highlighted a number of lapses in style. I hope that the book in its final shape will meet with their approval. Any remaining errors (and clichés) are my own.

Thanks to Julia Steer and Vicki Sunter of the Linguistics section, OUP, and to production editor Kate Gilks, for their unfailing help and courtesy during the process of seeing the book through the press. Copy-editor Jeremy Langworthy spotted many errors and infelicities of style, thus improving the overall presentation considerably. I also thank Joy Mellor for reading the proofs so thoroughly.

On the personal level, the support of my father, sister, and brother was a constant source of encouragement. Last but not least, there is the person whose idea it was that I should write this book, but who does not wish to be mentioned by name. In deference to her wishes, I can only quote the refrain of the old song: *Ar Éirinn ní ineosfainn cé hí.*

List of figures

List of abbreviations

A. Publications

CS	*An Claidheamh Soluis*
D	*Irish-English Dictionary* (= Dinneen 1904)
Des	*Desiderius* (= O'Rahilly 1941)
DIL	*Dictionary of the Irish Language* (= Royal Irish Academy 1983)
GJ	*The Gaelic Journal*
HM	*An haicléara Mánas* (= Stenson 2003)
FL	*Fáinne an Lae*
OD	*Foclóir Gaeilge Béarla* [Irish-English dictionary] (= Ó Dónaill 1977)
PB	*Párliament na mban* (= Ó Cuív 1977)
PCT	*Parliement Chloinne Tomáis* (= Williams 1981)
PF	*Párliment na bhfíodóirí* (= Ó Duinnshléibhe 2011)
TST	*Teagasc ar an Sean-Tiomna* (= Ó Madagáin 1974)

B. Terms and names

EMI	Early Modern Irish
LMI	Late Modern Irish
MI	Modern Irish
NUI	National University of Ireland
SPIL	Society for the Preservation of the Irish Language

C. Labels not found in Leipzig glossing rules

EMP	emphatic
NAS	nasalized consonant
PRS	present
PRT	particle

Conventions for spelling and transcription

Since many readers will not be familiar with the International Phonetic Alphabet, an attempt is made to represent the sounds of Irish using English spelling. Individual sounds are written between slashes, e.g. 'The first sound in the Irish word *sí* is pronounced as /sh/'.

When discussing spelling, graphs are written between angled brackets, e.g. '<ph> in the Irish word *phós* is pronounced as /f/'.

When discussing the provenance of words, a single angled bracket is placed before the source, e.g. *sagart* (< *sacerdos*).

Segments of words which have a grammatical function, such as prefixes, suffixes, and endings of verbs, are written in bold, e.g. 'The ending -**ann** in the Irish word *glanann* stands for the Present Tense'.

An asterisk before a word indicates that it is ungrammatical or misspelt, e.g. *mouses, *dogz.

Titles of publications in Irish are followed by an English translation in square brackets, e.g. *Cín lae Amhlaoibh Uí Shúilleabháin* [Humphrey O'Sullivan's diary] (de Bhaldraithe 1970).

Passages in Irish are followed by an English translation in square brackets, e.g. I ndán na nGall gealltar linn [In the poem for the foreigners we promise].

Linguistic examples which are discussed are numbered. When necessary, they are glossed word for word according to the Leipzig glossing rules.

Irish words which occur throughout the text and which are commonly used in English are not written in italics, e.g. Gael, Gall, Gaeltacht. Individual Irish words are written in italics and translated, e.g. the word *dún* 'close'.

Many Irish names occur in both Irish and English variants, e.g. Douglas Hyde = Dubhghlas de hÍde. In the text, the English variant is invariably used, but the reader should bear in mind that Irish variants may occur in quotations and references. The most common duplicates are cross-referenced in the index.

Likewise, the spelling of Irish words varies depending on whether they occur in texts before or after 1950, e.g. *Gael* (new) = *Gaedhal* (old). Except in quotations and references, the post-1950 form is used.

Unless otherwise stated, all translations are the author's.

1

Introduction

1.1 Writing the history of a language

Libraries and bookshops often have sections entitled Language, or Language Studies. Within these sections one will find a number of books dealing with the history of individual languages, like English or French. These histories can be divided into two types depending on the approach taken by the author.

Internal histories deal with concrete changes that have occurred in a language over the centuries. In the case of English we can observe a major difference if we compare the Old English period (*c.*450–*c.*1150 AD) with present-day English. Old English is closely related to Old German, and many of its linguistic features can still be found in present-day German: for example, the three genders for nouns—masculine, feminine, and neuter. Present-day English no longer has this grammatical gender, and its vocabulary has expanded considerably in the last millennium, by borrowing words or creating them out of existing resources. An internal history of English would describe all of the various changes in detail, and try to account for their occurrence.

Language history is also part of history in general, it does not exist in isolation from it. External histories describe changes that take place in the communities that speak different languages, linking these changes to events in politics, culture, and social structure. If we take again the case of English, an external history would refer to the effect that the Norman invasion of England in 1066 had on its linguistic community. It would describe among other things the wholesale borrowing of words like *dinner* or *baron* from French into English in the period following the Norman invasion, linking this to the prestige enjoyed by the language of the new ruling class, Norman French. External histories also deal with such matters as bilingualism, the rise and fall of languages, and written and spoken language. In brief, one might say that external histories deal with the social aspects of language use, or sociolinguistics.

To some extent, internal and external histories are independent of each other. Thus, it is possible to provide an outline of the development of a language and its interaction with society and culture without going into details of the internal changes within the language in the same period. Likewise, one could deal with the details of linguistic change by simply stating, for example, that a certain sound or grammatical structure was replaced by another one, without linking this to non-linguistic factors. However, if we compare the internal and external development of any language, we realize that the two are closely interconnected. Change is nearly always driven by some alteration in the linguistic community.

Consider for a moment the process by which a single language, Latin, developed in the period *c.*500–*c.*1000 AD into the various individual languages which we know today as the Romance languages—French, Italian, Spanish, and Rumanian. Before the break-up, there were regional dialects of Latin which prefigured the later languages. Now, one might argue that the dialects simply diverged and leave it at that. However, it is no coincidence that this divergence coincided with a period of great upheaval in the area of the Roman empire. Until the fifth century this single administrative and cultural unit had relied on a single language, Latin, as its medium of communication. Before the fall of the western empire in 476 AD it was necessary to have a language that could be used by all its citizens for communicating, whether they were living in Britain in the far west or in Northern Africa in the Mediterranean. With the break-up of the empire into smaller regions, such distant communication was no longer necessary; one only had to deal with the inhabitants of one's own region, at least in speaking. Population movements and invasions further disrupted the former unity, and the final outcome was the emergence of different languages about 500 years after the empire broke up.

Now it is not possible to state categorically that the change of a certain sound in Latin into another sound in Spanish is specifically linked to an event such as the invasion of the Iberian peninsula by the Vandals in the fifth century. Nevertheless, it could be argued that the political upheaval was indirectly responsible for the linguistic chaos which produced the new sound. To simply concentrate on the internal linguistic development without taking into consideration the external factors constitutes a very limited approach.

Likewise, social change often has as one of its consequences linguistic change. Irish society has undergone something of a transformation in the last forty to fifty years. This has had an effect on the English spoken in Ireland. In 1950, the regional dialects of the country were quite distinct, even in the case of educated speakers. As soon as somebody opened their mouth, one could identify them as coming from a particular region such as the south-west, or the north, or Dublin. Unlike Britain, where a standard kind of English had existed for sometime, there was no standard pronunciation for Irish English.

This situation has changed dramatically in the last half century. A new dialect has emerged which one might label standard Irish English, a dialect spoken by members of the middle classes all over the country, from the heart of Dublin to the Aran Islands on the western seaboard. It is based on the metropolitan dialect which has developed in Dublin in the last fifty years or so, but it is no longer confined to this area. The rise of this standard dialect has been accompanied by the decline of the traditional regional dialects. This particular case of linguistic change is not accidental. It is a direct consequence of the spread of education, the influence of the mass media, particularly television and radio, and the urbanization of Irish society.

The present work presents aspects of both the external and internal history of Irish. However, it is not intended as a systematic study of the internal changes that Irish has undergone in the period 1200–1922. For the most part, it is concerned with the shifting position of Irish in society over the centuries, with the way it is perceived by the Irish people, and with its interaction with various historical developments in Ireland. At the same time, it seemed a good idea to provide some information about how the actual shape of the language changed in tandem with the external developments. For this reason, I also provide a brief account of the more accessible and important internal changes which affected Irish over the centuries.

In theory at least, it would be possible to write an internal history of Irish without saying much about other languages. For an external history, this is simply not possible. The history of Irish is intimately bound up with the spread of English in Ireland. This in turn is the result of a complex array of political, cultural, religious, educational, and sociological factors. An alternative title for the book might be: *A history of the Irish and English languages in Ireland*. Thus, as the narrative progresses, I will have more and more occasion to refer to the rise of English.

1.2 Dates and periods

At this stage, it is necessary to define some terms that I will be using in the course of this work. Just as general historians divide the past into various periods such as the Middle Ages or modern times, historians of language use terms like old or modern when referring to the various phases of a language's life. However, the terms used in language studies, and particularly in the history of Irish, differ somewhat from those found in general history, and often cause confusion for students and readers. For this reason, I will try to present a succinct and precise definition of the labels attached to the various periods in the history of Irish.

Before 600 AD, our picture of what Irish might have looked like is very hazy indeed. Most of what we know comes from monuments called Ogham stones from the fifth and sixth centuries. These stones are marked with lines and notches which represent the letters of the Latin alphabet. For the most part, the inscriptions consist of personal names. On the basis of the Ogham stones and some other scraps of evidence, scholars have been able to put together a tentative outline of what is known as Primitive Irish.

The period c.600–c.900 AD is labelled Old Irish. In this era, we find texts written in manuscripts, on the basis of which scholars have been able to reconstruct reasonably completely the language of the time. In the 300 years after 900, the language underwent some far-reaching changes which resulted in a new kind of Irish. For this reason, the period c.900–c.1200 is called Middle Irish. Sometimes, the whole period c.600–c.1200 is called Medieval Irish. This can be a bit misleading, because the medieval era in history lasts longer, until about 1500.

The next phase of Irish, c.1200–c.1600, has traditionally been referred to as Early Modern Irish (EMI). This label has caused a lot of confusion. For historians, the Early Modern Period does not begin until at least 1500. Furthermore, Early Modern English is the name given to the English of the two centuries c.1500–c.1700. In terms of culture, the period c.1200–c.1600 in Ireland is part of the medieval era, or the Middle Ages, and in fact there is a remarkable continuity between Middle Irish and Early Modern Irish with respect to literature.

Modern Irish (MI), sometimes called Late Modern Irish (LMI), is regarded as beginning about 1600 and extending to the present day. This more or less corresponds to the modern period in general history, and so is unlikely to cause much misunderstanding. However, some authors use Modern Irish to include Early Modern Irish as well. This leads to an unfortunate mismatch, whereby Modern Irish begins in 1200, but Modern Irish history does not start until about 1550.

In what follows, I will stick to the traditional terminology, as to do otherwise would only confuse things further, but the reader should bear in mind the somewhat idiosyncratic nature of the terms used in relation to Irish in other works.

1.3 Some sociolinguistic terminology

In the course of this book I try to minimize the amount of technical jargon. However, it will be necessary to refer to some linguistic terminology which is widely used in works of this sort. I present here the most basic concepts of sociolinguistics, and I will gradually introduce some more terms in the course of the narrative.

1.3.1 Standard languages and dialects

Most living languages occur in more than one version in the modern world. If we consider English in Ireland, we can observe that there is one version that is used in what one might call public situations. Such situations include broadcasting, education, political speeches, religious ceremonies, and to a lesser extent written literature and drama. This version of English is standard English. It has a more or less homogeneous pronunciation, grammar, and spelling. For example, if you listen to newsreaders working in RTE (the Irish public broadcasting service), their accents sound more or less the same. At school, children are taught to write in a uniform way, for example, to write *night* instead of *nite*, or *bite* instead of *bight*.

Of course, we all know that people do not speak the same way, even if they are all living in a small country. If one compares somebody from Dublin and somebody from Cork, one will notice differences between their pronunciation, their vocabulary, and even their grammar, perhaps. These variants of a language we call dialects. Dialects can be subdivided further into regional dialects, which are based on geography, and social dialects, based on social class. For example, within Dublin one can distinguish middle-class and working-class pronunciation.

If there is a standard form of language, it contrasts with non-standard varieties, which may be confined to a particular region or social class. Non-standard versions of a language are sometimes referred to as substandard, but linguists try not to use this term, as it implies that one variety is somehow better than another. In terms of language, there is nothing inherently superior about saying 'I don't know anything', rather than 'I don't know nothing'—one might even argue that the latter is more logical, and so-called double negatives are common in other languages. One construction is standard, one is non-standard. Any additional evaluation exists only in the minds of the speakers and listeners.

Standard versions of languages are a relatively recent phenomenon, and usually are the result of a centralized authority like a state or church imposing its version of a language on other people. Standards are necessary when communicating with strangers, people outside your own locality or social group. They are more used in written communication than in speaking, more in formal situations than in casual ones.

1.3.2 Language contact

As we shall see, much of our story will be concerned with the way that English and Irish have influenced each other over the centuries. Language contact is a universal and age-old phenomenon. It is triggered by situations in which one needs to communicate with speakers of another language, which leads to speakers being exposed to and perhaps learning a different language.

A typical example of language contact would be an Irish or English tourist communicating with locals in Spain. If the communication were in English, the Spanish speaker would bring some features of his own language with him into the kind of English he spoke, e.g. the Spanish pronunciation of certain vowels. It is also possible that language contact would lead to new items of vocabulary being borrowed from one of the languages to the other.

In situations of prolonged contact, some individuals or communities may be exposed to two languages from childhood onwards, which results in their speaking the two languages with similar proficiency. This proficiency is referred to as bilingualism. As one would expect, if there is widespread bilingualism in a community it can lead to fairly radical changes in one of the languages. An oft-quoted example of this kind of bilingualism is the situation in England after the Norman conquest, in the period 1100–1300. Many groups—the new government functionaries and administrators, the clergy, and the merchants—were bilingual in English and French. As a result, English borrowed a vast amount of French vocabulary in this period through language contact. The bilingualism didn't last, but it did have a permanent effect on English.

Sometimes people with a knowledge of two languages will associate them with two very different spheres of activity. A common scenario is that one language is associated with more formal activities such as teaching or writing, and the other one is used more when speaking to members of one's family or to neighbours. This kind of situation is referred to as bilingual diglossia. It is very common in post-colonial countries in Africa and Asia, where it is not unusual for people to speak a local language at home, and to speak English or French at school or at work.

Diglossia can also occur between a dialect of a language and a standard version, particularly when the two are very far from each other. In many Arab-speaking countries, there is a standard form of Arabic used in official communications, in writing, or when dealing with people from other regions, while a local dialect is spoken in everyday communication.

1.4 Sources

As with any kind of history, the history of a language is based on various sources. The further back we go in time, the scarcer these sources become, and the more difficult they are to interpret.

Generally speaking, we have more information about the external history of Irish than its internal history, or at least the statements about the former are more straightforward. Frequently, these statements come from outsiders,

English speakers who were visiting Ireland, or inhabitants of the English-speaking parts of the country. For that reason, they have to be treated with caution. However, even if the writers did not know Irish, it is safe to assume that they would have recognized Irish when they heard it being spoken, and so their statements about the numbers of speakers, or the parts of the country they inhabited, can be taken as reasonably reliable.

We also have evidence in Irish about the language. There is less of this than the English evidence, but since it provides us with a view from the inside, in some ways it is more valuable. In contrast to the English evidence, the Irish evidence tends to be a source of information about the internal history of the language. A good example is the collection of texts known as grammatical tracts (Bergin 1916–55; McKenna 1944). These were commentaries on Irish compiled in the late medieval period by professional poets, probably as a kind of manual for students of poetry. One reason that they are a valuable source for the modern historian of the language is that they often provide us with information about particular words or forms or pronunciations which are labelled as lochtach 'faulty'. The fact that the poets felt the need to warn their students about these mistakes tells us that some speakers of Irish at the time were using these 'faulty' forms in their speech, and thus we are able to deduce something about dialectal and non-standard speech at the time. Most linguistic records before the twentieth century are written in standard or prestige varieties, and hence provide us with little information about colloquial or non-standard speech. For this reason, evidence of the sort provided by the grammatical tracts is particularly precious.

While the English-language sources for the external history of Irish are well known and readily accessible, the Irish-language sources are familiar only to those who can read them, and new evidence is still being collected and published. One purpose of this book is to point readers in the direction of both kinds of source, and especially to make them aware of the Irish-language ones.

1.5 Scope and lay-out

This book is primarily concerned with what happened in the period 1200–1922. The end of the twelfth century is regarded as a defining moment in Irish history, witnessing as it did the arrival of a new group of invaders, who brought with them a language that was eventually to dislodge the one spoken until then. This, and the fact that internally Irish entered into a new phase around 1200 (Early Modern Irish), makes 1200 a natural starting-point. In Chapter 2, I include a short note on Old and Middle Irish in order to provide a context for what follows. It should be borne in mind, though, that the language of the period 600–1200 is radically different from the later language, just as Latin is quite distinct from the Romance languages into which it metamorphosed in the Middle Ages. The history of Old and Middle Irish would require a separate study.

The end-point of my narrative, 1922, is less obvious. After all, the story of Irish does not stop there; it continues right up to the present day. A number of considerations prompted me to finish my narrative at this point. First, Ireland gained independence from Britain in 1922. For the first time ever, the Irish language now had the support of the state. Second, for reasons that will become clear in Chapters 7 and 8, in the period 1870–1922 Irish entered into a new phase. Responsibility for the language passed from the hands of native speakers into the hands of learners. This in turn had a huge impact on its structure, the echoes of which can still be felt. Future historians of Irish will be faced with the task of labelling and describing the new language which is still being shaped by second-language speakers, a language which is still in the process of becoming. In some ways 1922 marks the end of Late Modern Irish, the last variety of the language to be spoken by communities as a first language, rather than as one which they learned at school. Thus there are good reasons connected with the internal history of Irish for ending the narrative in 1922.

The book is divided into an introduction and seven chapters. Each of these chapters deals with a distinct period in the history of the language. The individual chapters are followed by a conclusion which relates the preceding discussion to present-day Ireland and the place that Irish occupies in its society. Each chapter is divided into two parts. The first part deals with the external history of Irish in the period in question. The second part provides a brief and concise account of the more important internal developments that occurred in this era. The drawback of this lay-out is that there is a certain abruptness about the transition from one section to the other, with the flow of the narrative being interrupted. On the other hand, many readers will want to concentrate on one section or another, and the unambiguous signposting of the contents will facilitate this. Each chapter ends with suggestions for further reading. The works listed there will enable those who are interested to delve more fully into both the literary/cultural and linguistic aspects of the history of Irish.

Because the work is intended for a general readership, linguistic terms have been kept to a minimum, but it has been necessary to introduce a limited amount of technical jargon. Linguistic terms which are used frequently are explained in the glossary.

A brief comment is in order on the maps in the book. I have included a number of maps with the aim of showing the geographical distribution of English and

FIGURE 1.1 Map of Ireland

Irish at various stages over the centuries. Unfortunately, two-dimensional maps, while helpful, are not able to display this coexistence of two languages in one geographical region. It is important that the reader bear this point in mind when interpreting language maps, both in this book and in other works. A map of Ireland from 1200 onwards is not like a map of present-day Western Europe, where it is more or less possible to delimit German-speaking regions from French-speaking territories. Within the core German-speaking region, we know that all social classes, from the ruling elite to the unskilled labourers, speak German. This was not the case in Ireland, particularly after 1500. For example, Irish was never spoken by the power elites in Dublin and other urban centres. An alternative way of trying to visualize the distribution of English and Irish would be to think of geological layers. On the bottom we would find Irish, then there might be a transitional layer of mixed language, and on the top would be a layer of English. The essential point to remember is that the distribution of languages is not merely geographical; it is also social and ethnic. The same two languages can, and often are, spoken in the same area, but by two different social and ethnic groups. The history that I have written is more about describing these groups and their interaction than about trying to identify regions where all the population spoke only one language to the exclusion of the other.

Finally, the book is written from an Irish perspective. Dublin, rather than London or New York, is the capital city; when I write about English, I am referring to the kind of English spoken in Ireland. The last chapter is focused on present-day Ireland. Given the subject matter, this seems to be a reasonable enough approach. In the same way, one could hardly fault an author of a history of English for writing from an English perspective. A map of Ireland is provided to enable readers to identify locations referred to in the book (Figure 1.1).

Further reading

For an introduction to the study of language, see Fromkin *et al.* (2007).

For a dictionary of linguistic terminology, see Crystal (2008).

For an accessible introduction to the study of language change in general, see Chapter 11 of Fromkin *et al.* (2007).

For introductions to sociolinguistics, see Chapter 10 of Trudgill (2001) and Fromkin *et al.* (2007).

For a history of English, see Mugglestone (2006). This does not require any previous knowledge of linguistic terminology.

Ó Murchú (1985), Ó Huallacháin (1994: 10–37), and Ó hUiginn (2008) provide concise accounts of different aspects of the external history of Irish.

For a history of Irish English, see Hickey (2007).

For a comprehensive collection of English-language comments on Irish from medieval times to the twentieth century, see Crowley (2000).

2

The Anglo-Normans and their heritage (1200–1500)

2.1 The Anglo-Norman invasion

2.1.1 Before the Anglo-Normans

Our earliest detailed knowledge about Ireland and its culture comes from the period 400–600 AD, after the introduction of Christianity. The new religion brought with it the Latin language and the alphabet. Before that the language spoken by the inhabitants of Ireland had never been written down.

The Christian missionaries soon established a network of monasteries all over the country, the remains of which can be seen to the present day in places like Clonmacnoise or Glendalough. These monasteries were centres of learning, and fulfilled a similar function in society as universities do today. Because the language of the church was Latin, many of the medieval texts that have been preserved are written in this language. The subjects are for the most part religious, such as commentaries on the Bible, theological tracts, and saints' lives. Latin was also the medium chosen for secular subjects such as history, law, or medicine, and even for poetry. One advantage that Latin had over Irish was that it was an international language, understood all over Europe, much in the way that English is today. This meant that Irish clerics could correspond easily with their counterparts on the Continent, and read new works being produced in other countries. Quite a few Irish clerics went abroad to study, teach, and evangelize non-Christian peoples, using Latin as a means of communication.

By the beginning of the seventh century Irish monks had adapted the Latin alphabet for the purpose of writing down their native language. A fairly large corpus of material survives from the period c.600–c.900, enough for scholars to compile a grammar for the language of this time, Old Irish. Most of this material survives in manuscripts preserved in monasteries in Continental Europe, such as St Gall in Switzerland or Würzburg in Germany. Very often they consist of brief explanations or translations, called glosses, of Latin sentences and phrases, which are written on the margins of manuscripts.

Ireland differs from the rest of Europe in the Middle Ages in that both clerics and lay writers began to use Irish to record longer texts at a relatively early date, from the eighth century onwards; elsewhere at this time written compositions still tend to be in Latin. Many of the treasures of medieval Irish literature have survived in manuscripts written in monastic centres in the era *c.*900–*c.*1200. Much of the literature, such as the nature poems attributed to hermits, is overtly religious. However, the monastic scribes were also quite happy to write down secular, pre-Christian tales like the saga *Táin Bó Cuailgne* [Cattle Raid of Cooley]. The most important categories of prose writing recognized are historical tales, otherworld tales, heroic tales, *Fíanaigecht* (tales about the warrior band called the *Fian*), legal texts, and saints' lives.

Around the year 800, Vikings from Scandinavia and Scotland started raiding Ireland. Initially they confined themselves to brief raids, but soon they began to stay for longer spells, and eventually founded a number of urban centres around the coast, the most important of these being Dublin. For a few hundred years, we can assume that there was a small community in Ireland which spoke the language of these Vikings, Old Norse. We can also be pretty certain that there were many people who were bilingual in Irish and Old Norse. However, by 1200 the Norsemen seem to have been relatively well assimilated into the general Irish community, at least as far as language is concerned. There was some borrowing of words from Old Norse into Irish. These were mostly terms connected with warfare, sailing, and commerce. Here are some examples:

(1)   *targa* 'shield' (< *targa*), *garrda* 'enclosure, garden' (< *garðr*), *stiúir* 'rudder, helm' (< *styri*), *trosc* 'codfish' (< *Þorskr*), *margad* 'market' (< *markaðr*), *beóir* 'beer' (< *bjórr*)

Eventually the newcomers adapted themselves to their new surroundings and took on the language of the host country, just as they had done earlier in northern England, Scotland, and Normandy in France.

The 300 years following the first Viking raids was a period of social and political upheaval, with alliances being formed between the various Gaelic and Viking dynasties which were trying to assume control over large parts of the country. Linguistically, the period *c.*900–*c.*1200 is referred to as Middle Irish, because Old Irish underwent a number of drastic changes then which ultimately produced a very different language. Some scholars have speculated that the linguistic change may have been partly driven by the social turmoil of the time. While this claim cannot be decisively proved, we know in the case of other languages that political and social change is often a catalyst for linguistic developments. A case often quoted is the change which English underwent after the Norman invasion of England (the language of this period is called Middle English).

It is worth remembering that Ireland was not the only territory where Irish was spoken in 1200. Beginning in the fifth century, invaders from Ireland had settled in large numbers in Scotland. Christianity gained its first foothold on the tiny island of Iona on the western coast, and spread from there to the south-western part of the country and the Highlands. A Gaelic kingdom was established in Scotland in the ninth century. Irish gave way to English in the south of the country in the twelfth century, but remained in the Highlands and Western Isles for many centuries after that, eventually becoming a separate language called Scots Gaelic. Irish also established itself as the language of the Isle of Man around the same time that it spread to Scotland. The language which later emerged on this island is referred to as Manx.

Returning to Old and Middle Irish, it must be emphasized that they are very different from Modern Irish. One example can serve to illustrate this. Most languages have a verb expressing the concept *to fear*, and this verb is followed by a direct object denoting the cause of the fear:

(2)   I fear the Lord.

Old Irish was no exception in this regard. It too possessed a verb expressing *to fear*, which took a direct object:

(3)   intí   adagadar   in Coimdid
       the.person   who.fears   the Lord
       'he who fears the Lord'   (DIL, under the entry *ad-ágathar*)

Here, the verb *ad-agadar* 'fears' takes the direct object *in Coimdid* 'the Lord'. Now compare sentence (2) to a similar sentence in Modern Irish:

(4)   Tá   eagla   orm   roimh   an Tiarna.
       is   fear   on.me   before   the Lord
       'I fear the Lord.'

Instead of a single verb, followed by a direct object, in MI we have a construction involving the verb *to be* + noun (*eagla*) + two prepositions. So the object of the preposition *ar* 'on' in MI corresponds to the subject *I* in the English sentence *I fear the Lord*, while the object of the preposition *roimh* 'before' in MI corresponds to the English object *the Lord*. On the other hand, the structure of the Old Irish sentence (3) is more or less identical to the English equivalent: there is just a subject, verb, and object, without any prepositions.

This is only one of the many significant differences between the language before *c.*1200 and the shape it took after that date. The verbal system in particular before 1200 was highly complex, and poses considerable difficulties for the learner. Even those students with a good command of MI have to learn Old and Middle Irish from the start.

2.1.2 The Anglo-Norman conquest of Ireland

Very often, certain dates and events come to have a special significance for the history of particular countries or societies. For French people, the year 1789, the year of the French Revolution, has a special resonance. For all Europeans, 1914 and 1939, the years in which the two world wars began, have powerful associations. Countries and nations that have been occupied by other countries frequently remember the years when the occupation began or ended. In the case of Ireland, one of the dates that stands out is 1169, the year in which, according to historians, the Anglo-Normans of England invaded the neighbouring country.

In military terms, the invasion was highly successful. Within a mere six years Henry II of England had been officially recognized as the Lord of Ireland, and his Anglo-Norman warlords had gained control over much of Leinster, Munster, and Connaught. Dublin became a new centre of government and administration, the seat of the English king's representatives in Ireland. Large numbers of settlers followed in the wake of the armies and soon had established themselves in a number of urban centres: Dublin, Cork, Limerick, Waterford, Kilkenny, Cahir, Galway, and Dundalk. The influence of the new rulers could be felt in the countryside as well, where they built castles to maintain their control of the Irish chieftains.

Despite this victory, the Irish chieftains gradually rallied and began to resist the newcomers. As well as this, as time went by many of the more powerful Anglo-Norman families became virtually independent of the king of England and his representatives in Dublin. The history of the period 1200–1500 is one of intermittent wars and truces between the king of England and the Irish and Anglo-Norman lords, without either side gaining a conclusive victory. Both the Irish and the Anglo-Normans seem to have had no hesitation in changing sides if it lay in their own interests to do so. With intermarriage between the two groups, the distinctions which had initially existed between invader and invaded became blurred, especially in the south-west and west of the country, where the English influence was weaker than it was closer to Dublin.

The Anglo-Normans brought with them a different social and legal system, and tried to impose it on the parts of the country under their control. Apart from the towns and cities, only in two regions can they be said to have succeeded in permanently establishing English law and customs. One was the Pale, the district comprising County Dublin and parts of Counties Louth,

Meath, Kildare, and Wicklow. The other was the south-east of Ireland, in County Wexford, the place where the invaders had landed in 1169. In the rest of Ireland, there was either a mixture of Irish and English law, or Irish law only.

From the point of view of this book, the main importance of the Anglo-Norman conquest of Ireland was the fact that it brought a new element into the linguistic landscape of the country, namely the English language.

2.1.3 The linguistic and cultural impact of the conquest

The group of people that invaded and settled Ireland in the period 1100–1200 was mixed in terms of language. Some of the aristocratic leaders like Richard de Clare or Hugh de Lacy spoke Norman French as well as English, but most of the soldiers and settlers were English speakers. For the next hundred years or so many French-speaking administrators and noblemen were sent over to Ireland to represent the interests of the king of England. A few pieces of literature in Norman French dealing with events in Ireland have survived from the thirteenth and fourteenth centuries. Despite this limited evidence for writing in French, it seems safe to say that by 1350 the new colonists of Ireland were nearly all solidly Anglophone. Like in England, French continued to be used for a few centuries more in legal and administrative affairs, but this was mostly at the written level. However, French did survive for a while as a spoken *lingua franca* in commercial transactions among the merchant families of the coastal towns who traded with the Continent, and was used among certain aristocratic circles and in some religious orders.

In the period 1200–1500, the English speakers were more or less confined to those areas under the control of the crown. We have good evidence that English was spoken in the main towns and cities, in the Pale, and in the south-east. It was also spoken to some extent in Anglo-Norman households outside these areas, by noble families like the Fitzgeralds of Desmond in the south of the country, or the Burkes of Clanricarde in the west. We know also that Irish still continued to be spoken by many of the inhabitants of the Pale, and even of Dublin. We can assume, then, that there must have been a high degree of bilingualism in those areas of the country where the writ of English law ran.

2.1.4 Hibernicis ipsis Hiberniores

As time went by, many of the Anglo-Norman families became Gaelicized and took on Irish language and customs. Writing of this development, the seventeenth-century historian John Lynch remarked that they became *Hibernicis ipsis Hiberniores* 'more Irish than the Irish themselves'.

We can illustrate this with a verse from a poem written in the fourteenth century by a leading poet of the day, Gofraidh Fionn Ó Dálaigh:

I ndán na nGall gealltar linn
Gaoidhil d'ionnarba a hÉirinn;
Goill do shraoineadh tar sál sair
i ndán na nGaoidheal gealltair.
[In the poem for the foreigners we promise that the Irish will be driven from
Ireland; in the poem for the Irish we promise that the foreigners will be
scattered eastwards across the sea.]

(Mac Cionnaith 1938: 206)

This verse is instructive for a number of reasons. First, it comes from a poem
written for Gerald, the Earl of Desmond, an important Anglo-Norman lord
from Munster (in the south of Ireland). It would suggest that Gerald and
people of his class felt comfortable speaking Irish; not only that, but they
actively embraced native cultural forms of expression such as poetry
and music. Second, in this poem we find the terms Gael (Gaoidheal) and
Gall juxtaposed.[1] The former refers to what we would nowadays call the Gaelic
inhabitants of Ireland, the latter to the descendants of the invaders, the Anglo-
Normans. Both groups speak Irish, but there is the implication in the poem
that there is an ethnic difference between them, a difference that at times
found expression in actual armed conflict.

The terms Gael and Gall survived the downfall of the Gaelic aristocracy in
the seventeenth century, and are widespread in the poetry of the period
1600–1850. In this latter period, though, there is a very clear divide between
the two groups. The Gael represents the ethnic, linguistic, cultural, and
religious values that the later poets identified with, while the Gall stands for
all that is alien and opposed to those values. In the fourteenth-century poem
by Gofraidh Fionn Ó Dálaigh, though, the poet does not identify with the
Gael. Both the Anglo-Norman lord and the Gaelic chief are potential patrons
for the poet. He acknowledges that there are differences between the two kinds
of patron, but the overall impression is that they are part of the same cultural
and linguistic milieu.

In his book *Mere Irish and Fíor-Ghael*, Joep Leersen points out that Gerald
the Earl of Desmond also wrote poems in Irish, and that in one of them he uses
the term *Éireannach* 'Irishman' to refer to the inhabitants of Ireland (Leersen
1996a: 169). Unlike Gael or Gall, *Éireannach* is not an ethnic name, but one
that refers merely to the country of residence. In Leersen's view, this shows
that some of the Anglo-Normans felt a strong affinity between themselves and
their Gaelic neighbours.

---

[1] Note that Gaeil is the plural of Gael, while Gaill is the plural of Gall.

There is other, more prosaic, evidence that the degree of assimilation of the Anglo-Normans was indeed far-reaching. One of the more important centres of royal rule and administration in medieval Ireland was the city of Kilkenny. In 1366 during a session there of the royal parliament of Ireland, a piece of legislation called the Statutes of Kilkenny was enacted. In these statutes, the legislators advert to the Gaelicization of the Anglo-Normans: 'But now many English of the said land, forsaking the English language, manners, mode of riding, laws and usages, live and govern themselves according to the manners, fashion and language of the Irish enemies' (Curtis and McDowell 1943: 52; quoted in Crowley 2000: 14). As a corrective, they recommend the following: 'It is ordained that every Englishman do use the English language, and be named by an English name... and use the English custom, fashion, mode of riding and apparel... It is ordained that the men of Ireland do not use the plays which men call hurling' (Curtis and McDowell 53; quoted in Crowley 2000: 14).

As far as we can tell, for the next 150 years the Statutes of Kilkenny were more honoured in the breach than in the observance. One might argue that the Norman conquest had as little impact on the linguistic landscape of Ireland as it had earlier on that of England. In both cases, it seemed, after an initial period when the language of the conquerors held sway, after a while the invaders adopted the language of the country. In England French yielded to English, while in Ireland English gave way to Irish.

However, this does not mean that English did not influence Irish in the centuries following the Anglo-Norman invasion. On the contrary, it made its presence strongly felt through an activity which seems to always thrive in situations where two languages are confronted with each other, namely translation. Large amounts of material were translated from English into Irish in this period. The texts translated are representative of the kind of material to be found all over Europe at the time: they comprise Romance tales such as those connected with King Arthur and his knights, as well as sermons, lives of saints, medical tracts, and travel books like the account of Marco Polo's visit to China.

On the spoken level, there must have been quite a lot of interpreting going on between the different linguistic communities, especially in spheres of activity such as trade. All this translation, both written and spoken, meant that there was considerable enrichment of the vocabulary of the Irish language, and also that the intellectual life of the literate Irish classes was enhanced. Comparing Ireland to the rest of Europe at the time, we get the impression of a language and society that is fully keeping pace with overseas developments. This contact with other countries would have been facilitated by the presence in Ireland of religious orders like the Franciscans, who had strong links with Britain and the Continent. Irish brothers and monks were constantly travelling abroad, bringing back with them knowledge of other cultures, a knowledge which found its way into the written texts produced in Irish in this period.

2.2 The shape of the language (1200–1500)

2.2.1 Early Modern Irish and Modern Irish

As mentioned in Chapter 1, it is common practice to refer to the language of the period 1200–1500 as Early Modern Irish (EMI). This might suggest that it is not that different from Modern Irish (MI), the language taught in schools in Ireland to the present day. There is some truth in this: if we compare the earlier language to the Irish that some readers will be familiar with from their schooldays, we can observe a remarkable degree of similarity.

Let's start off with a simple sentence, *The man kisses the woman*, in EMI and in MI:

(5) a. Póg-aidh   an fear   an mnaoi.   (EMI)
        kiss-es   the man   the woman

     b. Póg-ann   an fear   an bhean.   (MI)
        kiss-es   the man   the woman

The three key words here are *póg* 'kiss', *fear* 'man', and *bean* 'woman'. Two of them are the same in a. and b.: *póg* and *fear*. The only word in EMI that looks different from MI is *mnaoi*. The other big difference is the ending of *póg* 'kiss'. In MI it is **-ann**, while in EMI it is **-aidh**. In order to illustrate how the difference came about I need to use a little bit of technical terminology.

Words like *fear* 'man' and *bean* 'woman' are called nouns; they name some entity. Nouns can appear in different forms depending on the context. In English, we use the form *cat* (singular) when there is only one animal involved, and *cats* (plural) when there is more than one present in the discourse. There is a change in form from *cat* → *cats*, indicated by the presence of **-s**, but we are still talking about the same animal. The change in meaning might be described as grammatical, in the sense that we are not changing the object of discourse, merely providing some extra information about it. Languages which exploit this device a lot are called (highly) inflected languages.

Nouns can have different roles depending on their place in a sentence. A noun may be the entity initiating the action, or the entity being acted upon. If the former, we say it is the subject, if the latter, the object. Now in English, the same form is used for subject and object:

(6)   a. The man kisses the woman. (*woman* is object)
    b. The woman kisses the man. (*woman* is subject)

The same is true for MI:

(7)   a. Pógann   an fear   an bhean.   (*bean* is object)
          kisses   the man   the woman
          'The man kisses the woman.'

    b. Pógann   an bhean   an fear.   (*bean* is subject)
          kisses   the woman   the man
          'The woman kisses the man.'

All that distinguishes the subject from the object in MI is its position in the sentence.

EMI is more inflected than MI. Some nouns, when they are objects, take on a different form from when they are subjects. One such noun is *bean* 'woman'. When it is the subject, it is *bean*, just as in the modern language:

(8)   Pógaidh   an bhean   an fear.
      kisses   the woman   the man
      'The woman kisses the man.'

But when it is the object, it changes to *mnaoi*, as in (5a) above. So sometimes the inflection, the actual form of the noun, tells us what the semantic role is.

Another kind of word which takes on many different grammatical forms in the Irish of this time is the verb. In English, we usually need separate words like *I*, *you* and *he/she* to tell us who is doing the action (the person). These words like *I* and *you* are called pronouns. In English, the ending of the verb only changes once, when we have a subject who is a third party (not the speaker or the person being spoken to), and this subject is singular:

(9)   *clean*
      Singular   Plural
   1 I clean   we clean
   2 you clean   you clean
   3 he/she/Susan cleans   they clean

Obviously, we need a word like *I* or *you* for most verbs, or we wouldn't be able to figure out who was doing the action from the form alone. If we just said *clean*, the subject could be *I*, *you*, *we*, *you* pl, or *they*. This system for dealing with the person of the verb, whereby it is combined with a pronoun, is called analytic inflection. It's as if the verb is analysed (broken down) into two parts—the verb proper and the pronoun.

Some languages have a separate form for each person of the verb. We can observe this in Italian, for instance:

(10)   *comprare* 'buy'
        Singular   Plural
    1 compr-o 'I buy'   compr-iamo 'we buy'
    2 compr-i 'you buy'   compr-ate 'you buy'
    3 compr-a 'he/she buys'   compr-ano 'they buy'

Here, the endings tell us what person we are talking about: the -**o** in *compro* tells us that it is the first-person sg (*I*), so we don't need the pronoun *I* as well. Verbs which conform to the Italian system are called synthetic verbs—the verb and the ending are synthesized, or brought together.

MI is half-way between English and Italian in terms of the shape its verbs take. In the first-person sg and pl, we have an ending:

(11)   *glan* 'clean'
        Singular   Plural
    1 glan-aim 'I clean'   glan-aimid 'we clean'

This is like Italian: the ending -**aimid** for the plural tells us that the subject is *we*; there is no need for a separate pronoun as well. For the other persons, though, the system is like English. We find one verbal form *glanann*, and separate pronouns for the persons:

(12)   Singular   Plural
    2 glanann tú 'you clean'   glanann sibh 'you clean'
    3 glanann sé/sí 'he/she cleans'   glanann siad 'they clean'

In EMI, on the other hand, all the persons of the verb have separate endings, as in Italian:

(13)   Singular   Plural
    1 glan-aim 'I clean'   glan-maid 'we clean'
    2 glan-ae 'you clean'   glan-taoi 'you clean'
    3 glan-aidh 'he/she cleans'   glan-aid 'they clean'

As in Italian, the endings provide the information about who is doing the cleaning, so that we find the verb and the person all in one single word.

When we have a noun subject like *an bhean* 'the woman', or *an fear* 'the man', we can observe a further difference between MI and EMI. In MI, the common form ending in -**ann** is found with a noun subject, whether it is singular or plural:

(14) a. Glan-ann   an fear   an seomra.
          clean-PRS   the man   the room
          'The man cleans the room.'

      b. Glan-ann   na fir   an seomra.
          clean-PRS   the men   the room
          'The men clean the room.'

In EMI, when the subject is singular, the verb is singular, when the subject is plural, the verb is plural:

(15) a. Glan-aidh   an fear   an seomra.
          clean-PRS.3SG   the man   the room
          'The man cleans the room.'

      b. Glan-aid   na fir   an seomra.
          clean-PRS.3PL   the men   the room
          'The men clean the room.'

This matching between the singular noun and the singular verb, and between the plural noun and the plural verb, is called agreement. We can describe the difference between MI and EMI in terms of agreement: in EMI there is agreement between subject and verb, while in MI there is none.

These are only some of the most striking differences between MI and EMI, differences in inflection. There has been a huge reduction in the number of forms in Irish for nouns and verbs since EMI, so that in one sense it is easier to learn the modern language. The student who is approaching EMI for the first time has to master a multitude of forms, which obviously makes the task much more difficult.

2.2.2 Spelling and pronunciation

Rules for writing were not standardized for Irish until the twentieth century, so that the printed versions that we have nowadays of medieval texts are the result of editing. The scribes of the time simply wrote as they saw fit. We can see this if we look at a verse of poetry as it appears in the original manuscript (Figure 2.1).

The first thing that catches our eye is that the letters are written differently from nowadays; in fact, it almost looks as if the alphabet were different. This is not actually so, it is simply the case that scribes shaped the letters differently in the Middle Ages. Copying a long passage was a laborious task, and medieval scribes used short-cuts, just as we use short-cuts today when texting. The Irish name for a contraction of this kind is *nod*. You can see some examples of these contractions in Figure 2.2.

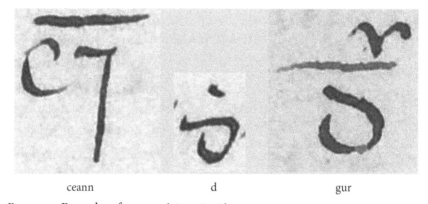

FIGURE 2.1 Quatrain from University College Cork, Irish MS 1, p. 6
Source: Irish Script on Screen (http://www.isos.dias.ie/)

ceann	d	gur

FIGURE 2.2 Examples of manuscript contractions

The first stage in editing a manuscript is to decipher the original spelling, and write the contractions out in full. With our manuscript this is relatively easy, as the scribe wrote clearly and the contractions are unambiguous. With older manuscripts, though, the modern editor has to struggle with ink-stains and other extraneous marks, with careless copying, and even with missing pages. A first transcription of the verse might look like this:

(16) Olc do thaigrais athorna
        ge bheith dfeabhas healadhna
        tar ceann leithe mogha muigh
        re niall cosgrach a ccrúachain

This first version, where the spelling of the scribe is reproduced exactly, is called a diplomatic edition. It is certainly an advance on the original, in that we can make out recognizable letters. But even for somebody who knows EMI well, it is hard to make sense of this version. That is because in modern printed texts in all languages, not just Irish, there are various conventions which help the reader make sense of what they are reading. For instance, proper nouns, names of people and places, are written with capitals. Then there are language-specific spelling rules. In the case of Irish, these were only established in the last hundred years. One convention is that short grammatical words like *the* or *a* are kept separate from other words. Thus *an* 'the' is separated from the noun that follows it, even though in speech the two seem to form a single unit. In MI we write *an fear* 'the man', not **anfear*. In the manuscripts, though, it is not uncommon to find the two written as a single word, and often the <a> of *an* is written as <i>, *so that we get infear for MI an fear*.

Returning to our quatrain in Figure 2.1, we know from other sources that a personal name *Torna* existed in the medieval period. When addressing somebody in Irish, we use a particle *a* before the name, e.g. *a Mháire!* 'oh Mary!' This, and our knowledge of the conventions of the scribes, enables us to rewrite the ending of the first line, so that we arrive at *a Thorna* for *athorna*. We are now beginning to make progress, we know that the poet is addressing somebody called Torna. Applying the same kind of process to the other lines of the verse, we can bring them into line with modern conventions for writing, and produce a version which is more or less intelligible to somebody who has studied EMI and is familiar with its grammar and vocabulary. In the final version, called a normalized edition, punctuation marks have been introduced, and words spelled in keeping with modern rules:

(17) Olc do thagrais, a Thorna,
    gé bheith d'fheabhas t'ealadhna,
    tar ceann Leithe Mogha amuigh,
    re Niall coscrach i gCruachain.
    [Despite your great learning, Torna, you pleaded badly on behalf of Leath Mogha with triumphant Niall from Cruachain.]

It should be noted that there are limits to how far one can go with normalizing a text. For example, in the case of Figure 2.1 above, it contains the word *ealadhna*, which is spelled *ealaíona* in modern dictionaries. The reason for not totally modernizing it is that the metrical scheme of EMI demands that it should be spelled in the old way. The old spelling indicates that the second syllable (-**ladh**-) has a short vowel, which is necessary for the metre. This effect would be lost if it were spelled *ealaíona*, with a long vowel (-**laí**-) in the second syllable. Note also that I have only dealt with one short, simple example of editing; with whole poems of fifty or more quatrains, often an editor will have to decide whether to change what was written by the original scribe or to leave it as it is. While there are general guidelines for editing, to some extent it involves subjective choices.

I have dwelt on the issue of manuscripts and editing because so much of written Irish was in manuscript form until the twentieth century, and we are only in the process of discovering what these manuscripts contain. It is important for the modern reader always to bear in mind that what we read in printed form is the result of choices made by editors over the years, and that the rules and conventions which guide them are arbitrary, and are constantly changing.

In my exposé of the structure of EMI, I have not yet touched on the most basic aspect of the language, namely pronunciation. Unfortunately, we can only form tentative proposals for EMI compared to what is possible for the twentieth century, when machine recordings of real speech became available for the first time. The poems of the EMI period were written in strict metre, with rhyme between the ends of the lines and assonance (vowel rhyme) between individual words, and with a fixed number of syllables in each line. The pronunciation demanded by the verse was conservative, in that it was often based on spelling rather than on the speech of the day. Spelling often lags far behind developments in the spoken language. In English, for example, we still write a <k> at the beginning of the word *knight*, even though this <k> has not been pronounced since at least the seventeenth century. In Irish in the period 1200–1500, many consonant sounds disappeared when they occurred between vowels. For instance, the word *croidhe* 'heart' originally had two syllables, with the <dh> in the middle being pronounced like the initial sound in British English *the*, so that the whole would have sounded something like /krithe/. By the fourteenth century the <dh> sound had disappeared and the vowel preceding it had been lengthened to /ee/. However, the spelling reflects the old pronunciation, and this pronunciation was maintained in the poetry. A word like *croidhe* would thus count as two syllables in verse, whereas its modern counterpart *croí* /kree/ has only one syllable. This is why modern editions of medieval poetry often retain the old spelling.

2.2.3 Classical Irish

In the introduction, I adverted to the fact that nowadays, many languages exist in two forms. One is the standard dialect, used in writing and in the public domain. The other form consists of regional and social dialects, usually associated with a more informal, spoken domain.

If we think of standard English in the twenty-first century, we can distinguish four main divisions of language where standardization might apply. These are:

a. pronunciation
b. grammar
c. vocabulary
d. spelling.

Grammar and spelling are often acquired at school. For example, a child who hears 'I done it' at home might be corrected by their teacher, and told to say 'I did it.' In the same way, speakers of English are taught to write in a certain way, regardless of how a word is pronounced. Both *though* and *enough* end with the letters <gh>, even though in one case the <gh> is not pronounced, and in the other it is pronounced as /f/.

With pronunciation, the school instruction is usually less explicit, so children acquire their accent from other sources. In Chapter 1, I mentioned the existence of standard Irish English pronunciation, based on middle-class Dublin speech. This pronunciation is absorbed through exposure to the speech of people in positions of influence, people such as broadcasters, politicians, and increasingly media celebrities of all sorts. However, this pronunciation is not explicitly taught at Irish schools. Similarly, with respect to vocabulary, there is no dictionary of Irish words in general use. Speakers of Irish English use British English dictionaries, even though they may also use some individual words and constructions which are specifically Irish. A case in point is the so-called *after*-perfect, as in the sentence *I'm after reading the newspaper* ('I have read the newspaper'), which is found in all regions and social classes in Ireland. Some Irish words have even enjoyed international careers, such as the word *feck* (mild expletive), which caught on with British TV viewers after the success of the series *Father Ted*.

From this brief discussion, we can see that in order for a standard to come into being, some kind of institution must exist which codifies and promotes a particular variety of language. In modern France, the Académie Française tries to regulate the French language, introducing various rules which accept certain linguistic forms and reject others. Ireland in the late Middle Ages did not have an academy of this sort, but it did have a highly organized and articulate literary class. These were the *filí* (pl of *file*). The word *file* is often translated as 'poet' or 'bard', but a *file* in the twelfth century was much more than a modern-day poet—he was more like a journalist, in that his task was to comment on current events which were of importance for his community. It is true that the *filí* wrote in verse, but the subject matter was not personal. First and foremost they celebrated the deeds of the dynasty they were attached to.

The *file* was employed by a patron, the local chieftain, to praise him and his family, to enumerate his illustrious ancestors, and to mourn his death. The poems produced were highly conventional, and were written in special metres. The language of the poems is based on the spoken language of *c.*1200, but it represents a high register. In the same way, nowadays the language of academic discourse is based on everyday speech, but differs from it in the kind of vocabulary and constructions it uses. The name given to the verse produced in this period is Bardic poetry.

The *fili* were an extremely influential group in society, and it was they who set the written standard for Irish. Poetry was a profession, usually handed down from father to son, and required a special linguistic training, which was provided in schools of poetry. Some manuals for the use of students have survived, called grammatical tracts (Bergin 1916–55; McKenna 1944), and these enable us to form some kind of picture of the language used in poetry. Scholars who have edited and deciphered these grammatical tracts comment on the fact that they provided a standard for the writing of poetry: 'As to how this standard was formed we have no information, but from about the beginning of the thirteenth century it must have been taught in all the schools, for the same dialect is found in all scholastic verse written in Ireland till the middle of the seventeenth century' (Bergin 1938: 207).

The standardization recommended by the grammatical tracts manifested itself mostly in the area of grammar, and specifically in the form that certain words take, what I called inflection in the previous section (2.2.1). Thus, the tracts provided information about the various forms of the noun and verb for the students of poetry, and thanks to this we are able to form a picture of nominal and verbal inflection in EMI. What is interesting about these tracts is that often the compiler labels the examples given as either *cóir* 'correct' or *lochtach* 'faulty'. Now, the so-called *lochtach* forms were not learners' mistakes; they were produced by native speakers of Irish. This means that they must have been common in speech. Consider once again example (5a) from section 2.2.1:

(5a) Pógaidh   an fear   an mnaoi.
     Kisses   the man   the woman

mnaoi is the form prescribed by the grammars when *bean* is the object of the verb, and the form *bean* is prohibited, labelled as *lochtach*. However, we know from prose sources that the old form *mnaoi* was disappearing as early as 1200 (Jackson 1990; McManus 1994b). So, using today's terminology, we could say that the form labelled *cóir* represents the written standard, and that labelled *lochtach* the spoken dialect.

In other cases, two different versions of a word are accorded the same status by the grammatical tracts, being regarded as acceptable variants. We can see this in the case of the verb. Recall that in section 2.2.1 we noted that there are two possibilities for expressing the person of a verb, either with a pronoun as in English, or with an ending, as in Italian. Some MI dialects resemble English in this regard, while others are closer to the Italian model. The same must have been true of dialects in the period 1200–1500, because the grammatical tracts explicitly allow students of poetry the choice of using one system or the other:

(18)   *glan*—first-person sg Past Tense

    a. do   ghlan-as   (ending)
       PST clean-1sg

    b. do   ghlan mé (separate pronoun)
       PST clean I
       'I cleaned'

Since the twentieth century, there has been an ongoing dispute in progress about which of the modern dialects of Irish is the oldest and purest. One of the criteria advanced for classifying a given dialect as older than another was the presence of the synthetic verbal system rather than the analytic one—synthetic verbal systems were considered by some scholars to be superior to analytic ones. As can be seen, neither system had precedence in EMI, which undermines spurious claims about one dialect being older, and hence better, than another. The truth is that all of the modern dialects contain traces of the older language. This is one reason why it is important to study the history of Irish— it enables us to form balanced and rational judgements about the shape of the modern language, by separating genuine linguistic facts from language myths.

As can be seen, then, there was a certain amount of flexibility in the grammatical tracts with respect to what was and what wasn't allowed. This has led scholars to claim that the language of Bardic poetry is the result of 'the formal adoption of vernacular speech as the basis for a new literary standard' (Ó Cuív 1973: 130). Some qualification is needed for this statement. As McManus (1994b) shows in detail, various strands were present in Bardic poetry and the grammatical tracts, some of which were conservative, some innovatory. Certainly, some of the rules reflect innovations in the spoken language, and other rules allow for both old and new forms. But many of the guidelines are conservative, and exclude developments taking place in the spoken language. Of course, as pointed out by McManus (1994b), one reason for retaining obsolete forms was that they gave the writers greater flexibility when writing verse, where one is confined by the demands of the metre. In any case, regardless of what the situation may have been in 1200, when the rules for writing poetry had been laid down, by 1500 the spoken language had changed considerably, just as the English of 2013 differs from the English of 1713. As a result, by the beginning of the sixteenth century, a typical Bardic poem would have been pretty unintelligible to anybody who hadn't received a special education in the language and metres found in this kind of writing.

We also have to bear in mind that poetry can never be said to be typical of the language as a whole, because it is an artificial creation. The composers of Bardic poetry were under pressure to conform to very strict metres and rhyming schemes. This led them to rearrange the normal word order of sentences. Consider the following couplet:

(19) Flaitheas   nach   gabhaid   Gaoidhil
      sovereignty   that.not   possess   Gaels
      geallmaid   dóibh   i nduanlaoidhibh.
      we.promise   to.them   in poems
      'We promise a sovereignty which the Irish do not possess to them in poems.'

                                                  (Mac Cionnaith 1938: 206)

In Irish, the verb normally comes first in the sentence, followed by the subject (if there is one), followed by the object, followed by the rest of the sentence. So the above verse, in normal prose, would read:

(20) Verb   Object   Rest
      Geallmaid   flaitheas nach gabhaid Gaoidhil dóibh i nduanlaoidhibh.
      we.promise sovereignty which the Irish   to them in poems
                  don't possess

Even when written like this, it still is difficult for the modern reader to make sense of the whole, but at least the verb and object are in the right place in the prose version, whereas in the poetry they have been moved about. In the same way, the English poet Milton uses a highly unnatural word order in *Paradise Lost*:

(21)   Of Mans First Disobedience … sing Heav'nly Muse

The normal word order at the time (seventeenth century) would have been:

(22)   Sing, Heav'nly muse, of Mans First Disobedience

In other words, poetry of any period in any language does not give us a very good idea of how people actually spoke, and this is especially true of Bardic poetry.

The Irish poets also had to make use of a highly stylized vocabulary, which made reference to figures from literature and mythology. There were set ways of describing such things as the appearance of the chieftain, or the place where he lived. The more allusive the approach and the less direct it was, the better, as far as the poets were concerned. One ornament that the bards were particularly fond of was compounding. This consists in putting two (or more) words together to make a new one, e.g. *black-board, house-wife*. Some of the compounds we find in Bardic verse are transparent, in that we can easily guess their meaning:

(23)   Compound   Meaning
    a. bog-chroidhe   soft heart
       soft-heart

    b. trom-ghonaidh   wounds heavily
       heavy-wounds

Very often, though, the two original elements are harder to discern, because of certain sound processes which take place at the juncture of the words which change the spelling:

(24) Original elements   Compound   Meaning
    deoch + gear   dig-géar   bitter drink
    drink + bitter
    bean + liaigh   beinliaigh woman doctor
    woman + doctor

In other cases, it takes the reader a while to work out the meaning:

(25)   Compound   Meaning
    a. barr-úr-thais   'with fresh and damp hair'
       head-fresh-damp

    b. Tadhg-mhac   'Tadhg the son'
       Tadhg-son

    c. ceann-las   'to light above'
       head-light

Because it was a vehicle of literary expression for 400 years, and because relatively little prose was written in the same period, this Bardic poetry has acquired a privileged status in the history of Irish. This is a common enough occurrence cross-linguistically. For reasons having more to do with literary achievement or the cultural influence of particular authors, certain varieties of language come to possess an authority that leads to them being held up as examples of how to write or speak. The best-known case of this in the Western world is Latin. Because of their political and cultural influence, writers like Cicero, Caesar, and Vergil came to be regarded as representing the last word in

Latin style and elegance, and the language found in their writings came to be called classical Latin. This classical Latin was based on the speech of educated Romans in the first century BC. Latin continued to be spoken for another 600–700 years after that, undergoing many changes in the meantime, but the written language taught in schools in late antiquity continued to be the same classical standard of the first century BC. When the study of Latin received a new impetus during the Renaissance, emphasis was placed once again on authors like Cicero, Caesar, and Vergil, and this tradition has remained with us right up to the present day.

The language of Bardic poetry is often referred to as classical Irish, because like classical Latin, its form remained unchanged for centuries. With respect to the study of Irish after 1200, classical Irish occupies a position not unlike that of classical Latin. The following passage is illustrative of the attitudes of present-day scholars to the language used in Bardic poetry:

From its creation in or around the thirteenth century to the middle of the seventeenth century classical Modern Irish was the subject of intense study by the Irish literati, in particular by the professional poets, whose genre it served. Never before (or since for that matter) had a more strictly regulated and beautifully balanced medium been devised for a specific task, and the Bardic grammarians guarded it jealously. As the vehicle for what, at that time at least, was the only cultivated medium, viz. verse, and the bread and butter of the learned classes in the form of the Bardic ode, classical Modern Irish was held in the highest esteem.

(McManus 1996: 165)

However, in a different work McManus (1994a), the author of the above passage, makes the point that classical Irish does not reflect the changes that were taking place in spoken Irish in the late Middle Ages. Spoken language is constantly changing, and Irish and Latin are no exceptions. What complicates the picture for these two languages is that the high status of a particular written variety meant that it was a long time before changes in speech made their presence felt in writing.

Fortunately, there is another source for EMI besides Bardic poetry, namely prose. Non-verse texts provide valuable evidence for the changes taking place in the language at the time, as we shall see in the next section.

2.2.4 The non-classical language

On the whole, prose tends to offer a better reflection of ordinary language than poetry. However, a word of caution must be sounded even here with respect to Irish. Because of the authority of tradition, many medieval scribes tried to make their texts look older than they were by employing outmoded grammatical forms. The effect was similar to what would happen if somebody living in

Ireland in the twenty-first century tried to write a text in what they thought was medieval English. In some cases the forms would be genuinely medieval, in others they would not. But one way or another, the result would not faithfully mirror English as spoken and written in the second decade of the twenty-first century. So we find a whole range of styles in medieval Irish texts. At one end of the scale we have archaizing texts, which deliberately use linguistic forms which are out of date. At the other end of the scale are pieces of prose which reflect contemporary usage. In the majority of cases, however, we find a mixture of the two styles.

Thanks to the work of modern editors of the medieval texts, we are in a position to judge which linguistic features are archaizing, and which might be described as reflecting the language of the time that they were written down. McManus (1994a) divides prose texts of EMI into two groups: those which more or less reflect the changes taking place in the language, and those which employ an artificial, pseudo-archaic style. There was a complex array of factors which influenced the choice of style, including the intended audience: if a text was meant to be read aloud to uneducated listeners, then it tended to reflect the changes taking place in the spoken language. One text which is relatively modern is *Smaointe beatha Chríost* [Meditations on the life of Christ], a translation from Latin of *Meditationes vitae Christi*, carried out sometime between 1430 and 1460. Here is an extract:

(26)   Ó, a Mhic milis díl, ca fuile, ocus cad do-ní, ocus cad is fuirech duit? Ocus guidim sibh, uair is ibh mu Mhac ocus m'Athuir ocus mu Maithius uile, ar ghradh Dia, mas edh, na cuir ar cairdi mé. Uair do gealluis éirghi an tres la, ocus cuimhnigh gurab e aniugh an tres lá, ocus nach e ane.

         [Oh, dear sweet son, where are you, and what are you doing, and what is keeping you? And I beseech you, since you are my Son and my Father and my whole Good, for the love of God, therefore, do not keep me waiting. For you promised to rise on the third day, and remember that today is the third day, and not yesterday.]

                                                                    (Ó Maonaigh 1944: 175)

For someone who knows MI, the above passage is partially intelligible. The biggest problem is the spelling, which has not been altered by the editor, but left just as the scribe wrote it. Thus, length marks which we would expect nowadays have been omitted over many of the vowels, e.g. *ane* 'yesterday' in the last line, which would be spelled *inné* now. Likewise, the markers of lenition and eclipsis (changes to initial consonants) are for the most part absent, e.g. in l.3 *do gealluis* 'you promised' for *do gheallais* (MI), where the lenition of the /g/ after the particle *do* is indicated in spelling by the insertion of <h>. Likewise, some grammatical forms used in the text are no longer to be found, like the synthetic *bhfuile* 'you are', instead of *bhfuil tú* (MI) in l.1. But the gist of the piece is more or less clear for a reader of MI.

In order for us to get a glimpse of how Irish had changed between *c.*1200 and *c.*1450, when *Smaointe beatha Chríost* was translated, it is worthwhile making a brief comparison between the above passage and one from late Middle Irish—that is, the period when EMI was coming into being. Here is a sentence from the late Middle Irish text *Merugud Uilix maicc Leirtis* [The wanderings of Ulysses son of Laertes]:

(27) Ocus   fúaratar   caerch-u   ollacha   móraidbli
      and   they.got   sheep-PL.ACC   wooly   big.huge
      ocus   ro   marbsatar trí   caerchu   dib.
      and   PST   they.killed three   sheep   of.them
'And they got big huge wooly sheep and they killed three of them.'

(Meyer 1886: 2)

We can observe here two major differences compared to the later text *Smaointe beatha Chríost*. The first concerns the noun. In Old Irish, the plural of *caera* 'sheep' was *cairigh* when it was the subject, and *caercha* when it was the object. Thus, there was a special ending for the plural object, namely **-a** (sometimes spelled with <u>). This special object case began to disappear in Middle Irish, but is still preserved in some texts, such as *Merugud Uilix maicc Leirtis*. By the time *Smaointe beatha Chríost* came to be written, there was no special object case, but the grammatical tracts continued to recommend it for students of poetry long after it had disappeared from the ordinary language.

The other change concerns the form of the third-person pl past of the verb *to kill*, *ro marbsatar* 'they killed'. The word *ro* was a preverbal particle used in Middle Irish to mark the past tense. In EMI it was replaced by the particle *do*—this is the marker that we find in *Smaointe beatha Chríost*, e.g. *do gealluis* 'you promised' in l.3 of the passage quoted. In this case, the grammatical tracts are in line with the contemporary language in that they recommend the new past marker *do*.

There is still much work to be done in sifting the evidence for the non-classical language, but through the efforts of scholars like McManus we are at least in a position to distinguish the two varieties from each other.

2.2.5 Borrowing

Up to now, I have written about the internal structure of Irish as if it existed in a vacuum without any contact with other languages. Yet, as we saw in section 1, after the Anglo-Norman invasion it had to coexist with English. It would be strange if this contact did not result in borrowing from one language into the other, and this is exactly what happened: hundreds of items entered Irish in the period 1200–1500, many of which have remained with us to the present day.

The most striking group of loan-words are personal names, both first names and family names. Nowadays, we think of names like *Seán*, *Nóra*, and *Liam* as typically Irish. The truth, alas, is more prosaic: they are simply borrowings into Irish of names that were common throughout Europe at the time. The source language for the Irish versions would have been either English or Norman French. The reason that the Irish forms seem so different from the English/ French ones has to do with the sound systems of the languages. In the Middle Ages, Irish had no sound corresponding to the initial sound in words like *John* (or French *Jehan*), which was the source of *Seán*. For this reason, speakers of Irish substituted a sound from their own language which was close to it, in this case a /sh/ as in the English word *she*. With other names like *Nóra* and *Liam* the Irish version is the result of the loss of the initial syllable. In English/French *Honore* the stress was on the second syllable, and the initial <h> was silent. Unstressed syllables are often lost in a language, and this is what happened when /O'nora/ was brought into Irish: the /o/ of the first syllable was lost, and the final result was *Nóra*. In the same way modern *Liam* was originally *Uilliam* (English *William*), with the stress on the second syllable, which was lost in speech, even though it continued to be written long after that.

We live in an era where many parents like to give new or exotic names to their children. A similar kind of craze seems to have affected Irish society after the Anglo-Norman invasion, with the Gaelic families eagerly embracing the new names. Even the conservative bards accepted them, incorporating them into the inflectional system for dealing with nouns and their various forms. Here are some more new names:

(28) *Aibhilín/Eibhlín* (*Aveline*), *Máire* (*Marie*), *Maighréad* (*Margaret*), *Síle* ((*Ce*)*cile*), *Sinéad* (*Jennet*), *Siobhán* (*Joanne*), *Éamonn* (*Edmund*), *Muiris* (*Maurice*), *Riocard* (*Richard*), *Séamas* (*James*), *Tomás* (*Thomas*)

Some names borrowed in this era were later reimported into English as Irish names:

(29) *Eibhlín > Eileen*; *Máire > Maura/Moya/Moira*; *Seán > Shawn*; *Síle > Sheela*

McManus (1994a) divides the loan-words of EMI into a number of groups according to the sphere of activity with which they were connected. Thus, we find a large number of words associated with the new legal and administrative system introduced by the Anglo-Normans. Words like *constábla* 'constable' belong to this group. Another important semantic division concerns military matters, e.g. *áirseoir* 'archer'. Many new items refer to domestic life and activities; an example would be *sabhsa* 'sauce'. Still others are connected with new kinds of buildings and architectural features, e.g. *seiminéar* 'chimney'. Finally, there are new consumer goods like *fínéagra* 'vinegar'.

Here are some words which entered Irish at this time and which are still part of the language:

(30)   *bagún* 'bacon', *buidéal* 'bottle', *captaoin* 'captain', *clóca* 'cloak', *clós* 'close, yard', *cófra* 'coffer, chest', *cóta* 'coat', *cúirt* 'court', *cupa* 'cup', *dínér* 'dinner', *gúna* 'gown', *méara* 'mayor', *ósta* 'inn' (< oste), *páipéar* 'paper', *paróiste* 'parish', *pláta* 'plate', *plúr* 'flour', *séipéal* 'chapel', *seomra* 'chamber', *siúcra* 'sugar' *ospidéal* 'hospital', *túr* 'tower'

Some new verbs entered the language as well at this time. These were frequently provided with a special ending **-áil**:

(31)   *giústáil* 'joust', *iontráil* 'enter', *ofráil* 'offer', *sábháil* 'save', *tástáil* 'taste'

It should not be forgotten that Irish had been borrowing words from Latin since the fifth century, and this language continued to be a source of new vocabulary right through the later Middle Ages. The Latin influence is particularly evident in the sphere of religious vocabulary. Here are some borrowings from Latin which found their way into Irish at this time:

(32)   *instruimint* 'instrument' (< *instrumentum*), *oific* 'employment, ritual' (< *officium*), *spongia* 'sponge' (< *spongia*)

2.3 Conclusion

In this chapter I discussed the arrival of English in Ireland, and the mingling of languages and cultures that followed as a result. The overall impression is that English exerted a moderate influence on Irish, mostly through translation and borrowing, but that, on the whole, Gaelic society remained unaffected by the presence of another language in the same geographical territory. The literary form of the language, and the kind of literature produced in Irish, are remarkably uniform over the whole period of 300 years from 1200 to 1500. It was as if nothing had altered, or at least as if nothing really significant had altered.

This situation was not destined to last for ever. Change was to come to Ireland with a vengeance with the rise of a new ruling dynasty in England at the end of the fifteenth century, the Tudors.

Further reading

For a political history of the Anglo-Normans in Ireland, see Dolley (1972).
For Gaelic literature before the Anglo-Normans, see Ní Mhaonaigh (2006). This essay describes the various genres of writing before 1200, and also deals with the question of literary style.
For an accessible description of Old and Middle Irish, see Greene (1969: 11–21). Russell (1995: 25–60) is a more technical account of the changes Irish underwent before 1200. The same author provides a brief characterization of Scots Gaelic and Manx, and how they differ from Irish (Russell 1995: 61–5).
Ó Cuív (1975) is a collection of essays on how the Vikings influenced the Celtic countries and their languages. Marstrander (1915) discusses in detail the borrowings form Old Norse into Irish.
For a recent survey of late medieval Irish literature, see Caball and Hollo (2006). The authors discuss in detail the impact of the arrival of the Anglo-Normans on Bardic poetry. In addition, they examine English, French, and Latin writings of this period from Ireland, and their interaction with Gaelic literature. O'Riordan (2007) examines in depth the rhetorical devices of Bardic poetry against the background of late medieval European literature.
For an anthology of late medieval Irish literature, adapted for students of MI, see Ó Doibhlin (2003).
For a recent account of Irish and its speakers in the late medieval period, see Mac Giolla Chríost (2005: 74–83). The author delineates in map form three linguistic zones—Irish-speaking, English-speaking, and mixed. Ó Huallacháin (1994: 10–18) covers much the same ground.
For source documents on Irish and English, see Crowley (2000: 12–17).
For a recent and comprehensive study of English in Ireland in this period, see Hickey (2007: 30–84). For a recent account of French in medieval Ireland, see Picard (2003).
For national identity in this period, see Leersen (1996a: 151–77); this study relies heavily on the evidence from Bardic poetry. Mac Mathúna (2007: 1–9) focuses more on linguistic identity.
For medieval translations into Irish, see Cronin (1996: 8–46).
For the writing and spelling of Irish over the centuries, see Ó Cuív (1969). Ahlqvist (1994) covers the same ground, but in a much more technical manner.

For classical Irish and the grammatical tracts, see Bergin (1938); Ó Cuív (1973); and McManus (1994a, 1994b, 1996). These are written for students with a good knowledge of traditional grammatical terminology. Knott (1957) provides a clear presentation of the metrical rules for Bardic poetry.

For the non-classical language, see McManus (1994a, 1994b). To follow these works one needs some familiarity with EMI.

For borrowing from English and French in this period, see Risk (1968–71, 1974) and McManus (1994a). For the borrowing of names, see Ó Cuív (1986b).

3

The Tudors (1500–1600)

3.1 A new era

Historians agree that the sixteenth century witnessed some enormous changes not just in Britain and Ireland, but right across Europe. Because they were to have quite profound effects on the Irish language, albeit indirectly, I begin this chapter with a brief account of these general developments.

When we look back at the Middle Ages from the perspective of today, it looks as though everyday life changed very little for a 1,000 years, from about 500–1500. This is a false impression, but compared to the hundred years following 1500, there is a certain validity to the claim that medieval Europe was in some ways a stable entity. Society was organized hierarchically, with the king and the church at the top, the aristocracy on the rung below them, and with most of the population living in the countryside, enjoying little control over their own lives. Towns and cities existed, but were quite small. This was especially true of Ireland and some other countries on the peripheries of European civilization. People's intellectual horizons were confined more or less to their immediate environment, and the church kept strict control over the dissemination of knowledge. Any ideas which it considered heretical were immediately stamped out.

Two movements were to change this state of affairs. The first was the Renaissance, which means 'rebirth'. The impetus for this intellectual movement was a desire to return to ancient Greek and Roman civilization. This exploration of the art, philosophy, language, and literature of the ancient world resulted in all kinds of scientific, artistic, and intellectual developments which had never been heard of before this. These included the geographical discoveries which led to Europeans taking part in voyages of exploration to places like Africa, India, and the Americas, the painting and sculpture of artists like Michelangelo Buonarroti and Leonardo da Vinci, and the writings of political theorists like Machiavelli. All of these currents were to fundamentally alter the way that Europeans viewed themselves and the world.

The Renaissance led to the spread of education, which in turn encouraged people to challenge the authority of the church. By 1500, corruption was widespread among the clergy. Popes fathered illegitimate children by their mistresses, bishops often drew large revenues from dioceses which they never visited, and many country priests could barely read and write. All of this led to demands for reform. In 1517, a German monk called Martin Luther published ninety-five theses (what we would call arguments, or points) criticizing various practices common in the church at the time. This single act sparked off a challenge to the authority of the pope right across Europe, resulting in a movement which came to be known as the Reformation. This challenge in turn led to the splitting of Christianity into two main branches: Catholicism, which continued to recognize the authority of the papacy, and Protestantism, which insisted that salvation was open to all individuals who believed in the word of God as revealed in the Bible. For the latter group, the pope was an unnecessary obstacle in the dialogue between God and man.

Political leaders were not slow to get involved in this religious dispute, and before long supporters of Protestantism and Catholicism were at war with each other, and were to remain at loggerheads for the best part of 200 years. Part of the reason for secular leaders becoming involved in religious affairs was that they could increase their control over ordinary people by reducing the power of the church. There were also rich pickings to be gained in the shape of revenues and property owned by the church, which now could be claimed by anybody powerful enough to take them by force.

This was the general background in Europe in the 1530s, when Henry VIII was making his mark as the king of England.

3.1.1 The Tudors

Henry VIII belonged to a new royal dynasty, the Tudors. Unlike their pre-decessors, the Tudors were not content to let their realm be run by warring factions and powerful aristocrats, but wanted to be firmly in control of their kingdom and subjects. Henry VIII in particular pursued this policy with vigour.

One concern of his, which later became an obsession, was to produce a male heir and so ensure that the Tudor line would continue to rule England after his death. When his first wife, Catherine of Aragon, failed to give birth to a son, Henry asked the pope for permission to divorce her. The pope refused, on political grounds, and after many years of negotiations Henry decided to break free of the papacy and have himself declared head of the Church of England. As a result of this many of the monasteries were dissolved, and their revenues passed to the crown.

Henry was not overly concerned with Ireland, but he wanted his authority to be recognized there as well. Accordingly, his Lord Deputy was instructed to bring the Gaelic and Anglo-Norman lords to heel, and to make every effort to ensure that English law was applied all over the island, not just in the Pale area around Dublin. A new archbishop was appointed to the Dublin diocese, with the task of introducing the reformed rites and prayers to the Irish hierarchy, and with overseeing the dissolution of the monasteries. The reformed Irish church was called the Church of Ireland, and was directly answerable to the king. The new version of Christianity introduced into England and Ireland at this time is called Anglicanism. While it rejected the authority of the pope, in many other respects it was closer to Catholicism than other Protestant churches such as Lutheranism and Calvinism.

While the political strategy of the Dublin administration met with some measure of success, from the beginning the ecclesiastical reforms came up against stiff resistance. This non-compliance was to last for centuries afterwards and colour Anglo-Irish relations in every sphere of activity. The long-term effect was the creation of a new kind of Irish identity, one based not on language or ancestry, but on religion.

For eleven years after the death of Henry VIII, there was turmoil in both England and Ireland. Under the short reign of Henry's son, Edward (1547–53), a kind of Protestantism close to Continental Lutheranism was enforced as the official state religion. After Edward died his sister Mary, who had been raised as a Catholic, came to the throne, and immediately began undoing the reforms of her father and brother. She in turn died in 1558, and her sister Elizabeth I succeeded her.

Elizabeth's reign was marked by a return to moderate Anglicanism. On the political front, however, her generals and political representatives in Ireland pursued an aggressive policy of subduing the rebellious Irish chieftains and Anglo-Norman lords, and of 'planting' the newly conquered territories with settlers from England. What this meant was confiscating land and dislodging the local population, and bringing over settlers from Britain to live on the confiscated land and to farm it.

Two leaders tried to rally the Irish against the crown in the period 1570–1603. The first was the Anglo-Norman noble, James FitzMaurice FitzGerald. In 1579 he arrived in Kerry in the south of Ireland with a force of Spanish and Italian soldiers, intent on winning Ireland back to the papacy and restoring dispossessed owners to their lands. This rebellion was quickly crushed. The second leader, Hugh O'Neill, was a more formidable opponent of English rule. In what came to be known as the Nine Years War (1595–1603), he and his Ulster allies successfully kept the English army at bay until their defeat at the Battle of Kinsale in 1601. Like Fitzgerald before him, Hugh O'Neill also tied religion to the struggle against the English invaders. Both attempts at resistance ended in defeat, and by the death of Elizabeth I in 1603, Ireland had been subdued militarily.

3.1.2 Language and identity under the Tudors

Language and culture feature prominently in both English and Irish writings in the Tudor era. Unlike the Anglo-Norman period, from which little explicit commentary has survived, there is quite a wealth of material written by courtiers, soldiers, and administrators involved in the conquest of Ireland, and these writings enable us to form a reasonably clear picture of the linguistic mosaic to be found in the country at this time. Likewise, many of the Gaelic texts of the period contain references to the relationship between English and Irish.

In Chapter 2 I introduced the terms Gael and Gall when referring to the ethnic distinction between the pre-Norman inhabitants and the Anglo-Normans, and I will continue to use these terms in what follows. English writers at the time used the terms Irish and English for the two groups in question. However, there were two kinds of English/Gall to be found in Ireland by 1500. There were the families which had been in Ireland since the twelfth century, many of which had become Gaelicized. These were known as the Old English, or Sean-Ghaill, to distinguish them from the Tudor officials and soldiers who were coming to Ireland in large numbers, and who were called the New English, or Nua-Ghaill. As the sixteenth century progressed, the Old English, even the ones living in Dublin, found their loyalties becoming divided. On the one hand, some of them felt an allegiance to the English monarch and to English culture. On the other hand, they felt themselves alienated from the new administrators because of religion—the Old English for the most part remained Catholic.

In 1485, at the beginning of the Tudor era, we can distinguish three linguistic communities in Ireland. The first was the Irish-language community. Ethnically speaking, there were two kinds of Irish speakers: the Gaeil/Irish, and some members of the Sean-Ghaill/Old English. Then there was the English-speaking community. This was made up of some Sean-Ghaill/Old English, and of the Nua-Ghaill/New English. Finally, there was a bilingual community. Bilinguals tended to come from the Sean-Ghaill and the Gaeil. Very few of the new Tudor officials or planters learned Irish.

Figure 3.1 locates the three communities of speakers on the map of Ireland. As can be seen, the purely English-speaking area is still very small, being centred on Dublin and the south-east. Two multilingual zones are distinguished. One of them rings the Pale in the east, extending up the coast as far as Antrim in the north-east. The other stretches east–west across the provinces of Leinster and Munster in the south. Figure 3.1 shows very clearly that Irish was still spoken over most of the country.

The increased presence of English speakers did not go unnoticed among the Gaelic community. In this context it is worth lingering for a moment on the history of the word *Béarla* 'English language'. As far as we can ascertain, until

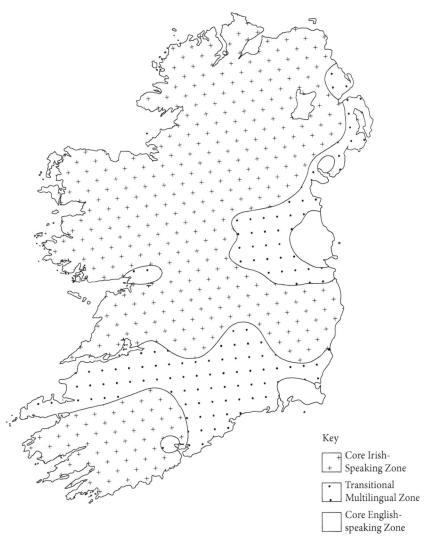

FIGURE 3.1 Language communities in Ireland c.1500

Source: Diarmait Mac Giolla Chríost (2005). *The Irish language in Ireland*. London/New York: Routledge. Figure 3.1

Key

⊞ Core Irish-Speaking Zone

⊡ Transitional Multilingual Zone

☐ Core English-speaking Zone

the sixteenth century this simply meant 'speech, language', and required some kind of qualifier in order to denote a specific language, e.g. *an berla Grecdaí* 'the Greek language' (DIL, under the entry *bélrae*). Obviously, the English language was a form of speech that the Gaelic literati were well acquainted with by 1500, and there are numerous references to it in the writings of the poets. However, before 1600 it seems that the word *béarla* had to be preceded by the element *gall* 'foreign' (*Gall-Bhéarla*) in order for it to mean 'English language' (Leersen 1996a: 397, n. 42). Beginning in the late sixteenth century, we find *Béarla* by itself increasingly being used to denote 'English language'. Other languages are pushed into the background, and the cultural opposition of Gael versus Gall is mirrored by the linguistic conflict of *Gaeilge* 'Irish' versus *Béarla* 'English'.

I mentioned in Chapter 2 that in medieval Europe, Latin was the international language, and the language used in such areas as law, learning, and even literature. The status of Latin was to change because of the two great events of the age: the Renaissance and the Reformation. The Renaissance placed great importance on returning to the languages of the ancient world, Greek and Latin. One might therefore expect the status of Latin to be raised as a result. In one way it was, in that more emphasis was placed on learning it properly, and on editing and publishing the writings of Roman authors like Vergil and Cicero. But paradoxically, the use of Latin as an everyday language was discouraged, mainly because of the very high standards expected of those who wrote in it. From this time onwards, Latin became more and more confined to the learned sphere. It did, however, maintain a strong presence in diplomacy and in international contacts right through the sixteenth and seventeenth centuries. Many of the historical sources we have for the history of Ireland under the Tudors were written in what is called Neo-Latin—that is, the Latin of the Renaissance.

The sphere of activity where Latin had its most visible presence in the Middle Ages was religion. The Reformation brought about a seismic change in the use of language in this sphere. All of the reformed churches, including Anglicanism, insisted on individual Christians having access to the scriptures, which in turn meant that the Bible had to be translated into the vernacular languages—up to this time it was available only in the so-called Vulgate, or Latin version. Likewise, Latin was removed from services and replaced by prayer books in the languages of the various countries where the Reformation took root. It was retained in the Catholic church, but its overall status suffered considerably during the sixteenth century.

In his essay 'The Irish language and Tudor government' (1973), Donald Jackson notes that Latin fell out of favour as a *lingua franca* in Ireland because of its association with Catholicism. For the new rulers of Ireland, English was a more acceptable medium of communication, a point which is made explicit in the following letter from the Lord Deputy to the Gaelic chieftain O'Carroll:

And where you would have answer in latyn, remember you lyve under a englyshe kyng, which requirythe in so gret a cyrcut of countrey as you occupy to have sum honest man whom you myght trust to wryte your letters in englyshe, and I lykewhyse trust to expound [explain] myne sent unto you.

(*Calendar of state papers relating to Ireland* 1509–73; quoted in Jackson 1973: 21)

This letter exemplifies the attitude of the people engaged in the conquest of Ireland. It was not enough to defeat the Irish in battle; according to the new way of thinking, one had also to colonize their minds. Richard Stanihurst, one of the Dublin Old English, saw it as only natural that the Irish should adopt the language of the conqueror: 'For where the countrey is subdued, there the inhabitants ought to be ruled by the same law ... and speake the same language, that the vanquisher parleth' (Stanihurst 1979 [1577]; quoted in Crowley 2000: 34). The poet Edmund Spenser, who lived in Ireland for sometime, put it more pithily: 'The speech being Irish, the heart must needs be Irish' (Spenser 1997 [1633]; quoted in Crowley 2000: 49). Spenser's statement illustrates very well the thinking of the Elizabethan courtiers with respect to Irish language and culture. Linguistic identity had become part of a broader political and cultural identity.

For their part, the Irish speakers were just as unenthusiastic about English, even though some of them seem to have had some knowledge of it. Stanihurst relates an anecdote about the Ulster chieftain Shane O'Neill, head of the powerful Uí Néill dynasty and an implacable foe of the English. The two sides met to parley during one of the many mini-conflicts of the Elizabethan era. The negotiations seem to have been conducted through an interpreter, for at one point in the proceedings, according to Stanihurst:

One Englishman demanded why O Neale would not frame himself to speak English? 'What,' quoth the other [Irishman], in a rage, 'thinkest thou, that it standeth with O Neale his honor to wryeth [= twist] his mouth in clattering English?'

(Stanihurst (1979) [1577]; quoted in Crowley 2000: 35)

Another observer, Fynes Morrison, comments on the reluctance of the Irish and Old English to speak English:

The meere Irish [= Gaeil] disdained to learne or speake the English tongue, yea the English Irish [= Old English] and the very Citizens (excepting those of Dublin where the lord Deputy resides) though they could speake English as well as wee, yet Commonly speake Irish among themselves, and were hardly induced by our familiar Conversation to speake English with us, yea Common experience shewed, and my selfe and others observed, the Citizens of Watterford and Corcke having wyves that could speake English as well as wee, bitterly to chyde them when they speake English with us.

(Kew 1998: 50–1)

This last anecdote is an example of a phenomenon known to us from modern times, namely the use of language to prevent rather than facilitate communication. The motivation for this is usually to make a political point. In our own day, it frequently happens that a politician from an English-speaking country meets somebody from a non-English speaking one. As often as not, the latter speaks English quite well, and could conduct the conversation in that language, but for reasons of prestige insists on using the services of an interpreter. Similarly, when a language is under threat from a stronger language, people will often insist on using the lesser-spoken one, even if that means excluding others from the conversation. Thus, in Wales speakers of English often find themselves obliged to resort to grunts and gestures to make basic purchases in shops owned by Welsh speakers, even though the shopkeepers can all speak English as well as they speak Welsh.

Generally speaking, though, pragmatism wins out over ideology, especially where trade is concerned, and there is some evidence that this was the case in Tudor Ireland as well. In his book about language contact, *Béarla sa Ghaeilge* [English in Irish], Mac Mathúna (2007) discusses a character with a foot in both the Gaelic and English worlds. Richard Weston came from an Old English background and lived in Dundalk, a town located on the border between the Pale and Ulster, the stronghold of Hugh O'Neill. He was a merchant who traded with the Continent, and thus was in an ideal position to receive and dispatch foreign intelligence. He also knew both Irish and English. This enabled him to act as a secretary and interpreter to Hugh O'Neill in his dealings with the authorities in Dublin. Historians disagree as to whether his allegiances lay with the Irish or with the English, and perhaps Weston himself did not know whose side he was on. Like many another spy before and since, he seems to have supplied information to both parties. Nevertheless, when Hugh O'Neill decided to leave Ireland for good in 1607, Weston followed him into exile. From the point of view of the interaction between English and Irish, it is clear that he was at home in both worlds. On the one hand, he wrote reports and letters to the English authorities in Dublin. At the same time, he wrote a poem in Irish which has survived in a number of manuscripts (see 3.2.2 for analysis).

There must have been more people like Weston in Ireland at the time, and in the state records we occasionally come across references to interpreters. The overall impression one receives from reading the various references to Irish and English in the Tudor era, though, is that of polarization. The two languages represented opposing world views, opposing religious values, and opposing legal and political systems. In such a context, there was less and less room for men like Richard Weston who were able to take part in both linguistic worlds.

3.1.3 The Tudor response to language conflict

The Tudors were not the first English dynasty to encounter opposition to the English language in Ireland. Like their predecessors, they responded to the lack of cooperation with coercive legislation. Under Henry VIII, a number of statutes were enacted calling on the inhabitants of Ireland to 'use and speak commonly the English tongue and language'. These statutes also mention education, which was now becoming available to the sons of the nobility and the new middle classes. In 1570, James Stanihurst, the speaker of the Irish House of Commons, called for 'the erecting of Grammar Schools, within every diocese'. He went on to say:

I doubt not...but this addition discreetly made, will foster a young fry, likely to prove good members of this commonwealth...when Babes from their Cradles should be inured under learned School-masters, with a pure English tongue, habit, fashion, discipline.

(Stanihurst (1970) [1633]; quoted in Crowley 2000: 28)

The policy of educating the sons of the nobility in England or in Anglicized environments is a classic technique of colonization, employed later by the administrators of the British Empire in India and Africa. It was pursued very vigorously by the representatives of the crown in Ireland. When the Lord Deputy struck deals with the Irish chieftains, one of the conditions was that they send one of their sons to England to be educated, the hope being that the son would change his allegiance as a result, and prove loyal to the monarch when he succeeded to his father's title. Like in India and Africa in the twentieth century, this method sometimes backfired on the rulers, with the English education only serving to better prepare the young Irish chieftain to resist the enemy. Hugh O'Neill, the most sophisticated and politically astute opponent of English rule in the Tudor period, had been brought up by Sir Henry Sidney in England. Without this education, it is unlikely that he would have been able to repulse the incursion of English rule so effectively for such a long period of time. Nevertheless, the overall effect of the legislation was to gradually wean the Irish nobility away from their traditions and language.

One of the main concerns of the Tudor administrators was to reform the Irish church in line with the changes introduced in England under Henry VIII, and later under Elizabeth I. Here they were faced with a dilemma. On the one hand, they wanted the Irish to use the *Book of Common Prayer*, the text officially recognized for conducting services in the new Church of Ireland, and the new translation of the scriptures into English, the *Great Bible*, published in 1539. Religion was seen as a key factor in civilizing the Irish. Sir Henry Sidney expressed this view trenchantly in his *Discourse for the reformation of Ireland*:

The Charge your Majesty committed unto me for the setting down of my opinion how your realm of Ireland might with the least charge be reclaimed from barbarism to a godly government is somewhat difficult...God's will and word must first be duly planted and idolatry extirped [cut out] … All brehons, bards, rhymers, friars, monks, Jesuits, pardoners, nuns to be executed by martial law.

(Brewer and Bullen 1867–73; quoted in Crowley 2000: 38)

The adoption of English, it was thought, would greatly hasten the embracing of the new religion.

At the same time, even the most bigoted English officials recognized the practical difficulties of preaching to the Irish in a language they did not understand. For this reason, it was recommended that ministers be allowed to preach and pray in Irish in those places where English was not understood. Here once again are the thoughts of Sir Henry Sidney on this subject:

In choice of which ministers for the remote places where the English tongue is not understood, it is most necessary that such be chosen as can speak Irish. For which, search would be made, first and speedily, in your own Universities.

(*Calendar of the state papers relating to Ireland* 1574–85; quoted in Crowley 2000: 31)

Some readers might be surprised at Sidney's suggestion of recruiting Irish-speaking ministers at Oxford and Cambridge. After all, the general impression nowadays is that Irish was anathema to Elizabeth I and her courtiers. In fact, Irishmen were encouraged to study at Oxford and Cambridge as long as they embraced the new religion and conformed to English customs and manners, and many of them availed of this opportunity.

The more enlightened members of the Anglican church hoped that Irish-speaking graduates could translate the Bible into Irish and help bring the new faith to their benighted countrymen. Sometime in the 1560s money was provided by the government in England for the manufacture of an Irish printing font 'to printe the New Testament in Irish' (Williams 1986: 22). In 1571 the first book in Irish was printed in Dublin, *Aibidil Gaoidhilge agus Caiticiosma* [Irish alphabet and catechism]. The author-translator, Seán Ó Cearnaigh, was from Sligo and seems to 'have had some training in a bardic school' (Ó Cuív 1994: 4). He graduated from Cambridge in 1564/5 and took a post in Dublin as a minister of the Church of Ireland. Another Irish speaker who followed the same career path was Uilliam Ó Domhnaill, who oversaw the translation of the New Testament (Ó Domhnuill 1602), and translated the *Book of Common Prayer* (Ó Domhnuill 1608).

Both Ó Cearnaigh and Ó Domhnaill were well versed in the Irish literary language, and at the same time they had a good knowledge of English and of Latin and Greek. Both of them sincerely believed in the necessity of converting their countrymen to Anglicanism. They failed because of the cultural chasm

between English-speaking Anglicans and Irish-speaking Catholics; later attempts to persuade the Irish to abandon Catholicism also foundered. As a
result, it came to be believed that there was some kind of organic link between
a particular language (Irish), and a particular religion (Catholicism). The
efforts of Gaeil like Ó Cearnaigh and Ó Domhnaill to promote Anglicanism
show how erroneous such a view is. There is no necessary link between a
particular language and a particular religion, even though in practice it may
happen that most speakers adhere to a particular set of beliefs. In Scotland,
most of the Gaelic-speaking communities eventually were converted to Presbyterianism, through the agency of other Gaelic speakers. Ireland could just as
easily have gone the same way if there had been more ministers like
Ó Cearnaigh and Ó Domhnaill, or if the English authorities had been less
aggressive in their approach.

   Despite the efforts of some Anglican churchmen to promote the use of Irish,
it must be stressed that this group was a minority. The overall policy of the
Elizabethan administration was to discourage the speaking of Irish and to
encourage the spread of English.

3.1.4 The Gaelic reaction

In Chapter 2 we saw that the poets or *filí* were the guardians of the traditions
of the community. The political and social developments of the Tudor era
were deeply disturbing for them, as they posed a direct threat to the way of
life that sustained their patrons, and thus indirectly threatened the existence
of the poets. Joep Leersen makes the point as follows:

> The poet's main task was to be the arbitrator of nobility, of honour...The encroach-
> ment of Tudor colonization was a complete disruption of this fabric of honour and
> nobility which, as far as the poet was concerned, was the main unifying, cohesive force
> both of (synchronically) Gaeldom, the Gaelic order, and of (diachronically) Gaelic
> history, the continuity of the Gaelic tradition.
>
> (Leersen 1996a: 180)

These poets were also under direct threat from the Tudor authorities, who
perceived them as trouble-makers who incited rebellion among the native
Irish, as this report from 1561 shows:

> The thirde sort is called the Aeosdan, which is to saye in English, the bards, or
> the riming septes; and these people be very hurtfull to the commonwhealle, for they
> chifflie mayntayn the rebells; and, further, they do cause them that would be true, to be
> rebelios theves, extorcioners, murtherers, ravners, yea, and worse if it were possible.
>
> (Smyth 1858 [1561])

While the above statement contains a measure of exaggeration, the work of the poets sometimes bore a resemblance to what nowadays we would call propaganda literature. One of their main concerns was blackening the reputation of the enemy and exhorting the chieftain and his henchmen to battle.

It is not surprising, then, that in sixteenth-century Bardic verse we occasionally find references to the new customs and fashions that were creeping into Gaelic regions. One of the best-known examples of Bardic disapproval is a poem whose first line reads *A fhir ghlacas an ghalldacht* [O you who take on foreign ways]. In it, the poet contrasts two brothers. One of them is infatuated with foreign customs and fashions, which provokes the poet's wrath. He singles out for derision the new hair-style of the foppish brother, who seems to have had his hair cut and curled—the poet uses the borrowed term *locuidhe* 'locks' to describe the new look. The effeteness of this wayward son is compared to the rugged, homely attire of Eoghan Bán: not for him the *brísdi* 'trousers', *coisbeirt* 'footgear', *sdocaidhe* 'stockings', *spuir* 'spurs', or *ráipéar* 'rapier' of his brother. Eoghan Bán is a real man, who prefers sleeping in rushes to a feather-bed, who wields a dagger instead of a rapier, and who delights in fighting against the foreigners (Gaill) that his brother apes.

In another composition, the poet compares the Irish to bees in a hive being tricked by a predator into leaving their refuge:

Teagar i dtimcheall na mbeach
do sheilg ortha go háiseach,
fir is mná éadaigh amhlaidh,
lá a mbréagaidh ó a mbeachadhbhaidh.
[The bees are surrounded in order to hunt them easily, men and women dressed in bright clothes do so, when coaxing them from their beehives.]

Mar sin do-níd gasraidh Ghall
re Gaoidhealaibh Guirt Fhreamhann,
na fir fhlaitheamhla ó Lios Bhreagh,
dá sgrios d'atharrdha a n-aithreadh.
[That is what the hosts of foreigners do to the Gaeil of Gort Freamhann, the generous men from Lios Breagh, banishing them from the patrimony of their fathers.]

Taisbéanaid cuilte clúimhe,
fíon dearg, brata bláthnúidhe
d'uaislibh slóigh bhaisghnéabhuig Bhreagh,
is taisbhéanaid bróin mbleidheadh.
[They show warm blankets, red wine, bright-flowered cloaks to the soft-handed nobles of Breagh, and they show (them) a quernstone.]

(Ní Dhomhnaill 1975: 96–7)

The gist is the same as in the previous composition, namely that the Irish are allowing themselves to be seduced by the comforts of the new civilization, which leads them to abandon their heritage.

Although the poets writing in the Tudor era cannot have been unaware of the dark clouds gathering on the horizon, they continued to write the same kind of praise poetry for their patrons as their ancestors had done from time immemorial. Towards the end of the sixteenth century, however, one occasionally comes across a note of bitter realism, a realization that the world has changed:

> Ceist! cia do cheinneóchadh dán?
> a chiall is ceirteolas suadh:
> an ngéabhadh, nó an áil le haon,
> dán saor do-bhéaradh go buan?
> [I ask: who will buy a poem? Its message only scholars could understand: will anyone take, does anyone want, a noble poem that will bring him immortality?]
>
> Gé dán sin go snadhmadh bhfis,
> gach margadh ó chrois go crois
> do shiobhail mé an Mhumhain leis-
> ní breis é anuraidh ná anois.
> [Though it's a poem skilfully woven, I have walked the whole of Munster with it, every market from cross to cross, and its value is no greater now than a year ago.]
>
> D'éirneist gémadh beag an bonn,
> níor chuir fear ná éinbhean ann,
> níor luaidh aoinfhear créad dá chionn,
> níor fhéagh liom Gaoidheal ná Gall.
> [No man or woman offered as much as a groat as an advance for it, no one gave a reason, neither *Gael* nor *Gall* paid me any heed.]
>
> (Bergin 1970: 145)

The poet is feeling the effects of the change in society. Patrons are in short supply, and the poet's product is no longer valued. Note that there is no difference made between Gael and Gall in this composition, both groups are equally indifferent to what the poet has to offer. There may also be some significance in the use of the word *margadh* 'market' in the second quatrain, which possibly refers to the new way of conducting trade: the towns built by the planters all had a marketplace, just as their counterparts in England had.

Before concluding this survey of the Gaelic reaction to the new civilization, it is worth pointing out that it was not entirely negative. Just as there were members of the nobility and learned classes who were happy to attend universities in England and embrace the new religion, so too were there some poets who were prepared to support the new order. In a recent article, Liam Mac Cóil discusses a number of compositions written for Tomás Dubh Buitléir, the Earl of Ormond. The Ormonds were one of the most important Anglo-Norman families in Ireland in the sixteenth century, and one which consistently remained loyal to the Tudor monarchs. In a picture painted at the time, Tomás Dubh is portrayed with a group of courtiers accompanying Queen Elizabeth I in a procession to Blackfriars. At the same time, his Gaelic poet in Ireland was writing verses in Irish, listing his accomplishments, one of which included being made a Knight of the Garter:

> Fuair sé d'airdchéim Ridireacht Gáirtéir,
> ainm nár ghnáth é ar Éirionnach.
> [He received the honour of a Knighthood of the Garter, a title unusual for an Irishman.]

(Mac Cóil 2008: 197)

Note that the poet uses the name *Éirionnach* 'Irishman' to refer to the earl, rather than opting for one of the contrasting terms Gael or Gall. Commenting on an earlier use of this word, Leersen writes:

The terminology is especially interesting in its use of the term *Éireannach*: the idea is that Desmond [the poet] swears by a country which is possessed co-jointly by the Gaels and by *Goill* like himself, and he brings these two groups ... together under the term *Éireannach*, derived from the country they both inhabit, and defined as against yet another group: the Saxons with their king in England ... This terminology not only begins to dissociate the Gaelicised *Goill* of Ireland from their English fellow–subjects, but in fact almost amounts to a geographical view of 'nationality', as distinct from the racial/genealogical one employed in the bardic system.

(Leersen 1996a: 169)

The later poet who composed the verses for Tomás Dubh Buitléir seems to have been striving for an equally inclusive view of what it meant to be an Irishman in the Elizabethan era. One could be a loyal servant of the queen, and yet speak Irish.

It has to be admitted that poems such as the above were the exception rather than the rule but, like the work of the Irish-speaking Anglican prose-lytizers mentioned earlier, they show that there was nothing inevitable about the Irish language being associated with resistance to English rule. That association, like the association with Catholicism, is due to the polarization of Irish society that occurred in the period 1600–1800. In the Tudor era, there was still scope for the language to be used to support other political and religious options.

3.2 The shape of the language (1500–1600)

3.2.1 Conservatism, innovation, and genre

Unlike political and social history, there was no major change in the language itself in the period 1500–1600. EMI is usually said to have lasted until *c*.1600. This statement is based on the written records which have come down to us, and on Bardic verse in particular. The poets continued to write poems in classical Irish right through the sixteenth century, and there is virtually nothing in the language of these poems to distinguish them from similar compositions written 300 years earlier.

With respect to prose texts, the situation is similar to that in the period 1200–1500. Some texts contain highly conservative and even archaizing language. These are usually versions of traditional tales, saints' lives, or annal entries. On the other hand, translations aimed at the common reader sometimes reveal developments that were taking place in the spoken language. One such text is *Aibidil Gaoidheilge agus Caiticiosma* [Irish alphabet and catechism] (Ó Cuív 1994). In the introduction to his edition of this work, Ó Cuív discusses the spelling found in the book and what it tells us about the spoken Irish of the day. One example will illustrate the kind of information that can be derived from such sources.

From independent evidence, we know that in the period 1200–1600 the pronunciation of Irish changed with respect to certain groups of consonants containing <h> and another consonant, e.g. <gh>, <dh>. Around the year 1200, these were both pronounced in the same way, like the <ch> of Scottish loch, but with the vocal cords vibrating (this is one of the most challenging sounds for learners of Irish). By 1600, <gh> and <dh> were no longer being pronounced in the middle or at the end of a word, and the vowel near them was lengthened by way of compensation for this loss. Therefore, by 1600 the traditional spelling was highly misleading as far as pronunciation was concerned. We can see this if we compare the spelling of late EMI with MI:

(1)   EMI   MI
   a. bailighim   bailím
   b. cruinniughadh   cruinniú

In b, a sequence of seven letters, <ughadh>, has been replaced by a single long vowel, <ú>, because the <gh> in the middle and the <dh> at the end are no longer pronounced. Clearly, the older orthography was cumbersome and downright misleading, but it continued to be used long after it ceased to reflect pronunciation.

In *Aibidil Gaoidheilge agus Caiticiosma*, the author tried to write in the traditional way, but sometimes his misspellings reveal something about his pronunciation. The consonant groups <dh> and <gh> are still written in the middle of a word, but as well as that, the preceding vowel is spelled with a length-mark, to indicate that it is long:

(2)   Spelling in AGC   Traditional spelling   MI spelling
  a. fhúathaígheas   fhuathaigheas   fhuathaíos
     ainmnígthear   ainmnighthear   ainmníthear

  b. beathúghadh   beathughadh   beathú
     ghortúghadh   ghortughadh   ghortú

     (examples from AGC taken from Ó Cuív 1994: 23)

The hybrid spellings of the translator of *Aibidil Gaoidheilge agus Caiticiosma* show that the change discussed above had taken place by the late sixteenth century, but the traditional spelling masks this to some extent.

Another area where translations prove innovative is in the introduction of loan-words. A lot of religious material was translated into Irish by both Catholic and Protestant clergymen in the sixteenth and seventeenth centuries. Not surprisingly, this material contains many loan-words, usually taken either from English or Latin. Here are some which according to Ó Cuív (1994: 42) are first attested in *Aibidil Gaoidheilge agus Caiticiosma*:

(3)   *aldarman* 'alderman', *caiticiosma* 'catechism', *coimisinéar* 'commissioner', *cusdum* 'custom', *prionnda* 'print', *priuáideach* 'private', *reuerensach* 'reverent', *translásion* 'translation'

By and large, though, the prose texts of the Tudor era, like the poetry, belong to the higher register, and hence tend to be more formal and conservative in terms of language. Only in a very few items do we find anything that might be said to reflect everyday speech. One fascinating source of information is a kind of guide-book to Ireland for English people, written by Andrew Boorde and published in 1547. It contains what must be the first ever phrasebook of Irish for visitors, entitled *A talk in Irish and English*. Below are some examples of what were considered useful expressions for tourists in the sixteenth century. I give the original spelling and gloss, and below them a putative transcription in standardized EMI:

(4)   a. English   Irish
         You be welcome to the town   De van wely
                                          Dé bheatha do-chum an bhaile

b. How do you fare?   Kanys stato?
                                 Cionnus a-tá tú?
   I do fare well, I thank you. Tam agoomwah, gramahogood
                                 A-táim go maith, go raibh maith
                                 agat.

c. Wife, have you any good meat? Benitee, wyl beemah hagoot?
   [*meat = food* in 16th-cent   A bhean an tí, an bhfuil bia maith
   English]   agat?
   Sir, I have enough.   Sor, tha gwyler.
                                 ?Sor?, a-tá go leor.

d. What is it o'clock?   Gaued bowleh glog.
                                 ?Gad? buille den gclog.
   It is vi. o'clock   She wylly a glog.
                                 Sé bhuille den gclog.

(based on Boorde 1870 [1547]; quoted in Crowley 2000: 25)

When the spelling is normalized, the above phrases and dialogues are more or less intelligible to somebody who knows MI, in fact, some of them, like (b) *kanys stato*, are still to be found in text-books of Irish. We also find here the character of *bean an tí* 'hostess', a figure who was to become familiar to generations of schoolchildren in the twentieth century. Finally, note the presence of the lexical item *sor* 'sir'. Irish at the time lacked a neutral form of respect for addressing strangers, so it was only natural that it should borrow this item from English.

The above phrases provide a tantalizing glimpse of the potential there was for Irish to develop in the sixteenth century. In the mini-dialogues of Boorde's book, we have moved outside the inward-looking, hermetic world of Bardic poetry, with its fixed formulae and conventions, to the world of cultural and linguistic contact, such as was to found in other societies at the time. Had the circumstances been different, one could imagine Irish being adopted by the New English in the towns and smaller urban centres that were being built at the time, which would have led to a considerable broadening of its register to embrace such areas as commerce, administration, law, education, and printing—in short, what we nowadays would call the public domain.

Another kind of writing which offers us valuable insights into the less conventional language are private letters. With the spread of education in Europe in the period 1450–1600, letter writing became much more common between ordinary people. Collections of letters from the fifteenth and sixteenth centuries are a valuable source of information for historians of various languages. For example, the letters of the Paston family in England provide us with much data for the study of Early Modern English. Epistolary material in

Irish is much more meagre, but a few letters from the sixteenth and seventeenth centuries have survived. Here is an extract from one sent by the Ulster chieftain Seán Ó Néill to the Lord Justice of Ireland, the Earl of Sussex, in 1561:

(5)   Beandacht ó Ua Néill docum an Iústís mar dhligheas sé agus dochum na coda ele don Chomhairle: agus atáim agá fhiarfaighe díobh créd do rinne mé do ní do rachadh a n-easonóir nó a ndíghbháil don Bhanríoghain nó dhaoibhsi as ar bhriseabhair orum gan fhátha gan ádhbhur, agus tairgsin gabháltus do dhénamh orum gan ghiolla gan liter do chur chugam ó do thángabhair a nÉirinn.

[Greetings from O'Neill to the Justice as is his due and to the rest of the Council: and I'm asking you what did I do that would dishonour or harm the queen or yourself, which led you to attack me without reason or cause, and try to seize my lands without sending messenger or letter to me since you arrived in Ireland.]

(Ó Lochlainn 1939: 28)

One difference between this letter and the more common prose texts like tales or saints' lives is the relative directness and brevity of O'Neill's style. In the above passage, the only redundancy is in the use of a pair of synonyms in the phrase *gan fhátha gan ádhbhur* 'without reason without cause'. Otherwise the writer gets to the heart of the matter almost straight away. Apart from the spelling, the language is reasonably comprehensible to a modern reader. True, there are some verbal forms which might be puzzling to students familiar with standard MI: *dhligheas* (= *dhlíonn*), *bhriseabhair* (= *bhris sibh*), *thángabhair* (= *tháinig sibh*). All of these forms, though, are to be found in twentieth-century dialects. Another feature worth commenting on, and one which is found in other letters written around the same time, is the use of the second person pl in addressing a stranger. Both *bhriseabhair* and *thángabhuir* are plural in form, but singular in meaning—they refer to the Lord Justice. This is a common device in many languages, the so-called polite form of the second-person pronoun (usually equivalent to the second-person plural) for addressing strangers. In French we have *vous*, in German *Sie*. MI and Modern English are unusual in not having a polite form of the second-person pronoun. It is clear that in the sixteenth-century Irish was well on the way to developing a polite-familiar system like other languages did at this time. Later changes in the social circumstances of Irish speakers meant that such a system became unnecessary, as Irish became used less and less in formal or impersonal contact.

Now compare this letter to a passage from a text written nearly forty years later, *Turas na dtaoiseach nUltach as Éirinn* [The journey of the Ulster chieftains from Ireland], describing the voyage of Hugh O'Neill and Hugh O'Donnell to France in 1607:

(6)   Timchiol medhóin oidhche éirghiss in fhairrgi i n-a tonnoibh tul-borba
       tinneasnacha trén-tuinnsemhacha dóip. Trócaire na Trínóite ri-s-tesairc
       gan in long co n-a mbuí innte do bháthadh.

       [About midnight the sea rose towards them in rough, violent, strongly
       buffeting waves. It was only the mercy of the Trinity that saved them, and
       [prevented] the ship and all who were in her from being drowned.]

                                                        (Ó Lochlainn 1939: 75)

We can observe here a stylistic feature much beloved of EMI writers, namely
the use of strings of alliterating words: *tonnoibh tul-borba tinnesnacha trén-
tuinnsemhacha*. The three adjectives *tul-borba, tinnesnacha*, and *trén-tuinnsemhacha* are near synonyms, and the presence of the last two is not really
necessary as far as the content is concerned. Literary devices like this cause
considerable difficulties for modern readers, if only because the compound
adjectives like *tul-borba* or *trén-tuinnsemhacha* are no longer to be found in
Irish, and there is no proper dictionary of the older language.

   Another complication of the above passage is grammatical in nature. The
verbal form *éighiss* is an old third-person sg past tense, used in narrative. Even
by the fifteenth century it was obsolete (see Ó Catháin 1933; Ó Maonaigh
1944). And yet writers like Tadhg Ó Cianáin, the author of the above passage,
continued to use it right into the seventeenth century. The verbal form in l.2,
ri-s-tesairc, is equally archaic. The -s- in the middle represents the object
pronoun, 'them', which is as it were inserted into the verb, between the particle
ri- and the main part of the verb, *tesairc* (a similar phenomenon in French
involves the placing of object pronouns between the subject and the verb, e.g.
je-t-aime 'I-you-love', where -**t**- 'you' comes before the verb *aime*). These
infixed pronouns were the norm in Old and Middle Irish, but by 1200 they
had been replaced by independent object pronouns placed after the verb,
e.g. *insaig-siu é* 'attack it' (Breatnach 1994: 271). However, the poets and
other literati continued to use infixed pronouns for 400 years after they had
disappeared from the spoken language.

   The above brief discussion once again illustrates how difficult it is to make
hard-and-fast statements about Irish in the period 1500–1600. Some texts are
archaic, while others more or less reflect contemporary developments. It is
therefore vital that historians of the language have an intimate acquaintance
with the sources that they are dealing with.

3.2.2 Diglossia and bilingualism

We saw in the previous section that the majority of texts, whether poetry or
prose, were written in a language that was largely unintelligible for an average

speaker of Irish. This was not just a question of literary style. One might also argue that nowadays certain novelists or poets writing in English are hard to understand, but this is (usually) more a question of style and vocabulary than grammar. However, as we have just seen, the actual grammatical forms being used in literature had become very far removed from everyday speech by 1600.

In Chapter 1, I referred to the concept of diglossia in sociolinguistics. This comes into play when two different language codes are in use in a speech community. Very frequently, one of them is a high register, and the other a low one. One oft-quoted example of diglossia is standard written Arabic versus local dialects. Speakers of modern Arabic dialects have to learn the standard written variety in a formal educational setting. Some people would go so far as to claim that traditional written Arabic is a dead language. Thus one author, discussing the attitudes of twentieth-century Egyptian nationalists to the traditional written register, remarks that for them it had 'fossilized to the point where it could be declared (almost) a dead language' (Suleiman 2008: 34).

By 1600, it seems that a similar kind of diglossia had developed in Irish. Those who went through the formal education of the poetic schools were able to understand, and to some extent reproduce, the fossilized grammatical forms that I discussed in the previous section. The rest of the population was unable to enjoy the products of the literati. This is overtly acknowledged both by native and foreign commentators. Edward Campion in his *Historie of Ireland* comments as follows:

The [Irish] tongue is sharp and sententious, and offereth great occasion to quick apothegms and proper allusions, wherefore their common Jesters, Bards, and Rhymers, are said to delight passingly those that conceive the grace and propriety of the tongue. But the true Irish indeed differeth so much that they commonly speak, that scarce [one] among five score, can either write, read or understand it. Therefore it is prescribed among certain [of] their Poets and other Students of Antiquity.

(Campion 1970) [1571]; quoted in Crowley 2000: 29)

In a number of Bardic poems from the end of the sixteenth and the beginning of the seventeenth century, the poet refers sarcastically to the necessity of dumbing down for the new audience. Here is an extract from one such composition:

Do thréig sind sreatha caola
foirceadal bhfaobhrach ffrithir
ar shórt gnáthach grés robhog,
is mó as a moltar sinde.
[I have given up the delicate lines of pithy lessons for a common kind of facile composition, and I get more praise for it.]

Maithim, giodh mór an sonas,
énbhonn feasda dá thoradh,
má théid énrand gan tuigse
dom dhánsa ó dhuine ar domhan.
[I will not take a single groat of profit, though it were good for me, if as much
as a single verse of my poem is not comprehensible to anyone in the world.]

(Bergin 1970: 127–8)

Formerly, the whole point of Bardic poetry was to be as obscure as possible
(an activity that most poets seem to have excelled in). Now, because of the
lack of patrons, they were forced to try to make their work accessible to all. It
would be sometime before accessibility became reality rather than mere
rhetoric, but eventually poetry adapted to the new conditions, and started
using a language closer to the spoken Irish of the day.

Bilingualism is simply an extreme form of diglossia, involving two different
languages, rather than two registers. As we saw earlier, bilingualism was on the
increase in Ireland in the Tudor era. From about 1600 onwards, we come
across evidence for the kind of English spoken by Irish speakers who had to
learn the other language. However, we have virtually no records of Irish
spoken by English speakers, with one exception. This is a work by the
character we have already introduced in section 3.1.2, Richard Weston, the
intermediary between Hugh O'Neill and the authorities in Dublin. After he left
Ireland in 1607, Weston composed a poem addressed to the family and friends
he had left behind. As Mac Mathúna (2007) points out, the poem provides
fascinating evidence of the kind of Irish spoken by bilinguals in seventeenth-
century Ireland. The following verse is illustrative:

(7) B'éigean   dom   fágbháil   mo bean
     was.necessary to.me   leave.INF   my wife
     is   gan gabháil   mo cead   leis,
     and   not take.INF my leave   with.him
     ná   fuirreach   d'éis   Ó Néill   sa   tír
     or   stay.INF   after   O'Neill   in.the   land
     och   a   turrus   is   bocht   sin.
     oh   VOC   journey   is   poor   that
     [I had to leave my wife without saying goodbye to her, or stay after
     O'Neill in that land, oh journey, that is sad.]

(Ó Fiaich 1970: 283)

When somebody speaks or writes a language that they have learned, they
normally make mistakes, and the same is true of Weston. Two kinds of errors
can be identified in the above quatrain. First, there are deviations in the shape

of individual words. After the possessive pronoun in the first-person sg, *mo* 'my', a following consonant undergoes a modification called lenition. This sound change is marked in spelling by the presence of <h>:

(8) Unlenited consonant   Lenited consonant
     bád   mo bhád [vawd] 'my boat'
     cat   mo chat [hat] 'my cat'

Judging by the spelling throughout the poem, Weston failed to lenite his consonants. In both l.1 and 2 above, there is a possessive in the first-person sg, but no lenition is marked: *mo bean* instead of *mo bhean* (l.1), *mo cead* instead of *mo chead* (l.2). Another error is the use of the masculine *leis* 'with.him' in l.2, referring to the noun *bean* 'wife' in l.1. Here and in other places in the poem the two genders, masculine and feminine, are confused with each other.

The second kind of error concerns word order. To illustrate this, I need to introduce a little bit of new terminology. Consider the English sentence:

(9) I had to leave my wife.

We have two verbs here: *have* and *leave*. When a verb occurs with *to* before it, we call it an infinitive. So in (9) above *to leave* is an infinitive. Irish also has infinitives, and there is a special ending for them:

(10)   Verb   Infinitive
     a. fág   fág-bháil
         leave   leave-INF
                 'to leave'

     b. gabh   gabh-áil
         take   take-INF
                 'to take'

However, there is a further complication in Irish about these verbs, concerning word order. Sometimes there is an object with an infinitive verb, as in the English sentence above: *wife* is the object of the infinitive *to leave*. In Irish, the object of an infinitive comes before the verb, so that the Irish version of (9) is:

(11) B'éigean   dom   mo bhean   a fhágbháil.
      was.necessary to.me   my wife   to leave.INF
      'I had to leave my wife'.

Learners of Irish have great difficulty with this word order, and as often as not keep the order verb–object, just as Weston does in l.2:

(12) B'éigean   dom   fágbháil   mo bean.
      was.necessary to.me   leave.INF   my wife
      'I had to leave my wife'.

If we take another quatrain, we can witness another phenomenon typical of bilingual and second-language speakers:

(13)   Do gheibh mise aig Í Néill
       Mass inné is *Mass* inniu,
       ní déara Mineistéir liom,
       a Ristird Buistiún, *Come to Church*.
       [I got with O'Neill a Mass yesterday and a Mass today, no minister will
       say to me, Richard Weston, 'Come to Church!']

(Ó Fiaich 1970: 284)

Here we see an example of code-switching, which means mixing two languages within a single utterance or text. As one might expect, code-switching is typical of bilingual situations. Very often it is found when somebody wants to give the exact words of a speaker, as in the quatrain above, where the poet quotes the English-speaking minister verbatim, rather than translating what he said into Irish.

What is interesting about Weston is that despite his errors, he writes in a high register. While his verses may lack the elaborate ornamentation of the professional poets, the metre he chooses is similar to those found in Bardic poetry in general. Many of the phrases he uses are part of the stock of Irish poetry at this time, e.g. the opening line:

(14)   Beir mo beanocht go Dún Dalck.
       [take my blessing to Dundalk]

(Ó Fiaich 1970: 283)

This was a typical way of starting a Bardic poem, by referring to a place as if it were a person. Obviously, then, Weston picked up his Irish from mixing with the nobility, the likes of his patron Hugh O'Neill and, unlike many bilinguals, he must have been able to read Irish well in order to achieve some mastery of the literary style. At the same time, his poem is full of grammatical mistakes, the kind of errors that teachers of Irish come across nowadays in the classroom.

3.3 Conclusion

The Tudor era in Ireland was marked by a series of seismic changes. The most long-lasting was the military conquest of the island, which had been more or less completed by the time the last Tudor, Elizabeth I, died in 1603. The other big change, which accompanied the subjugation of the Gaelic and Anglo-

Norman lords, was the Reformation. Although it failed to take root, it quickly became part of the ongoing struggle between the new arrivals, the New English and the old Catholic ruling class, which consisted of both Gaelic and Anglo-Norman lords.

On the linguistic level, the initial impression is that there is a remarkable continuity with the late Middle Ages, in that the written language remained largely the same right up to 1600 and even beyond that date. What did change was the status of Irish in relation to English. As the sixteenth century progresses, we find more and more references to attempts by the government to suppress Irish. By the end of the Tudor era, the poets were reacting in their writing to the reality of change. The cultural and political change was accompanied by subtle but significant alterations in the shape of the language. When we look more closely at the written records, then, it is possible to discern indications of many of the developments that Irish would undergo in the next century.

Further reading

For Tudor Ireland, see MacCurtain (1972: 1–88).

For a general survey of language and literature 1500–1600, see Ó Cuív (1976).

Mac Craith (2006: 192–210) is a succinct account of the new religious prose writings of the late sixteenth and early seventeenth centuries.

Ó Doibhlin (2006) contains the key Irish-language texts of the period, along with commentary.

Leersen (1996a: 177–90) discusses the sense of Gaelic identity which can be discerned in the Bardic poetry of this period, while stressing that this was not developed into a coherent political philosophy. O'Riordan (1990) deals with the Bardic response to the erosion of the old Gaelic way of life.

For a recent account of Irish and its speakers in Tudor and Stuart Ireland, see Mac Giolla Chríost (2005: 84–96). This contains details about the spread of English through Gaelic society in this period. The author subscribes to the thesis that in the Tudor era religion began to replace language as a badge of national identity.

For source documents relating to language in Tudor Ireland, see Crowley (2000: 18–53).

For language contact and conflict in Tudor Ireland, see Mac Mathúna (2007: 9–26).

For Irish and the Reformation, see Williams (1986: 21–43) and Mac Craith (2006: 192–6).

For a survey of Neo-Latin writing from Ireland in the Tudor period, see Millett (1976). Harris and Sidwell (2009) is a collection of essays on individual Neo-Latin texts.

For innovation and conservatism in EMI, see Mac Manus (1994b). This is directed at the specialist rather than the general reader.

For a detailed analysis of Richard Weston's Irish, see Mac Mathúna (2007: 66–87).

4

The Stuarts (1600–1700)

4.1 A new dynasty

We saw in the last chapter how the rebellion of Hugh O'Neill and Hugh O'Donnell was finally brought to an end in 1603. The treaty which concluded the Nine Years War, the Treaty of Mellifont, allowed the defeated Gaelic leaders to retain their lands, but they were now subjects of the new king of England, Scotland, and Ireland, James I. Elizabeth I had died unmarried and childless, and the throne passed to her Scottish cousin, James, after her death. James was a member of the Stuart dynasty which had been ruling Scotland since the fourteenth century.

Because of the cultural links between Ireland and Gaelic Scotland, the Gaelic leaders and their poet spokesmen hoped initially that James would prove more favourably inclined towards Irish Catholics than his cousin Elizabeth. In an article about the Gaelic reaction to the accession of James, Breandán Ó Buachalla quotes a passage in a letter from Hugh O'Neill to the king of Spain:

When the Queen died and this King, who was before King of Scotland, succeeded to her, the Irish hoped, on account of their old friendship with the Scots, that they would receive from the King many favours and, in particular, their liberty of conscience.

(Walsh 1962: 225; quoted in Ó Buachalla 1983: 83)

Even the poets joined in the general rejoicing, as this couplet illustrates:

An ghrian loinneardha do las;
scaoileadh gach ceo Cing Séamas.
[The bright sun shone, King James broke up the fog.]

(Breatnach 1978: 174)

Michelle O'Riordan comments on the poem that this couplet comes from: 'Ó hEodhusa [the poet] makes extensive use of contrasting evil and good, attributing everything bright and good to James' presence, everything dark and evil to his absence. This is the traditional bardic practice of associating prosperity and fertility with a good or popular ruler' (O'Riordan 1990: 170). So as far as the poets were concerned, nothing much had changed; if anything, there was a change for the better—the Tudors were gone, and the new Stuart dynasty, it was felt, would be well disposed towards the Gaelic order.

Unfortunately for the Irish, their hope in the new king proved unfounded, and before long they realized that he and his administration were determined on pushing through the policy of colonization begun under the Tudors. As a result, the Gaelic chiefs of Ulster decided to leave Ireland in 1607 and to seek refuge with the Catholic rulers of the Continent, in the exodus referred to as the Flight of the Earls. This meant that the government could confiscate their lands and bring in people from Scotland and England to settle them. Thus began the Plantation of Ulster, which resulted in significant changes in the social and cultural make-up of Ireland. The old landowners were dispossessed and replaced by outsiders. Many of the newcomers were from Scotland, and were Presbyterian in religion, which in turn meant that they had a more implacable attitude towards Catholicism than the Anglican Church of Ireland.

Until 1616 there existed the possibility that Hugh O'Neill would return to Ireland at the head of a Spanish army and succeed in wresting power from the English. With the death of O'Neill in 1616 that hope was dashed. Nevertheless, under the reign of James I and his son Charles I, who came to the throne in 1625, many of the Irish civil and religious leaders tried to reach some kind of accommodation with the new rulers. In this they were not wholly successful, but it is true that the Stuarts, while not Catholic themselves, were moderate Anglicans, and as such were relatively tolerant of Catholics. Under Charles the Catholics of Ireland enjoyed a limited measure of religious freedom. This period of relative calm lasted until 1641.

The history of Britain in the period 1600–1700 is essentially the story of the struggle between the traditionalist Stuart monarchs and the parliament, which aimed at forcing those same monarchs to give up their power to the elected representatives of the people. The struggle also had a religious dimension. The anti-Stuart faction in the English parliament drew its support from the Puritans, who were more much anti-Catholic than the established Anglican church.

In 1641 a rebellion broke out in Ulster, and by 1642 it had spread to other parts of the country. Normally, the English government would have suppressed such an uprising. However, Charles I had little room for manoeuvre, because in 1642 civil war broke out between him and the Parliamentarians led by Oliver Cromwell. As a result, Charles needed the help of the Irish Catholics and entered into negotiations with them, promising them various concessions in return for their help against the Parliamentarians. The Catholic camp in Ireland was divided. The remaining Gaelic chiefs and some Old English sided with the king, while the Old English of Dublin and the Pale supported the Parliamentarians. On the other hand, the Ulster Scots sided with Cromwell and resisted the rebellion.

By 1646 the king had been defeated and captured. Charles continued to try to do deals with various groups during his captivity. For this reason, he was finally tried for treason and beheaded in January 1649. This left Oliver Cromwell free to turn his attention to Ireland, where the Royalists, the supporters of the monarchy, were still holding out.

One historian describes Cromwell's pacification of the country as 'swift, terrible and decisive' (Mac Curtain 1972: 151). By 1653 the country had been subjugated once again, and as before, retribution was not slow in coming. Large amounts of land were confiscated and distributed to soldiers and financiers who had backed the winning side. Many of the previous owners who had survived the Cromwellian invasion were transported to the West Indies. Others were granted land in Connaught, west of the Shannon, to compensate them for the losses they had sustained. Not surprisingly, this new plantation of Ireland, and the terrible war which had preceded it, caused much bitterness in the folk-memory of the dispossessed.

Charles's son, also called Charles, had fled to France in 1651. After the death of Charles I, Cromwell had replaced the monarchy with what was called the Commonwealth, ostensibly a republic, but in reality a semi-dictatorship. After his death in 1658, his son Richard tried to follow in his father's footsteps and continued to act as Lord Protector of the Commonwealth. Richard lacked the force of character required for such a task and in 1660 the exiled Stuart monarch, Charles II, returned to the throne of England in what became known as the Restoration. His reign lasted until 1685.

Despite their unfavourable experiences with his father and grandfather, the Irish greeted the return of Charles II with enthusiasm, hoping to have their lost lands returned to them and to be allowed to practice their religion. Some of these hopes were realized. Because the Cromwellian army was dominated by Puritans, members of the Catholic clergy had suffered death and imprisonment under the Commonwealth. Under Charles II, the position of Catholics improved considerably, and the clergy were allowed to minister to their congregations, although they still were persecuted from time to time. The land question was a different matter. Complicated legislation was enacted to enable dispossessed landowners to sue for the regaining of their property, but few of them managed to repossess what they had lost.

The Restoration era was by and large peaceful. However, politics and religion raised their ugly heads again when Charles II died in 1685 and was succeeded by his brother James II. James had converted to Catholicism in 1668, and immediately set about appointing Catholics to positions of influence in the administration and the army, which caused fear and resentment among his predominantly Protestant subjects. In 1688 the English parliament decided for the second time that its monarch was interfering with its liberties. This time they opted to retain the institution of the monarchy, but to change the person occupying the throne. Parliament offered the crown to James' Protestant nephew and son-in-law, William of Orange in Holland, who readily accepted it. Shortly after William's forces invaded England, James fled to France, and soon afterward set sail for Ireland in the hope of rallying support for his cause there.

As always, the Irish flocked to the standard of the Stuart king. This time there was a further dimension to the struggle, in that the French king, Louis XIV, had decided to lend his aid to James. Ireland was to become the main arena of the struggle sometimes known as the Williamite War. One of the larger battles in the war took place in Ireland, on the river Boyne in the north-east of the country, when the Williamite army routed the joint Franco-Irish forces under the command of James. James himself fled to France, leaving his generals to carry on the war without him. In 1691 the Franco-Irish army was defeated again at the Battle of Aughrim, this being followed soon afterwards by the Treaty of Limerick, which concluded the war. The Irish soldiers were given the option of leaving the country, and many availed themselves of this opportunity.

England was now firmly in control of Ireland, and there were no further attempts to overthrow its rule for a long time. Most of the land remaining in Catholic hands passed to members of the Protestant minority; this group was to rule Ireland for the next hundred years.

4.1.1 The linguistic effect of the conquest

As far as language was concerned, the seventeenth century witnessed the completion of the process begun in the sixteenth century, by which English spread to every part of Ireland. This dissemination of English had two sources. First of all, it was caused by the deliberate planting of large swathes of the country, particularly in Ulster and the midlands. As a result of the change in land ownership, large numbers of Irish speakers were dislodged from their hereditary homelands and replaced by English and Scottish settlers. As can be seen on Figure 4.1, the eastern part of Ireland and a large part of Ulster were by 1700 mixed in terms of language, with both English and Irish being spoken.

As well as this, English began to make its presence felt even in those parts of the south and west where the population was predominantly Irish-speaking. Urban centres were being set up right across the country, where new consumer goods could be bought and sold at the market through the medium of English. New law-courts were in operation, and at a time when one had to prove one's right to hold land, it was vital to be able to plead one's suit in the language of the law, English. For those who could afford it, education was available, once more in English. Thus as well as the geographical spread of

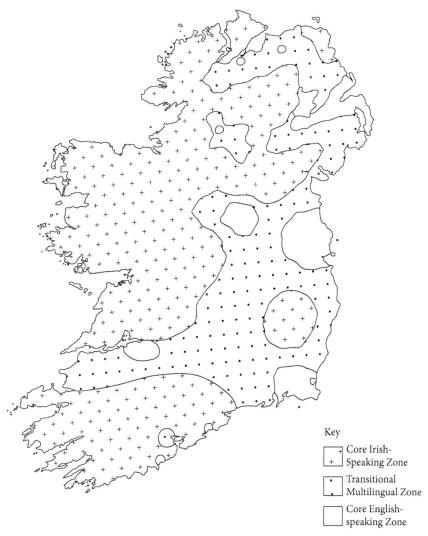

FIGURE 4.1 Language communities in Ireland *c.*1700
Source: Diarmait Mac Giolla Chríost (2005). *The Irish language in Ireland*. London/New York: Routledge. Figure 4.1

English reflected in Figure 4.1, there was, as it were, the vertical imposition of a stratum of English all over Ireland, from the far west to Dublin. The provinces of Connaught and Munster may well have been predominantly Irish-speaking, but there was a now a cluster of English speakers in every parish, and what was more important, this cluster held the reins of power.

Smyth (2006) takes into account both the geographical and the social/ethnic dimensions of the spread of English. The regions he identifies as

English-speaking correspond more or less to those in Figure 4.1. His summary of the sociolinguistic situation is worth quoting:

When we look at the crucial domains of language for Irish and English by, say, the early 1660s, the following picture emerges. At the military/political/administrative level a whole array of New English officials and agents have become established in Dublin, with all its key ruling institutions, in the county/shires, in town government, as well as in other customs functions in the port-cities. Backing up this new official 'civil service' world were close on 300 'officered' garrisons of various sizes, ready to defend and uphold the rule of English law by physical coercion. Judges and lawyers exercised that law through the courts... This island-wide spread of colonial courts and garrisons was dominated by English speakers, as were the administrative arms of county and town government. Likewise, the landlord estate system, established across the island, printed its leases, managed its rent books and, where necessary, used writs and summonses in the English language only. At the level of the barony and parish, the Protestant constable or subconstable—outside of Connacht and Clare—were almost invariably English speakers. This prestigious ruling caste of landlords, judges, barristers and attorneys, officers, officials and agents came to constitute the ruling Protestant Ascendancy—the apex of the English language and cultural system in Ireland.

(Smyth 2006: 403–4)

The same author tries to quantify the numbers for the three linguistic communities, Irish-speaking, English-speaking, and bilingual. He estimates that about one-third of the country could speak English, although many of these spoke Irish as well. Smyth reckons that more than 80 per cent of the population spoke Irish, and that many of these were bilinguals.

The recognition of the last group, those who belonged to two linguistic and cultural worlds, is a crucial element in this analysis. Smyth describes the bilinguals thus:

A whole series of contact zones of interpenetration between Irish and English speech can also be inferred from the 1660 map. A hybrid linguistic group has emerged in these middle spaces, which include the old port-cities. In 1660 it is likely that this mediator group, which understood if not spoke both English and Irish, constituted at least one-fifth of the population. This group of middlemen/women, agents, innkeepers, shopkeepers, pedlars, carters, artisans, midwives, seasonal migrants and servants, and other more mobile classes in the population occupied key cultural hinge positions, facilitating and lubricating the workings of the deeply divided society. At this language interface, ambivalence, hybridity, opportunism and indeed, sadness and shame were often intermingled.

(Smyth 2006: 408)

Smyth's assessment of the linguistic situation in 1660 is a recent contribution, one which does not yet appear to have made a significant impact on the debate about the history of Irish. I have dwelt on it because, if correct, it will entail a radical reappraisal of the language shift from English to Irish. The 33 per cent English speakers might seem an insignificant number compared with the 85 per cent Irish speakers. But in language change it is not so much a question of how many speakers a particular language has, but of who these speakers were. The English speakers were those who were in control of the country. And they were not just speakers; they were also writers of English. Previous histories of Irish have tended to concentrate on numbers of speakers only, without taking literacy into account. A growth in the numbers of those who were able to read and write was very much a feature of Anglophone society in the seventeenth century, while even before the incursion of English, literacy levels among the Gaelic population were extremely low. English did not introduce writing to Ireland, but it did introduce an omnipresent writing and print culture which was absent from traditional Gaelic society. Not surprisingly, this culture was attractive to everybody, including those whose first spoken language was Irish.

The other point that arises in Smyth's analysis which was to prove crucial in the 150 years after 1660 was the presence of a bilingual community that constituted about 20 per cent of the population. While it is true that some of the settlers acquired a certain communicative facility in Irish, this bilingualism was heavily weighted in favour of English because of the plethora of social and economic factors mentioned above. The implications for the future of Irish could not be anything but negative. Bilingual communities tend to be unstable, with one language or the other winning out in the end. In a situation where one language enjoys high prestige, and the other is perceived as the language of defeat, it is usually not long before the former replaces the latter.

4.1.2 Language attitudes in the Stuart era

In the last chapter, we saw that at the end of the Elizabethan age some bards became aware of the winds of change that were blowing in Ireland. This awareness intensified under the Stuarts. The English language was forcing itself into the consciousness of the Gaelic community in ways which could no longer be ignored.

This new linguistic reality was summed up pithily by the poet Dáibhí Ó Bruadair:

> Is mairg atá gan béarla binn
> [Woe to him who knows no fancy English.]
>
> (Mac Erlean 1910: 18)

The big problem for poets was that the society which had supported them was collapsing. The chiefs who had provided patronage were losing their lands and their status. The intermittent wars and general upheaval in the country made it difficult for the Bardic schools to continue their activity. The religion which had been so much a part of Gaelic society was under threat. Last but not least, there was linguistic and intellectual competition from the powerful newcomer, the English language.

The initial reaction of the poets and literati was derision for the new order, and sorrow at the passing of the old ways. The change in society and culture meant that the old esoteric Bardic poetry with its strict rules had to give way to new, simpler, song metres. The poets reluctantly began to compose in the new mode, which they considered common and vulgar. But they still maintained their disdainful attitude to the new culture. In the following quatrains, the poet connects the arrival of the new language to the embracing of English dress by the plain people of Ireland. Both are regarded as a symptom of the lower orders getting above themselves:

Och! mo chreachsa faisean chláir Éibhir!
loca cas ar mhac gach mná déarca,
cufa geal 'ma ghlaic is fáinne aerach,
mar gach flaith d'fhuil Chais dár ghnáth Éire.
[Och! I am aghast at the fashion of Ireland! Every beggar's son with his hair curled, a white cuff on his wrist and a sparkling ring, as if he were a prince of noble blood whose home is Ireland.]

'S gach mogh nó a mhac go stairs go hard lé smig,
cor tar ais dá scairf is gáirtéar air,
stoc tobac 'na chlab dá lántséideadh,
's a chrobh ó alt go halt fá bhráisléidibh.
[Every serf and his son covered up to the chin in starch, his scarf thrown back and he wearing a garter, blasts of smoke from the pipe-stem in his mouth, and every joint of his hand covered in bracelets.]

Is cor do leag mé cleas an phlás-tsaoilse:
mogh in gach teach ag fear an smáilBhéarla,
's gan scot ag neach le fear den dáimh éigse
ach: 'hob amach 's beir leat do shárGhaelgsa'.
[The tricks of this false world have laid me low: every house where tainted English is spoken has a servant, and no heed paid to the poet but: 'Clear out! and take your fine Irish with you!']

(de Brún et al. 1971: 11)

The overthrow of the old Gaelic order was a revolution. Like all revolutions, there were winners and losers. The losers were the Gaelic and Old English aristocrats and the poets that they had maintained, and also the clergy. However, there is some evidence that the fortunes of the better-off Irish tenants improved in the new order of things. *Pairlement Chloinne Tomáis* [The parliament of the Clan Thomas] (PCT) is a satire on the 'economic and social ambitions of an emergent entrepreneurial class, which had exploited the uncertainty of the late sixteenth and early seventeenth centuries to better its lot' (Caball 1993: 48–9). In the text, the peasants hold an imaginary parliament where they decide to throw off the yoke of their old masters, the native Gaelic aristocracy, and ally themselves with the new rulers. In a later version of PCT, one of the characters even composes a poem in the Bardic style, praising Oliver Cromwell. One of the signs of social climbing which the author objects to is the participation of the upstarts in the new craze for smoking tobacco. In the following passage, the 'parliamentarians' see an English tobacco-pedlar coming towards them. They want to buy some tobacco from him, but are faced with the dilemma of lacking a common language. One of them, Tomás an Trumpa [Thomas of the trumpet], has no such inhibitions, and blithely undertakes to purchase the tobacco on behalf of his companions:

Níor chian dóibh annsin an tan do-chunncadar óglách gallda chuca. 'Cia an fear gallda úd chugainn?' ar fear díobh. 'As aithnid damhsa é', ar fear eile, '.i. Roibín an Tobaca é siúd, agas is maith an tobac bhíos aige do ghnáth'. 'Ceannócham cuid de', ar Bernard Ó Bruic, 'agas cia aguinn laibheorus Béarla ris?' 'Mise féin', ar Tomás. Táinig an t-óglách gallda agas beannuigheas go ceannsa agas adubhairt: 'God bless you, Thomas, and all your company'. Do fhreagair Tomás dó go neamhthuaisceartach agas as eadh adubhairt: 'Pleshy for you, pleshy, goodman Robin'. 'Dar anmuin mo mháthar', ar Bernard Ó Bruic, 'do dhubhshloigis rogha an Bhéarla'. Do thionólsad cách 'na thimpchioll ag machtnughadh uim Bhéarla Thomáis. 'Fiafruigh cunnradh an tobaca', ar Bernard. Do labhair Tomás agas as eadh adubhairt: 'What the bigg greate órdlach for the what so penny for is the la yourself for me?' Adubhairt Roibín: 'I know, Thomas, you aske how many enches is worth the penny', agus do thóguibh a dhá mhéar mar chomhartha, agas adubhairt: 'Two penny an ench'. Dar láimh mo chairdios Críost, maith an cunnradh', ar Tomás. 'Créad é?' ar Diarmuid Dúr. 'Órdlach ar an dá phinginn', ar Tomás. 'Déana tacuigheacht oruinn', ar cách. 'Do-dhéan', ar Tomás agas adubhairt: 'Is ta for meself the mony for fart you all my brothers here'. Adubhairt Roibín: 'I thanke you, honest Thomas, you shall command all my tobaco.' 'Begog, I thanke you', ar Tomás. Fuair Tomás an tobaco ar a fhocal agas tug do chách é.

[It was not long before they saw a young Englishman coming towards them. 'Who is that Englishman coming towards us?' said one of them. 'I know him,' said another of them, 'that's Robin of the Tobacco, and he usually has good tobacco.' 'We'll buy some of it', said Bernard Ó Bruic. 'Which of us will speak English to him?' 'I will', said Tomás. The young Englishman came up and greeted them civilly and said: 'God bless you, Thomas, and all your company.' Tomás answered him not uncivilly and said: 'Pleshy for you, pleshy, goodman Robin.' 'Upon my mother's soul,' said Bernard Ó Bruic, 'you really have absorbed the choicest English.' Everybody gathered around him marvelling at Tomás's English. 'Ask what the deal is with the tobacco', said Bernard.

Tomás spoke and said: 'What the bigg greate órdlach for the what so penny for is the la yourself for me?' Robin said: 'I know, Thomas, you aske how many enches is worth the penny', and he lifted up his two fingers as a sign, and said: 'Two penny an ench.' 'By the hand of my godparent, it's a good bargain', said Tomás. 'What is it?' said Diarmuid Dúr. 'Twopence an inch', said Tomás. 'Talk to him for us', said the others. 'I will', said Tomás and said: 'Is ta for meself the mony for fart you all my brothers here'. Robin said: 'I thanke you, honest Thomas, you shall command all my tobaco.' 'Begog, I thanke you', said Tomás. He got the tobacco and distributed it to the rest.]

(Williams 1981: 40)

The above passage is illuminating for a number of reasons. First, the author knows English quite well. When Robin talks, he speaks standard Early Modern English. What comes from the mouth of Tomás, on the other hand, is a garbled mish-mash of English words and Irish. To manipulate different registers like this requires more than a passing acquaintance with a foreign language. In the previous chapter, we noted the presence of a degree of bilingualism in Ireland at the end of the Tudor era. Judging by the surviving Irish texts of the seventeenth century, the learned class had a reasonable acquaintance with English, even if they didn't approve of it.

What Caball (1993) calls the *arriviste* class, on the other hand, may not have known any English, but they seem to have been keen to learn it. It is true that PCT is a work of fiction, and one would not wish to read too much into one single passage. Nevertheless, it is striking how little animosity there is between the Irish characters and the English peddler. If we are to believe some history books, the encounter described above should have epitomized the clash of two cultures. But contrary to all expectations, the commercial transaction took place in an atmosphere of peace and to the mutual satisfaction of both parties. For Tomás and his friends, English represents not a threat, but new opportunities.

Caball (1993) discusses a real-life figure who, he argues, may have been a prototype for the kind of *parvenu* satirized in PCT. The person in question, Patrick Crosbie, came from a Gaelic family, but for many years he served the English interest in Ireland. In order to gain a foothold in the new order, he Anglicized his surname from Mac an Chrosáin to Crosbie, and had his daughter marry a settler. There must have been other people like Crosbie active in the political and legal worlds of early seventeenth-century Ireland, men who used their knowledge of the Gaelic legal and cultural systems to feather their own nests and aid the colonization project. Thus, although it is not a historical document in the modern sense of the word, PCT seems to be based on the realities of the rapid changes which Ireland was undergoing at the time of composition.

Mac Mathúna (2007) notes that the use of English is characteristic of a number of seventeenth-century texts which satirize the lower orders. Just like PCT, in these later texts we observe great admiration on the part of the native Irish for the new language, and for those who speak it. The editors of a recent work on the interaction between Irish and English sum up the diverging responses of the different interest groups to the spread of English as follows:

> Moreover, though it is not difficult to locate poets and poems that characterized this development as profoundly regressive, the generality of the Irish-speaking Catholic population were more pragmatic.
>
> (Kelly and Mac Murchaidh 2012a: 23)

Pragmatism, rather than idealism, was to become even more widespread in the years to come.

4.1.3 Interaction between English and Irish at the written level

Up until the seventeenth century, while there was a good deal of translation from English to Irish, there was little activity in the opposite direction. Certain Irish words and phrases found their way into legal and historical documents, but there is no evidence of any major text being translated from Irish into English. After 1600, this was to change, as English landowners took possession of the whole country. The new ruling class was initially hostile to the Irish language and to Irish culture. However, as that class settled in Ireland and put down roots there, its more enlightened members began to take an interest in the history and traditions of their adopted homeland. Even as the old Gaelic learned class began to decline, certain individuals found new patrons among the New English, the group which came to prominence in this era.

In the early seventeenth century, two leading scholars, Sir James Ware and Archbishop James Ussher, began to collect Irish-language manuscripts in order to acquire sources for investigating early Irish history. Antiquarians like these were handicapped by their ignorance of Irish, and therefore had to turn for help to Gaelic scribes who knew English to read and translate the works in question for them. Thus began a tradition of collecting and translating which was to continue right up to the middle of the nineteenth century. In an article on this subject, Bernadette Cunningham and Raymond Gillespie demonstrate the degree of collaboration between Anglo-Irish and English manuscript collectors and Irish scribes and literati. Here is their description of one of these scribes:

> MacGeoghegan was a man who straddled two worlds, native Irish yet literate in English. He was a new landowner who had connections with the old order and this

ensured that he was well placed to act as a conduit between two traditions of manuscript use and to facilitate the circulation of manuscripts and printed books among
different cultural groups.

(Cunningham and Gillespie 2012: 70)

Thanks to the work of MacGeoghegan and other Gaelic scribes like Dubhal-
tach Mac Fhirbhisigh, works like Keating's *Foras Feasa ar Éirinn* [History of
Ireland] (Comyn and Dinneen 1902–14) or the *Annals of Clonmacnoise*
(Murphy 1896) were translated into English. In some cases the translations
were published in book form, so that the texts made the transition from the old
manuscript culture to the new world of printing.

We saw in the last chapter how attempts had been made in the reign of
Elizabeth to provide reading matter in Irish for the new Church of Ireland.
This trend continued in the seventeenth century. The most notable achievement was the translation of the Old Testament into Irish. The initiator of this
project was an Englishman, William Bedell. In 1627, when he was 56, he was
made provost of Trinity College in Dublin, and later transferred to the diocese
of Kilmore. Bedell was passionately interested in languages, and set about
learning Irish as soon as he arrived in Ireland. Despite the fact that he was a
Puritan, and as such an opponent of Catholicism, he seems to have been a
benevolent man, lacking the prejudice towards the Irish so often found in
other Englishmen at the time. Sometime in the 1630s he formed the project of
translating the Old Testament and Apocrypha into Irish. For this purpose, he
engaged the services of two Irishmen, Séamas de Nógla and Muircheartach Ó
Cionga. Bedell translated the original texts into English, and then the Irishmen
translated them into Irish, the final result then being compared with the
original. The work was completed in 1638, and published in 1685 (*Seintiomna*
1685); Robert Boyle, the Oxford scientist, covered the cost of the publication.
The whole of the Bible was now available in Irish. Shortly afterwards the Old
and New Testaments were published together in a single volume. The Irish
translation of the books of Scripture is known popularly as Bedell's Bible.

4.1.4 The Irish abroad

The translation activity described above took place in Ireland with the sanc-
tion of the new authorities. Meanwhile, an important centre of learning and
translation had come into being in Louvain in the Low Countries, which at the
time was ruled by Catholic Spain. In 1606 an Irish College was established
in Louvain for the education of Franciscans. This attracted a group of priests
who were also well versed in the manuscript tradition of their native country.
By 1611 the Franciscans in Louvain had acquired a printing press with Irish

characters, which they used to publish a number of works designed for use in Ireland.

Most of these works were religious in nature. These include Flaithrí Ó Maolchonaire's translation of the Catalan allegory, *Desiderius* (Des), into Irish (O'Rahilly 1941), and Aodh Mac Aingil's *Scáthán Shacraimint na hAithridhe* [Reflection of the sacrament of penance] (Ó Maonaigh 1952). However, the best-known enterprise in which the Franciscans were involved was the compilation of *Ánnala Ríoghacht Éireann* [Annals of the Four Masters] (O'Donovan 1990 [1854]), a history of Ireland based mostly on manuscript sources. This is an invaluable source for historians of medieval Ireland.

There seems to have been a growing awareness in the seventeenth century that the old written language was becoming increasingly inaccessible to speakers of Irish. For this reason, the Franciscans also published what might be described as language-teaching materials. One such work was *Rudimenta grammaticae Hiberniae* [Basics of Irish grammar] by Bonaventure Ó hEodhasa (Mac Aogáin 1968). Another was one of the first Irish dictionaries, *Foclóir no sanasan nua* [Dictionary or new etymology] (Miller 1879–80, 1881–3), by Micheál Ó Cléirigh.

The scholars of Louvain were operating in a different milieu to their Anglo-Irish counterparts in Ireland. Latin was still the language of the Catholic church. The Franciscans were anxious to make their Continental colleagues aware of the existence of Irish saints and their work. To this end, they translated into Latin and edited a huge body of material concerning these saints. This material was published in three books in Louvain in the 1640s.

Other Neo-Latin writers in the seventeenth century drew on the Gaelic literary tradition for their material. Thus Dermot O'Meara published in 1615 an epic poem called *Ormonius* [Ormond], in which he extolled the life and military prowess of Thomas Butler, Earl of Ormond. In an essay on this poem, Keith Sidwell and David Edwards (2009) argue that the poem was partly inspired by native literary genres. Another important Neo-Latin text by an Irish author was the *Commentarius Rinuccinianus* [Rinuccini commentary] (Kavanagh 1932), which dealt with the wars of the 1640s. McLaughlin (2009) shows that one of the authors of this work, Robert O'Connell, actually translated some Bardic verses into Latin and included them in the *Commentarius*. Writers like O'Meara and O'Connell were writing for the benefit of an international community which still used Latin as the language of communication; their concern was to put forward particular versions of recent events. Their work thus may be regarded as political propaganda.

4.2 The shape of the language (1600–1700)

4.2.1 Late Modern Irish (LMI)

The Early Modern phase is usually said to come to an end between 1600 and 1650. The reason that this date has been selected is that a gradual change can be observed in the language found in written records after 1600. This is mainly due to the change in poetic practice described in section 4.1.1, whereby the old syllabic metres were replaced by stressed ones. These stressed metres reflected more faithfully the pronunciation of the time than the Bardic ones had done. Take these lines from a poem written about 1650:

(1)   Do lag mo chreat gan neart mná seolta,
       gan bhrí gan mheabhair gan ghreann gan fhónamh.
       Adhbhar maoithe scaoileadh an sceóil sin,
       cás gan leigheas is adhnadh tóirse.

       [It weakened my frame so that I hadn't the strength of a woman in labour, deprived of vigour, sense, joy, or worth. The broadcasting of this story is a source of sadness, a plight without cure, and kindling of sorrow.]

                                                    (de Brún *et al.* 1971: 31)

In l.2, we find the word *meabhair* 'sense'. In a Bardic poem, this would have been pronounced as two syllables, /mavir/. However, in the metre of the seventeenth century, there has to be an assonance or vowel-rhyme between it and the word *greann* 'joy', which only has one syllable. We know from twentieth-century Irish that *meabhair* and *greann* rhyme, both being pronounced with a vowel like English /ow/: /miowr/, /grown/. The conclusion we can draw is that this change in *meabhair*, from two syllables to one, and from the vowel /a/ to /ow/, had already taken place in the seventeenth century. In the same way, in l.4 above, *leigheas* 'cure' rhymes with the first syllable of *adhnadh* 'kindling', both being pronounced like /ai/ in the English word *like*: /lais/, /aina/. In Bardic poetry, though, *leigheas* would have had two syllables, /leghas/. The <a> in the first syllable of *adhnadh* would have been pronounced /a/ not /ai/, and the <dh> in *adhnadh* would have been pronounced like the first sound in British English *that*.

The poetry of this period is useful, then, as it reveals changes that had taken place in the spoken language but which are not reflected in spelling: only the rhymes tell us what the pronunciation would have been. After 1600, scribes begin to write more and more as they speak, although they try to follow the old spelling as far as possible. For this reason, from the beginning of the seventeenth century onwards we can form some picture of Irish dialects. Before this, as we saw, there was one standard written language for Ireland and Gaelic

Scotland. After 1600, various regions were gradually to go their own way, as it were, which led to the rise of different dialects.

It would be wrong to think that there was a sudden overnight change, whereby a single, totally homogenous language broke up into widely diverging dialects. The writers of Irish were conservative, and still tried to imitate the writers of the past. Some of them continued to use forms of the language that had long become obsolete, because they felt that they were more prestigious. This tendency is very noticeable in prose tales written in seventeenth-century manuscripts. While it is true that Irish developed some new forms of literary narrative in this era, such as the satire and morality tale, there is a preponderance of romance tales in the surviving manuscripts. These romance tales were written down in the seventeenth century, but they display archaic features from earlier eras. It is debatable to what extent we are justified in referring to these as compositions of the period 1600–1700, especially since they are based on earlier exemplars.

Other genres were intended for a wider, more popular audience. Religious works, such as sermons or translations of theological tracts, are abundantly represented in this era. These works were probably intended to be read aloud to large audiences. The language in them represents a high register, but is firmly grounded in the Irish of the day, not of the past. The texts contain numerous references to contemporary events, and also large numbers of new loan-words or coinings. The editor of one such text, *Párliament na mBan* [The parliament of women] (PB), written about 1697, describes the language in it in the following words:

The Irish of Párliament na mBan is interesting, for it represents a stage of development intermediate between Early Modern Irish and current Cork Irish ... The developments which had taken place in the spoken language during the preceding centuries are reflected to a considerable extent in Párliament na mBan, and indeed, we may feel sure that apart from the points I have already mentioned, the Irish ... is very little removed from the Irish spoken in County Cork at the end of the seventeenth century.

(Ó Cuív 1977: xxxi)

We can illustrate the change from EMI to LMI by comparing PB with a text belonging to the same genre, *Desiderius* (O'Rahilly 1941) (Des). The latter was published in 1616, and represents a much more conservative strain of Irish than does PB. The following two examples are illustrative of this conservatism. In EMI, the noun *corp* 'body' had a special form *curp*, which was used after certain prepositions, e.g *ar churp* 'on a body'. In the later language, this distinction has been lost, with the basic form *corp* being used after prepositions: *ar chorp*. The text of Des contains examples of both the old and new forms. In PB, on the other hand, the older *curp* has been replaced everywhere by the basic form after prepositions, as in twentieth-century Irish; we only find forms like *ar a chorp* 'on his body' (Ó Cuív 1977: 5).

The second example relates to verbs. In section 2.2.1, we saw that in EMI the present tense of the verb ends in -(a)idh when the subject is *he/she*, e.g. *molaidh* 'he/she praises'. In twentieth-century Irish, on the other hand, the verb ends in -(e)ann followed by *sé/sí*, e.g. *molann sé/sí* 'he/she praises'. Des only contains verbs with the -(a)idh ending like *molaidh*. In PB, on the other hand, we only find modern forms like *molann sé/sí*.

Just how tricky and complicated the dating of language in this period is can be illustrated by the different manuscript versions of PB. There is another version of PB besides the one from 1697; the second manuscript dates from 1703. Despite the fact that the second version is more recent than the first, the language in it is older and more artificial. In contrast to the earlier version, we find here the ending -(a)idh for the third-person sg of the present tense of the verb, e.g. *cuiridh* 'he/she puts'.

One reason why written records from 1600 onwards are so valuable is that Irish was still spoken all over the island, including the province of Leinster in the eastern part of the country. By the time scholars began collecting specimens of spoken Irish around 1900, there was hardly any Irish left in Leinster. Thus, with the aid of texts from LMI, scholars have been able to reconstruct a pretty accurate picture of the Irish spoken in areas where it has been long dead.

4.2.2 Borrowing and code-switching

We have already noted the spread of English and bilingualism in the seventeenth century. Not surprisingly, then, we also find English making its presence felt in the Irish records of the time.

The poets and literati were firmly opposed to the new language and all it stood for. Nevertheless, their writings are liberally sprinkled with borrowings from English. One area where there was extensive borrowing was legal terminology, which was to be expected, given that English common law was being imposed all over the country. The following extract may serve as an example of the introduction of English, Latin, and French legal terms into Irish texts:

(2)   Is docht na dlithe do rinneadh dár ngéarghoin:
       siosúin cúirte is téarmaí daora,
       wardship livery is Cúirt *Exchéquer*,
       cíos coláisde *in nomine poenae*;
       greenwax, capias, writ, replévin,
       bannaí, fíneáil, díotáil éigcirt,
       provost, soffré, portré, méara,

sirriam, sionascáil, marascáil chlaona.
Dlí beag eile do rinneadh do Ghaeulaibh,
surrender ar a gceart do dhéanamh.

[Severe are the laws which were made to heavily wound us: court sessions
and harsh terms, wardship livery and Exchequer Court, greenwax, capias,
writ, replevin, bail, fining, wrongful indicting, provost, suffrain, portreeve,
mayor, sheriff, seneschal, crooked marshals. Another little law that was
enacted for the Gaels, to surrender their rights.]

(O' Rahilly 1952: 73–4)

As Mac Mathúna (2007) remarks, passages like the above display varying
degrees of integration of English words into the borrowing language. Some, like
siosúin 'sessions', look like ordinary Irish words. English /s/ has been replaced by
Irish /sh/, as regularly happens in borrowings from English to Irish, and the new
word has been assigned to the group of nouns whose plural is formed by adding
<i> to the singular: siosún (sg), *siosúin* (pl). This is a case of total integration.
On the other hand, some items are left in their English guise, words like *greenwax,
writ, provost, surrender.* This last option is a case of code-switching.

Sometimes the code-switching is more extensive, with whole phrases of
English being placed in a text side by side with the Irish. Here are some lines
from a different poem, describing the events taking place during and after the
Cromwellian pacification of Ireland:

(3)   *Transport, transplant*, mo mheabhair ar Bhéarla [is what I understand of
       English.]
       Shoot him, kill him, strip him, tear him,
       A tory, hack him, hang him, rebel,
       a rogue, a thief, a priest, a papist.

(O'Rahilly 1952: 90)

In this poem the framework is Irish, but whole passages of English have been
inserted into it. As we will see in the next chapter, code-switching was to
become even more common in the following century.

4.3 Conclusion

The historical background to this chapter were the turbulent events which led
to Ireland being totally subjugated to English rule. Not surprisingly, this
military and political conquest was accompanied by social and linguistic
change. As a result, English language and culture spread all over the country.

Up to 1550, English and Irish occupied more or less separate geographical and
intellectual domains. One could live one's life through the medium of Irish

without having to bother too much about the existence of English, any more than an Irish person in the twenty-first century worries too much about the influence of French on his life. After 1700 nobody, not even the inhabitants of the remotest island off the west coast of Ireland, could ignore the presence of English.

At the beginning of Tudor rule, language and ethnic identity were closely intertwined. While it is true that the Old English were a mixed group, containing both Irish and English speakers, members of the Gaelic families spoke almost exclusively Irish. By 1700 that situation had changed completely. English was now a badge not of ethnic but of social identity. It was spoken by the Protestant Ascendancy and the townspeople, which is not surprising, but it was also spoken by the Catholic landowners and middle classes, and even the common people were taking an interest in it. This in turn meant that the Irish language was increasingly coming under its influence.

Further reading

For Stuart Ireland, see Mac Curtain (1972: 89–196).

For general surveys of language and literature 1600–1700, see Ó Cuív (1976) and Mac Craith (2006). Ó Háinle (1978) deals with new forms of prose fiction in the seventeenth century.

Cunningham (2000) is a monograph on the historian Geoffrey Keating and the context in which he was writing. Ó Buachalla (1996: 3–228) is an exhaustive study of the reaction of the Gaelic literati to the Stuart monarchs of the seventeenth century and the key events that accompanied their reigns. It explores in depth many of the themes touched upon in this chapter, such as the connection between religion and identity, or the work of historians like Keating and the Four Masters.

Ó Doibhlin (2007) is a collection of extracts from texts written in the years 1616–41. These include many classics of Irish literature like Keating's *Foras Feasa ar Éirinn* (Comyn and Dinneen 1902–14), or various poems lamenting the downfall of the old Gaelic order. Ó Doibhlin (2008) covers the period 1641–1704, which witnessed the final conquest of Ireland. It contains poems from important literary figures like Dáibhí Ó Bruadair, which rail against the incursion of the English settlers and their impact on Gaelic culture.

Smyth (2006) explores the effect of colonization and plantation on the physical landscape, and also its impact on social, economic, and cultural life. The author's use of statistics and maps makes this an invaluable contribution to our understanding of this era.

Mac Giolla Chríost (2005: 84–96) describes the linguistic changes which overtook Ireland in the seventeenth century. He provides a clear summary of the spread of English in various parts of Ireland. Smyth (2006: 401–15) provides a detailed account of the geographical distribution of English and Irish on the basis of such tools as the poll-tax of 1660, the depositions of witnesses to the 1641 Ulster rebellion, and the evidence of English and Scottish surnames.

For source documents relating to language in Stuart Ireland, see Crowley (2000: 54–78).

For language attitudes in the Stuart era, see Mac Mathúna (2007: 89–181).

For the reaction of the poets to linguistic and cultural change, see Leersen (1996a: 190–228).

For the translation of Irish antiquarian texts into English, see Cunningham and Gillespie (2012). For the translation of the Old Testament into Irish, see Williams (1986: 43–55); McCaughey (2001); and Caball (2012).

For Irish scholarship on the Continent, see Leersen (1996a: 254–77); Mac Craith (2006: 197–214); Jennings (2008); and Cunningham and Gillespie (2012).

For Neo-Latin writings in this period, see Millett (1976) and Harris and Sidwell (2009).

For the development of LMI and the emergence of dialects, see Williams (1994). This contains a useful map showing the three main dialects which began to make themselves visible in this period. A further advantage is that the presentation is not over-technical.

For borrowing and code-switching in this period, see Mac Mathúna (2007: 89–114).

5

Two Irelands, two languages (1700–1800)

5.1 The Anglo-Irish Ascendancy

The Treaty of Limerick brought to an end the wars which had ravaged Ireland for over a hundred years. The period 1700–1800 was one of peace. However, this peace was based on an oppressive legal system which discriminated against that part of the population which did not conform to the established religion, the Church of Ireland.

5.1.1 The Penal Laws

The Protestant ruling class in Ireland had been badly shaken by the accession of the Catholic James II to the throne in 1685. If he had kept his crown, they would have had to give up many of their privileges. The Stuarts had gone into exile, but they continued to lay claim to the throne of the three kingdoms—England, Scotland, and Ireland—right up until the death of James II's son in 1766. After the death of Queen Anne in 1714, there was the danger of her half-brother James III succeeding to the throne. To avert such a possibility, the English parliament invited George, the Elector of Hanover, to accept the crown. Thus began the rule of the Hanoverian (also called Georgian) dynasty, which was to last right through the eighteenth century.

In order to copper-fasten the Protestant grip on Ireland, a series of laws were enacted which made second-class citizens of the Catholics. They were forbidden the right to bear arms, or to have their children educated abroad in Catholic schools. Their clergy were not allowed to operate openly in Ireland, although many bishops and priests continued to carry out their duties right through the eighteenth century in defiance of the law. The new restrictions also made it difficult for the children of the few remaining Catholic land-owners to inherit property. Catholics were not allowed to sit in the parliament in Dublin, or to vote unless they took an oath abjuring the Stuarts and the Catholic religion. Because Catholics were banned from the only university in the country, Trinity College in Dublin, they were denied access to the professions. They were also unable to take commissions in the army.

Apart from Catholics, various non-Anglican Protestant churches were discriminated against, although they were not treated as severely as the Catholics. The most numerous Protestant group were Presbyterians, who were concentrated in the north-east of the country. Unlike the Catholics, they did not lose their lands, and they managed to achieve economic prosperity in agriculture, trade, and industry.

The net result of these Penal Laws, as they were called, was to create a three-tier society, with the Anglican minority, the Anglo-Irish Ascendancy, dominating the economic, legal, and cultural life of the country. This minority was concentrated in Dublin and the larger towns. In the countryside, the landowners built imposing mansions for themselves, many of which, like Castletown House and Carton House in County Kildare, are still standing. The Ascendancy was responsible for giving the centre of Dublin the shape which it maintains to the present day, particularly for the wide streets and squares so typical of what is now called Georgian architecture. Dublin was an important urban centre in eighteenth-century Europe, and had a number of imposing features, including the House of Parliament (now the Bank of Ireland on College Green), Trinity College, the Customs House, and the Four Courts, as well as St Stephen's Green and the Phoenix Park.

Meanwhile, the majority of the inhabitants of Ireland, the Catholics, were living in conditions of extreme poverty. Most of them were tenant farmers, dependent for their livelihood on the good will of the landlord. One burden which was the source of much complaint was the obligation to pay tithes to the local Church of Ireland minister, even though most of the parishioners were not members of his flock. Not surprisingly, housing and food were of the most basic kind, with the potato being the only source of nourishment for the majority of the population. Visitors to Ireland like the English traveller Arthur Young were horrified by the conditions that they found there. Lord Chesterfield, who was Lord Lieutenant of Ireland in the 1740s, wrote that 'The poor people in Ireland are used worse than negroes by their lords and masters' (Dobrée 1932: VI, 2617).

From 1770 onwards, conditions for the Catholic middle class began to improve as the severest of the Penal Laws were rescinded or at least toned down. Simultaneously, there was a move among liberal members of the Ascendancy to provide everybody with the same civil rights as they themselves enjoyed. By 1793 the only barrier that remained to full emancipation was the right to be a member of parliament, although there was still much unofficial discrimination against Catholics in everyday life. Nevertheless, the ground had been prepared for them to attain full citizenship in the following century, and the days of the Ascendancy were numbered.

5.1.2 The hidden Ireland

After 1600, Gaelic Ireland began to diverge more and more from the mainstream of European social and cultural development. As we have seen, while there continued to be writing in Irish in the period 1600–1700, there was very little engagement with the world of print. After 1700, speakers of Irish were excluded from the centres of power and education which would have facilitated participation in the kind of intellectual activity found in other linguistic communities at the time. For this reason, they became, as it were, inaudible to outsiders, even if those outsiders lived in geographical proximity to them.

It was this low profile of Gaelic society which led Daniel Corkery to choose the title *The hidden Ireland* for his study of the Irish-language poetry of eighteenth-century Ireland (Corkery 1924). So influential has this work been, that the very title has become part of the permanent vocabulary of the debate on Ireland in this era. Modern scholars have rejected many of Corkery's views and statements (see Further reading for references), but the basic thesis cannot be denied: the Gaelic literature which was circulated in oral form and manuscript was to remain hidden from the English-speaking world until he and others like him wrote about it two centuries later.

At the same time, the fact that it was invisible to the ruling class did not mean that Gaelic Ireland did not have its own means of disseminating ideas:

Gaelic Ireland possessed its own public sphere and that this was defined by the existence of networks of communication and by its Irish-language manuscript culture, particularly the copying and exchange of political verse.

(Ní Mhunghaile 2012: 228)

Thus, although writers in Irish were excluded from the world of print, they were not totally disempowered; they simply expressed themselves through a different medium. Poems were recorded in manuscripts, but they were usually recited aloud to a large audience, so that everybody in the community, not just the literate, could enjoy them.

Until recently Irish history was based on state records and other texts like personal letters and diaries, all of which were written by members of the upper or middle classes, in English. The publishing in the twentieth century of Irish-language poetry gives us a glimpse of what was going on in the lives of the ordinary people at the time, and so is a valuable source not just for literary scholars but also for social historians. We can see this by comparing how one particular subject, the authority of the Hanoverian monarchs, was treated in English and Irish. The English-language writings of the time nearly all accepted the status quo of English rule in Ireland. Even a work like *Ireland's case briefly stated* (Reily 1720), an *apologia* for the Catholic position, is careful not to offend the government authorities: 'Reily's position, therefore, although Jacobite, is loyal and legalistic, stressing the injustices done to the Catholic élite and the need to redress them' (Ó Ciosáin 1997: 116).

In the Gaelic poetry there was no need to be so circumspect, and the poets gave free vent to their support for the Stuart cause, and also to their religious sectarianism. Much of the writing of the time was what might be called political poetry. In it, the poets express their hope that the Stuarts will return to the throne of the three kingdoms, bringing with them religious freedom, the return of confiscated lands, and the restoration of Gaelic culture. These poems are called Jacobite poetry, from the Latin *Jacobus* 'James', because they were written in support of James II, and later his son, James III (1688–1766). They usually end with a prophecy:

> Beidh Éire go súgach's a dúnta go haerach
> is Gaedhilg 'gá scrúdadh n-a múraibh ag éigsibh;
> Béarla na mbúr ndubh go cúthail fá néalaibh,
> is Séamus n-a chúirt ghil ag tabhairt chonganta do Ghaedhealaibh.
> [Ireland will be joyous and her settlements will be gay, and scholars will be studying Irish within their walls; the English of the dark churls will be brought low and disgraced, and James in his bright court will be helping the Gaels.]

> Beidh an Bíobla sin Liútair 's a dhubhtheagaisc éithigh,
> 's an bhuidhean so tá cionntach ná humhluigheann don gcléir chirt,
> 'gá ndíbirt tar triúchaibh go Neuland ó Éirinn;
> an Laoiseach 's an Prionnsa beidh cúirt acu is aonach!
> [That Bible of Luther and his false black teaching, and the guilty crew who do not submit to the rightful clergy, will be banished afar to New Land from Ireland; Louis and the Prince will hold court and assembly!]

(Dinneen and O'Donoghue 1911: 166)

The style of this poetry is closer to the vernacular speech of the time than the works of the medieval bards, but there are still a lot of references to figures from Irish mythology, and there is much use of stock epithets to describe nature or the human figures who appear in them. The poems are verbose, with strings of near synonyms and compound nouns and adjectives used more for their sound than for their meaning, a quality which is virtually impossible to preserve in translation:

> Do dhearcas-sa réilteann ghréagach ghreanta
> ghlé, a bhí gasta gnúis-gheal,
> banúil, béasach, béal-tais, blasta,
> céimeach, cneasta, cumtha,
> maisiúil, méineach, maorga, measta,
> aerach, aibí, iúlach.

[I saw a fair lady, splendid, shapely, bright, who was neat and radiant of countenance, womanly, mannerly, moist-lipped, gracious, distinguished, kind, comely, decorative, high-minded, stately, esteemed, cheerful, ripe, knowledgeable.]

(Ua Duinnín 1901: 23)

As can be seen, each line of the Irish contains strings of alliterating words, whose main purpose is to ornament the verse rather than provide information. It is a composition for the ear rather than the intellect.

This, then, was the kind of literature being produced by the less visible of the two worlds I have briefly described, the world of the hidden Ireland. Over and over again we find the same motif: things are bad now, but everything will be alright as soon as the rightful king returns to the throne. There were two attempts made by James III to regain the throne of his ancestors, both of which failed. Even after the collapse of the last Jacobite rebellion in 1746, the Irish poets continued to express their hope that one day the Stuarts would return. Their longing is made all the more poignant by the fact that even if the Stuarts had been restored to the English throne, it is unlikely that they would have reinstated the Irish language to its former position. As the author of a recent publication remarks, 'James II shared the general antipathy of anglophones to the Irish language' (Kelly 2012: 193).

James's son and grandson were to spend most of their lives in France, and would have had no sympathy with Gaeldom. But in their desperation the Irish refused to believe that they had backed a dynasty which cared nothing for them.

5.1.3 Language contact and macaronic poems

Reading Corkery, one has the impression that the Anglophone and Irish-speaking worlds existed in virtual isolation from one another. In linguistic terms, this would imply that bilingualism was not common at the time. Recent work by Mac Mathúna (2007, 2012) has demonstrated that this is far too simplistic a picture of the eighteenth-century reality. This author shows that as well as monolingual Gaelic writings, there have been preserved a large number of bilingual texts which reveal a remarkable degree of language contact.

These texts belong to the genre called macaronic, in which two languages are freely mixed. In the Middle Ages, Latin was often combined with vernacular languages in this way:

Omnes gentes plaudite,
I saw many birds sitting on a tree;
they took their flight and flew away,
with, *ego dixi*, have a good day!

(Ó Muirithe 1980: 28)

The authors of such medieval verses were learned, and often mixed the languages for comic effect, or simply to show off.

We have already seen some examples of this kind of composition in Irish in the previous chapter, but the genre become much more widespread in the eighteenth century. Furthermore, the amount of English in them far exceeds that found in the seventeenth-century compositions, where we only find individual words and phrases in what are essentially Irish texts. In macaronic verse, Irish and English are found in equal measure. Sometimes we find both languages in the same line:

Angelical maid, i do dhéidh ní fada mé beo [I won't live long pining after you]
your virtues so rare a mhéadaíos m'aicíd gach ló [that aggravate my disease every day]
your excellent features, ag déanamh solais i gceo, [lightening the fog]
have power to raise from graves an iomad gan gó. [a crowd without doubt]

(Ó Muirithe 1980: 98)

In other cases, we find whole verses in Irish and English alternating with one another:

Is tá cluanaí de bhuachaill óg 'mo mhealladh gach lá
is níl spuicéad ón tsluasad ach a ghunna ina láimh,
cúilín dúghlas ar mo bhuachaillín is é fite go barr,
is nach trua sin mo ghrá á lua liom is nach bhféadaim 'fháil.
[A young flattering boy is coaxing me every day, and no shovel in his hand but a gun, my little boy has dark hair, tied up to the crown, and isn't it a pity that he's being spoken of as my love and I can't be with him.]

And how late I'm captivated by a handsome young man,
and daily complaining for my own darling John,
I'll be roving all day until the long nights come on,
and I'll be shaded by the green leaves of the *draighneán donn*.

(Ó Muirithe 1980: 62)

Here, the second verse is a partial translation of the first one.

The first text mentioned above, *Angelical maid*, comes from a manuscript source, the second, *An draighneán donn*, survived as a folk-song and was only collected in the twentieth century, but is much older than that. The existence of such texts enables us to form some picture of the linguistic reality of eighteenth-century Ireland. First of all, the poets display an equal mastery of both languages, Irish and English. In fact, many of the best-known poets of this era also wrote whole poems in English. This contrasts with the situation in the seventeenth century, where an active knowledge of English, judging by the literary evidence, was much more limited. Second, the audience for these poems must have had a good passive knowledge of English in order to be able to follow the narrative.

When a speaker can understand another language but is unable to produce utterances in it, linguists use the term receptive bilingualism to describe the competence that the speaker has. There is some evidence that in those parts of the country where there was a sizeable English-speaking population, many people became receptive bilinguals of this sort. The following poem is a literary composition, and cannot be taken as hard scientific evidence, but it is probably indicative of the general trend at the time. In it, the poet-narrator, an Irish speaker, is working when he is addressed by a passing girl in English. A bilingual conversation ensues, in which each party seems to have no difficulty in understanding the other:

The man:
Bhíos-sa lá ar thaobh an chnoic ag treabhadh i ndiaidh mo chéachta,
cé chasfaí chugam ach ainnir chiúin gur deas a súil is a héadan.
Bhí a píob is a bráid mar eala ar linn is a leaca mar na caora,
isé a dúirt sí liom 'god bless your work', is bheannaíos di as Gaelainn.
[One day I was on the side of the hill following my plough, and who should I meet but a gentle maid whose eye and face were pleasant. Her neck and her breast were like the swan on the lake and her cheeks were like berries, she said to me 'God bless your work', and I greeted her in Irish.]

The girl:
In Castletown I took a tour and found no man to please me,
I praised the town and took a rest till I'd relieve some tradesmen.
I am a sporting roving lass with beauty in my favour,
and I was told along the road that you were fond of raking.

The man:
Mhaise, a ainnir chiúin, is ionadh liom go dtabharfá dóibh siúd géilleadh,
go mbeadh mo dhúilse i radaireacht is gan tointe orm den éadach.
Mise ag síorchur allais díom is mo chapaill bhochta á dtraochadh,
sin é an ní is measa liom, is duit ní thabharfainn géilleadh.
[Oh, gentle maid, I am surprised that you would believe those people, that I could be interested in flirting and I without a stitch of clothes. That I am constantly sweating and tiring my horses, that's what I'm concerned about, and I don't believe you.]

The girl:
Give your horses ease and rest 'tis early in the season,
give 'em ease and liberty and don't kill 'em with hard labour.
'Tis now I crossed the country and I hope that you will treat me,
I'll be at your service, sir, for only sixpence ha'penny.

(Ó Muirithe 1980: 43)

From the last line of stanzas 2 and 3, and the first lines of stanzas 3 and 4, it is clear that this is a coherent dialogue, despite the mixture of languages. In stanza 3, the man replies to the girl's suggestion that he might be interested in her services, while in stanza 4, she dismisses his excuse that he has too much work to do. Everything points to their being able to understand each other.

There are so many examples of this kind of bilingual dialogue that it is hard to believe that they do not reflect some kind of linguistic reality. In the seventeenth century, bilingual encounters tended to be between natives of Ireland and newcomers, like Robin of the Tobacco in *Pairlement Chloinne Tomáis* (section 4.1.1). We also saw that English tended to have strongly negative associations for the poets of the time, particularly after the Cromwellian conquest. The eighteenth-century bilingual encounters, on the other hand, seem to be between members of the same class, and possibly even of the same ethnic origin. As Liam Mac Mathúna puts it:

By the eighteenth century much of the rancour associated with the use of English within the Irish textual tradition was yielding to a mixture of pragmatism and literary exploitation, as the Irish were transforming themselves into *lucht an Bhéarla* [English speakers], the formerly despised 'others' of poets such as Mac Cumhaigh.

(Mac Mathúna 2012: 137)

5.1.4 The Anglo-Irish and the Irish language

At the beginning of the eighteenth century, the new ruling class, the Anglo-Irish, were violently opposed to all things Irish, including the language. The attitude of Jonathan Swift, the author and pamphleteer, is illustrative. Like many members of the Anglo-Irish, Swift felt himself to be English, even though he had been born in Ireland. He spent much of his life bemoaning the fact that he had ended up in Ireland as dean of St Patrick's cathedral in Dublin. His attitude to the indigenous language of his country can be deduced from the following quotation from his pamphlet *On barbarous denominations in Ireland*:

I am deceived, if any thing hath more contributed to prevent the Irish from being tamed, than this encouragement of their language, which might easily be abolished, and become a dead one in half an age, with little expence, and less trouble.

(Davis and Landa 1964: 280; quoted in Crowley 2000: 114)

Sentiments like these could be heard from various members of the Protestant elite for many years after Swift's death. However, in the course of the eighteenth century, some of the Anglo-Irish came to form for themselves a new identity as Irishmen, one which was distinct from both Gaelic and English culture, but contained elements of both. One of the reasons for this growth in national awareness among the Anglo-Irish was an interest in the Gaelic past. Following in the tradition of the seventeenth century, members of learned bodies like the Dublin Philosophical Society set about investigating the linguistic and material remains of ancient Ireland. As far as language was concerned, they were mostly interested in old manuscripts and in translations of the same. However, some of them were prepared to learn the living contemporary form of Irish in order to further their antiquarian studies. One of the best-known examples of a member of the Anglo-Irish with an interest in Gaelic culture was the Church of Ireland minister Anthony Raymond. While rector of Trim in County Meath, he learned Irish from his parishioners, utilizing this knowledge to make translations from Irish manuscripts. He was friendly with a family of Irish scribes living in Dublin, the Ó Neachtains, and employed them to make copies of manuscripts for him. The rector showed a remarkable degree of adventurousness by reaching out to the despised 'Popish natives', as Swift and his like would have described them. The natives in turn seem to have had a genuine affection for him, and went so far as to Gaelicize his name to Uaithne Réamond.

This kind of collaboration between the old Gaelic culture and the new Anglo-Irish one continued right through the eighteenth century. A major impetus to this interest in the Gaelic past was provided by the publication in 1760 of the work *Fragments of ancient poetry* by a Scotsman called James Macpherson. It was claimed that this was a translation of poems about the hero Ossian (Oisín), collected by Macpherson from illiterate Gaelic-speaking peasants in the Highlands of Scotland. The work was an outstanding success among the English reading public, and it was soon translated into all the major languages of Europe. Thus began the craze for all things Celtic, or allegedly Celtic, which has persisted to the present day.

After the publication of Macpherson's Ossian poems, Irish became more respectable in the eyes of scholars and literati. Charles Vallancey compiled a grammar of Irish in which he tried to create a link between it and other ancient languages. In 1789 Charlotte Brooke published *Reliques of Irish poetry* (Ní Mhunghaile 2009), containing translations of a number of Irish poems. In his discussion of Brooke's work, Leersen makes the important comment that:

She saw the introduction of the Gaelic literary heritage to an Anglo-Irish readership, not, like Macpherson or Gray, as an opportunity to capitalize on its exotic value, but rather ... as a Patriot endeavour in the service of her country: hoping to instil some appreciation for native Gaelic culture among the lettered Irish, and hence, to raise Ireland and its culture in the British estimate.

(Leersen 1996a: 363)

It would be wrong to imagine that people like Anthony Raymond or Charlotte Brooke were representative of the Anglo-Irish community as a whole. Nevertheless, their work is indicative of a change in consciousness among the ruling class, a sign that this class was beginning to feel more comfortable with Ireland's past, including its language.

Finally, I should mention one other manifestation of an interest in Irish, from the closing years of the eighteenth century. The United Irishmen movement of the 1790s was supported by Protestants of various sorts, particularly Ulster Presbyterians. Some of these enthusiastically advocated the printing and learning of Irish, as a result of which in 1795 the first ever periodical in Irish was published in Belfast (*Bolg an tSolair; or Gaelic Magazine* 1795). Only one issue ever appeared, and soon afterwards the whole United Irishmen initiative collapsed, but this publication is yet another sign of change in the attitude of Protestants towards Irish.

5.1.5 The churches and the Irish language

As mentioned earlier, the Church of Ireland had made sporadic attempts in the period 1550–1700 to convert the native Irish to Anglicanism through the medium of Irish. Some well-meaning clergymen continued these efforts in the eighteenth century, but without any great success, partly because many bishops and influential public figures opposed this policy, arguing that it would make more sense to provide religious instruction through the medium of English.

One might have thought that the Catholic church would be more active in the use of Irish, given that large sections of the population and clergy were Irish-speaking. Admittedly, the Penal Laws made it difficult for the Catholic church to operate openly, particularly in the first half of the century. However, after the failure of the Jacobite rebellion of 1745 in Scotland, the fear of a Catholic restoration began to diminish among the Anglo-Irish, and the church could catechize and preach more openly.

The Irish Catholic clergy were recruited from the small class of well-to-do farmers and merchants. In keeping with the overall trend among what we might call the Catholic middle class, the priests and other religious increasingly found their linguistic identity in the English language. One writer on the subject has commented that 'While the clergy did not purposely seek to neglect the Irish language in the eighteenth century, they did not champion it in the manner of the Franciscans at Louvain in the early seventeenth century' (Mac Murchaidh 2012: 164). The same author further remarks that 'The generality of the Catholic clergy possessed neither the linguistic skill nor pastoral will to ensure that the [Irish] language remained central to its evangelizing mission' (164).

One factor which compounded the language problem was the fact that priests had to be educated abroad, in the seminaries of the Catholic countries of the Continent. Right through the eighteenth century, various commentators drew attention to the fact that Irish students tended to lose their active command of Irish while studying on the Continent (Mac Murchaidh 2012). Given that the students were at least 12 years old when they left Ireland, it is difficult to see how they could have lost their command of Irish entirely. What the commentators probably had in mind was that because the language of instruction for the religious studies of the seminarians was not Irish, priests who returned to Ireland later on experienced severe difficulties in speaking, and particularly in writing of such matters in Irish. This would certainly be in keeping with the general tendency to associate Irish entirely with non-written communication concerning everyday matters. Anything demanding a more formal and rigorous approach, like theology and writing sermons, was increasingly conducted through the medium of English.

Another element which must be borne in mind in trying to assess eighteenth-century reports of lack of proficiency in Irish is what we nowadays call language attitude. This refers to the positive or negative feelings which people have to a given language, which can lead them to claim a greater or lesser competence in the language than they actually possess. If one has positive feelings towards a language and the culture that accompanies it, one tends to overestimate one's actual command of the language. If one associates negative values with a language and its speakers, one often downplays one's knowledge of this language.

It is in this light, perhaps, that we ought to interpret the remarks of a priest called James Lyons, discussed in Mac Murchaidh (2012). After eight years spent in Rome studying for the priesthood, Lyons returned to the west of Ireland to work in a parish. In one of his letters he tells us that he has been allowed to return to Dublin 'because of my deficiency in my native language, which for the greater part I forgot in the College' (Fenning 1965: 104; quoted in Mac Murchaidh 2012: 177). A year later he was back in the west of Ireland, from where he wrote, 'I am much occupied in learning the Irish language, and I almost despair of ever learning it to perfection'(Mac Murchaidh 2012: 178). Assuming that Lyons had been brought up speaking Irish, and had not left Ireland before the age of 10 or 11, it is simply not possible that he could have forgotten it to such an extent that he had to start all over again. What is possible is that he had been brought up in a bilingual environment, and had never acquired an active knowledge of Irish, or else that he knew Irish, but simply did not wish to admit to this, because of the low status of the language.

Despite the overall apathy among the clergy regarding the presence of Irish in their work, there were individual bishops and priests who encouraged the use of Irish, and even tried to provide religious material for this purpose. The most outstanding example of this is Bishop James Gallagher, who published a collection of sermons in Irish (Gallagher 1736). This book became very popular and was reprinted several times in the next hundred years. Another work which proved a success was Andrew Donlevy's bilingual catechism, published in Paris (Donlevy 1742).

In 1795, following the relaxation of the Penal Laws, permission was given to the Catholic church to establish a seminary in Maynooth, County Kildare. From now on priests could be trained in Ireland. Now that the conditions were finally favourable for training clergy to conduct their work through the medium of Irish, it turned out to be too late for such a venture, as society at large, and the Catholic church as part of that society, had already embarked on a journey of Anglicization.

5.1.6 A private document

Most of the material from this era written in Irish tends to be very formal in nature. The poetry and prose which have been preserved were composed for public consumption. Very little has survived of what we would regard as personal documents.

Against this background, one text from the eighteenth century stands out. This is a journal for the years 1736–47 (Ní Chinnéide: 1954, 1957). The author was Charles O'Conor of Belanagar, a member of one of the few Catholic families which managed to hold on to their lands in this period. O'Conor was an antiquarian of note who wrote a history of ancient Ireland in which he defended his country against the charges of barbarism which had been laid against it by a number of historians. He was also a founder member of the Catholic Committee, a group of well-off Catholics which successfully campaigned for an easing of the Penal Laws.

Although O'Conor was bilingual, one would have expected somebody of his background and education to have written exclusively in English. For some reason or other he decided to keep a journal in Irish for a period of just over ten years. The subject matter mostly concerns the minutiae of country life: the weather, farm-work, crops, and animals are what we most frequently encounter in it. People figure less often in the happenings recorded by O'Conor. Thus, the deaths of two sons of the diarist are alluded to with a brevity which surprises the modern reader. In one case the death is juxtaposed with a reference to the fermentation of hops:

Mebhair laethach siosana. 1741
Ian.21. mo mhac Sean do chur aníu a gcill chorcaidhe tededh nuadh cheithre mbairille bracha an so aníu.

[The journal follows. 1741
January 21. My son John buried today in Cill Chorcaidhe; a new fermenting of four barrels of malt here today.]

(Ní Chinnéide 1957: 15)

Another entry records the death of Toirdhealbhach Ó Cearbhalláin [Turlough O'Carolan], a famous harpist and composer, who would have been a frequent visitor to the O'Conor house:

1739. an snechta gan leaghadh a nedh ar chuid den bhaile so. bliadhain sa la aníu cuireadh toirrdhealbhach .h. cearbhullain. an toirfidech orrdherc gaodhalach; a naimsir is fearr chonairc sinn ré leaithbhliadhain iso.

[1739. Yesterday the snow had not melted in part of this townland. A year ago on this day Turlough O'Carolan, the illustrious Gaelic musician, was buried. This is the best weather we have seen for six months.]

(Ní Chinnéide 1957: 9)

Occasionally we find references to events taking place in the greater world of Europe. Here is an entry written in 1740:

Octobris.3.1740. comhairle na Saxan agus gíustis na hEreann do chur Embarcco agus toirmiosg aníu ar loinges agus trácht na Rioghochta co hiomlan, tri baramhail cogaidh ris a bhfrainc, o a congnamh don Spainnech agus athogbhail Dhúncerc doich agom do dtiocfaidh chum maithesa dhuinne, gi gan amharus co millfidh moran fúin a lathair. As e an timbargo sin nuaidhecht is mo do Erinn re 20 bliadhain.

[October 3 1740. The English council and Irish [Chief] Justice today put an embargo and ban on shipping and trade throughout the Kingdom, on the grounds that war with France is predicted, because of her giving help to Spain and recapturing Dunkirk. I feel that it will be to our benefit, although undoubtedly it will cause us much harm at the present moment. That embargo is the biggest news for Ireland in 20 years.]

(Ní Chinnéide 1957: 14)

The years covered by the journal coincided with the Jacobite rising in 1745. Charles Edward Stuart (Bonny Prince Charlie), the grandson of James II, landed in Scotland with a small French force, in the hope of regaining the three crowns from George II. The Gaelic clans of Scotland rallied to his side and for a while it looked as if they might succeed in defeating the government forces, but they were eventually routed at the Battle of Culloden in 1746. The journal entries of 1745–6 make interesting reading for the historian:

Sep. 22 1745. Aimsir ro bhredha. Gidhedh, gan ní ar bith don choirce ar fiú a luadh bainte. Mac Mic Rígh Sémuis anos a n-Albain ag buaidhirt na dtrí ríoghacht. Níl fhios nach amhlaidh as férr.

[September 22 1745. Very fine weather. Nevertheless, no corn worth mentioning has been harvested. King James's grandson in Scotland now disturbing the three king-doms. Who knows but that this is for the best?]

Feb. 14 1745–6. Aimsir mhaith. An Stibhardach do dhíbeirt astech go Gaodhaltacht na hAlban a mesg na sléibhte, agus an chuid as mó dhá mhuintir do imthecht uadha. Ag sin drithle d(h)édhionach do choindil taoi dol as re trí fichitt bliadhoin, mur dtoir-miosgan Dia. [Good weather. Stuart driven into the *Gaeltacht* [Gaelic region] of Scotland among the mountains, and most of his people gone from him. That's the last flicker of a candle that has been going out for 60 years, unless God prevents it.]

Marta 31, Luan Casg 1746. Buaireadh anocht orm gan fhios agom ga ní tá na hAlbanaigh dhénamh fón amso, ga treisi nó mí-threisi d'éirigh dháibh re sechtmhuin, nó an críoch ar a gcogadh catharrdha so.

[March 31, Easter Monday 1746. I am troubled tonight because I don't know what the Scots are doing by now, were they victorious or were they defeated, or is their civil war at an end?]

An 18ú lá don Oibrén. Aimsir ro aoibhinn re mí. Mé faoi chéibh ó gach sgél dá gcluinim. Cuid dom dhith céille. An giúsdís dhá innsin dhúinn sechtmhuin sa lá aniú go ndechaidh an cogadh catharrdha go huile a n-aghaidh na n-Albanach. Más fíor so as amhlaidh as ferr é.

[April 18. Very fine weather for the last month. I'm anxious because of the stories I hear. That's part of my foolishness. The justice was telling us a week ago that the civil war went totally against the Scots. If this is true it's for the best.]

Mai 3 17(46). Aimsir ro mhaith agus na hAlbanaigh buailtidh ar dubh ón 16 lá don Oibrén, amhail tharrnghair mé.

[May 3 1746. Really good weather and the Scots routed since the 16th of April, as I predicted.]

(Ní Chinnéide 1954: 39–40)

Like others in Ireland, O'Conor was keenly aware of what was going on in Scotland and must have followed the events of the rising closely. In his journal, he is very careful not to commit himself to one side or the other. In the first entry, he seems mildly optimistic, in so far as one can make anything of the last sentence, 'Who knows but that this is for the best?' By February 1746, he has clearly concluded that the Stuarts' cause is a hopeless one. When the final defeat comes in April, he seems to be relieved. These journal entries are in keeping with what we know of O'Conor otherwise: he believed in proceeding with caution, using constitutional means rather than rebellion to improve the lot of his co-religionists.

The journal kept by Charles O'Conor is not very long, only about sixteen printed pages in all. Its value lies in its uniqueness in terms of genre in the eighteenth century. The author straddled two worlds, that of English and of Irish. In the journal, he tried to transfer to one language a literary form which was totally new. In doing so, he moulded and adapted traditional Irish to suit the journal style. His example was not followed by others, but it offers us a glimpse of how Irish might have developed to meet the needs of the new world of the eighteenth century.

5.1.7 Bilingualism, diglossia, and language statistics

I have referred before to the phenomenon of diglossia, whereby two dialects or registers of a language are used for specific purposes. Sometimes we find diglossia with two different languages, not just dialects of the same language. Fishman (1967) is a classic study of this bilingual diglossia.

A modern example of diglossia involving bilingualism would be an immigrant community in Dublin with its own language, versus the surrounding community which speaks English. The immigrant community uses its own language in more or less clearly delimited situations: at home, talking to family members, and also, perhaps, in situations like church services where other members of the same language group are to be found. English will be used in official or neutral contexts like work, education, or visits to government offices.

We also find bilingualism but without diglossia. This involves people mixing languages without any detectable social pattern in the switch from one to the other. According to Fishman, this arises in 'circumstances of rapid social change' (1967: 35). A common example is when a whole community gradually abandons one language for another. This often occurs with second-generation immigrants.

We must also bear in mind that two language communities can live in close geographical proximity, but without much interaction. When this is the case, diglossia exists, in that there are two distinct contexts for the two languages, but the speakers of the individual languages are not themselves diglossic. Examples of this from pre-war Eastern Europe are the traditional Jewish communities of countries like Poland, Russia, and Lithuania. In the countryside and in small towns, Jews spoke Yiddish, and because of strict segregation, many of them did not learn the national language. Their non-Jewish neighbours only spoke their own language (Polish, Russian, or Lithuanian). There would also have been some members of the Jewish community who were bilingual, and used the national language in a diglossic setting, when dealing with non-Jews, but they were a minority.

In eighteenth-century Ireland, two languages were spoken in rural areas. Life in a country parish centred round the Big House, the dwelling of the landlord. He, his family, and some employees like his agent, would have spoken English, as would the local Church of Ireland rector, and the middle-class inhabitants of the nearest town or village. In the south and west of Ireland, most of the tenants on an estate would still have spoken Irish, and many of these knew no English.

What we don't know for certain is the degree of diglossia and bilingualism present in rural Ireland at the time. As I mentioned earlier, Corkery seems to have viewed the two worlds as adjacent but separate, much like the Jewish and non-Jewish communities of Eastern Europe. But the evidence of the macaronic poems suggests rather a high degree of bilingualism. There is other evidence that the Catholic, Gaelic population was becoming more and more interested in English. While education at higher levels was only available to members of the Church of Ireland at this time, there was an informal kind of schooling for the sons of Catholic farmers. Itinerant teachers, the so-called Poor Scholars, travelled the country, setting up schools for the winter months in any district that would supply them with paying pupils. These schools were known as hedge-schools. Neither the pupils nor the teachers were well off: 'Teaching prospects, especially before mid-century, were often poor, tutoring spells short, and further movement the inevitable outcome. The scholar's services were sometimes offered for as little as a night's lodgings... This was at the margin of economic survival' (Cullen 1990: 25).

Because there were so many of these Poor Scholars travelling around, supply exceeded demand, and hence wages were low, often being paid in kind. This in turn meant that some kind of education was within the reach of even the less well-off members of society. By and large the medium of instruction in the hedge-schools was English, and there was a strong emphasis on the teaching of English in the curriculum. This emphasis was driven by demand on the part of the parents, who were paying for the education, and felt that they could choose what was to be taught. Literacy was becoming more and more associated with English: 'Because literacy was usually acquired in English, even for Irish speakers, the spread of literacy paralleled the spread of English' (Ó Ciosáin 1997: 178). Even among the scribes who transcribed Irish manuscripts, and who might justifiably be regarded as the guardians of the literary tradition, the use of English was growing:

The amount of English in the manuscripts, first added by the owners and increasingly by the scribes themselves, increased massively in the manuscripts from the 1750s and 1760s... Increasingly, and certainly from the beginning of the nineteenth century, the atmosphere of the manuscripts is bilingual. Phonetic scripts [based on English spelling] were unknown in the mid-eighteenth century, emphasising that the acquaintance with literacy first derived from Irish and from the literary moulds of the language.

A generation later, *circa* 1790, the phonetic scripts begin to appear. These were not numerous in the south, but where they appear they emphasised that individuals were drawing their reading knowledge from English, and that they proceeded to literacy in Irish by models already picked up from English.

(Cullen 1990: 32)

Putting all these threads together, we can hazard a tentative description of the linguistic reality of rural Ireland in the eighteenth century. The upper classes were monolingual in English, although they must at least have been aware of the existence of Irish. The Catholic middle classes, comprising clergy, school-teachers, better-off farmers, merchants, landlords' agents, and the like, were bilingual-diglossic. They would have used Irish when speaking with the peasants, and English when talking to townspeople and the upper classes. More and more, diglossia was becoming a feature of a written–spoken opposition: English was for reading and writing, Irish for speaking.

It is difficult to give more than a very rough estimate of the number of Irish speakers in this period for two reasons. First, we do not have reliable statistics before the end of the eighteenth century. Second, in a bilingual context, there is a problem about defining a speaker of a language. If we take again the macaronic exchange in section 5.1.3 between the girl and the ploughman, is the girl a speaker of Irish or not? Is the ploughman a speaker of English? Writers in the eighteenth century sometimes provide estimates of the number of speakers of Irish, but their statements are often wildly at odds with each other. One thing that does seem to be reasonably certain, though, is that there was a decline in the overall proportion of the Irish population who spoke Irish. According to the estimates of Fitzgerald (1984), only 45 per cent of the children born in the decade 1771–81 were brought up speaking Irish. Because the population of Ireland was growing at the end of the eighteenth century, there were still a lot of speakers, but what is important for language maintenance is not so much absolute numbers as the social status of the speakers, the presence or absence of another language in the community, and, most important of all, the numbers who pass the language on to their offspring.

The work of Smyth (2006) strongly supports the notion that Irish was in decline in the eighteenth century. His yardstick for estimating the numbers of Irish and English speakers is literacy in English, on the grounds that 'high levels of literacy presumed a prior capacity to know and speak English' (Smyth 2006: 411). The projected figures for literacy in English lead him to sum up the linguistic situation as follows:

Between 1660 and 1750, the number of both English-speakers and bilingual speakers increased significantly. By the early 1750s, it is likely that at least half the Irish population knew and understood English. Equally, it is likely that well over half were still primarily

Irish-speakers…The mid-eighteenth century, therefore, marks a fundamental watershed in the fate of both languages.

(Smyth 2006: 411)

Twentieth-century commentators have tended to see the nineteenth century as the decisive period for the decline of Irish, but the last sentence in the above passage suggests that this change was well under way by 1750.

5.2 The shape of the language (1700–1800)

5.2.1 Representing dialects in writing

In section 4.2.1, I drew attention to the fact that after 1600 we begin to find evidence for differences between the different regional dialects of Irish. This trend accelerates in the eighteenth century.

For sometime there had been a tension between the way that Irish was written and the way that it was pronounced, with the traditional spelling reflecting the spoken language less and less adequately. As far back as 1639 Theobald Stapleton had suggested simplifying the spelling and bringing it into line with current pronunciation. In the eighteenth century, others took the same approach. One of these was Francis Hutchinson, who was responsible for the publication in 1722 of a catechism for the use of the inhabitants of Rathlin Island, situated roughly half-way between Northern Ireland and Scotland. Although Hutchinson himself did not know Irish, he employed two Irish-speaking clergymen to compile the catechism for him.

The spelling of this catechism is peculiar. In the words of one commentator, 'The form of orthography used is based on that of Irish, with considerable modifications in the directions of English' (Ó Dochartaigh 1976: 183). The main justification provided for these modifications was the fact that many consonant groups which were found in writing were not actually pronounced any more. This is a common phenomenon in the history of languages. For example, at one time the <gh> in English words like *thought* and *though* was pronounced. The digraph continues to be written in the twenty-first century, even though there is no need for it. The introduction to the Rathlin catechism takes a different approach to spelling, arguing that letters should not be written if they are not found in speech. Thus it is recommended that the word *ionfhoghlamtha* 'learnable' should be written *inolama*, because the combinations <fh>, <gh>, and <th> are silent. In another part of the book, it is pointed out how economical the new system is compared to the old one: '*koivhervantee* Communis Servus, Fellow Servant…in the Highland Bible printed in the English Karakter, this word is *Coimhshearbfhoghantuighe*, four and twenty Letters instead of 12' (Williams 1986: 124).

Below, I give an example of the new spelling, juxtaposed with the same words in the traditional orthography. The example consists of short dialogues:

(1) a.   Question   What is your name?
         New spelling   Kest   Ka hainim ta ort?
         Traditional spelling   Ceist   Cá hainm atá ort?

     b.   Answer   N:M
                                           Fregra   N:M
                                           Freagra   N:M

     c.   Do you speak English?
         New spelling   In lavirin tu Bearl?
         Traditional spelling   An labhrann tú Béarla?

     d.   I do, I don't, I speak a little.
                                           Lavirim, nee lavirim, lavirim began.
                                           Labhraim, ní labhraim, labhraim beagán.

     e.   Where do you live?
                                           Kam bee tu ad chovnee?
                                           Cá mbídh tú i do chomhnaidhe?

     f.   In Lisburn.
                                           An Lisnegarvah.
                                           I Lios na gCearrbhach.

                                           (based on Williams 1986: 181)

Texts like the one above are an invaluable source of information for historians of the language. Precisely because the orthography deviates from the historical spelling, we are able to form a better idea of the way words were pronounced in the eighteenth century in the north-eastern part of the country. Take the sound [v], for example, normally represented in writing by <bh>. In other parts of the country this sound was lost in the middle of words like *labhrann* 'speaks', and the vowel preceding it modified as a result:

(2) EMI   MI
     labhrann   lowrann (as in Eng *cow*) / loreann (as in Eng *lore*)

However, we know from records of Rathlin speech collected in the twentieth century (Holmer 1942) that the /v/ sound was retained in the north-east. The use of <v> in the word *lavirin* in (1c) above reflects this more unequivocally than traditional <bh>.

    On the other hand, reforms can go too far and remove some features of the original system that were useful. In Irish, vowel length is indicated by an accent, e.g. <á> (long) versus <a> (short). The Rathlin catechism discards length-marks entirely. In (1c) above, the word *Béarla* 'English' is spelled *Bearl*, with no length-mark over the <e>. Now Holmer (1942: 45) maintains that 'in front of a double consonant, éa is often shortened to ɛ, as in Béarla'. It would be helpful to know whether this shortening of the vowel had taken place in the eighteenth century, but because all the vowels in the Rathlin catechism are written short, we have no way of finding out.

As more and more texts like the Rathlin catechism are edited and annotated, our knowledge about dialects and changes taking place in the eighteenth century will increase, and we will be able to form a much fuller picture of the state of Irish at the time.

5.2.2 Vocabulary

We can say that in the eighteenth century we are dealing with the stage of the language I identified in Chapter 4, namely Late Modern Irish. As in previous eras, it is necessary to separate deliberately archaizing material, such as copies of heroic tales, from contemporary texts, like the dialogues in the Rathlin Catechism, in order to arrive at a true picture of the Irish of the day. Nevertheless, there do not seem to have been any major changes in the hundred years following the composition of *Párliament na mBan* [The parliament of women], the work I identified in 4.2.1 as definitely representing LMI.

One area where it is possible to detect change relatively easily is vocabulary. In English, numerous words entered the language in the eighteenth century due to the huge advances being made in science and learning. Many English words that we still use are first recorded in this era. A recent article on the history of English mentions the following items as first making their appearance at this time:

(3)   *heroism, bother, growl, pork-pie, descriptive, dressing-gown*

(Tieken-Boon van Ostade 2006: 264)

For Irish, however, we do not have the same wealth of material entering the language. Furthermore, we lack anything like the OED which would enable us to track the first appearance of words in minute detail, although we do have a valuable tool in *Corpas na Gaeilge* [Corpus of Irish] (Royal Irish Academy 2004), an electronic dictionary based on printed texts from the period 1600–1882.

As we saw earlier, Irish was now confined to a small number of registers. Nevertheless, it is worth noting that there were individual scholars who tried to compile dictionaries which added to the stock of words in the language. One of these was Tadhg Ó Neachtain's word-list of 1739, which still exists only in manuscript form. Ó Neachtain lived in Dublin and had an excellent command of English. In his word-list, he often coins new terms to make up for deficiencies in the Irish of his day. Tomás de Bhaldraithe cites derivatives of the word *leabhar* 'book' as an example of Ó Neachtain's coining. At least some of these seem to have been thought up by him to find equivalents for English words or phrases:

(4)   *leabhr-amhail* 'bookish', *leabhr-óg* 'bookish woman', *leabhar-lann* 'library', *leabhar-lann-aire* 'librararian', *leabhr-aím* 'book' (verb)

(de Bhaldraithe 2004: 83)

One of these new words, *leabharlann*, was taken up in the twentieth-century revival of Irish and has become the standard term for *library*. However, the further derivative found in Ó Neachtain's word-list, *leabharlann-aire* 'librarian', has been replaced by *leabharlann-aí* in twentieth-century Irish. As far as I can ascertain, the other derivatives coined by Ó Neachtain in the above list—*leabhramhail, leabhróg, leabhraím*—have not survived into the modern language.

It is highly unlikely that Ó Neachtain's efforts at expanding the vocabulary of Irish with respect to more learned registers had any impact in its day. For the most part, if ordinary people needed a new word, they borrowed it from English. Even the clergy of the day who wrote sermons in Irish, or translated them, had recourse to this stratagem. In his introduction to his Sermons, Bishop James Gallagher wrote:

I have sometimes made use of words borrowed from the English, which practice and daily conservation have intermixed with our language, choosing with St Augustine rather to be censured by the critics than not to be understood by the poor and illiterate, for whose use I have designed them.

(Gallagher 1736; quoted in Mac Mathúna 2007: 211)

Mac Mathúna (2007: 212) mentions some of Gallagher's loan-words: *drag-áil* 'drag', *druinc-éir* 'drunkard', *siút-áil* 'shoot'. The suffixes -**áil** and -**éir** had long been in use in Irish for borrowing from English, but it is evident that they were being called upon more and more in the eighteenth century. Some of Gallagher's loans would seem unnecessary, in that equivalents existed already in the borrowing language: *tarraing* 'drag', *pótaire* 'drunkard', *lámhach* 'shoot'. Such duplication is typical of bilingualism. In the case of Gallagher, the author seems to have felt that a word like *druncaeir* would be more accessible to his audience than *pótaire*, even though *pótaire* does not seem to be a particularly learned word, judging by the genres in which it occurs.

If we compare Tadhg Ó Neachtain with Gallagher, we can detect two different devices for forming new words, the learned one and the more colloquial one. These two approaches are to be found right up to the present day. The learned register tries to expand the vocabulary by making use of existing resources. Thus, Ó Neachtain took the obsolete suffix **-lann**, which originally was a separate word meaning 'building, house', to derive *leabhar-lann*, 'library', literally 'a house for books'. To perform this operation, he had to be able to analyse the word *library* itself, into **libr** + **ary**, and then to identify the meaning of the two parts: **libr-** = *book*, **-ary** = *place* (compare *dispensary, bakery*). This in turn required a knowledge of Latin (or French), in order to make the connection between **libr-** and *book*. Obviously, an operation of this sort can only be carried out by somebody with the education and time to investigate the etymology of words, and the resulting new word will not always be immediately accessible to an ordinary speaker—by the eighteenth century the word *lann* 'place' no longer existed in everyday speech.

For somebody working under pressure, e.g. a priest preparing a sermon with the help of an English exemplar, it would have been much easier to simply import a foreign word in its entirety. Most Irish speakers in the eighteenth and nineteenth centuries would never have encountered a library, and so would have had no need of the term for it. However, there were other English institutions that would have had a much more direct impact on their lives. One of these came to prominence in the nineteenth century, namely the *poorhouse*, the institution which provided relief for the destitute. This term was borrowed into Irish and survived into living memory, in the form *púrous* (de Bhaldraithe 1953: 369). Sometimes a word itself has such powerful con-notations that no translation, no matter how accurate, contains the same degree of expressiveness. Thus, while *poorhouse* was also rendered into Irish more transparently as *teach na mbocht* 'house of the poor', this expression would not have had the same terrible associations as *púrous* for those who actually experienced the reality of poverty in the nineteenth century.

Not surprisingly, then, the eighteenth century is the era when the borrowing of English words into Irish really begins to make its presence felt, even in written documents. Other words which first make their appearance at this time are:

(5)   *bolta* 'bolt', *boxáil* 'to box', *búistéir* 'butcher', *cic* 'kick', *friseáilte* 'fresh',
       pléideáil 'to plead', *retréut* 'retreat', *saidléir* 'saddler', *siúráilte* 'sure'

(based on Ó Fiannachta 1978: 31)

Many of these are everyday words in the language of the twentieth and twenty-first centuries.

5.2.3 The language of Charles O'Conor's journal

In section 5.1.6 I examined an example of an untypical kind of document, namely a private journal kept by a member of the Catholic upper classes, Charles O'Conor. In this section, I mention some linguistic features to be found in this diary.

O'Conor had been well trained in the reading and writing of manuscripts. The language of his journal reveals a mixture of the conservative written language and the contemporary spoken dialect of the west of Ireland. On the conservative side, O'Conor continues to write medial consonants which had disappeared in speech, e.g. *bliadhain* (written) for *bliain* (spoken) 'year'. Likewise, we find in his journal the preposition *re* 'towards, with' which had been replaced by *le* by 1700 (Williams 1994: 462).

On the innovative side, the author sometimes provides spellings which reflect the spoken dialect of north Connaught, the region he came from. In the twentieth century, the scholar Seán de Búrca collected material in this area which enables us to form a good picture of what Irish sounded like when it was still spoken there. One noteworthy feature of this region was the replacement of /ch/ by /f/ in the past tense of the verb *téigh* 'to go' (de Búrca 1958: 129):

(6)   Traditional   North Connaught
       chuaidh   fuaidh 'went'

O'Conor consistently writes this verb with initial <f> in his journal:

(7)   an bhliadhainsi   fuaidh   thorainn
       the year.this   went   past.us
       'this past year'
                    (Ní Chinnéide 1957: 8)

With respect to grammar, O'Conor at times uses a form which is typical of later dialects. In most dialects of the twentieth century, English *we* is *muid* or -**mid**, written either together with or separately from the verb:

(8)   cuirimid   /   cuireann   muid
       put.PRS.1PL   put.PRS   we
       'we put'

An alternative word for *we, sinn*, is confined to the north-west of Ireland:

(9)   cuireann   sinn
       put.PRS   we
       'we put'

In his journal, O'Conor also uses *sinn*:

(10)   An   lá   as flithe,   fuaire,   anfadhaighe,
        the   day   wettest,   coldest,   stormiest
        chonairc   sinn   san   am   so   riamh.
        saw   we   in.the   time this ever
        'The coldest, wettest, most miserable day we ever saw at this time.'
                    (Ní Chinnéide 1954: 38)

So, it can be seen that he sometimes follows the spoken language in the way he writes. However, in another entry his conservatism manifests itself when he uses an obsolete verbal particle **ro-** to mark past tense:

(11)   Ferthain   shíorruidhe   re   sé   sechtmhuine,
       rain   continuous   for   six   weeks
       ro   mhill   mórán   faoi   fherrtha
       PRT   ruin.PST   much   under   grasses
       'Continuous rain for six weeks, which ruined much hay and corn.'

(Ní Chinnéide 1954: 37)

ro- had not been in common use in Irish since about 1200. By choosing to use it, O'Conor reveals his familiarity with old manuscripts.

O'Conor's vocabulary is mostly connected to farming and the weather, but he occasionally displays creativity, as when he uses the word *nuaidheacht* 'newness' in the sense of *news*:

(12)   Núaidhecht   gabhala   portobello   san   Nindia shíar ra Saxoibh
       news   of.capture   of.Portobello in.the   India   west by Saxons
       'News of the capture of Portobello in the West Indies by the English.'

(Ní Chinnéide 1957:12)

Likewise, his use of the preposition *as* 'out of' to indicate *lack, scarcity* is possibly due to the influence of English:

(13)   Me   as   moin   anos   agus   ni   hengnamh.
       me   out.of   turf   now   and   no   wonder
       'I'm out of turf now and it's no wonder.'

(Ní Chinnéide 1957: 10)

I have dwelt on this particular text because it illustrates a mixture of styles. On the one hand it strikes the reader as quite formal, employing as it does obsolete grammar and vocabulary. This is in keeping with the purpose of the journal, namely to record facts and figures. On the other hand, the author occasionally departs from the impersonal style and allows himself a moment of emotional reaction. When this happens, the language changes accordingly, as in the final line of the passage below:

(14)   Aimsir   ro   fhleoch   agus   Arbur   ar sraith   accuinn
       weather   very   wet   and   corn   in swathes   by.us
       o   thosach   na   miosa dha   sceth   agus dha loghadh.
       since   beginning   of.the month PRT   crumbling and   PRT rotting
       Dia   dha   reidhteach.
       God   PRT   settling

> 'Very wet weather and we have the corn cut since the beginning of the month.
> It is crumbling and rotting. God help us.'
>
> (Ní Chinnéide 1957: 14)

The interjection *Dia dhá réiteach* 'God help us' can still be heard on the mouths of the older generation of Irish speakers in the west of Ireland.

The journal of Charles O'Conor is unique for this time because it is a private document. Other texts, being intended for a public audience, tend to be more conventional, but they nearly all contain traces of the spoken language. Only a painstaking examination of them all will reveal the full truth about what was going on in Irish at this time.

5.3 Conclusion

In the eighteenth century, Ireland appeared to be divided into two classes, each with its own language, religion, and culture. However, a closer look at society reveals a much more complex situation than one might initially assume. The more mobile members of Gaelic society were acquiring literacy in English, and using this skill to compose macaronic verse which reflected the bilingual society in which they operated. At the same time, the more enlightened members of the Ascendancy gradually began to think of themselves as Irish and to acquaint themselves with the linguistic and literary heritage of Gaelic Ireland.

In terms of the language itself, we can observe the vernacular increasingly intruding into the literary language. This trend is manifested in the evidence for dialect differences and in the high percentage of colloquial borrowings to be found in written texts from this period.

Further reading

For eighteenth-century Ireland, see Johnston (1974).

For challenges to Corkery's view of the two cultures, see Cullen (1969); Ó Buachalla (1979); and Ní Mhunghaile (2012).

For a general survey of language and literature in the period 1700–1800, see Ó Cuív (1986a). Buttimer (2006) deals with the same period thematically, employing headings like 'Politics' and 'Quotidian life'. Another innovation of Buttimer's is that he provides a section on poetic style, which is an invaluable tool for anybody approaching eighteenth-century Gaelic verse for the first time.

Ó Buachalla (1996: 231–596) is an in-depth study of Irish Jacobitism and its representation in Gaelic poetry in the eighteenth century. No fewer than four chapters are devoted to the poetical genre which is referred to as the *aisling* 'vision'; this was a kind of political poem which foretold the return of the Stuarts to the throne, and the restoration of the old Gaelic order. Ó Ciardha (2002) covers much of the same ground, but is written more from a historical than a literary perspective.

Ó Doibhlin (2009) contains the key poems discussed in Ó Buachalla and Ó Ciardha, as well as some macaronic prose texts dealt with in Mac Mathúna (2007).

For recent accounts of Irish and its speakers in the period 1700–1800, see Mac Giolla Chríost 2005 (96–100); Smyth (2006: 408–15).

For source documents relating to language in eighteenth-century Ireland, see Crowley (2000: 83–132.)

For bilingualism and diglossia in general, see Fishman (1967).

For education and literacy in this period, see Cullen (1990) and Ó Ciosáin (1997).

For macaronic literature in Irish, see Mac Mathúna (2007: 116–27, 183–217; 2012).

For the Anglo-Irish Ascendancy and the Irish language, see Harrison (1999); Kelly (2012); and Ní Mhunghaile (2012).

For the churches and the Irish language, see Mac Murchaidh (2012).

For the representation of dialects in writing, see Williams (1986: 119–28), (1994).

For the coining of new words and borrowing, see Mac Mathúna (2007: 116–27).

6

A new language for a new nation (1800–70)

6.1 Change comes to Ireland

Up to now, I have based my chapter divisions on centuries, but in this chapter, I stop at the year 1870. This is because there is a fundamental shift in the fortunes of Irish after this date. Up to 1870, Irish was being abandoned in favour of English on a massive scale, with hardly anybody attempting to learn it. After 1870, the decline continued, but side by side with this there began an attempt to arrest the decay and to encourage people to learn it. For this reason, it is necessary to divide the nineteenth century into two chapters. Another reason for this division is related to non-linguistic history. After 1870, there was a general movement of cultural regeneration in Ireland, and the revival of Irish was very much a part of this. On the other hand, the decline of Irish in the first half of the century was bound up with the forging of a national identity which found its linguistic expression in English.

The eighteenth century was a relatively stable era. What change occurred came at a very slow pace. The nineteenth century, by contrast, led to seismic upheavals in Irish society. We need to have some grasp of these in order to understand the linguistic change that accompanied them, particularly as many of these changes are connected with the decline of the Irish language in this period. In this chapter, I will examine the causes of this decline one by one and try to assess their real impact. This task is complicated by the fact that the replacement of Irish by English is an emotional issue, and has given rise to a number of myths in the popular imagination, some of which have filtered through into academic discourse. It is important, therefore, that we try to disentangle myth from reality in discussing these issues.

The first sign of change came in 1798 when, after a century of peace, a rising broke out aimed at overthrowing British rule and establishing a republic in Ireland. The rising was led by the United Irishmen, a society which subscribed to the same ideals of fraternity and equality which had brought about the American and French revolutions towards the end of the eighteenth century.

The rising was suppressed savagely, and shortly after that, in 1800, the Act of Union was passed. This deprived Ireland of its parliament: from now on, Irish deputies would take their seats at Westminster.

After the failure of the armed rising, opponents to British rule turned to constitutional methods to achieve their goals. Two issues were to dominate politics for the next fifty years. One was the winning of civil rights for Catholics, referred to as Catholic Emancipation. Even though the worst of the Penal Laws had been relaxed, Catholics were still not allowed to sit in parliament or occupy higher government positions, and so were effectively deprived of political power. The other issue was the repeal of the Act of Union and the restoration of the parliament in Dublin. The Repeal movement, as it was called, did not wish to achieve full independence, only a limited control of those matters that affected Ireland directly.

6.1.1 Daniel O'Connell

One person dominates public life in this era, namely Daniel O'Connell. Born into a well-to-do Catholic family, he was educated in France during the French Revolution of 1789–93, and later studied for the bar in London. Returning to Ireland, he set up as a barrister in 1798, and soon joined the Catholic Committee, an organization whose aim was the winning of Catholic Emancipation. O'Connell injected new vigour into what up till then had been a deferential but ineffective body. As a result, a Catholic Relief Bill was put before the London parliament in 1821, but opposition in the House of Lords led to its defeat. Following this, O'Connell and his followers set up a new pressure group in 1823, the Catholic Association. With the support of the Catholic church, this association harnessed the masses of Irish peasantry who until now had had no say in the running of their country. A subscription of a penny a month provided funding for the organization. Before long, so-called monster meetings were being held all over the country, at which O'Connell agitated for Emancipation. The importance of the press was growing at the time, and the support of some Dublin newspapers undoubtedly helped to further his cause.

In 1828 O'Connell himself stood for election against a government candidate and defeated him. This victory raised the political temperature in Ireland to such a degree that there was fear of violence breaking out. In these circumstances, the king's representative in Ireland, the viceroy, advised the British government to grant emancipation to the Catholics. The Act of Emancipation became law in 1829.

Encouraged by this success, O'Connell established the Society for the Repeal of the Union in 1830. For the next seventeen years, until his death in 1847, he campaigned tirelessly for this cause, in the hope that an Irish parliament would

enable Catholics to finally take control of their own affairs. Unlike Emancipation, the Repeal movement failed, mainly because it did not have the support of
any political party at Westminster. After O'Connell's death, the movement
collapsed, and the idea of a Dublin parliament was not to be revived until
after 1870.

O'Connell enjoyed a degree of popularity that a modern politician can only
envy. The peasants in particular idolized him, and folk-tales about him
survived in both English and Irish versions for more than a hundred years
after his death. A number of folk-poets composed verses about him and his
exploits, describing him in heroic terms. Here is an extract from such a verse
by Tomás Rua Ó Súilleabháin:

> Is é Dónall binn Ó Conaill caoin
> an planda fíor den Ghaelfhuil,
> gur le feabhas a phinn a's meabhair a chinn
> a scól sé síos an craos-shliocht;
> go bhfuil sé scríofa i bPastorini
> go maithfear cíos do Ghaelaibh
> a's go mbeidh farraigí breac le flít ag teacht
> isteach thar Phointe Chléire.
> [Sweet, gentle Daniel O'Connell is the true scion of Gaelic blood, with the skill
> of his pen and his wits he flayed the greedy gang alive; it is written in Pastorini
> that the Gaels will have their rents remitted, and that the sea will be dotted
> with ships coming in by Cape Clear.]

(Ní Shúilleabháin 1985: 57)

The above passage is composed in the same style as the Jacobite poetry
described briefly in section 5.1.2. The rhetoric of the poem is not very
sophisticated. On the one hand we have the hero, Daniel O'Connell, who is
brave and clever and resourceful. Pitted against him are the English/Protes-
tants ('the greedy gang'). Pastorini was the pen name of an English Catholic
who wrote a book in which he prophesied the downfall of the Established
Church and the restoration of Catholicism. Not surprisingly, the work sold
well in Ireland. The last two lines above predict the arrival of a foreign fleet
which will enable the Gaels to overthrow the thrall of the British. Apart from
the first line, in which O'Connell is named, the verse could have been written
in the eighteenth century, foretelling the return of the Stuarts.

The poet goes on to tell us what will happen when O'Connell wins
emancipation:

> Beidh ministrí gan strus, gan phoimp,
> a's ní rithfid chun cinn mar a théidís;
> ní bhainfid cíos de Chaitlicigh

mar cuirfear síos na méirligh.
Beidh Dónall choíche ar a dtí
go nglanfar cruinn as Éilge iad
nuair a bheidh an dlí fúinn féin arís
ar theacht *Emancipation.*
[Ministers will lose their wealth and pomp, and a halt will be put to their
gallop; they won't take rents from Catholics, because the villains will be put
down. Daniel will be constantly pursuing them until they are kicked out of
Ireland completely, when we are laying down the law after Emancipation
comes.]

(Ní Shúilleabháin 1985: 58)

O'Connell would probably have appreciated the flattery of the above lines.
He had been born into an old Gaelic family, one of the few who had held
onto their lands in the eighteenth century, where the tradition still survived of the aristocrat as head of the clan, protecting the rights of the
tenants and commanding their love and respect. In the words of one
commentator:

He [O'Connell] enjoyed the sport and amusements of the 'local' characters in Uíbh
Ráthach [his birthplace]. He humoured and encouraged the local poet Tomás Ruadh
Ó Súilleabháin, and the songs and dances of the locality seem to have given him
genuine pleasure.

(Ó Tuathaigh 1974: 26)

However, O'Connell would not have been happy with the threat of violence
that the poem contains, or the idea of himself leading the hunt of Protestants.
When it came to political activity, he belonged to the new age of democracy
and constitutionalism. He wanted to lead his people, not as a hereditary
monarch, but as a democratically elected parliamentarian.

His approach to life was pragmatic, and that included his approach to
language. One statement that he was alleged to have made about Irish and
English, quoted by a biographer of his, has become a permanent part of the
debate about the decline of Irish in the nineteenth century:

Someone asked him if the use of the Irish language was declining among our
peasantry. 'Yes,' he answered, 'and I am sufficiently utilitarian not to regret its gradual
abandonment...It would be of vast advantage to mankind if all the inhabitants spoke
the same language. Therefore, although the Irish language is connected with many
recollections that twine around the hearts of Irishmen, yet the superior utility of the
English tongue, as the medium of modern communication, is so great, that I can
witness without a sigh the gradual disuse of the Irish.'

(Daunt 1848 vol. 1: 14–15; quoted in Crowley 2000: 153)

The above passage led later commentators to regard O'Connell as a traitor to his people and his heritage. Thus, the authors of what is still one of the standard text-books on the history of Irish literature write:

Tá an ráiteas...ó bhéal Dhomhnaill Uí Chonaill faoin nGaeilge ina ainimh ar chlú duine a rinne mórán ar son an chine.

[The statement...from the mouth of Daniel O'Connell about Irish is a blemish on the reputation of somebody who did much for the [Irish] people.]

(Williams and Ní Mhuiríosa 1979: xxiv)

For his critics, O'Connell's felony seems to have been compounded by the fact that he was a speaker of Irish: 'O'Connell, a native speaker, held that the superiority of English as a language of modernity was sufficient cause to think of the passing of Irish without regret' (Crowley 2000: 134). The historian John A. Murphy sums up the prevailing twentieth-century view of O'Connell's cultural philosophy in these words:

According to the canons of the nationalism that became the later orthodoxy, Daniel O'Connell was the great West Briton of the nineteenth century, explicitly and deliberately rejecting his priceless cultural heritage for the English fleshpots. That stern moralist of the Irish cultural revolution, Daniel Corkery, speaks about O'Connell's 'callousness' and the 'harm' done by him...Even such admiring biographers as 'Sceilg', Fr. Antoine Ó Duibhir and Domhnall Ó Súilleabháin either reproach him for not having been a language enthusiast or feel they must really explain anew what they believe to have been his attitude to Irish.

(Murphy 1984: 36)

Part of the motivation for censure of O'Connell in the twentieth century may have been based on a somewhat limited view of what constitutes a native speaker. O'Connell's critics seem to think that there was only one language present for the formative years of his life, and that he then wilfully and perversely chose to replace his native language with a foreign one. Such a view makes no allowances for the existence of bilingualism, and the complex patterns of diglossia that so often arise when two languages are in daily use in a community. For many bilinguals, there are two native languages, and the question of chronological replacement of one by the other simply does not arise.

In the case of O'Connell, he was fostered out to an Irish-speaking family for the first four years of his life, so that chronologically his acquisition of Irish would have preceded his acquisition of English. Certainly, four years is long enough for a child to acquire native competence in a language. But that competence can be lost if it is not reinforced after the age of 4; in fact, it is not unusual for children to entirely forget their first language if they are taken out of the linguistic community into which they were born. All the evidence suggests that when O'Connell returned to his uncle's house at the age of 4 there was a change for him from Irish to English. According to MacDonagh (1988: 8) 'the male O'Connells had become bi-cultural. Irish was their working language with servants, labourers and tenants. But among themselves, they spoke, and wrote, in English only.' All Daniel O'Connell's writings and speeches are in English, including letters written to his family when he was in France. His education was obtained through the medium of English and French, and his working life was spent in a completely Anglophone environment. He did not lose the ability to speak Irish, but there is a strong possibility that his command of that language was underdeveloped compared to this command of English. Rather than describing him as a native speaker of Irish, we might want to say that he was bilingual-diglossic, with a bias towards English in his adult life.

Like many people in Ireland at the time, O'Connell seems to have associated literacy exclusively with English. It is highly improbable, for instance, that he would have been able to read a manuscript in Irish, or would have wished to do so. In 1826 Anthony O'Connell, whose uncle Peter had compiled an Irish–English dictionary, approached Daniel O'Connell with a request to aid in the publication of the work. Daniel is said to have 'dismissed his namesake, telling him that his uncle was an old fool to have spent so much of his life on so useless a work' (MacDonagh 1988).

Given these circumstances, there is nothing even vaguely remarkable about O'Connell addressing political rallies in English. He had been trained as a barrister in London and Dublin, where he would have studied the speeches of previous generations of English lawyers. It made more sense for him to speak in English and have the speeches translated into Irish for the benefit of those who only knew Irish. However, the whole point about bilingual diglossia is that it avoids absolute binary choices between language A and language B. It is more a question of choosing the appropriate language for the appropriate task. Murphy (1984) provides ample evidence of O'Connell using Irish when he saw fit to do so. For example, he is said to have moved his listeners to tears on one rare occasion when he addressed them in Irish (Murphy 1984: 37). As I mentioned earlier, it is likely that he would have been pleased with the panegyric composed in his honour by Tomás Rua Ó Súilleabháin. Poems like this appealed to his sense of pride in his ancestry, to his feeling of being the leader of his people. It is untrue to say that he turned his back on Irish—he simply assigned it a certain role in his life which was different to that of English.

There is little evidence for any kind of conscious language policy on the part of O'Connell. He valued his Gaelic heritage, but did not regard it as a strait jacket which prevented him from taking part in the world of politics. His attitude towards Irish did not in any way affect his popularity with the adoring Gaelic-speaking peasants. A twentieth-century folk informant described O'Connell's views on the language: 'They used to say that he wasn't in favour of Irish, although he had plenty of Irish himself' (Uí Ógáin 1984: 39). Compared to some of the later criticisms I have quoted, this is a simple, neutral statement. Part of the reason why the plain people of Ireland did not object to O'Connell's views was that they identified with them. They too were trying to negotiate a *modus vivendi* for themselves in the complex cultural landscape of the time.

In the view of one twentieth-century historian, Gearóid Ó Tuathaigh, not only was O'Connell representative of the Catholic community in general, but his views were even shared by the Gaelic literati:

It is, perhaps, necessary to point out that in refusing to take up the issue of cultural nationalism, O'Connell was in no sense disappointing any clearly-expressed political aspirations of the Irish-speaking community. Most of the Irish writers—who are, after all, the sole authentic voice of Gaelic Ireland in the eighteenth and nineteenth centuries—accepted the fact that the Irish language was in decline, that it was being set aside by those who could choose their medium of communication.

(Ó Tuathaigh 1974: 25)

Thus, we can see that there is quite a discrepancy between the way O'Connell was viewed by nineteenth-century Gaelic society and by later twentieth-century commentators. He was very much in tune with the Gaelic tradition, in fact far more so than his detractors, but later accounts tended to overlook that.

O'Connell's influence reached its peak in 1829, with the granting of Catholic Emancipation. From about 1830 onwards, a new kind of nationalism was coming to the fore in Ireland which represented a different philosophy to that of O'Connell. In order to understand the nature of this new movement, we need to broaden our perspective somewhat and take a glance at what was happening in Europe at the time.

6.1.2 Language and national identity in Europe and Ireland

After the Napoleonic wars at the beginning of the nineteenth century, the great powers of the day—Britain, France, Prussia, Austria, and Russia—reached a peace settlement at the Congress of Vienna (1815). This settlement resulted in a number of small nations losing their independence and being absorbed into larger political entities like the Austro-Hungarian empire or the Russian empire. Right through the nineteenth century there were risings by the smaller nations against the larger powers. In 1830 and 1848 in particular, there was a rash of revolutions right across Continental Europe.

The European nationalist struggles for independence drew their inspiration from Romanticism. This was a cultural movement which emphasized the particularity of ethnic groups and their right to self-determination. It especially emphasized the link between language and national identity. Many of the foremost ideologues of the Romantic movement were from German-speaking regions. One of these, Johann Gottfried Herder, saw languages as reflecting the character of the peoples who spoke them and of the regions where they were spoken:

When the children of dust undertook that structure that menaced the clouds—the Tower of Babel—...there came into being a thousand languages according to the climate and the customs of a thousand nations. If the oriental burns here under a hot zenith, then his bellowing mouth also streams forth a fervid and impassioned language. There the Greek flourishes in the most voluptuous and mildest climate...his organs of speech are fine, and among them, therefore, originated that fine Attic speech. The Romans had a more vigorous language...Thus transformed itself this plant—human speech—according to the soil that nourished it and the celestial air that drenched it.

(quoted in Chambers 1995: 249)

Passages like this led nineteenth-century nationalists to believe that each ethnic group had its own territory, its own culture, and its own language, with an organic connection between the three. Losing one's language as a result of colonization by another power was therefore tantamount to losing one's ethnic identity. In places like Bohemia (present-day Czech Republic) or Lithuania, then part of the Russian empire, public leaders like teachers and members of the clergy became actively involved in supporting native languages. They engaged in such pursuits as compiling grammars and dictionaries, agitating for the inclusion of national languages in the educational curriculum, or simply going among the peasants and collecting folk-tales.

One might expect events to have taken a similar course in Ireland, which was also a small country under the heel of a foreign power, but there were specific factors at work there that made Irish nationalism different. For one thing, from the time of the United Irishmen onwards there had been a tension between the modern, internationally orientated republicanism that this movement represented, and the old, monarchist tradition of the Gaelic world. One author, Seán Cronin, describes the attitude of the new republicans towards Irish, pointing out that 'The United Irishmen took their political ideals from many sources, none Gaelic' (Cronin 1980: 40). Alan Titley elaborates on this tension between the old and the new nationalism in the following passage:

Deinimse amach go raibh dhá intinn pholaitiúla Éireannacha ann roimh theacht Dhónaill Uí Chonaill ar an bhfod, dhá intinn pholaitiúla go teoiriciúil ar aon nós.

Ceann acu siud bhí sí bunaithe ar an náisiúnachas nua polaitiúil, ar an bpoblachta-nachas go minic. Bhí sí ina seasamh ina dhiaidh sin ar chearta an duine; bhí sí neamhsheicteach ina cuid reitrice; bhí sí daonlathach, cuid mhór dá mheanma ba ea an frith-Shasanachas, agus b'é an Béarla a teanga. B'é an dara hintinn pholaitiúil ná an ceann a fhaighimid go minic i litríocht na Gaeilge. Bhí a seasamh sin ar shinsearacht, ar leanúnachas cine, ar dhílseacht do sheanchultúr; bhí sí ríoga nó prionsúil seachas daon-lathach; bhí sí Caitliceach don chuid is mó agus 'seicteach' frith-Phrotastúnach—bíodh go mbíonn eagla ar dhaoine é sin a admháil go hoscailte inniu—agus b'í an Ghaeilge a teanga.

[In my opinion there were two political outlooks in Ireland before Daniel O'Connell came to prominence, at least in theory. One of them was based on the new political nationalism, frequently on republicanism. On top of that it stood for the rights of man; it was non-sectarian in its rhetoric; it was democratic, to a large extent it was anti-English, and English was its language. The second political outlook was the one that we often find in Gaelic literature. That one stood for ancestral heritage, for racial con-tinuity, for loyalty to the old culture; it was royalist or princely rather than democratic; it was Catholic for the most part and 'sectarian', anti-Protestant—although people are afraid to admit this openly nowadays—and Irish was its language.]

(Titley 2000: 40)

While it is difficult to put Daniel O'Connell as a politician into one or other of Titley's categories, there is no doubt where he stood in terms of language—he belonged to the new Ireland. However, after 1830 another political force began to grow which challenged O'Connell's hegemony. This was the group referred to as Young Ireland. Its name was meant to echo the better-known movement called Young Italy, which had been set up after the 1830 revolution to further the cause of Romantic nationalism in Italy. The main ideologue of Young Ireland was Thomas Davis. He offers an interesting contrast to O'Connell, in that he was a member of the Protestant middle classes, and had no inherited connection with Gaelic culture. Davis added a new strand to nationalist thinking by emphasizing the importance of language, just as his European counterparts had done earlier. Compare this passage from Davis's writings with the one by Herder quoted earlier:

The language, which grows up with a people, is conformed to their organs, descriptive of their climate, constitution and manners, mingled inseparably with their history and their soil, fitted beyond any other language to express their prevalent thoughts in the most natural and efficient way.

(Davis undated: 172; quoted in Crowley 2000: 161)

It is clear that the Romantic philosophy of language had made its mark on Davis by the time he came to write this.

Later in the same essay Davis wrote the following words, words which have been quoted again and again by various writers:

A people without a language of its own is only half a nation...To lose your native tongue, and learn that of an alien, is the worst badge of conquest.

(Davis undated: 173; quoted in Crowley 2000: 161)

The contrast with the pragmatism of O'Connell could not be greater. Davis was giving voice to the philosophy which would fuel the Gaelic Revival half a century later, namely that a language is innately connected with a place and its inhabitants. For him there could be no two ways about it, no choices, no jumping from one language to another as the occasion demanded: if you claimed to be Irish, you should be speaking Irish. It was as simple as that for Davis.

Unfortunately, it was considerably more complicated than that. To begin with, Davis himself did not know a word of the language he was advocating. This did not prevent him from laying down simplistic guidelines about how Irish might be revived:

What we seek is, that the people of the upper classes should have their children taught the language which explains our names of persons, our older history, and our music, and which is spoken in the majority of our counties, rather than Italian, German or French.

(Davis undated: 178; quoted in Crowley 2000: 163)

In fairness to Davis, a similar policy had been adopted in other countries, or at least there had been sufficient people of influence who had been prepared to promote the endangered national language and thus ensure its survival. The problem with Ireland was that by the time he was writing, 1843, there were hardly any Irish speakers who had sufficient training to act as tutors for the children of the upper classes. There were few teaching aids that they could call upon for such an endeavour. And more important than anything else was the fact that most of the progressives, those who were most sympathetic to Davis's cause, had no interest in Gaelic culture. Like many an Irish-language activist since then, Davis had some brilliant ideas which he could present in powerful rhetoric, but he provided no practical tips for how these ideas might be implemented.

Ironically, even while he was advocating the preservation and revival of Irish, Davis himself was strengthening the position of English. In 1842 he and two friends had set up a newspaper called *The Nation*. In it, they and others published (in English) essays and poems which aimed at inculcating a spirit of nationalism in their readers. The newspaper proved popular and was soon being read aloud in every village in Ireland. Davis himself was a talented balladeer, and many of his compositions, set to music, found their way into the repertoire of Irish folk-singers. Other literary contributors included the poets

James Clarence Mangan, A. M. Sullivan, and Thomas D'Arcy Magee; these authors often drew on old stories and legends for their compositions. *The Nation* is a vital link in the forging of Irish nationalism in the middle of the nineteenth century. Once again, though, its very success ensured that English would become the language of separatist rhetoric. Irish, indeed, could not fulfil this role, because the only Gaelic compositions available fitted the description of Alan Titley quoted above: backward-looking, monarchist, and violently anti-Protestant. One wonders if Davis would have been so enthusiastic about the revival of Irish had he been aware of the sentiments expressed in the Gaelic poetry of his day.

There was an abortive attempt by the Young Irelanders to start a rising in 1848. After its collapse, many republicans fled the country to avoid imprisonment. In 1858 James Stephens set up the Irish Republican Brotherhood (IRB) in France. A like-minded organization, the Fenian Brotherhood, was established in America under the control of John O'Mahony. This group, commonly referred to as the Fenians, organized another rising in 1867. It too failed, but the IRB continued to agitate for Irish freedom in the United States afterwards. Like the Young Irelanders, the Fenians encouraged the writing of popular ballads and political articles, which were published on the pages of its paper, *The Irish People*. Once again, though, the writings were in English. By and large, the Fenians, and later the IRB, were considerably more pragmatic than the Young Irelanders. For them, military training and fundraising took precedence over the promotion of Irish.

Summing up, then, we can say that while the period 1800–70 was a formative one for the development of Irish nationalism and for separatist republicanism in particular, for the most part it ignored the existence of the Irish language. A new identity was being forged for Ireland, but it was happening through the medium of English. The legacy of Thomas Davis remained unexploited until after 1870.

6.1.3 Education and literacy

In the previous two sections I briefly described the main political developments in the period under scrutiny. These political events were accompanied by momentous social changes which also had an impact on language. I begin with education and literacy.

I have already adverted to the fact that, in the eighteenth century, English had become strongly associated with reading and writing. This trend accelerated considerably in the first half of the nineteenth century. One of the main reasons was the spread of education to the masses in this era. On the one hand, the existing private schools continued to expand, particularly those run by Catholic religious orders. As well as this, in 1831 the government set up a National Board of Education to provide free elementary education for all. This was a controversial scheme, and came under fire from the clergy of the Established Church, the Catholic bishops, and the Presbyterian synod. Nevertheless, by 1849 the National schools were catering for nearly half a million pupils.

Histories of the Irish language written in the twentieth century all stress the negative impact of the national schools on the Irish language. One of the main attractions of the new system, from the point of view of the parents, was that English was the language of instruction. This point is brought out in the report of a schools inspector from 1856 which stated that 'It is natural to inquire how this strong passion for education could have possessed a people who are themselves utterly illiterate . . . Their passion may be traced to one predominant desire—the desire to speak English' (GJ, March 1884: 90; quoted in Crowley 2000: 165). In other words, the enthusiasm for the new schools was part of the more general trend in Irish society towards becoming part of the Anglophone world.

When dealing with the education system of the nineteenth century, Ireland is often compared to other countries where local populations resisted the imposition of a foreign language at school. An oft-cited case is western Poland, which was under Prussian rule from 1795–1918. Under the government of the Prussian chancellor Bismarck, an intense policy of Germanification was applied to schools in western Poland in the 1870s. German became the language of instruction in all schools, even if the population was mixed. The only exception was the teaching of religion, but in 1900 an order came to teach even this subject through the medium of German. This led to a famous strike by schoolchildren in 1902 who refused to say their prayers in German even at the risk of being beaten.

This attitude of non-compromise in places like Poland is often cited as an example of how the Irish could have behaved. Even in regions like Wales and Brittany which were under the control of administrations hostile to the indigenous cultures, there was more resistance to the imposition of non-native languages in the education system than in Ireland. One significant ally that the native language found in Poland, and also in Wales and Brittany, was the church of the common people. In Ireland, by way of contrast, the Catholic church aided and abetted the process of Anglicization. To understand this more fully, we must take a closer look at religious affairs in the first half of the nineteenth century.

When dealing with the Reformation in Chapter 2, we saw that it never really succeeded in Ireland. The north-east of the country was an exception, Here, the Presbyterianism imported from Scotland managed to take root. The rest of the country remained mainly Catholic. Even the Penal Laws of the eighteenth century failed to induce most Irish people to abandon their religion in favour of Anglicanism. The nineteenth century gave a tremendous boost to Catholicism. After Emancipation, Catholics were free to advance socially and to take up professions and occupations that had hitherto been barred to them. A national seminary had been established in Maynooth in 1795, and similar training colleges soon sprang up around the country. Continental religious orders like the Poor Clares and the Ursuline nuns, or native ones like the Christian Brothers, assumed an active role in health and education. The church also was free to publish religious material for the instruction of the faithful.

Until recently, it was commonly accepted that there was little demand for printed books in Irish, mainly because people could only read, and only wanted to read, English. Ó Ciosáin (1997) shows that this is not entirely correct. He admits that 'the spread of literacy paralleled the spread of English' (Ó Ciosáin 1997: 178). However, he also points out that 'Literacy could be acquired independently of English. There was a continuous and substantial production of Irish-language manuscripts throughout the eighteenth and early nineteenth centuries, as well as a minor explosion in Irish-language printing between 1800 and 1850' (Ó Ciosáin 1997: 179). Contemporary nineteenth-century sources back up Ó Ciosáin's claims about literacy. Whitley Stokes gave an estimate of 20,000 people who could read Irish in 1806 (Ó Cuív 1986: 381). This is not a huge number, but it effectively supports Ó Ciosáin's statement that 'literacy in Irish therefore existed, with a potential readership for printed works in Irish' (1997: 181). Ó Ciosáin examines one work in particular in detail, the *Pious miscellany* of the poet Tadhg Gaelach Ó Súilleabháin, which was a collection of religious verse. This was printed no fewer than eighteen times between 1800 and 1850. Given that the Irish language was in severe decline by then, this is a striking testimony to the potential demand for religious books in Irish. And yet, compared to the amount of English-language Catholic material published in Ireland in the same period, the number of books which appeared in Irish is insignificant.

Ó Ciosáin links this paucity to the role played by religion in the spread of literacy. In Wales the effectiveness of the eighteenth-century Methodist mission led to a high level of literacy among Welsh speakers. In Brittany, the Catholic Counter-Reformation in the seventeenth century boosted literacy and encouraged printing in the Breton language. In Ireland, the Protestant Reformation never really took off, and the unfavourable political climate meant that the Catholic Counter-Reformation could not be effective either. By the time the Catholic church began its missionary work in earnest after 1800, it was simply too late for it to start operating in Irish. As one report from 1823 puts it, 'It very frequently happens that even the priest himself is incapable of instructing members of his own people from want of a common medium of communication' (de Brún 2009: 123).

At the same time as the Catholic church was reclaiming lost ground, the Church of Ireland and other Protestant denominations were making one last attempt to convert the Irish, in a movement which became known as the Second Reformation. This movement, which was closely connected to the teaching of literacy, was to have important implications for the Irish language.

6.1.4 Bíoblóirí, *Jumpers, and* An Cat Breac

In the early nineteenth century the various non-Catholic religious denominations in Britain and Ireland experienced an evangelical revival, which involved prosletyzing members of other churches. In Ireland, this led to a kind of struggle between the Catholic church and the other Christian churches for the souls of the people, which was to cause much bitterness in Irish society for years to come.

The Protestant churches conducted their mission primarily through Bible societies, which taught children and adults to read the scriptures and some other Protestant writings. Most of the evangelizing work was conducted through the medium of English, but in those parts of the country where Irish was still widely spoken, it was felt that it would be a good idea to teach people to read the Bible in their native tongue. A number of societies undertook missionary work in Irish, the most important being the Irish Society for Promoting the Education of the Native Irish through the Medium of their Own Language. Ultimately the Society hoped that the Irish would learn to read English, but as an aid to that, and for their short-term moral improvement, it decided to employ teachers to instruct them in the reading of Irish. It also printed and distributed copies of Bedell's Bible and Ó Domhnaill's *Book of Common Prayer* (see sections 2.1.3 and 3.1.2). It specifically stated in its rules that it renounced 'all intention of making the Irish language a vehicle for the communication of general knowledge' (de Brún 2009: 1). This last point shows how the Church of Ireland viewed the use of Irish in religious instruction: it was not meant to strengthen the language. Most of those who advocated using the native language were not in favour of Irish as such, but reluctantly agreed that it was a necessary evil in the short term. There were also some exceptions to this generalization, people such as the clergyman scholar Whitley Stokes, who were genuinely interested in both promoting the language and converting the Irish speakers to Anglicanism.

To carry out the actual day-to-day instruction, the Irish Society employed schoolmasters from among the native population, most of whom were Catholics. They were called *Bíoblóirí*, from the Irish word for Bible, *Bíobla*, and the agentive suffix -óir. One of the main incentives to become a teacher was the salary, rather than any great religious fervour. At the time, most country schoolmasters eked out a precarious living as Poor Scholars. In this context, the relatively high salaries offered by the Bible societies would have been hard to resist. Activity commenced in 1818 and by 1825 the work was in full swing all over the western and southern part of the country, with a total of 144 teachers employed. It is difficult to form an accurate picture of how successful the Society was, as some of the teachers seem to have exaggerated numbers of pupils in order to keep their jobs (de Brún 2009: 83), but there is no doubt that quite a few people learned to read Irish by attending the Society's classes.

Conversion was another matter entirely. Most of the teachers were Catholics. The hope was that both they and their pupils would convert to Protestantism by reading the scriptures, and there are accounts of relatively large numbers joining the Church of Ireland in the early years of the Society's activity, as in a report from 1827 which declared that 'You hear of a wonderful work in Cavan, where 500. Catholicks [sic] have read their recantation and near sixty are rejected until they read and reflect more' (de Brún 2009: 95). On the whole, though, the number of genuine, lasting conversions was low (de Brún 2009: 97).

One factor that militated strongly against the work of the Society was the fierce opposition of the Catholic church to the whole enterprise. Teachers were denounced from the pulpit by the local Catholic priests, and in some cases parents of children attending the Society's schools were excommunicated. In County Cavan, in Ulster, four teachers were murdered. As a result of the Catholic church's denunciation of the Society and its activities, the ability to read and write Irish became something suspect, a sign of having being involved with the *Bíoblóirí*. The historian John O'Donovan reported in 1836 that 'the teachers of the Bible through the medium of the Irish language have created in the minds of the peasantry, a hatred for everything written in that language' (de Brún 2009: 124–5). A former teacher who had repented of his ways denounced the Society: 'If the teaching or learning of Irish ... should be the cause of sin to the Teachers, the scholars, or others, it instantly changes its nature, and ... becomes a sinful one ... Who will deny that the teaching or learning of Irish, in connection with the Irish Society, is not the cause of sin?' (de Brún 2009: 125). Bedell's Bible became *an Bíobla Gallda* 'the Protestant Bible', and an ability to read it marked one out as a Protestant. Pádraigín Ní Uallacháin cites the words of a song-collector from south-east Ulster, to the effect that the use of Irish in general became associated with Protestantism because of the activities of the various Bible societies and the reaction of the Catholic clergy:

When the priests decided that Irish was a danger to the faith...the weaker scribes discontinued...I became aware that a granduncle of mine, a namesake Thomas Holly-wood, was a scribe and had accumulated a considerable quantity of manuscripts...His son told me that his father stopped the copying of manuscripts when the clergy advocated the abandonment of Irish in the interests of the Faith.

(Ní Uallacháin 2003: 22)

Another collector tells of the experience of one of his informants in her youth:

D'inis seanbhean dúinn go mbíodh eagla orthu nuair a bhí sise óg aon Ghaeilge a labhairt dá mbeadh sagart nó maistir scoile i láthair—go raibh sé crosta orthu aon leabhair Gaeilge a léamh ar eagla gur chuid den Bhíobla Ghallda a bheadh ann.

[An old woman told us that they used to be afraid when she was young to speak Irish if there was a priest or a school-teacher present—that they were forbidden to read any Irish books in case they contained part of the Protestant Bible.]

(Ní Uallacháin 2003: 24)

The bitterness caused by the clash between the two churches persisted in the folk-memory well into the twentieth century, long after the main period of proselytizing. In the west of Ireland, converts were referred to disparagingly as Jumpers, and in the latter half of the nineteenth century often came under attack from the local community. The following verses from a folk composi-tion are illustrative of attitudes:

Féuchaidh na 'Jumpers' nach iad atá á mealladh!
a' léamh bíoblaí Liútair ar stiúir an fhir shalaigh
siúd é an t-údar ar dtús lena dtarraingt
go b'é deire na dúthracht é 'phlúchadh ar a leaba.

[Look at the Jumpers, oh they're being fooled!
reading Luther's Bible under the guidance of the awful man.
He was the initial cause for their being attracted
and after all this zeal he was smothered in his bed.]

(Moffitt 2008: 187)

As a result of the pressure exerted by the Catholic Church, many of the Jumpers reverted to Catholicism, having signed statements in which they admitted the error of their ways.

Another name which found its way into both English and Irish in this era was Catbrack/*An Cat Breac*, which literally meant 'speckled cat'. The term came from a primer which was widely used for instruction in reading: *An Irish and English spelling-book. For the use of schools, and persons in the Irish parts of the country* (Goodwin 1837). One of the first phrases in Lesson Two of the primer was *cat breac* 'speckled cat'. As a result, Catbrack/*An Cat Breac* came to stand for the primer itself and those who taught or learned from it:

Lucht Bíobla a léigheadh nó Bible Readers a bea na daoine a bhíodh a' múineadh ar dtúis ins na scoileanna. Tugtaí an Cat Breac ar na leabhra bhíodh aca agus ar a gcúram, agus Lucht an Chait Bhric ortha féin is ar a lucht leanúna.

[The people who taught in the schools initially were those who read the Bible or Bible Readers. The books that they had and the work that they did were referred to as *An Cat Breac*, and they themselves and their followers were referred to as the people of the *Cat Breac*.]

(Ó hAilín 1971: 138)

Like the name Jumper, Catbrack became a term of abuse for those who converted to Protestantism or supported the Bible Societies (de Brún 2009: 113).

The missionary activities of the Protestant churches and the war with the Catholic church which ensued have been blamed for the decline of the Irish language in the period 1800–70. Undoubtedly, this episode in Irish history did not help Irish, but it is unlikely to have played a major role in the abandoning of the language. Long before the missions got underway, the Catholic church had decided that it would conduct its own campaign in English. The opportunity existed for it to have fought back through Irish. In fact, the Catholic Archbishop of Tuam, John McHale, who was violently opposed to the Protestant missions, published an Irish translation of the New Testament so that his flock could read the scriptures without being perverted by the *Bíoblóirí*. Anti-Protestant rhetoric was to be had in abundance in the Irish language poetry of the period 1550–1800—the verse about the Jumpers quoted above is simply a nineteenth-century take on a theme that we have encountered already in the eighteenth century, namely the iniquity of the Protestant heretics. Thus there would have been absolutely no problem about conducting a campaign against the missionary schools through the medium of Irish, and such a campaign would have met with a ready response. Had the Catholic church decided to set up its own schools teaching the people to read the Catholic catechism in Irish, it would certainly have succeeded where the Protestant missionary societies had failed. But this was not a serious option for the Catholic church by the time Maynooth was founded in 1795. The following quotation sums up the church's position on the two languages:

The Irish peasant is not so deficient in Scriptural knowledge as Mr Anderson imagines; thousands of catechisms in Irish are annually printed, and O'Gallagher's sermons have now gone through a fourteenth edition. These were useful, but we question the utility of that which would lead to perpetuate the Irish as a spoken dialect; the English is a much more convenient language—it is more extensively used, and is a key which unlocks more intellectual sources of information. Perhaps it was a misfortune that Irish did not continue to be the language of the country; but now regrets are unavailing. English is the language of the majority, and must finally become the language of the whole; and the sooner it does so the better for Ireland.

(*Catholic Miscellany* 1828; quoted in de Brún 2009: 124)

For Daniel O'Connell and the Catholic church, a key part of the new Irish identity was religion. In fact, the popular poetry of the period which has come down to us in folk-memory reflects this shift of consciousness. As pointed out by Gearóid Ó Tuathaigh, in eighteenth-century Gaelic poetry the non-Gaelic foreigners in Ireland were distinguished by their language and their religion, whereas by the nineteenth century the main source of otherness was religion:

It must be noted that in the vast majority of the eighteenth-century *aislingí* [political poems] the role-reversal forecast by the poet as a consequence of Ireland's deliverance is described with reference to religious and linguistic labels . . . By the early nineteenth century, however, the linguistic label is found less often in the poems, and the religious distinction becomes the primary test in discussing the past and future.

(Ó Tuathaigh 1974: 29)

The revived Catholicism could be more effectively inculcated through the medium of English, if only because the clergy for the most part were unable to preach through Irish. The laity seem to have accepted this state of affairs— at any rate, there is little evidence of protest on their part in the nineteenth century. The limited success of the schools of the Irish Society and other missionary bodies was due to the hunger for literacy and English on the part of the Irish peasantry. Even without the condemnation of the Catholic clergy, it is unlikely that many would have embraced Protestantism when the only attraction which that offered was the possibility of reading the Bible in Irish. The people wanted a better preparation for the confrontation with the English-speaking world than Bedell's Bible and the *Book of Common Prayer*. This need became even stronger after the defining event of nineteenth-century Ireland, the Famine.

6.1.5 The Famine and emigration

The population of Ireland increased dramatically in the period 1791–1841, from about 4.7 million to about 8 million. Unlike other countries, this rise in population was not connected with industrialization. Ireland remained a largely agricultural country, with two-thirds of the population living on the land. What enabled the demographic growth was the dependence of the majority of the rural dwellers on the potato as their main source of sustenance. Even a very small holding could support a family if it was planted with potatoes. This in turn led to subdivision of holdings into smaller and smaller units, especially in the west of the country.

   Disaster struck in 1845 when a new virus, potato blight, arrived in Ireland, quickly spreading over the whole country. The summer crop failed, and whole families were left with nothing to eat. This situation persisted until 1849, by which time the blight had begun to recede. The government in power in 1845, headed by Robert Peel, was completely unprepared for the disaster. It set up a scheme of relief-works, and also distributed maize free of charge, but the aid provided was unequal to the scale of the calamity. To make matters worse, Peel's Conservatives were replaced in the 1846 election by the Whigs, who believed that there should be a minimum of government intervention in the lives of citizens. This in turn led to a reduction in the amount of aid for those in need. By 1847 famine was widespread. People fled to the workhouses in search of help, but these quickly became overcrowded and diseases like typhus and dysentery spread, causing as many deaths as starvation did. The death toll was at least 800,000—that is, one-tenth of the population.

The Famine is usually seen as weakening the Irish language. In a very direct way it did weaken it, in that many of those who died were Irish speakers. Emigration increased at an enormous rate during the Famine itself and in the years that followed. Since the emigration was exclusively to English-speaking countries, it has been argued, this led to a greater demand for English on the part of parents. Whereas before the Famine children could have stayed in Ireland, after 1850 holdings tended to be consolidated rather than subdivided, which meant that only one son could inherit the farm. With little employment to be had in Ireland, the only alternative for the rest of the family was emigration. This led to large numbers of Irish speakers leaving the country after 1850, and even those who remained had little incentive to continue to speak Irish.

This explanation for the weakening of Irish after 1845 seems plausible enough, although, as we have seen, there was not much enthusiasm for Irish before the Famine. Nevertheless, it would seem reasonable to suggest that the fact that emigration became a permanent feature of life in Irish-speaking districts would have reinforced existing attitudes about the usefulness of English and the uselessness of Irish.

English may also have become more attractive because from 1850 onwards it was associated not just with England, but also with the United States of America. People are often surprised that Irish nationalists who denounced Britain as an enemy in the nineteenth century had no compunction about speaking English, the language of their alleged foe. However, English was also the language of the New World, of the land of freedom and hope that the Irish emigrants were travelling to. It is not entirely surprising that they associated the language of this country with positive values: freedom, prosperity, a better life. Irish was the language of the country they were leaving behind, the language of poverty and failure. It is significant that of the hundreds of ballads composed about emigration to the United States, hardly any are in Irish, even though there were many Irish speakers among the first waves of emigrants after the Famine.

America's language policy did not encourage linguistic diversity. Here are Theodore Roosevelt's thoughts on the subject around the time of World War I:

We have room for but one language in this country and that is the English language, for we intend to see that the crucible turns out our people as Americans, of American nationality and not as dwellers in a polyglot boarding house, and we have room for but one loyalty and that is a loyalty to the American people.

(Roosevelt 1926: XXIV, 554)

Commenting on American language policy in the 1960s, the sociolinguist Joshua A. Fishman wrote:

There is a 'message' which immigrants, other ethnics, and their children quickly get—that ethnicity is foreignness, that both have no value, they are things to forget, to give up. The frequent and enduring contrast between war, disharmony, and poverty abroad, and relative peace, acceptance, and prosperity here clearly shouts this message.

(Fishman 1972: 23)

The Irish immigrants to the United States seem to have embraced Roosevelt's language policy with enthusiasm. If we compare them to other immigrant groups, such as Eastern European Jews or Italians, what is striking is how quickly the Irish language disappeared from view once the immigrants landed in America, even though many of them would have spoken little English when they arrived. Various factors played a role in this assimilation to the language of their adopted country. By 1850, most Irish people had some knowledge of English, and had at least come into contact with English speakers. Switching to English, both in linguistic and psychological terms, was a far smaller leap for them than for somebody from Eastern or Southern Europe who had never left their village before this. Furthermore, unlike Italians or Poles, say, the Irish immigrants comprised a linguistically mixed group. In this situation, where one of the languages of the newcomers was also the language of the new country, it was entirely natural that English should become the language of the immigrant community as a whole. Another factor was politics. As mentioned earlier, the United States became a base for the independence movement in the years 1850–70, which led Irish immigrants to look to their new homeland for leadership and inspiration. As is well known, the Irish were quicker to get involved in American politics than other immigrant groups. Had they chosen to live in a linguistic and cultural ghetto, it is debatable whether they would have achieved so much at the political level, an arena which demands a certain degree of assimilation.

Some immigrant groups in the United States have maintained their ethnic language much better than others. According to one recent author:

There is evidence that the most successful language maintenance occurs in groups for whom language is intertwined as a core value with other core values, such as religion and historical consciousness or family cohesion, rather than those for whom language stands in isolation as an identity marker. This might explain the success of Greeks but also why Hasidic Jews, who have no ideological commitment to Yiddish, maintain it much better in the US than do Yiddishist ideologues, because the former have specific domains in which they have to use it, owing to religious considerations.

(Clyne 1997: 310)

Religion is often a key element in the maintenance of linguistic identity. Writing on this subject, Fishman draws attention to an interesting difference between Catholicism and other churches in America:

Whereas the other immigrant Churches lacked de-ethnicized, English-speaking American roots, the Roman Catholic Church as a result of over a century of effort had already developed such roots by the time masses of non-English-speaking Catholics arrived. Horrified by the 'regressive' centrifugal prospects of re-ethnicization, the Catholic hierarchy in America may well have become (and remained) the second major organized de-ethnicizing and Anglifying force in the United States, next to the American public school system.

(Fishman 1972: 68)

Writing specifically about Irish in the USA, a more recent commentator confirms Fishman's remarks on Catholicism:

Unlike the role of Hebrew in Judaism, Arabic in Islam, Greek, Armenian, and Serbian in Eastern Orthodox churches, the role of Irish in Catholicism was not one of religious necessity. Although more recent movements within the Catholic Church to use vernaculars could work to the benefit of American minority languages, the marginal position of the Irish language in American Catholicism must be understood as part of a specifically religious determination as to which languages are necessary or sanctified and which are simply instrumental.

(Kallen 1994: 35)

I should add that Irish was not totally abandoned as a language of religious activity in the USA. There is limited evidence that individual priests from Ireland preached in Irish to congregations of immigrants, particularly before the Famine:

Fleeting glimpses of Irish-speaking communities exist for the early nineteenth century. I. D. Rupp (1845, p. 18) reported that within communities of recent Irish immigration in Schuylkill and Carbon counties in Pennsylvania, 'the greater proportion...are

Catholics, and have priests officiating in the Irish language, which is spoken by many of the laboring classes'.

(Kallen 1994: 31–2)

However, for the Irish who emigrated after 1850, the Catholic church they left behind them in Ireland had already become Anglicized, and it would only have seemed natural to them that its members should function through English in the United States. Writers on the fate of Irish in America stress the indifference, and sometimes downright hostility, of the Catholic church there towards the language: 'The Catholic schools that most Irish-Americans attended were all but inimical to the language' (Callahan 1994). Thus, another important ingredient in the maintenance of language among immigrant communities was lacking.

The Irish-American community did establish for itself a very distinct identity in the United States, but it was one from which language was almost totally absent, one that relied more on political allegiances and religion. The only presence that the Irish language had was a symbolic one, consisting of Anglicized versions of Irish words and phrases like *Erin-go-breagh*, which had no communicative function.

Because of the pervasiveness of emigration to America from the remaining Irish-speaking communities after 1850, cities like Boston became more famil-iar to these communities than Dublin. Unlike Britain, America offered its immigrants a chance to advance socially and economically in ways undreamt of at home in Ireland. Small wonder, then, that the Irish who went there so readily embraced the culture and language of their new homeland.

6.1.6 The extent and pace of the language shift

Because of administrative developments in the nineteenth century, we are in a much better position to form a reasonably accurate picture of the numbers of Irish and English speakers than we were for previous centuries. For the first half of the century we have to rely on estimates, sometimes varying consider-ably from person to person, but the 1851 census gives reasonably precise figures for numbers of speakers.

For the 1820s, Ó Cuív (1951) suggests a figure of 'well over two million people'. What percentage of the total population this represents is not very clear. Twentieth-century accounts have tended to exaggerate the numbers. Thus, the authors of a history of Irish literature recommended for third-level students write that 'There were four million speakers of Irish out of a popula-tion of five million at the beginning of the nineteenth century in Ireland. That is, Ireland was for the most part Irish in language and custom as late as that' (Williams and Ford 1992: 255). Four million speakers would be 80 per cent of the population. But, as I pointed out in section 5.1.7, an in-depth longitudinal analysis of census figures (Fitzgerald 1984) claims that only 45 per cent of the children born in the decade 1771–81 were brought up speaking Irish. This creates a very different impression from saying that 'There were four million speakers of Irish.' Certainly, many parents who did not pass Irish on to their children could speak Irish, and spoke it to people of their own generation, but clearly a massive language change was already under way. In terms of the future of Irish, 45 per cent reflects the real situation at the beginning of the nineteenth century.

Furthermore, given that the population in general was growing rapidly in the years 1800–20, and that some of the new arrivals must have been Irish speakers, Ó Cuív's estimate of 'well over two million' for the 1820s would suggest a dramatic overall decrease in just twenty years (2 million) if the Williams and Ford figure were correct. In the light of this evidence, the conclusion we are forced to draw is that the estimate of 4 million for 1800 is incorrect. A more likely figure is 'about half of the population' (Ó Tuathaigh 1972: 140). Ireland was not 'for the most part Irish in language and custom' in 1800, contrary to what Williams and Ford claim (Figure 6.1).

Whatever the correct figure for 1800 was, by 1851 the proportion of Irish speakers had fallen to 23 per cent, and less than a third of these spoke Irish only (Figure 6.2). In a context where bilingualism was widespread, and the balance had shifted in favour of English, this 23 per cent represented in fact a much smaller number using Irish on a day-to-day basis. Brian Ó Cuív draws the same conclusion in reference to the 1851 census:

If I have stressed unduly this difference between Irish-speaking monoglots and bilingual speakers, it is because I attach great importance to it. I consider that the acquiring of English as a second language by one generation was the first step in the transition in the succeeding generations, firstly to the position where Irish was a secondary language, and ultimately to that where Irish was unknown, the stages being expressed thus: Irish only: Irish and English: English and Irish: English only.

(Ó Cuív 1951: 26–7)

In this and the previous chapter, I have tried to show that the language shift from Irish to English was a gradual process. If we take a generation as representing approximately twenty-five years, Ó Cuív's schema above supports this view. The process began in earnest about 1750, and had only reached completion a century later. The author of a recent study of this question seems to be of the same opinion: 'The abandonment of Irish was a gradual affair, a matter of evolution rather than revolution, and that would persist through the nineteenth century as well' (Mac Giolla Chríost 2005: 98).

FIGURE 6.1 Language communities in Ireland c.1800

Sources: based on Diarmait Mac Giolla Chríost (2005). *The Irish language in Ireland.* London/New York: Routledge. Figure 4.3; Garret Fitzgerald (1984). 'Estimates for baronies of minimum level of Irish-speaking amongst successive decennial cohorts: 1771–1781 to 1861–1871'. *Proceedings of the Royal Irish Academy* C, pp. 117–55. Map 1

Irish and English

English

N

0   50
Miles

FIGURE 6.2 Language communities in Ireland 1851

Sources: based on Brian Ó Cuív (1951). *Irish dialects and Irish-speaking districts*. Dublin: Dublin Institute for Advanced Studies. Map 1; Brian Ó Cuív (ed.) (1969). *A view of the Irish language*. Dublin: The Stationery Office. Map 1

The interpretation that I propose here is not particularly novel; similar accounts have been put forward by others in the last thirty years. The reason I have been at pains to stress the gradualness of the change is that this view of events has failed to filter down into popular consciousness. Indeed, the old view, which saw the change as cataclysmic and sudden, even lingers on in academic debate on this subject. This is largely due to another factor, namely the response of later generations to the loss of Irish.

6.1.7 Later attitudes towards the language shift

One of the modern legacies of the language shift is the belief that the Irish people sold their birthright for a mess of pottage, and that this betrayal, no less than the Famine, has had a traumatic effect on Irish society to the present day. Here is a particularly forceful expression of that position:

For to the extent that we lost Irish, to that extent we lost the cohesion, the continuity, the consciousness of belonging and the sense of personal and national worth that is the basis of all significant achievement; and with it too we lost the self-knowledge, the understanding of our personality in its origins and in all its moods and tenses that gives a purpose to that achievement. For in Irish not merely does our mind react to the same beauty, the same delicacy of inflection and suggestion that delighted our fathers; but we can still share through it the desires and hopes, the failures and successes, the nobility, and even, in a healing manner, the human weaknesses of practically the whole of our recorded history and literature.

(Brennan 1969: 76–7)

In the schools of the nineteenth century, punishment was meted out to children by means of a measuring instrument called the tally-stick. This was a stick worn on the neck of the child; for each misdemeanour, a notch was entered on the stick, and at the end of the day the child was beaten, the number of blows depending on the number of notches. One of the misdemeanours for which children were punished was speaking Irish.

The tally-stick and its relation to Irish has entered the folk-memory of the Irish nation. Thus in the historical poem *The Rough Field* by the contemporary writer John Montague, the tally-stick becomes a potent symbol of the loss of the language and the cultural trauma that this entails:

A grafted tongue.

An Irish
child weeps at school
repeating its English.
After each mistake

the master
gouges another mark
on the tally-stick
hung about its neck.

(Montague 1995: 8)

Montague's imaginative recreation of the teaching of English presents it in an overtly negative light. The child 'weeps'; the master doesn't just put a notch in the tally-stick, he 'gouges another mark' in it. The title of the section from which the quotation is taken is itself loaded: the new tongue, English, is not natural, but 'grafted'.

Imaginative recreations like Montague's are presumably based on contemporary nineteenth-century descriptions of the tally-stick. The following piece by Sir William Wilde (father of Oscar Wilde) describes the consequences for children caught speaking Irish by their parents:

> The children gathered round to have a look at the stranger, and one of them, a little boy about eight years of age, addressed a short sentence in Irish to his sister, but, meeting the father's eye, he immediately cowered back, having, to all appearance, committed some heinous fault. The man called the child to him, said nothing, but drawing forth from its dress a little stick, commonly called a scoreen or tally, which was suspended by a string round the neck, put an additional notch in it with his penknife.
>
> (quoted in Greene 1972: 10)

With respect to the scene described above, Wilde's sympathies are with the child. His attitude is very close to what our own would be. Few people nowadays would approve of children being beaten by their parents for speaking their mother tongue, whatever that may happen to be.

Wilde's account is not an isolated instance of parental punishment of children who spoke Irish. We know from other sources that parents actually collaborated with school teachers to ensure that their children spoke only English:

> The master adopts a novel mode of procedure to propagate the new language. He makes it a cause of punishment to speak Irish at school, and he has instituted a sort of police among the parents to see that in their intercourse with one another the children speak nothing but English at home. The parents are so eager for the English they exhibit no reluctance to inform the master of every detected breach of the school law.
>
> (GJ, March 1884: 91; quoted in Crowley 2000: 166).

Passages like the above have been used to condemn nineteenth-century attitudes as backward and brutal. We feel that we live in a more enlightened era, one in which a multiplicity of languages and cultures can peaceably coexist for the benefit of all. Modern educationalists, in particular, are horrified at the practice of not using the children's home language in the educational setting as well.

However, it is worth bearing in mind that in twenty-first-century Ireland we also countenance education in a language other than the mother tongue, albeit without the tally-stick. A large number of parents in present-day Ireland send their (English-speaking) children to schools which use Irish as the medium of instruction. This has been argued to be beneficial for the children's develop-ment: 'International research has consistently shown that second-language immersion-education improves children's general linguistic skills to a degree not always attained in first-language schools' (Mac Murchaidh 2008: 219). Not all educationalists agree with this statement; for example, Williams (1989) argues that Irish-language schools are not beneficial for children. Nevertheless, let us assume for the moment that it is correct, and that 'second-language immersion education' is a good idea. In modern terms, the national schools in the nineteenth century offered immersion education in English for Irish-speaking children. This in turn provokes the question: if immersion education is good in twenty-first-century Ireland, why was it bad in nineteenth-century Ireland? In both cases we are dealing with the native language of the home being replaced by a non-native language of instruction. Either this is beneficial for children or it isn't. The advocates of Irish-language immersion-schools seem to be saying that it's good when it's a lesser-used language (Irish), but bad when it's a widely used language (English).

A possible reply to this is that English-speaking children in modern Ireland do not lose their command of English, and are not pressurized by their parents and society to do so. Many Irish people today would argue that their ancestors could have taken a similar stance in the nineteenth century, encouraging their children to retain Irish while learning English at school. Thus, the author of the entry on the Irish language in the recently published *Atlas of the Great Irish Famine* writes:

The Irish are effortlessly speaking and writing a language that enables them to communicate with millions worldwide. And yet there is the niggling suspicion that more has been lost than has been gained. If English had been acquired and the Irish language maintained, what could have been achieved? Why was it assumed that only one language could be spoken properly when the rest of Europe seems perfectly capable of speaking several without difficulty?

(Nic Craith 2012: 587)

Those who share this view would advocate bilingualism for a society which is obliged to come to terms with a powerful linguistic neighbour like English. The assumption underlying this position is that one can have one's cake and eat it.

However, a recent study of the decline of Irish in the period 1960–2010 challenges this assumption:

Cruthaíonn mórán gach staidéar idirnáisiúnta nach mbíonn an dátheangachas seasm-hach trí na glúinte san áit a bhfuil mionteanga ar marthain le hais mórtheanga. Ré eadrána idir aonteangachas sa mhionteanga agus aonteangachas sa mhórtheanga a bhíonn ann . . .

Léiríonn an t-eispéireas domhanda go mbíonn *duine* dátheangach ar bhonn aonair, go mbíonn *tír* nó *náisiún-stát* dátheangach ar bhonn siombalach ach nach mbíonn *sochaí* datheangach ar bhonn seasmhach. I sochaí ina bhfuil mionteanga agus mórtheanga á labhairt, is dátheangachas dealaitheach a bhíonn ann agus faigheann an mhórtheanga an lámh in uachtar luath nó mall. Ní léiriú é an dátheangachas, mar sin, ar iolrachas ná ar ilchultúrachas fadsaoil, ach ar phróiseas comhshamhlaithe agus comhionannaithe.

[Nearly every international study proves that bilingualism is not stable over successive generations where a minority language is in coexistence with a majority one. It is an intermediate stage between monolingualism in the minority language and monolingualism . . .

The global experience shows that a *person* is bilingual on an individual basis, that a *country* or *nation-state* is bilingual on a symbolic level, but that a *society* is not bilingual on a permanent basis. In a society where a minority language and a majority language are spoken, the bilingualism is subtractive, and the majority language wins out sooner or later. Bilingualism, then, is not a manifestation of long-term pluralism or multiculturalism, but of a process of assimilation and homogenization.]

(Lenoach 2012: 93, emphasis original)

The author of the above passage is writing about more recent times, when Irish is much weaker than 200 years ago. At the same time, the Irish-speaking community of the present day is well educated and enjoys a measure of support from the state, as well as from academic institutions and individuals throughout Irish society. If this modern community cannot resist the pressure of English, then how could the downtrodden peasantry of the nineteenth century have done so? To expect them to have had the linguistic sophistication and awareness required for this kind of conscious language-planning is naïve in the extreme.

From the time of the language revival onwards, the relation between Irish and English has been viewed as a kind of military struggle, with Irish fighting a valiant rearguard action against superior English forces. Indeed, as we saw in Chapter 4, the same kind of metaphor was common in the reaction of the Gaelic poets of the seventeenth century to the spread of English. Against this background, it is instructive to examine briefly a text which describes a mixed-language community in Galway in the first half of the nineteenth century, at the time when the language shift was in full swing. The text, *An Haicléara Mánas* [Manus the Hackler] (Stenson 2003) is a comic account of the adventures of a hackler (somebody who prepared flax for weaving) when he goes to north Conamara to do some work. Part of the humour in the tale arises from misunderstandings between the Irish-speaking locals and the English-speaking soldiers and coastguards who live in their midst. What is important for our purposes here is that the existence of two languages is not a source of tension or discord; it is simply a matter of fact. One of the characters, Conán, is described as follows:

Conán, nach raibh cur amach an mhadra aige i mBéarla, ach fé ar bith mar bhí sé, bhí grá mhór aige a bheith dhá labhairt le tiarnaí talún agus le *waterguards*, mar bhíodh sé ag díol bainne is ime leo, agus bhí aithne mhaith acu uilig air.

[Conán, who hadn't a word of English, but however that was, he loved to be talking it to landlords and to waterguards, because he used to be selling milk and butter to them.]

(Stenson 2003: 59)

There follow two exchanges between Conán and English-speaking customers of his. Here is a short sample of one of these dialogues:

'*Hello there*, Conán,' arsa [said] Murphy.
'*Hello*,' arsa Conán. '*What you want?*'
'*I want some milk. Got any?*'
'*Milk*,' arsa Conán.
'*Yes*,' arsa Murphy.
'Bláthach, bainne géar, nó leamhnacht [buttermilk, sour milk, new milk], *you want, Mr Murphy?*' arsa Conán.

(Stenson 2003: 61)

This dialogue recalls the exchange we presented in Chapter 4 (section 4.1.1) between Tomás and the tobacco pedlar, Robin. Like that exchange, there is no tension here between the two parties, they are simply interested in effecting a commercial transaction. The lack of a common language is a hindrance, but it is entirely devoid of ideological significance. The members of the two language communities are merely trying to negotiate a deal with each other. There is no conflict, covert or overt, between the world of English and the world of Irish.

An Haicléara Mánas is a literary text, and there is a danger in taking it too literally as a social document. Nevertheless, it is a document produced by an insider, by a member of the Irish-speaking community, hence one might expect to find an anti-English bias there if this bias existed. After all, there is no shortage of anti-English vitriol in the folk-poetry of the time. Yet in An Haicléara Mánas we witness the peaceful, undramatic coexistence of two languages. Whatever tensions existed in Irish society at the time are not visible at the linguistic level.

It must be admitted that the particular interpretation that I have put forward is not one which receives widespread support among other commentators. Most writings in the last thirty-odd years on the subject of the language change are similar in tenor to the passage from Brennan quoted earlier, the only difference being that they make use of the framework of post-colonial theory:

This process of language change was not so passive or voluntary as is sometimes claimed, and it is not just the inevitable result of the modernizing process during imperialist times. Language change and cultural shift is, I would claim, the second phase of the colonial process, the subjugation of the mind and spirit after the subjugation of the body, and is often brought about with the full cooperation, indeed connivance, of certain elements of the colonized group. This concept lies at the heart of much postcolonial analysis, and it gives rise to some hard questions and, indeed, in the Irish situation, to some uncomfortable answers.

(Denvir 1997: 45)

For the post-colonialist critics, then, the Irish speakers of the nineteenth century had internalized the colonization process to such a degree that they were willing to collaborate in the destruction of their own culture.

Niall Ó Ciosáin proposes a way of approaching the question that does not involve making binary choices between what one might call the cataclysmic account (as in the above passage) and the casual, dismissive approach, which views the change as natural and inevitable:

The challenge, in other words, is to give due causal weight to the process of language shift in nineteenth-century Ireland without making it equivalent to other forms of change that were intimately linked with it. A more satisfactory approach to the subject could proceed along at least two lines of inquiry, both of which would shed much light on the culture of nineteenth-century Ireland more generally. The first would focus, not on two separate languages, but on the ways in which they were both used simultaneously by individuals and groups. In sociolinguistic terms this involves an 'ethnography of speaking' in a profoundly, if momentarily, bilingual and diglossic society... The other line of inquiry would be to consider the impact of language shift in areas and phenomena which were not strictly linguistic. To illustrate this, we can consider one of the principal popular religious manifestations of the later part of the century, the Marian apparition in Knock, County Mayo, in 1879.

(Ó Ciosáin 2005: 150–1)

The first line of inquiry mentioned by Ó Ciosáin strike me as particularly promising, that which focuses 'not on two separate languages, but on the ways in which they were both used simultaneously by individuals and groups'. To illustrate the kind of material which could be scrutinized under this approach, let us consider an account written by Douglas Hyde, one of the founders of the Gaelic League. In it he describes two encounters he had with young people about 1890, not long after the language shift had taken place:

I met a young man on the road... I saluted him in Irish, and he answered me in English. 'Don't you speak Irish,' said I. 'Well, I declare to God, sir,' he said, 'my father and mother hasn't a word of English, but still, I don't speak Irish'... The children are not conscious of the existence of two languages. I remember asking a *gossoon* [youth] some questions in Irish, and he answered them in English. At last I said to him, Nach labhrann tú Gaeilge? [Don't you speak Irish?] and his answer was, 'And isn't it Irish I'm spaking?...He was quite unconscious that I was addressing him in one language and he answering in another.

(Hyde 1986e [1894]: 160–1, n. 1; quoted in Mac Mathúna 2007: 225)

The above passage is revealing, in that it provides an answer to the frequently asked question: how could the Irish people have abandoned their linguistic heritage in such a casual fashion? Perhaps, though, that is the wrong question, as it assumes that there was a single moment when the whole population of Ireland consciously decided to reject one language totally, and totally embrace another. In fact, there never was such a moment. For the young man and the *gossoon* in Hyde's account, the two languages coexisted peacefully side by side; in fact, for the *gossoon*, they were one and the same language. The passage also supports the notion that the language shift was gradual rather than abrupt, taking place over successive generations. It shows that bilingualism itself is a term that needs to be treated with caution. It does not necessarily imply equal competence in the two languages. Hydes' interviewees still had a good passive knowledge of Irish, although we can be certain that they would not have transmitted this knowledge to their children. But what is important is that Irish declined slowly and imperceptibly for those who participated in the process. In such circumstances, there can be no question of clear choices or individual responsibility. This in turn may explain why many people at the time appear to have had no feeling of loss or traumatization, as pointed out by a recent commentator: 'For the most part, those who shifted languages did so fatalistically and without fuss' (Ó Gráda (2012). The sense of trauma and loss was to come much later, and was experienced vicariously on behalf of those who, according to the twentieth-century writers, had sold their birthright.

The subject of the language change is one which arouses strong emotions, and it is impossible to do it justice in a brief study like the present one. What is clear, though, is that all the evidence about the language shift, including attitudes at the time, needs to be reconsidered and reappraised in order to arrive at an adequate understanding of what really happened.

6.1.8 Attempts to preserve and strengthen Irish

Up to now I have concentrated on the decline of Irish and its causes. However, it would be creating a false impression if one were to ignore certain initiatives aimed at stimulating interest in Irish in this period.

As mentioned in Chapter 5 (section 5.1.4), towards the end of the eighteenth century some members of the Ascendancy began to take an interest in Irish and its literature. This tendency became stronger in the nineteenth century. New antiquarian societies sprang up, such as the Gaelic Society of Ireland (1806), the Iberno-Celtic Society (1818), the Irish Archaeological Society (1840), the Celtic Society (1845), and the Ossianic Society (1853). While these were mostly concerned with collecting and editing old manuscripts, their work did help to increase public awareness of the existence of Irish, and they often employed the services of scholars like John O'Donovan or Eugene O'Curry who also spoke the contemporary language. As a result of this antiquarian activity, a lot of important material was published, such as Eugene O'Curry's *Lectures on the manuscript materials of ancient Irish history* (O'Curry 1995 [1861]).

The work of these learned societies received a fresh stimulus from abroad in the 1850s, when Johann Kaspar Zeuss established a definite link between Old Irish and Indo-European languages like Greek, Latin, and Sanskrit; the results of his investigations were published in 1853 under the title *Grammatica Celtica* (Zeuss 1853). The exploration of the Indo-European family was one of the most exciting linguistic enterprises of the nineteenth century, and the fact that Irish had a role to play in this work lent it a respectability which it had hitherto lacked.

It has to be admitted, though, that such scholarly activity, important though it was, largely ignored the contemporary spoken language. There were exceptions to this general trend, in that some individuals took an interest in a language which could still be heard in almost every part of Ireland. One of the main centres of activity with regard to the living language was Belfast. In 1808, the Reverend William Neilson published his *Introduction to the Irish language*. In the preface to this book, he wrote: 'But it is, particularly, from the absolute necessity of understanding this language, in order to converse with the natives of a greater part of Ireland, that the study of it is indispensable ... In travelling, and the common occurrences of agriculture or rural traffic, a knowledge of Irish is absolutely necessary' (Neilson 1990 [1808]: x). The view put forward here strikes a modern reader as eminently reasonable—after all, the usual motive for learning another language is to be able to communicate with other people. At the time it was written it represented a revolutionary attitude to Irish, particularly for a Presbyterian minister. Ten years later, Neilson went so far as to set up an Irish class in the Belfast Academical Institution.

Another Belfastman, Robert McAdam, helped to found the Ulster Gaelic Society. Its aims were threefold: (a) to collect Irish manuscripts, (b) to set up Irish classes, and (c) to publish Irish books. As part of the-last named project, the Ulster Society published in 1833 an Irish translation of Maria Edgeworth's novels *Forgive and forget* and *Rosanna* (Edgeworth 1833). It also published some primers and grammar books of Irish for learners.

In other parts of the country, individuals here and there tried to cultivate the living language. Philip Barron from Waterford set up a college in 1835 in which Irish was the language of instruction, but it lasted only six months. Archbishop McHale translated part of Homer's *Iliad* (Mac Héil 1981 [1844]) and also *Moore's melodies* (Mac Hale 1871) into Irish.

None of these efforts made much of an impact at the time. It is not entirely true that there was no market for books in Irish, as we saw in section 6.1.3. However, works like the *Iliad* or the novels of Maria Edgeworth were too sophisticated for the market that existed. The potential readers of Irish were peasants, not members of the middle class. These were people who were eager to read works of popular piety or simple folk-tales. Ó Ciosáin (1997) identifies two kinds of secular literature that enjoyed great popularity in Ireland in the period 1750–1850: chivalric romances and tales of highwaymen. Very often books were read out loud to illiterate listeners, so the story-line had to be relatively straightforward. Not every kind of literature lent itself to such forms of transmission. The members of the Ulster Gaelic Society were middle-class intellectuals who had for the most part learned Irish. They provided the Irish speakers with books that they would have liked to read themselves, rather than trying to find out what their intended readers would have liked. They failed to grasp that the Irish-speaking peasants were of a different frame of mind. It would be a long time before Irish country-people would read the works of Ascendancy writers like Maria Edgeworth, either in the original or in translation.

If the market for translations into Irish was limited, the demand for translations and adaptations into English was growing. A number of dual-language collections of Irish poetry appeared in this period, such as James Hardiman's *Irish minstrelsy* (1971 [1831]). Other works which proved popular with the English-speaking readership were collections of folk-tales in translation, such as T. C. Crofton Croker's *Fairy legends and traditions of the south of Ireland* (1998 [1825]), or William Wilde's *Irish popular superstitions* (1979 [1852]).

Many authors writing in English drew heavily on Irish literature for their inspiration. Thomas Moore's *Irish melodies*, although composed in English, contains many poems based on older Irish legends like the story of the children of Lir. Poets like Samuel Ferguson and James Clarence Mangan reworked Gaelic poetry into new compositions. The novelist and short-story writer William Carleton is particularly interesting in that he grew up in a bilingual rural environment. Unlike other writers of the time, he knew the world of the Irish peasant from the inside, and his *Traits and stories of the Irish peasantry* (Carleton 1990 [1830]) is a vivid portrait of pre-Famine Ireland.

Translation and original composition in English hardly strengthened the position of the Irish language; if anything, they might be said to have weakened it. Nevertheless, by dealing with themes and stories taken from the Irish-language tradition, the Anglo-Irish writers of the period 1800–70 made the Gaelic world more accessible to the middle classes of Dublin and other cities. This in turn prepared the ground for the language revival movement which developed after 1870.

6.2 The shape of the language (1800–70)

Despite the fact that the numbers speaking Irish declined significantly in this period, plenty of evidence about the language has survived. The most reliable linguistic sources are prose texts, particularly religious writings. We can discern two strands in the language of these texts. One is what one might call innovative, in that it exhibits drastic changes in spelling and grammar compared to traditional written material. The other is conservative, maintaining as it does the spelling, grammar, and style inherited from the past.

6.2.1 The innovative strand

I have already referred to the fact that when people learned to read in Ireland in the nineteenth century, they usually were taught from books in English rather than in Irish. Once somebody had mastered the alphabet, there was no shortage of English-language reading material in the form of books, pamphlets, and newspapers. As a result, most of those who read printed matter at this time were more familiar with the English characters and alphabet than with the Irish ones.

As early as the eighteenth century, publishers were using the English alphabet and its conventions to represent Irish sounds in print, or else mixing the two alphabets. This non-traditional orthography was to become very common after 1800. Ó Ciosáin (2012: 275) makes the important point that 'no norm for a popular readership existed'. Some Irish books were printed using Gaelic fonts and traditional spellings, while others were in Roman type and used the conventions of English orthography to render the sounds of Irish. This new way of writing is also to be found in some handwritten records from this period.

We can illustrate this development by comparing two versions of the opening of a text I have already referred to, *An Haicléara Mánas* (HM), written about 1850. Nancy Stenson, the editor of this tale, describes its spelling: 'Lyden was a native speaker of Irish, but could read and write only English, the text is written in a quasi-phonetic orthography based mainly on

English spelling' (Stenson 2003: ix). Stenson has normalized the spelling, which means rewriting it using the conventions established in the twentieth century—that is, the spelling that readers who learned Irish at school would be familiar with. Now let us look at the first paragraph in the original spelling and in her transcription:

(1)   a. Original
         noar a cholee a Hack- soh hanick fied aun agas Crunnee a tees oag
         astach agas beagan gun Hack- Croppo Soas agas noar a Veen teach
         reah hussee a fara vus agas a far haul laggan amach a mead ibra a
         hūrach diess gun Hack- agas vee ahas more air mar vee Sule eggah
         Sheashure mah a yeenue fee Claddach Sol a diech Shea Wallah
      b. Transcription
         Nuair a chuala an Haicléara seo, tháinig foighid ann, agus chruinnigh
         an t-aos óg isteach, agus b'éigean don Haicléara crapadh suas, agus
         nuair a bhí an teach réidh, thosaigh an fear abhus agus an fear thall
         [ag] leagan amach an méid oibre a thabharfaidís don Haicléara, agus
         bhí áthas mór air, mar bhí súil aige séasúr maith a dhéanamh faoi
         chladach sula dtéadh sé abhaile.

                                                          (Stenson 2003: 2–3)

When the Hackler heard this, he relaxed, and the young people gathered in, and the Hackler had to sit back; and when the house was ready, a man here and another man there started to lay out the work that they would give to the Hackler, and he was delighted, because he hoped to do a good season's work on the coast before he went home.

                                                          (Stenson 2003: 141)

If we look at (b), what strikes us is how close it is to twentieth-century Irish. Thousands of pieces like this are to be found in the manuscripts of the Irish Folklore Commission, the body which collected oral records from speakers of Irish in the twentieth century. The vocabulary and grammatical forms differ hardly at all from those of the Conamara dialect as we know it today.

The author, Patrick Lyden, was trying to reproduce the sounds of his own speech by adapting the English characters he knew. The problem is that he is not consistent in this. For instance, in some cases he uses <ee> to represent a long /i/, e.g. *crunee—chruinnigh*, but elsewhere he uses <ie> for the same sound, e.g. *hūrach diess—thabharfaidís*. The digraph <oa>, on the other hand, represents both long /o/, as in *oag—óg*, and the diphthong /ua/, as in *soas—suas*. With respect to consonants, the author uses English <sh> to represent the /sh/ in the word *sé*, e.g. *shea—sé*. On the other hand, the final sound in *amach* is represented by the digraph <ch> in Lyden's system, just as in the older Irish spelling, which suggests that he had some acquaintance with traditional Irish orthography. The reason he chose <ch> probably was that <ch> in English represents the final sound in the word *each* or *church*, which is totally different from the final sound in Irish *amach*, so it was necessary to go outside the English system in this case.

It should be pointed out that there is nothing about the English system of writing which makes it more suitable for rendering sounds than the Irish system. English orthography is just as cumbersome and misleading as Irish, or perhaps even more so. The other difficulty with the English-style spelling is that each author has his own system, so that every time a reader encounters a new text they have to get used to the orthographical idiosyncrasies. For this reason, modern editors tend to normalize the spelling so that a present-day reader can follow the text without difficulty.

Having said that, there is information to be gleaned from texts like HM about the language in the nineteenth century, but extracting that information is an arduous task. An example of the kind of information to be found is the fact that before the consonant /m/ Lyden writes <oo> instead of traditional <o>, *croom—crom*. We know from twentieth-century evidence that many dialects of Irish have a long /u/ instead of /o/ before /m/, so Leyden's spelling tells us that this was also true of the dialect of north Conamara in the period 1800–50.

6.2.2 The conservative strand

It is important to remember that the manuscript tradition did not disappear when books began to be printed in Irish. In some parts of the country, it continued to flourish well into the nineteenth century.

The scribes who copied manuscripts do not seem to have received any formal training, to judge by the account given by one of them, Micheál Óg Ó Longáin, of how he learned to write:

Féach a léitheoir . . . ní bhfuil mé ach óg ar an scríbhneoireacht so agus bíodh a fhios agat ná fuair mé comhairle ná teagasc inti ó neach ar bith.

[See, reader . . . I am new to this writing and I'll have you know that I didn't get any advice or training in it from anybody.]

(Ó Conchúir 1982: 102)

Ó Longáin does, however, mention that he was educated as a Poor Scholar, and he worked in several households as a tutor. During this period in his life he would have come into contact with samples of Irish writing. According to Cullen (1990) manuscript transcription and tutoring often went hand in hand: 'Hence the links between transcription and teaching were complex. It was not simply that transcribers became teachers, but that tutors desperately needed transcribing to supplement their income or prolong the periods of maintenance' (Cullen 1990: 18). Manuscripts would even have been circulating in the houses of the farmers in the areas where Ó Longáin worked as a labourer in later life. Some of these manuscripts were commissioned specially by patrons, but most were written to provide reading material for the communities in which the scribes lived. The stories and poems in the manuscripts would be read aloud to neighbours in the kitchens of farmers in the long winter nights. Books were still luxury items for most people, which may explain the persistence of the manuscript tradition after the arrival of printing.

The scribes tended by and large to stick to the traditional spelling. As well as that, their style was more conventional than that of people like Patrick Lyden, who was not able to read or write traditional Irish manuscripts, although he was literate in English. To illustrate the contrast between the old and the new, I will take a sample of a text written in 1826—that is, about twenty-five years before HM. The author was Dáibhí de Barra. As well as producing original compositions and translations, de Barra was a scribe, and hence steeped in the manuscript tradition. Here is the opening paragraph of the second part of *Párliment na bhFíodóirí* [The weavers' parliament] (PF). First I give the text as it appears in the manuscript (the diplomatic version), and then I give the editor's normalized version:

(2)   a. Diplomatic version

Air mbeith iomorra do thomás fíréast a ccarruig thuathail an easbog dámhna le linn Shéamuis ui Achíairuinn do bheith an Árd easbog air na fighdóirighe, et air bhfághail bháis do Shéamus do luig an cúram uile air thomás, ionnus go raibh dá ccúbhdach et dá ttreórughadh ris go socair saáil air lúth lámhaig et marcuígheachta re rae tríchatt bliaghain, acht oídhche naon dár luig tomás air aleaba lán do imshníomh et do smaointe, gur thit fá dheoig 'na thorchím suain et sámhchodlata, go bhfeacathus do neach, nó guit, fán bhfroi, nó air mullach an tíghe fá sgéimh sheirgthe thanuídhe lomm, et adúbhairt an cómhrádh so ris.

(Ó Duinnshléibhe 2011: 313)

b. Normalized version

Ar mbeith, iomarra, do Thomás Fíréast i gCarraig Thuathail in' easpag-d[h]amhna le linn Shéamuis Uí Achiarainn do bheith in' ardeaspag ar na fíodóirí agus ar bhfáil bháis do Shéamus do luigh an cúram uile ar Thomás, ionnas go raibh dá gcumhdach agus dá dtreorú ris go socair, sádhail, ar lúth lámhaigh agus marcaíochta re ré tríochad bliain. Acht oíche n-aon dár luigh Tomás ar a leaba, lán do imshníomh agus do smaointe, gur thit fá dheoidh 'na thoirchím suain agus sámhchodlata, go bhfeacathas do neach nó guth fán bhfroigh nó ar mullach an tí fá scéimh sheirgthe, thanaí, lom, agus adubhairt an comhrá so ris.

[Now after Thomas Forrest had been bishop-designate in Carrigtoole while James Aherne was archbishop of the weavers and after James had died, the whole responsibility fell on Thomas, so that he was protecting them and guiding them steadily, easily, vigorously, and forcefully for thirty years. But one night when Thomas lay down in his bed, full of care and thoughts, he finally fell into a heavy and overwhelming sleep, and there appeared to him a person or a voice under the rafters or on top of the house, looking withered, thin, and bare, and spoke to him thus.]

(Ó Duinnshléibhe 2011: 104)

If we compare (a) and (b), we can observe certain differences:

1. The punctuation has been regularized in (b). In l.4 of (a), a list of adverbs is given with no comma separating them—*go socair saáil air lúth lámhaig et marcúigheachta*. In (b), there is a comma after the first two adverbs—*go socair, sádhail, ar lúth lámhaigh agus marcaíochta*.
2. The initial letters in names have been capitalized, e.g. *thomás* → *Thomás*.
3. Dáibhí de Barra, like other scribes, uses the Latin word *et* for 'and'. This has been replaced by Irish *agus*.
4. With some consonants, de Barra indicates the sound modification called eclipsis (*urú*) by doubling the original consonant. For example, the preposition *i* 'in' (*a* in the ms) causes an initial <c> (pronounced /k/) to be changed to /g/, e.g. *Carraig* /karig/—*i* /garig/ 'in Carraig'. In present-day Irish, this is indicated by writing <g> before the original <c>—*i gCarraig*. De Barra indicates the change by doubling the initial <c>—*a ccarruig*.

The main difference, though, between the traditional manuscript spelling and present-day orthography is one that I have mentioned before a few times, namely the presence of consonant groups in the old spelling which are no longer pronounced (cf. sections 3.2.1, 4.2.1, 5.2.1). These silent consonants have been dispensed with in twentieth-century spelling, and the vowel preceding them is lengthened as a result and marked as long by means of an acute accent:

(3) Traditional New
     figheadóir   fíodóir
     amugha   amú

De Barra tries to follow the old system, but there is constant interference from his own pronunciation, so that we end up with both the consonant groups being written and the vowel being marked long:

(4) Traditional de Barra
     figheadóir   fíghdóir
     adubhairt   adúbhairt

On the whole, though, once we have got used to the older spellings, we see that there is not such a great gap between them and present-day orthography, in that the conventions used are broadly the same. For example, the sound /v/ is represented by either <bh> or <mh>, as in present-day Irish. In HM, by way of contrast, it is represented by the English character <v>.

One might expect, then, that it would be easier to read PF than HM once the text has been normalized. But for the modern reader de Barra's tale presents all kinds of difficulties that are absent from Lyden's. One difference is that we come across grammatical forms in PF that are not intelligible to the modern reader. Take the opening words in (2) above: *ar mbeith, iomorra, do Thomás Fíréast*. One will not find a phrase like *ar mbeith* in the standard modern Irish–English dictionary (Ó Dónaill 1977) (OD). *ar* is actually a variant of *iar*, which in turn is an old conjunction meaning 'after'. Another form that is confusing to the modern reader is *ris* in l.4 and 7 of (2b) above. This means 'with him', but is not found in the modern language, being replaced there by *leis*. In other sections of PF we find strange verbal forms, like the initial word of the following:

(5)   Féachas   Rúraoi na Ruacan   ina thimpeall.
      looked   Rúraoi na Ruacan   in.his around
      'Rúraoi na Ruacan looked around him'.

                    (Ó Duinnshléibhe 2011: 110)

The word *féachas* means 'he looked'; it is the same archaic past tense that we met in section 3.2.1 in a text from the early seventeenth century, and even then it was obsolete in speech. The modern equivalent would be *d'fhéach sé*. This old past tense seems to have been reserved for literary tales as distinct from ordinary narratives concerning everyday events. Presumably, when placed in the right context, it would still have been accessible to an early nineteenth-century audience, in the same way that English forms like *thou art* are still comprehensible to a twenty-first-century audience. However, present-day students of Irish have not been exposed to forms like these in their reading, and have no idea what they mean.

Apart from the grammar, what one might call the style of the tale presents difficulties for the modern reader. We find strange words like *iomorra* in l.1 of (2b), and the idiom *ar lúth lámhaigh agus marcaíochta* in l.4 is somewhat obscure. One notes in PF the same pairs of near-synonyms, often alliterating, that are so common in EMI: *socair, sádhail* 'steadily and easily'; *suain agus sámhchodlata* 'sleep and deep slumber'. With regard to *iomorra* in l.1 of (2b), it is to be found in OD, but is labelled Lit[erary]. This label is the key to understanding the kind of material often found in the nineteenth-century manuscripts. The material is written in a high register, aimed at imitating the heroic style of the late Middle Ages. In everyday life, de Barra would not have spoken the way he wrote—or, if he did, nobody would have understood him. But because of the written–spoken diglossia that I adverted to in section 3.2.2, it was still acceptable to use this archaic style in prose narratives.

Both PF and HM are humorous tales set in a community of craftsmen in the nineteenth century, but in terms of their linguistic presentation they are worlds apart. Were it not for the fact that there are references in PF to certain dates and places which enable us to locate it in the early years of the nineteenth century, it could almost have been written at any time between 1500 and 1650. HM, on the other hand, could have been written as late as 1900, judging by the language alone. In trying to establish what nineteenth-century Irish really looked like, then, it is essential that we take genre and register into account.

6.2.3 Borrowing

As one would expect, with bilingualism becoming the norm, the level of borrowing in everyday speech increased significantly in this period. Borrowing is a blanket term for a number of different ways of introducing a foreign element into a language. One can simply import the foreign word without integrating it into the existing sound system. We have already observed instances of this in the seventeenth and eighteenth centuries. Alternatively, one can replace a foreign sound with a native one. An example of this would be the word *séipéal*, from English *chapel*. Because the initial sound in the English word did not exist in Irish at the time of borrowing, the native sound [sh] was substituted for it.

If the grammatical structures of two languages differ significantly, then it is necessary to adapt a loan to the system of the borrowing language. I illustrate this by means of the grammatical category of verbs. In Irish, we find a greater range of endings on the verb than in English (see section 2.2.1). Verbs also are divided into different groups, called conjugations, according to the endings added to them:

(6)   Conjugation 1   Conjugation 2
      dún-ann sé/sí   ceanna-íonn sé/sí
      close-PRS he/she   buy-PRS he/she
      'he/she closes'   'he/she buys'

In Conjugation 1, the ending for the present tense is -**ann**, but in Conjugation 2 it is -**íonn**. The meaning is the same; it is just that certain verbs are grouped together depending on their shape, and then one or other of the two endings is attached to them.

Sometimes borrowings are marked by some grammatical feature to distinguish them from native words. In the last few centuries, many verbs have been borrowed from English into Irish. When this happens, they get a special marker, to show that they are borrowings. Take the verb *péinteáil* 'paint'. The ending -**eáil** has been added to the English word, and the result is a new Irish verb, to which we can add the Conjugation 1 endings:

(7) péint-eál-ann   sé/sí
     paint-eál-PRS   he/she
     'He/she paints.'

Even though *péinteáil* is a loan-word, it has been integrated into the grammar of Irish, and behaves like an Irish verb. Some older loan-words of this sort are perhaps no longer felt to be borrowings, e.g. *sábháil* < *save*.

In the nineteenth century, we find both kinds of borrowing, with and without assimilation. Compared to earlier centuries, though, the unassimilated borrowings have increased in number. There was much technological development going on in Europe at the time, with new words being coined or their meaning extended every day to describe new inventions and consumer goods. The words *industrialism, urbanization, railway, cab, omnibus, bicycle, telegraph, cardigan,* to name but a few, all entered the English language in this era. Lacking as it did institutional support, Irish became increasingly unable to absorb new words, particularly those associated with science, medicine, and technology. One lexical area where we can note a huge increase in unassimilated loan-words is the building industry. We find the following items attested for the period 1800–70 in contexts referring to housing and building: *foundation, drains, shutters, front, repairs* (Mac Mathúna 2012: 135–6). No attempt is made to provide an Irish equivalent, the words are simply inserted into the text in their English spelling.

Examples of both assimilated and non-assimilated loan-words are to be found in PF and HM. Given that HM is written in a colloquial style, and PF in a literary register, one might think that there would be more new English borrowings in the former than in the latter, and this is indeed the case. But even in PF we find a good number of assimilated borrowings. They are of apparently recent origin, in that *Corpas na Gaeilge* doesn't record them before 1750. Here is the list of assimilated borrowings from PF:

(8) *capar* 'copper coin', *conafás* 'canvas', *custamaeirí* 'customers', *dosaen* 'dozen', *fleainí* 'flannel', *paisteáil* 'patching', *printíseach* 'apprentice', *rapair* 'wrapper' (clothing), *slipéir* 'slipper?', *stróinséirí* 'strangers', *struisín* 'starching', *stufálta* 'stuffed', *taimí* 'tammy'

We also find quite a few unassimilated borrowings, written in English orthography:

(9)   *bird eye, brush, cryer, diaper, fees, Freeholder, Hedge-freemason, huckabag, informer, job, Peelers* 'policemen', *price, profit, scotch tabby, ticking, tomtit*

Apart from the dialogues between English speakers and Irish speakers, HM has a lot of borrowings in the Irish text. The following is the list of assimilated borrowings of recent origin found there:

(10)   *aicsean* 'action', *badráil* 'bothering', *blaistéara* 'blaster', *bocstaí* 'boxty' (kind of food), *búistéara* 'butcher', *caidséara* 'cadger' (street seller), *canbhás* 'canvas', *carraera* 'carman, carrier', *ceaig* 'keg', *cíléar* 'keeler, tub', *cniotálach* 'knitter', *coca* 'cock' (of hay), *craeinéara* 'craner' (crane operator), *damáiste* 'damage', *drár* 'drawers' (clothing), *drive-áil* 'driving', *flapáil* 'flapping', *fuisce* 'whiskey', *haicléara* 'hackler' (somebody who prepares flax for weaving)', *jabaire* 'jobber' (cattle-dealer), *muigín* 'little mug', *muist* 'power' (< *must*), *ocastóir* 'huckster', *péintéara* 'painter', *pinsean* 'pension', *pinsinéara* 'pensioner', *píolótaí* 'pilot', *piontaí* 'pints', *plaistéara* 'plasterer', *pressáil* 'pressing' (into service), *printíseach* 'apprentice', *raiceáilte* 'wrecked', *rap* 'rap', *sáibhéara* 'sawyer', *sáspan* 'saucepan', *scláitéara* 'slater', *seaicéad* 'jacket', *settáilte* 'settled', *siúinéara* 'joiner', *siúráilte* 'sure', *stil* 'still' (for distilling), *stiléara* 'stiller', *suinc* 'sink', *tincéara* 'tinker', *treabhsar* 'trousers', *truic* 'trick', *trust* 'trust', *túicneáil* 'tucking' (cloth), *veidhleadóir* 'fiddler', *veist* 'vest'

The list of unassimilated loans is much shorter:

(11)   *away* le 'off with' (of movement away), *bedad* (< *by God*), *bias, fair play, mister, pilot, sou'wester, steam, tin can, waterguards*

If we compare the two texts, we observe that there are more unassimilated loans in PF (16) than in HM (10). On the other hand, the number of assimilated recent loan-words in HM far exceeds the number in PF: 50 versus 14. Even allowing for the fact that HM is longer than PF, the rate of borrowing is much higher in the former than in the latter. This is what one would expect, given the difference in register between the two texts. Literary authors like de Barra usually resist borrowings more than authors like Lyden who write pretty much as they speak.

I leave HM and PF now, and move on to another text. One genre which displays strong English influences is sermon writing. At first this seems strange, in that one normally associates this genre with a high register. Liam Mac Mathúna offers an explanation for the presence of English loan-words in many of the sermons which have come down to us, namely that 'Sermons were composed under two quite different, and to a certain extent conflicting, linguistic pressures: the desire on the one hand to be understood by the congregation in accessible, everyday language, and, on the other, to reflect the loftiness of the thoughts and teachings pertaining to the sacred and the supernatural' (Mac Mathúna 2012: 136).

This mixture of high and low can be observed in a collection of sermons called *Teagasc ar an Sean-Tiomna* [Teachings on the Old Testament] (TST), written in the 1860s. At times the language is dignified and biblical:

(12)   Ar bheith do Abraham ag tionlacan an bheirt aingeal agus mac Dé, adúirt se sion: 'An ceart dhúinn an gnóth a mheasaimíd a dhéanamh do cheilt ar an bhfear so atá ina cheap as na bhfásaig mórán náisiúin agus rithe comhachtach, agus na mbeannófar go aon chine insa domhan ina shliucht? Atá fhios againn go gciomádfaig sé fhéin, agus go n-achtóig sé dhá mhuintir, cóir agus ceart Dé a leanúint, agus go gcólíonfaig Dia gach ní a gheall sé dho'.

[While Abraham was accompanying the two angels and the son of God, he said: 'Should we conceal the deed we mean to do from this man who is the progenitor from whom many nations and powerful kings will spring, and every race in the world will be blessed in his progeny? We know that he himself will keep, and that he will enjoin his people to follow, the law of God, and that God will fulfil everything which he has promised to him.']

(Ó Madagáin 1974: 38)

In this passage, the choice of vocabulary like *ar bheith* 'while' instead of the more common *nuair*, and *achtóig* 'will enjoin', lend an air of solemnity to the text, as does the use of a pair of synonyms *cóir agus ceart* to translate *law*.

In other passages in TST, when the priest paraphrases what is happening in the Bible or comments on something contemporary, we find a much more colloquial kind of language. In the next extract he is commenting on Ishmael's persecution of Isaac and echoes of this in more recent times:

(13)   Gnóth eile as ceart a thabhairt fá ndeara as ea fé mar a rin Ishmael, an mac a bhí ag Abraham le Agar, *persecuting* ar Isaac, a cheap Dia mar oidhre ar na geallúna móra iontach a thug sé don nduine beannaithe úd: amhla sin a dhéanfaig, do shíor agus do ghnáth, leas-chlainn na Eaglaise, na eiricidí, a éirionn uadh am go am, *persecuting* agus géir-leanúint ar chlann fhírinneach na Eaglaise, na Catailicí.

[Another thing which ought to be noted is how Ishmael, the son that Abraham had with Agar, persecuted Isaac, who God had made heir to the great, wonderful promises that he had given to that holy person:

likewise the false children of the Church, the heretics, who rise up from time to time, will persecute the true children of the Church, the Catholics.]

(Ó Madagáin 1974: 47)

The native term for persecution is *géir-leanúint*, which occurs side by side with the English word *persecuting* in l.4 of the Irish text. There are two interesting aspects to the author's use of the English word here. First, it reflects a way of borrowing verbs from English into Irish that became widespread in the twentieth century. In this process, an unassimilated English word is combined with the Irish verb *déan* 'do' and the preposition *ar* 'on':

(14) English   Irish
     phone   déan fón   ar
                  do   phone   on
                  'to telephone'
     boycotting   déan *boycotting*   ar
                  do   boycotting   on
                  'to boycott'

Second, in l.4 of the extract the English word is followed immediately by the Irish equivalent: '*persecuting* agus géir-leanúint'. Commenting on speakers' awareness of language mixing in present-day Irish, one author writes that 'To some extent speakers mark interlingual transitions during discourse by means of what has come to be known as "flags"' (Wigger 2000: 174). What he means by this is that speakers tend to provide some kind of clue for their listeners that they are mixing languages. Various strategies can be employed to mark the transition from one language to another. One of these is the one used above by the author of TST. Wigger describes this strategy as follows:

A particularly interesting type of flag consists in immediate translation, i.e. juxtaposition of a semantic equivalent taken from the other language. Usually the sequence is English > Irish, as in:

   Tá fear a dtugann siad *sailmaker* air, fear déanta seolta.
   'There is a man they call *sailmaker*, a man for making sails'.

(Wigger 2000: 175)

The same mechanism seems to have been applied by the author of TST when he wrote 'a *dhéanfaig*...persecuting *agus géir-leanúint*' [will do persecuting and persecution]. Perhaps he chose *persecuting* because he was translating from an English sermon, and wished in particular to stress this lexical item, or considered it highly effective. At the same time, he would have been conscious that for his listeners this would have been an unfamiliar item, and hence felt the need to provide a translation.

It must be borne in mind that borrowing is not the only strategy available when a community of speakers come into contact with a new concept for which there is no existing word in their language. One can also try to provide a semantic equivalent for the word with the aid of existing resources in the language. We already encountered an example of this in section 5.2.2. We noted there that Tadhg Ó Neachtain tried as it were to invent an Irish word for English *library*, using the native elements *leabhar* 'book' and *lann* 'place'. As we saw in Chapter 5, this kind of conscious word-formation is much more time-consuming than straightforward borrowing of the kind we have been looking at up to now.

One writer who made such a conscious effort to avoid unassimilated borrowings was Amhlaoibh Ó Súilleabháin, a schoolteacher and merchant from County Kilkenny. Ó Súilleabháin kept a diary in Irish for the years 1827–35, *Cín Lae Amhlaoibh Uí Shúilleabháin* [Humphrey O'Sullivan's diary] (de Bhaldraithe 1970). In it he frequently coins new terms for concepts that he comes across in English. Thus, he makes new words from nouns by means of suffixes:

(15) Noun   Derivative
     cuile 'fly'   cuilearacht 'fly-catching'
     Márta 'March'   Mártúil 'March-like'
     rothán 'small wheel'   rothánach 'circulating' (applied to *library*)
     ubh 'egg'   ubhúil 'oval'

The word *rothánach* is more a description of *circulating* than an actual translation. Presumably, the reference was to the fact that a *circulating library* was on wheels. With *ubhúil* 'oval', in order for Ó Súilleabháin to coin the new term he had to be aware that English *oval* comes from Latin *ovalis*, this in turn being derived from *ovum* 'egg'. The Irish *ubhúil* only makes sense in this context. This, then, is a very learned kind of word-formation, requiring a knowledge of etymology.

As well as words like the above, Ó Súilleabháin was given to coining his own compounds for English items. In the following examples, we see that a single English word has been rendered into Irish by means of a compound, consisting of two parts:

(16) English   Irish
     barracks   tigh dragúin
                house of dragoons
     doctor   ollamh-leá
                sage physician

Colloquial Irish had the word *beairic* for *barracks* at the time that Ó Súilleabháin was writing, while the borrowing *dochtúir* 'doctor' had been in Irish since the Middle Ages. Strictly speaking, there was no need for the new compounds.

However, speakers frequently display a resistance to borrowing, as they feel that words composed of native elements are somehow more authentic. This was probably what motivated Ó Súilleabháin to coin the above items.

Other compounds of his fulfil a genuine need for Irish equivalents to English words:

(17) English   Irish
      patriotism   grá   dúchais
                       Love   of.heritage/native place
      snow-drop   cloigín   sneachta
                       small-bell   of.snow
      ventriloquist   goile-labharthóir
                       belly-speaker

Once again, for Ó Súilleabháin to coin a term for English *ventriloquist*, he had to know the Latin etymology—*ventriloquus* < *venter* 'belly' + *loquor* 'speak'.

Like Tadhg Ó Neachtain in the eighteenth century, Amhlaoibh Ó Súilleabháin was exceptional for the mid-nineteenth century. He was attempting to create a learned written register for Irish which it did not possess. Unlike Dáibhí de Barra, he was not just concerned with imitating the style of old tales, for in his diary he described the day-to-day reality of life in a small town in the 1830s. He differed from people like Patrick Lyden, the author of HM, in that he wanted to extend the spoken language, to enrich its lexical resources. Even when he borrows words directly from English, he attempts to assimilate them to the sound system and grammatical structure of the language.

If there had been more like-minded people among the Irish-speaking community at the time, and if they had had the backing of educational institutions and the world of print, they would undoubtedly have managed to make Irish a fit medium for dealing with the whole spectrum of nineteenth-century life. Sadly, this was not the case, and Ó Súilleabháin's contribution to Irish was only recognized a century after his death.

6.2.4 Grammars and primers

Paradoxically, even while spoken Irish was declining, there was an increase in the number of primers (text-books) and grammars of Irish. Some of these were printed by Bible societies, e.g. *An Irish English primer, intended for the use of schools; containing about four thousand Irish monosyllables with their explanation in English: together with a few of Aesop's Fables in Irish and in English, by T. Conellan* (Conellan 1815). Others were produced to meet the demand for reading older manuscripts, such as John O'Donovan's *Grammar of the Irish language* (O'Donovan 1845).

Works like these can often yield valuable nuggets of information about the language of the time, but like the texts described in the previous section, they must be handled with care. Scholars like John O'Donovan were only interested in old manuscripts dealing with history and genealogies, and regarded the spoken Irish of the day as inferior to that of the Middle Ages. Osborn Bergin, writing nearly a century later, criticized O'Donovan's methodology:

But a graver defect is the lack of precision with regard to Modern Irish. Sometimes it means the language of the Early Modern period, such as Keating [seventeenth century], whom he calls 'one of the last of the correct writers'. Sometimes it is the spoken Irish of his own day. Sometimes he denounces the spoken usage as 'corrupt', or 'barbaric', as 'not found in correct writers', 'a local jargon', &c.

(Bergin 1938: 226)

A more serious shortcoming, and one shared with other grammarians of the day, was that at times O'Donovan simply falsified the data. In the words of Bergin, 'The paradigm must be complete, and if the form is not known it must be invented. There are forms in his Grammar, such as 2 pl. *biadhaídh* or *beidhídh* "you will be" . . . which never existed in the language' (Bergin 1938: 227).

Fortunately for the historian of Irish, some grammarians also included in their works short samples of everyday dialogues, and these give us a much better idea of how people might have spoken to each other in the early nineteenth century. William Neilson, who I mentioned in section 6.1.8, took a more modern approach to language-learning than his contemporaries, as this sentence from his *Introduction to the Irish language* shows: 'The phrases and dialogues in the second part are calculated for general use; and the dryness of grammatical precepts will be relieved by the simple and original specimens of native manners and superstitions, contained in the latter dialogues' (Neilson 1990 [1808]: xii). The dialogues are divided by subject, such as buying and selling, health, and travelling. The speakers seem to be well-to-do farmers and merchants, rather than impoverished peasants. It is difficult to judge how realistic the dialogues are, but it is possible that in County Down, where Neilson was born, the Irish speakers were better off than in other parts of the country. The following phrases occur in a dialogue entitled *Teach oidheachta tuaithe* [A country inn]. The information in square brackets has been added to make the dialogues easier to follow.

(18) [Traveller] Ca mheud mìle uaim an baile is neasa damh?
      How many miles am I from the next town?
      [Local farmer] Ta deich mìle, maithe, go hairighthe; agus nil an bothar ro mhaith ann àiteachuibh.
      At least ten long miles; and the road is not very good in some places.

[Traveller] Is gann damh bheith ann a nocht. Nach aon ionad oidheachta, eadruinn agus è?

I can hardly reach it to night. Is there no place of entertainment between this and it?

[Local farmer] Ta brugh oidheachta ro ghleasta, a dtimchioll chùig mhìle romhad, ionn a bhfuighir gach comhgair go sàsta; agus beidh tu a gcontabhairt cuideachta fhaghail ann, mar is è so an bealach go haonach Bhaile na slogha.

There is a very decent inn, about five miles forward, where you can be well accommodated; and you will be apt to find company there, as this is the way to the fair of Balinasloe.

Gheabha tu proinn maith, agus leaba saimh ann, agus aire maith dod chapall.

You will get a good dinner and bed, and your horse will be well treated.

[At the inn]
[Traveller] Ca bhfuil fear an tigh?

Where is the master of the house?

[Innkeeper] Taim ann so, a dhuine uasail.

I am here, Sir.

[Traveller] Go de ta agad a Oghasdoir?

What have you for me, landlord?

[Innkeeper] Rogha gacha bidhe, is togha gacha dighe. Ta mairt fheoil mhaith, is caoirfheoil ùir; ta feoil laoidh biadhta, uain fheoil ro mhaith, is feoil mheith mhionann.

Choice of meat and drink. I have fat beef, and fresh mutton, fed veal, very good lamb, and fat kid.

[Traveller] Go de an seoirt dighe ta agad?

What kind of drink have you?

[Innkeeper] Ta leann donn, laidir, blàsta, brioghmhur; uisge beatha is fearr càil; biotailte bioracha o thìr fa thuinn; agus fionta na Fraince, is phort na ngall.

I have strong, well flavoured brown ale; whiskey of the best quality; spirits from Holland; and wine from France and Portugal.

(Neilson 1990 [1808]: 60–2)

The above dialogues are typical of what we still find in phrasebooks for travellers to foreign countries. On the whole, comparing them to what we know of twentieth-century dialects from the same region, they have an air of authenticity. Here and there we find errors, e.g. in l.6 of the first dialogue *Nach aon ionad oidheachta, eadruinn agus è?*, the verb *bhfuil* 'is' seems to be missing. Some of the vocabulary is archaic, which is only to be expected in dialogues written 200 years ago. For example, *brugh oidheachta* 'inn' is not attested in twentieth-century sources; it is not clear whether it reflects the common usage of Neilson's times or whether he invented it himself. Other words like *proinn* 'dinner' have disappeared from the spoken language but are attested in other nineteenth-century sources, and so presumably were still in use in Neilson's day. As regards the food and drink on offer, the menu is similar to various meals described by Amhlaoibh Ó Súilleabháin in his diaries from the 1820s and 1830s (de Bhaldraithe 1970).

Neilson's *Introduction to the Irish language* is by no means flawless, and at times the terminology and lay-out are confusing for the modern reader. At the same time, he displays a sensitivity to the problems encountered by English speakers when they first come into contact with Irish. For example, Irish distinguishes between actions and states quite systematically. Thus, for the verb *stand*, we find two separate constructions, depending on whether we want to express an action or a state:

(19) a. Sheas sí   ag an doras.
         stood she   at the door
         'She took up a standing position at the door.' (action)
      b. Bhí sí   ina seasamh   ag an doras.
         was she   in.her standing   at the door
         'She was standing at the door.' (state)

Students of Irish have great difficulty mastering the second construction, because it is so different from English. That is why Neilson devotes a whole section to what he calls 'reflected verbs', i.e. constructions like (19b) above. In it, he provides a list of commonly used expressions like *be asleep, be awake, be sitting, be living, dwelling, be silent* (Neilson 1990 [1808]: 125).

Another source of difficulty for learners is that very often, where English has a single verb, Irish has a construction involving a verb like *be* and a preposition. The best-known case of this sort is the expression of possession. Irish has no single verb *have*, but uses the verb *bí* 'be' and the preposition *ag* 'with, at, by':

(20) Tá   leabhar   agam.
      is   book   at.me
      'I have a book.'

The above is not an isolated example: *can, must, love, hate, want*, and many other common verbs are all expressed by means of a verb + preposition in Irish. Likewise, where English uses an adjective to describe a state, Irish will often use a verb + noun + preposition:

(21) Tá   ocras   orm.
      is   hunger   on.me
      'I am hungry'

Neilson is aware of the great difference between the two languages in this respect, and attempts to give the student some idea of the semantics of the various prepositions, illustrating with examples:

(22) Irish   English
      Ta   sgian   agam.
      is   knife   at.me   I have a knife.
      Ni   bhfuil   sgian   agam.
      not   is   knife   at.me   I have not a knife.
      Ta   sgian   uaim.
      is   knife   from.me   I want a knife.
      Ni   thig   liom   a dheanamh.
      not   come   with.me   its doing   I cannot do it.
      Is   eigin   damh   sgriobhadh.
      is   force   to.me   write.INF   I must write.
      Ta   gradh   agam   air Dhia.
      is   love   at.me   on God   I love God.
      Ta   fuacht   orm.
      is   cold   on.me   I am cold.
      Is   liom   sin   fòs.
      is   with.me   that   still   That is mine too.
                                (based on Neilson 1990 [1808]: 126)

In general, then, even while the spoken language was declining, there was a growth in demand for teaching aids for learners. The grammars and primers produced by men like Neilson offer us a glimpse into the language of the time, and also into the teaching methods of their authors.

6.3 Conclusion

The period 1800–70 is a period of far-reaching political, economic, cultural, and social change in Ireland. It is a crucial era for the shaping of modern Irish society. Part of the change that took place on the socio-cultural front concerned the relative roles of Irish and English. In 1800, Irish still had a strong presence in the daily life of rural dwellers; by 1870 it had retreated to the margins of society.

Few subjects have attracted so much attention in the history of the Irish language as the change to English. In this chapter, I have attempted to show that the change was quite a gradual one, spanning several generations. We have also seen that the conditions for the language switch existed as early as 1800. The acceleration after that date was due to the increased opportunities for education and mobility in Irish society. Only a very determined nationalist movement which stressed the centrality of language to ethnic identity could have turned the tide in favour of Irish. As we have seen, the kind of nationalism that emerged in Ireland was based on an identity which expressed itself in a new language, English. This new language was not just the language of Ireland's colonial master, England. It was also the language of the country which was fast becoming the ideal to which most Irish people aspired, namely the United States of America, a country which was to attract millions of Irish emigrants for the next hundred years. English was also the language of the church which provided an identity for the majority of Irish people, Catholicism.

Nevertheless, there are plenty of Irish-language sources for this period, if one is prepared to seek them out. Books printed using English orthography, manuscripts written in the old Gaelic character, and new grammars and language primers all contain copious examples of the Irish of the nineteenth century. As we have seen in the second part of this chapter, even in its period of decline Irish was still a language containing a range of registers. Contact with English was on the whole a negative influence in that it weakened the position of Irish, but it also resulted in an enrichment of the colloquial language with a whole spectrum of borrowings, some of which were to survive into the twentieth-century dialects.

Further reading

For Ireland 1800–50, see Ó Tuathaigh (1972).

For a general survey of language and literature 1800–70, see Ó Cuív (1986) and Denvir (2006). The latter also contains a section on language shift and on the societies and scholars who cultivated Irish in the first half of the nineteenth century.

Ó Doibhlin (2011) contains poems about Daniel O'Connell, and the Famine, as well as longer extracts from some of the prose texts discussed in section 6.2. For Daniel O'Connell and his Irish identity, see Ó Tuathaigh (1974); Murphy (1984); and Geoghegan (2008). Uí Ógáin (1985, 1995) deals with folk-memories of O'Connell.

For cultural nationalism in eighteenth- and nineteenth-century Europe, see Hutchinson (1987: 8–47).

For language and national identity in Ireland in the nineteenth century, see Leersen (1996b) and Titley (2000). Morley (2011) disagrees strongly with the thesis put forward by Leersen (1996b), namely that nineteenth-century Gaelic Ireland lacked a public sphere in which its culture could find expression.

For education and literacy, see Cullen (1990) and Ó Ciosáin (1997: 30–58). For literacy and the Catholic church, see Ó Ciosáin (1997: 134–51, 177–95).

For the Catholic church and the Irish language in this period, see Ó Tuathaigh (1986). Blaney (1996) contains much information on nineteenth-century Presbyterians who made a contribution to the study of Irish. For the Bible societies and their work, see Moffitt (2008) and de Brún (2009).

For an account of written Irish-language sources about the Famine, see Buttimer (2012). Ó Gráda (1994) is a collection of oral records in prose and verse about the same event.

For the Irish language in America, see Ó hAnnracháin (1979); McGowan (1994); and Callahan (1994).

For the language shift from Irish to English, see Ó Cuív (1951: 20–7); Wall (1969); Fitzgerald (1984); Ó Huallacháin (1994: 24–33); and Ó Murchú (1998). Durkacz (1983) compares the change in Ireland with similar events in Scotland and Wales; another distinguishing feature of his work is the emphasis on the role of religion, either as facilitating or impeding the advance of English. Nic Craith (1993) and Ní Mhóráin (1997) are longitudinal studies of language patterns in counties Cork and Kerry, respectively. Ó Ciosáin (2005) offers a comprehensive overview of the literature on language in the nineteenth century, subjecting the various works to a rigorous assessment in which he draws attention to their merits and shortcomings.

With respect to twentieth-century attitudes towards the language shift, de Fréine (1965) is an example of the cataclysmic approach to the language question. De Fréine's work is written from an unapologetically nationalist standpoint. Later writers like Nic Craith (2012) describe the change from Irish to English more in terms of the loss of cultural diversity. Mac Mathúna (2007: 219–68) is more neutral in his stance; he discusses how attitudes to the language shift varied over time and between different social classes.

For antiquarian societies and the preservation of Irish, see Ó Huallacháin (1994: 27–31) and Murray (2000). Ó Buachalla (1968) is a study of individuals and organizations who cultivated Irish in Belfast in the period covered by this chapter.

For source documents relating to language 1800–70, see Crowley (2000: 133–74).

For an account of editing and transcribing texts written in English orthography, see Stenson (2003: viii–xxiii).

Williams (2010) deals with attempts over the centuries to represent Irish in adaptations of English orthography.

For the background to scribes and authors like Dáibhí de Barra and Amhlaoibh Ó Súilleabháin, see Ó Conchúir (1982); Cullen (1990); Ní Urdail (2000); and Ó Duinnshléibhe (2011: 1–89).

For borrowing into Irish, see Stenson (1993); Doyle (1996); and Wigger (2000).

For a survey of nineteenth-century sermons in Irish, see Ó Dúshláine (1996).

For a history of Irish grammars before 1900, see Bergin (1938).

7

Revival (1870–1922)

7.1 Political and social developments (1870–1922)

After the failing of the Fenian rising in 1867, most Irish nationalists turned their backs on revolution and decided to concentrate instead on constitutional reform. Essentially, this was a return to the politics of Daniel O'Connell and his Repeal movement. The new political initiative, the Home Government Association, was founded by Isaac Butt in 1870, and soon became popularly known as the Home Rule movement. The Home Rulers contested the 1874 general election as a party and succeeded in winning 59 of the 105 Irish seats in the Westminster parliament. This faction became known as the Irish Party or the Home Rule Party.

In 1875 a young man called Charles Stewart Parnell joined the Home Rule Party. He rose quickly to prominence, replacing Butt as president of the Home Rule Confederation of Great Britain in 1877. Soon afterwards events occurred in Ireland which gave a new impetus to the struggle for self-government. Another agricultural crisis began as a result of the failure of the potato crop, and also because of the slowing-down of emigration to the United States. Unlike the Famine of 1845, this smaller famine provoked a strong political and social response. An ex-Fenian, Michael Davitt, set up the Land League in Mayo in 1879 to defend the rights of tenant farmers against the landlords, and Parnell threw the support of the Irish Party behind him. Thus began what came to be known as the Land War. This was a campaign conducted through the 1880s and 1890s which aimed at achieving fair terms for the small tenant farmers. It involved various forms of agitation, ranging from mass-meetings to withholding rents. The Land War gave the word *boycott* to the English language, after a community in Mayo refused to work for the local landlord Captain Boycott and subjected him to a process of ostracism, eventually forcing him to leave the district. Landlords hit back by evicting tenants who refused to pay their rents. At times the campaign spilled over into violence, and the British government of the day responded by imposing tough coercive legislation, even going so far as to imprison Parnell and Davitt at one stage.

Gradually the tactics of the Land War leaders bore fruit, and the Liberal government under Prime Minister William Gladstone introduced legislation in 1881 which provided fair rent, free sale, and fixity of tenure to the farmers. Later Land Acts provided government credit to enable small-holders to buy out their farms, and by 1900 the Land War was more or less over. The great estates of the past were no more, and rural Ireland had a new political and social class, the small owner-farmers, who were passionately attached to their land.

Meanwhile, Parnell and the Irish Party continued to agitate for Home Rule. In 1885 the Irish Party held the balance of power in the British parliament, and Gladstone agreed to introduce a Home Rule bill if Parnell supported him. The 1886 Home Rule Bill was narrowly defeated. Four years later, Parnell fell from grace because of a love affair with a married woman, and died in 1891 while fighting an election campaign. The scandal surrounding his fall caused a division in the ranks of the Home Rulers, which was not helped by the failure of the second Home Rule Bill of 1893 to be passed. After 1893, the Home Rule movement began to lose steam, and by 1900 there seemed little chance of Ireland achieving self-government in the near future. The government's land legislation had removed many of the grounds for complaint, and further economic measures aimed at alleviating the poverty of the west of Ireland helped to pacify the people even further. This policy of appeasement on the part of the British government is often referred to as killing Home Rule with kindness.

At the same time, the separatist tradition of the Irish Republican Brotherhood (IRB), which had never totally disappeared, began to make headway again. This was partly in response to developments in the North of Ireland. Alarmed by the prospect of a Home Rule bill being passed, the Irish Unionist Party was founded to preserve the link with Britain. Most of its support came from the Protestant community of Ulster. After 1900, this party began to adopt a more aggressive tone, hinting that it would fight to protect its rights if necessary. The nationalists in turn became more radical in the early years of the twentieth century. By the time that the third Home Rule Bill came to be passed by the House of Commons in 1913, the two sides were squaring up for a confrontation. In 1913 two paramilitary organizations were founded: the Ulster Volunteers to protect unionist interests, and the nationalist Irish Volunteers, which supported Home Rule. However, the outbreak of World War I in 1914 prevented matters from going any further.

Most nationalists and all unionists supported the British side in the war, with large numbers of Catholics and Protestants joining up to fight against Germany and her allies. In 1916, a small extremist faction within the Irish Volunteers, headed by Patrick Pearse, began to plot an armed uprising; they were joined by the socialist Citizen Army led by James Connolly. Their goal was to win total independence for Ireland. The Easter Rising was a military failure, but the execution of its leaders afterwards led to an upsurge of support for the separatist tradition. In the 1918 elections which followed the ending of World War I, Sinn Féin, a party which demanded complete independence, won an overwhelming majority of the Irish seats outside of Ulster. Soon afterwards in 1919, the military wing of the separatist movement, which had managed to reorganize itself, decided to begin attacking representatives of British rule, and thus began the War of Independence, which lasted until 1921. Following the signing of the Anglo-Irish Treaty in December 1921, the Free State was established in 1922. Ireland, with the exception of six of the counties of Ulster, became virtually independent under the terms of the treaty, with almost total control over its own affairs.

7.2 Cultural developments (1870–1922)

One result of the Land War described above was a growing self-confidence in Irish society. No longer did the rural Catholic masses feel that they were second-class citizens. For the first time ever in their history, they began to see themselves as masters of their own destinies.

This sense of empowerment led to a new kind of nationalism, which manifested itself in non-political activity. In the economic sphere, one of the more far-reaching initiatives of the 1890s was the cooperative movement. This encouraged small farmers to join together and form creameries, which would then sell their dairy products to the retailers directly, thus cutting out the middleman. In the same spirit Arthur Griffith's Sinn Féin party, founded in 1905, agitated for economic self-sufficiency, urging Irish people to buy only Irish products.

Another area which experienced a kind of revolution was sport. Until the 1880s, various games had been played in Ireland. Like in Britain, soccer, rugby, cricket, and golf were popular in the towns and cities. In the countryside, two specifically Irish games existed, hurling, and a kind of football which had its own rules, distinct from soccer and rugby. In 1884 a group came together to form an association for the native games, the Gaelic Athletic Association (GAA). The new movement proved a huge success, especially in the country-side. Branches were established at parish and county level, which led to a new sense of local pride.

The leading figure in this new association, Michael Cusack, was a nation-alist, and saw in the cultivation of Gaelic games a way of resisting the Anglicization that he witnessed all around him. The GAA from its foundation adopted a strong anti-British stance. For example, members of the Royal Irish Constabulary and the British army were not allowed to play in its competitions, and members of the GAA were forbidden to take part in what were called 'foreign games'. The founding of the GAA drove a wedge into Irish society which persisted until very recently. Certain members of the upper middle classes, usually with an urban background, continued to send their children to schools that played rugby and cricket, while Gaelic games became associated with rural Ireland and the working-class areas of the cities.

In the realm of literature, we saw in Chapter 6 how a new kind of writer had come to the fore in the period 1800–70, one who wrote in English, but who dealt with specifically Irish themes. In the period after 1870, Irish writers were preoccupied with creating a literature in English that at the same time would be a national literature. One stratagem that they adopted was to write in the vernacular of the country people, in what later came to be known as Hiberno-English. This dialect more or less corresponded to the speech of ordinary rural dwellers. Members of the Ascendancy or the Protestant middle classes, people like Lady Gregory, W. B. Yeats, and John Millington Synge, took this dialect and created out of it a new kind of literary language, one which was very different from the standardized language of mainstream British literature at the time. The literary movement that they led was known as the Anglo-Irish Revival. Due to the efforts of Lady Gregory and Yeats in particular, the Abbey Theatre was established in 1904 as a national theatre, and it was here that the plays of Synge and Sean O'Casey were staged for the first time. Meanwhile, Yeats was establishing himself as a major English-language poet in the successive volumes he published.

The question of nationality, of what it meant to be really Irish, was very much present in public discourse at the time. The foremost proponent of an Irish-Ireland, one which would be distinct from a British colony, was the journalist D. P. Moran, editor of the influential weekly *The Leader*. Moran espoused self-sufficiency in all realms of life, from literature to industrial production, excoriating at the same time those whom he saw as being lukewarm in their patriotism, like the Irish Party in the House of Commons, who only wanted to obtain Home Rule. For him there could be no true nationalism that was not based on cultural distinctness. There were two civilizations, according to Moran, the British and the Irish, and there was no possibility of compromise between them. Either Ireland succumbed to British influence and became 'West Britain', or it broke free of the intellectual and cultural tyranny that had bound it and became a nation in its own right.

It was in this general cultural milieu that the movement for reviving Irish began, a movement which was to become an important force in Ireland at the beginning of the twentieth century.

7.3 A precursor to the Gaelic League

One subject that has attracted much attention in the history of the Irish language is the founding of the Gaelic League in 1893. However, before this event took place, a lot of work had been done by another organization to promote an awareness of Irish among the public. Much of the activity of the Gaelic League was a continuation of projects which had been initiated by this earlier organization, and hence it is necessary to take a closer look at its achievements.

As we saw in the previous chapter, Irish was in serious decline by 1870, and this process continued in the following twenty years. By 1891, the areas where Irish was spoken had shrunk even further (Figure 7.1). It seemed that it was doomed to extinction in a few decades.

This was the general linguistic background to a new initiative aimed at protecting Irish. In 1876 a group of people came together in Dublin to form the Society for the Preservation of the Irish language (SPIL). This was not the first society founded in the nineteenth century with the purpose of cultivating Irish. However, in a number of respects it differed from previous initiatives of this sort. First, it had the support of people representing a broad spectrum of society, rather than just academics and antiquarians. Some idea of the composition of its membership can be gleaned from the minutes of the first meeting:

A meeting was convened at No. 4 Bacheler's [sic] Walk, December 29th 1876, 'To take the necessary steps for the formation of a Society for the Preservation and Cultivation of the Irish Language and Literature'. There were present: Charles Dawson Esq., High Sheriff of Limerick; William Dillon Esq., Barr.; T. D. Sullivan Esq., Editor of 'The Nation'; Bryan O'Looney M.R.I.A., Professor of Irish Language, Literature and Archaeology C.U.; Rev. H. P. Kelly O.D.C.; H. J. Gill Esq. M.A. T.C.D; P. W. Joyce LL.D. T.C.D.; Rev. J. E. Nolan O.D.C.; D. Comyn.

(Ó Murchú 2001: 14)

Second, it had the express purpose of preserving the living language, whereas previous societies of this sort had tended to be more antiquarian in spirit. This aim was clearly present in the mission statement of the SPIL:

After some discussion the meeting became unanimously of opinion that it is possible and desirable to preserve the Irish Language in those parts of the Country where it is still spoken, with a view to its further extension and cultivation.

(Ó Murchú 2001: 15)

Finally, the public response to the founding of the Society was far more enthusiastic than the response to previous organizations of this sort. Those

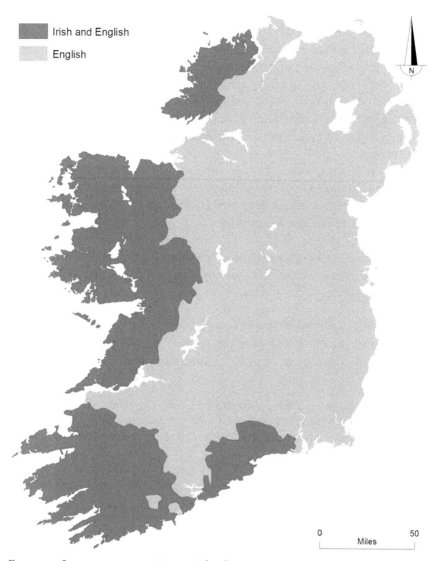

- ■ Irish and English
- ▒ English

FIGURE 7.1 Language communities in Ireland 1891

Sources: based on Brian Ó Cuív (1951). *Irish dialects and Irish-speaking districts*. Dublin: Dublin Institute for Advanced Studies. Map 2; Brian Ó Cuív (ed.) (1969). *A view of the Irish language*. Dublin: The Stationery Office. Map 2 who joined included members of the clergy, both Catholic and from the Church of Ireland, teachers and academics, parliamentary deputies, and representatives of the Anglo-Irish aristocracy.

One of the main aims of the Society was to introduce Irish into the educational system. To this end, it sent a petition to the Commissioners for National Education in 1878 requesting that Irish be recognized as an optional subject in primary schools. The permission was granted without any fuss, but only for schools located in districts where Irish was still spoken by the local community. Getting permission was one thing, but implementing the teaching of Irish was quite another. Many National School Teachers did not speak Irish, and even if they did, they were often unable to read or write it, and had no training in how to teach it. There were virtually no teaching aids available to them. Furthermore, because Irish was an optional subject, parents had to pay a fee of two shillings a year if they wished their children to attend the classes. Most parents in Irish-speaking districts were very poor, and saw no advantage in learning how to read and write Irish, for the reasons we explored in Chapters 5–6. In one school in County Clare, for example, the response to the idea of including Irish in the curriculum was somewhat less than enthusiastic: 'All can speak Irish; [the teacher] has no class, as the parents of the children would not like them to speak Irish' (Ó Murchú 2001: 161).

The SPIL tried to overcome these difficulties by publishing text-books and by providing training for teachers. A primer entitled *An chead leabhar Gaedhilge. First Irish Book*, appeared in 1878. The problem with this text-book was that it was geared towards second-language learners, while the children using it were not learners, but first-language/bilingual speakers. Like other books for teaching foreign languages at the time, the model adopted was very much based on the teaching of Latin, with little emphasis on contemporary everyday usage. Despite these shortcomings, the publication of this teaching aid marked a new beginning in the teaching of Irish.

After a few years, a certificate of proficiency in Irish was given recognition by the Commissioners of National Education. Existing teachers were required to pass an exam in order to be granted this certificate. Nearly all the teachers who took the exam in the 1880s were native speakers of Irish. However, there were complaints that the exam was too difficult, and not many teachers applied for the certificate. Right through the 1880s and 1890s the Society pressed for the appointment of professors of Irish in the various teacher-training colleges. In 1892 a motion was passed at the annual conference of the National teachers, which made Irish a part of the curriculum of the teacher-training colleges, and in 1897 the first professor of Irish was appointed in the main training centre, St Patrick's College in Drumcondra in Dublin.

The SPIL also wanted to have Irish included in the secondary school curriculum. Here, the situation was somewhat different, in that there was nothing preventing secondary schools from teaching Irish if they so wished. It was not until 1878 that legislation was passed providing for secondary education, the Intermediate Education (Ireland) Act. Due to the efforts of the SPIL, Irish was included in the list of subjects drawn up in 1878 for the official secondary school exam, the Intermediate Certificate. The same problems faced the teaching of the language at secondary level as at primary level. They were compounded by totally unrealistic expectations on the part of the Commissioners of Education as regards the abilities of pupils. More than in the case of the national schools, the teaching of Irish at secondary level was modelled directly on the teaching of Greek and Latin. The exam in Irish for the Intermediate Certificate tested pupils' knowledge of Early Modern Irish, a version of the language which had not been spoken for nearly 300 years. One of the pieces to be translated was written in 1627 in an archaic style by the historian and annalist Micheál Ó Cléirigh, one of the Four Masters mentioned in section 4.1.4. In terms of difficulty, this would be like requiring a present-day pupil of English to be able to read and translate a passage from Chaucer. It was not until the 1900s that a more realistic approach was taken, which was helped by the publication of a school's grammar and book of reading passages by the Christian Brothers. This last-named teaching order was responsible for the running of the majority of secondary schools for boys at this time, and from the start supported the teaching of Irish. By 1900 Irish had been accepted as part of the secondary school syllabus, even if many parents and teachers were still reluctant to have it taught.

At tertiary level, there had been sporadic attempts to include Irish in the list of subjects taught before 1870, and professors of Irish had been appointed in various institutions from time to time. The introduction of Irish into the secondary syllabus created a new situation, since it was possible for subjects taught at secondary school to be taken in the entrance exams of the Royal University of Ireland which was set up in 1879. As a result of pressure from the SPIL, Irish, along with French and German, was recognized as a subject in which students could matriculate. Some appointments were made to facilitate the study of Irish at third level. In 1891, Eugene O'Growney was appointed professor in Maynooth. Unlike previous holders of chairs in the subject, he was interested in the modern, spoken language rather than in the contents of ancient manuscripts. However, we must bear in mind that this was the only appointment of its sort at the time, and that it was made at an institution that did not have full university status. Elsewhere Irish, or Celtic as it was commonly called, continued to have a strong focus on the older language and its links with Indo-European. Nevertheless, O'Growney's appointment is some indication of the growing awareness of Irish as a living language.

The other main area where the SPIL wished to make its mark was the publishing of new and old literature. In 1882 a breakaway faction of the Society, the Gaelic Union, published the first edition of *Irisleabhar na Gaed-hilge/The Gaelic Journal* (GJ), a bilingual periodical. In terms of its contents, it steered a midway course between esoteric antiquarianism and more popular subjects. Its aim, in the words of its first editor, David Comyn, was 'to teach the Irish-speaking population to read their own language, which so few of them can do' (Nic Pháidín 1998: 16). At the same time, its subscribers tended to come from the English-speaking middle classes, so it had to provide material for them in English which they could identify with. Its main achievement was that it was the first periodical which published writing in Irish which had some relation to current affairs. It was by no means a newspaper as we would understand that term, but it did rescue the language from the druidic mists in which it had been shrouded before this. Much of the space of its columns was taken up with persuading its English-language readers that the preservation of Irish was a worthy and viable cause. It published Eugene O'Growney's series *Simple Lessons in Irish* which proved to be a great success; these later appeared as a single volume (O'Growney 1896). Readers of the GJ encountered in serial form the tale *Séadna* (Ó Laoghaire 1920), especially written for adult learners. More than anything, according to Nic Pháidín (1998), it prepared the ground for later Irish-language newspapers which had a more modern approach.

One other kind of publication which proved popular with the public were collections of tunes and songs, such as *Ancient Irish Music* (Joyce 1888). Collectors like P. W. Joyce understood that one way of coaxing people into learning Irish was through the medium of music. Later, this tactic was taken up by the Gaelic League, and to this day folk-music and dancing are seen as an indispensable part of the Irish-language movement.

In his book about the history of the Society, Máirtín Ó Murchú observes that the SPIL tended to get a bad press after the more radical Gaelic League came on the scene in the 1890s. He cites the following passage, written in 1949, as an example of the low opinion of the Society in later years:

Burdened, however, by dilettante membership the Society grew more academic than practical in outlook ... The more practical-minded grew dissatisfied with the lack of real progress, the perfunctory methods and the loss of time.

(Ó Murchú 2001: 3, n. 1)

The account given earlier of the various efforts of the Society to induce the Commissioner of Education to admit Irish to the school curriculum gives the lie to the above evaluation. Such efforts are not the kind of stuff that makes the headlines, but the aims of the SPIL, and the methods it employed to achieve them were anything but impractical.

Another myth that grew up about the Society, according to Ó Murchú, was that hardly any of the members could speak Irish: 'In 1878 a priest from Cork, later to become famous as one of the best stylists of Modern Irish prose, wrote to the Society for the Preservation of the Irish Language for some Irish books—but the letter could not be understood, because it was written in Irish!' (Mooney 1944: 12; quoted in Ó Murchú 2001: 4, n. 1). In fact, as Ó Murchú (2001: 19–21) shows, not only was the letter from the 'priest in Cork' answered, but a translation of it was published in the journal *The Irishman* soon afterwards.

One reason that the Society fell from favour in the twentieth century was that it was not anti-British in its attitude. Indeed, there were many representatives of the Dublin establishment among its members, people like Lord de Vesci and Colonel W. E. A. MacDonnell. While it pressurized the Commissioners of Education and the Westminster Parliament in order to win support for Irish, its general approach was conciliatory rather than confrontational, and it worked closely with the Irish parliamentary party to achieve its aims. After 1900, this kind of mild agitation was no longer acceptable to many Irish-language activists. That it was not is in large measure due to the activities of the Gaelic League, and to the main personality behind it, Douglas Hyde.

7.4 Douglas Hyde

In the course of this book, we have seen how sometimes certain individuals assume an importance in relation to events which far outstrips the influence of others. In the case of the Gaelic League, one of its founders stands head and shoulders above the rest—Douglas Hyde.

Born in 1860, Hyde was the son of the Church of Ireland rector of Frenchpark, County Roscommon, in the west of Ireland. He was a bookish child with a marked interest in languages. In the district in which he grew up, Irish was still spoken by older people. When Hyde was about 13, he began to learn Irish informally from the local gamekeeper, a fact he records in a diary entry written in a mixture of Irish and English:

29 December 1875 Cold stormy day. Foor sé Sémuis bás nae. Fear oc a ganool sin oc a firineach sin oc a munturach sin ní chonairc mé riamh. Bhí sé tin himpul a teachgin agus neii sin foor se éag. Sémuis ucht rina mé foghlamin gaodoilig uet. Fear le Gaelic oc a maith sin ni bhi sé 'a teis so. Ni higlum daoine a be dhecall feasda atá beidh dool agum oc a maith lé hu.

[Seamus died yesterday. A man ?so? kindly, /so truthful, so friendly, I never saw. He was ill about a week, and after that he died. ?Poor? Seamus, I learned my Irish from you. A man with Irish ?so? good there will not be after this. I cannot see people ?...? from now on that ?I will want? ?as well as you?]

(Daly 1974: 8)

The author of the biography of Hyde containing the above diary entry, Dominic Daly, provides an intelligible translation for the whole passage. I am afraid that I am unable to do more than guess at what many of the words might mean. Comprehension is not helped by the use of an idiosyncratic orthography based on English spelling. However, when we consider that the writer was only 15 and was working out the rules of the language for himself without the aid of formal instruction, the achievement is remarkable, and shows us just what an accomplished learner of languages Hyde was.

Within a year he was writing Irish more or less grammatically, and more importantly for the modern reader, in more conventional spelling:

7 December 1876 Fine calm day with a little frost. A and I went out shooting to the lake. A shot a waterhen and 5 snipe and I [shot] *3 snipe.* O rugadh mé ni chonnairc me leithid a snuaidh air a loch no uisge comh ciún no [r]adharc cho deas. Bhi an t'uisce gus an aéir mar aón rud, 'gus connairc me gach uile oileán so t'uisce co plánálta gur ni rabha fhios agam cé bhi an oileán, cé bhi an t'uisce. Deirigh ceo ro mhór nuair a bhi sinn tioct abhaile ach stiur mid abhaile le realt amháin a bhi ann. ach bhi dansér mor ann.

[Since I was born I have not seen such a sheen on the lake or water so calm or a sight so lovely. The water and the air were as one, and I saw every single island in the water so clearly that I didn't know which was the island, and which was the water. A very big fog rose up when we were coming home but we steered home with one star that was there. But it was very dangerous.]

(Daly 1974: 8)

Hyde had learned to read and write properly by studying various books published in the nineteenth century, including a version of Bedell's Old Testament and Neilson's *Introduction to the Irish language*.

By now the young Hyde was studying for an entrance scholarship to Trinity College Dublin. For the modern reader, his regime of study appears formidable: '19 January 1877 Before dinner I spent at least two hours at Latin, and between that and supper I did a little Irish. After supper I did Greek for an hour, then an hour at Latin, and before I went to bed I spent a good hour at French. In all, five good hours' (Daly 1974: 10). Hyde's biographer assures us that despite the long hours of study 'he was never in danger of developing into a bookworm' (Daly 1974: 11). He spent a lot of time in the open air, hunting and fishing. In this way he got to know the local people quite well. Unusually for one of his class and religion, he became friendly with a Fenian neighbour and soon developed a passionate enthusiasm for the nationalist cause. He occasionally gave vent to his patriotism in verse:

> When in its full intensity
> a patriot spirit burned,
> that clung to what was native
> and what was foreign spurned.
>
> ...
>
> Then fire upon fire
> on every hilltop high
> in Leinster, Meath and Connacht
> rose red into the sky.
> That was no smouldering fire
> of artificial flame,
> the fuel was a nation,
> the match was Freedom's name.

> (Dunleavy 1974: 28–9)

The author of the above lines seems to have seen no inconsistency in espousing such sentiments, while at the same time enjoying hunting rights on the estate of the local landlord, Lord de Freyne. It is clear that even at this young age he had begun to think of himself as a true Gael, rather than as a member of the ruling class.

By now, Hyde was visiting Dublin regularly. There, in 1877, he met some of the members of the SPIL and began to attend their meetings from time to time. He also continued to buy whatever Irish books he could find at auctions and in second-hand bookshops. In 1882 he moved to Dublin as a student in Trinity College. Here, he continued to express a radical anti-British philosophy, something virtually unheard of in the Anglicized atmosphere of the university. Hyde was also making the acquaintance of literary figures like the young W. B. Yeats and T. W. Rolleston, figures who were at the centre of the debate about what a national literature for Ireland should look like. It was at this time that he began to publish essays on Gaelic literature. In an article published in the *Dublin University Review* in 1885 he drew readers' attention to the fragile state of Irish and to the literary riches which Ireland was in danger of losing together with the language:

A few verses are jotted down here, nearly at random, from these unknown and unpublished songs, and the wish to preserve what a score or so of years will find disappeared off the face of the earth must serve as an excuse for reproducing the *ipsissima verba* [actual words], for slowly but surely those who knew them are disappearing; those who sung them are passing away; and soon, very soon, the place that knew them shall know them no more.

> (Hyde 1986a [1885]: 70)

In another article, written in 1886, Hyde formulated his thoughts on the Irish language and its place in Irish society. In this article, he presents what might be called a Romantic nationalist argument for Irish:

The language of the western Gael is the language best suited to his surroundings. It corresponds best to his topography, his nomenclature and his organs of speech, and the use of it guarantees the remembrance of his own weird and beautiful traditions... Every hill, every *lios* [fairy fort], every crag and gnarled tree and lonely valley has its own strange and graceful legend attached to it, the product of the Hibernian Celt in its truest and purest type, not to be improved upon by change, and of infinite worth in moulding the race type, of immeasurable value in forming its character.

(Hyde 1986b [1886]: 77)

A number of features are observable here which are to recur in Hyde's later writings. One is the use of the term Gael instead of Irishman. This was to become a corner-stone of the Gaelic Leaguers and of other nationalist ideologues like D. P. Moran: there were two kinds of Irishmen, the Gaels (true Irishmen), and the English speakers, often referred to disparagingly as West Britons or *shoneens*. The other feature is the connection made between ethnic purity and language. It is the Irish tongue that moulds 'the race' 'in its truest and purest type', that is best suited to the physical environment, and even to people's 'organs of speech'.

Without any sense of irony, Hyde includes himself in the Gaelic race:

To be told that the language I spoke from my cradle, the language my father and grandfather and all my ancestors in an unbroken line leading up into the remote twilight of antiquity have spoken, the language which has entwined itself with every fibre of my being, helped to mould my habits of conduct and forms of thought, to be calmly told by an Irish Journal that the sooner I give it up this language the better, that the sooner I 'leave it to the universities' the better, that we will improve our English speaking by giving up our Irish, to be told this by a representative Irish Journal is naturally and justly painful.

(Hyde 1986b [1886]: 75)

Hyde himself, as we have just seen, learned Irish only in his teens. It certainly was not the language of his forebears either on his father's or his mother's side. On his father's side, the Hyde family had come to Ireland in the Elizabethan era, having been granted land in County Cork as a reward for services to the queen. This hardly constituted a robust Gaelic genealogy. What is interesting is that Hyde, like many others in the Gaelic League later on, was trying to create an Irish identity for himself that was based more on wishful thinking than on fact. Up to now, people had been trying hard to Anglicize themselves, to deny their Gaelic heritage. Here we witness for the first time the reverse process, whereby somebody convinced himself that Irish was his language, that it had 'entwined itself with every fibre' of his being, even though this was totally at odds with the facts.

This kind of reasoning was to become widespread ten years later when the Gaelic League had been established, and it has persisted to the present day in some circles. A normal definition of native language is one's mother tongue, the language spoken in a child's environment by family, friends, and the wider community. For Hyde, and the Gaelic League, however, one's native language was what one wished it to be, what one felt it would have been if certain events had not taken place in the past. Because Hyde felt himself to be Irish, there was no choice for him but to claim that Irish was his language. However, it is important to remember that this claim was based not on linguistic facts, but on nationalist emotions, and that it implies a use of the term 'native language' at variance with the commonly understood meaning of those words.

Commenting on the article cited above from the *Dublin University Review*, Daly draws attention to one point which was to change in Hyde's philosophy as time went by. At the time of writing the article, 1886, he was not countenancing the revival of Irish for the whole country:

There is no use in arguing the advantage of making Irish the language of our newspapers and clubs, because that is and ever shall be an impossibility; but for several reasons we wish to arrest the language in its downward path, and if we cannot spread it (as I do not believe we very much can), we will at least prevent it from dying out and make sure that those who speak it now, will also transit it unmodified to their descendants.

(Hyde 1986b [1886]: 75)

At this stage, Hyde was advocating more or less the same kind of policy as the SPIL, namely the preservation of Irish in those places where it was spoken. Only later would he change that policy and urge people to learn Irish in order to make it their main language.

In the second half of the 1880s, Hyde spent much time in the company of literary figures who were trying to work out a solution to the problem of creating a national literature for Ireland. By now he was acting as a mediator of Gaelic culture for writers like W. B. Yeats who did not know Irish. He had also made the acquaintance of Yeats' muse, Maud Gonne, and undertaken to teach her Irish. The lessons with her don't seem to have gone very far. His diary records many meetings with her of a social nature, usually ending with the words: 'we did not do much Irish' (Daly 1974).

At this time, Hyde was making trips to the west of Ireland, collecting stories and songs from the older people. Beginning in 1889 with *Leabhar*

Sgéulaigheachta [Book of stories] (Hyde 1889), over the next decade he was to make much of this folk material available, publishing tales and poems in Irish with English translations. With respect to his translations, Daly remarks:

Next to guaranteeing the authenticity of his Gaelic originals, Hyde's main concern was to find the form of language best suited to their presentation in English. Here we come to one of the most important aspects of Hyde's work, the fact that he pioneered a manner of speech that was to become the vernacular, so to speak, of the Anglo-Irish literary movement, the model for Lady Gregory's 'Kiltartenese', Synge's plays and indeed the standard speech of the early Abbey Theatre.

(Daly 1974: 106–7)

Although he translated in order to reach a wider audience, Hyde always regarded composition in English as inferior to Irish: 'It is as though its own bark had rudely been stripped off the Irish tree, and a new artificial covering wrapped around it, and it is only now that [it] is beginning to absorb the sap and to cling to the trunk like something natural' (Hyde 1986c [1888]: 83). We do not know his views on the macaronic compositions discussed in section 5.1.3, with half the verse in Irish and half in English, but it is unlikely that he would have approved. For Hyde and the Gaelic League, choices were binary: one spoke either Irish or English, but not both in the same discourse.

Despite his reservations, it is Hyde's translations from Irish that have secured him a lasting place in the history of Irish literature. His most famous publication was his *Love Songs of Connacht* (Hyde 1971 [1893]), a collection of forty-five songs with verse translations of twenty-five of them. As well as the verse translations, he provided literal translations in prose for all forty-five items. It was these literal translations that won Hyde favour with the Anglo-Irish writers, particularly Yeats and Synge.

In 1892 he became president of the National Literary Society. His inaugural address, entitled the 'Necessity for de-Anglicising Ireland', is regarded as the point of departure for the Gaelic League, so it is worth looking at more closely. The address starts with what Hyde regards as a paradox, namely the fact that Irishmen profess to hate England, but at the same time seem to imitate it:

It has always been very curious to me how Irish sentiment sticks in this half-way house—how it continues to apparently hate the English, and at the same time continues to imitate them; how it continues to clamour for recognition as a distinct nationality, and at the same time throws away with both hands what would make it so.

(Hyde 1986e [1894]: 154)

Hyde goes on to analyse the reasons for this paradox, attributing it mainly to his countrymen's neglect of the Irish language. He first paints a glorious picture of the past:

What we must endeavour to never forget is this, that the Ireland of today is the descendant of the Ireland of the seventh century; then the school of Europe and the torch of learning... The bulk of the Irish race really lived in the closest contact with the traditions of the past and the national life of nearly eighteen hundred years, until the beginning of this century. Not only so, but during the whole of the dark Penal times they produced among themselves a most vigorous literary development.

(Hyde 1986e [1894]: 156–157)

This state of affairs, said Hyde, came to an end with the founding of Maynooth and the rise of Daniel O'Connell:

This training, however, nearly every one of fair education during the Penal times possessed, nor did they begin to lose their Irish training and knowledge until after the establishment of Maynooth and the rise of O'Connell. These two events made an end of the Gaelicism of the Gaelic race... within the last ninety years we have, with an unparalleled frivolity, deliberately thrown away our birthright and Anglicized ourselves.

(Hyde 1986e [1894]: 158)

For Hyde, the solution was simple—Irishmen must undo the pernicious effects of Anglicization:

I have no hesitation at all in saying that every Irish-feeling Irishman, who hates the reproach of West-Britonism, should set himself to encourage the efforts which are being made to keep alive our once great national tongue. The losing of it is our greatest blow, and the sorest stroke that the rapid Anglicization of Ireland has inflicted upon us. In order to de-Anglicize ourselves we must at once arrest the decay of the language.

(Hyde 1986e [1894]: 160)

The content of this speech is not very different from the article Hyde had published in the *Dublin University Review* seven years previously, but the tone is more forceful, the rhetoric stronger. The immediate response of the audience of the National Literary Society was unenthusiastic, as this passage from Hyde's autobiography shows:

Is cuimhin liom go maith an oidhche thug mé an óráid sin uaim, ag céad-chruinniughadh na bliadhna do bhí ag an gCumann Liteardha Náisiúnta. Do bhí céad duine nó b'éidir céad go leith i láthair. Níor mhúsgail an méid a dubhairt mé aon mhacalla 'na measg. Chuala cara dham beirt fhear óg ag caint le chéile ag dul amach an dorus, agus dubhairt fear aca leis an bhfear eile, 'An dóigh leat nó an measann tú gur féidir go mbeidh gluaiseacht de'n tsórt sin go deó in Éirinn?' 'Seafóid!' arsa an fear óg eile, 'Ní bheidh!'

[I remember well the night that I gave that address, at the first meeting of the year which the National Literary Society held. There were a hundred, or maybe a hundred and fifty people present. What I said did not produce any response among them. A friend of mine heard two young men talking to each other as they went out the door, and one of them said to the other, 'Do you suppose or do you think that there will ever be a movement of that sort in Ireland?' 'Nonsense!' was the reply. 'There never will be!']

(de hÍde 1937: 34)

The young man was wrong in his prediction. Within a year, a society had been founded with the express purpose of putting Hyde's ideas into action.

7.5 The Gaelic League

Inspired partly by Hyde's speeches and writings, a number of enthusiasts came together in Dublin in 1893 and founded the Gaelic League. The meeting was called at the instigation of Eoin MacNeill, a young historian from County Antrim. Hyde merely chaired the meeting, and mentions it almost in passing in his diary. He had just got engaged to his future wife, Lucy Kurtz, which may explain his apparent failure to attach much importance to the founding of the new association.

Unlike previous societies like the SPIL, the Gaelic League stressed that the only way to keep Irish alive was to speak it. Hyde, in a speech delivered in New York in 1891, suggested how this was to be done:

Anois a dhaoine uaisle, má's mian libh an Ghaedhilg do chongbháil beo in bhur measg ní'l aon tslighe ná aon mhodh eile le sin do dhéanamh acht amháin í do labhairt i gcómhnuidhe—i gcómhnuidhe adeirim, eadraibh féin. Leanaigí mo shompla-sa impidhim orraibh. Tá mé faoi gheasaibh mar dubhairt siad ins an tSean-Ghaedhilg, tá mé faoi gheasaibh nó faoi mhóid, gan aon fhocal Béarla do labhairt a-choidhche ná go deo, acht amháin an uair nach dtuigfidhear mé i nGaedhilg.

[Now, ladies and gentlemen, if you want to keep Irish alive in your midst there is no way or method to do that but to speak it all the time—all the time, I say, among yourselves. Follow my example, I beseech you. As they said in Old Irish, I'm under injunction, under injunction or under oath, not to speak a single word of English ever, except when I will not be understood in Irish.]

(de hÍde 1937: 40)

This was to be the cornerstone of Gaelic League activity: speak Irish on every possible occasion.

As a way of keeping a language alive among native speakers, this approach can hardly be questioned. Among learners, however, it is not at all clear that speaking a language without constant supervision from a teacher is an efficient practice. It is well known that learners perpetuate each other's mistakes and transfer features of their first language to the second language. By encouraging people to speak freely, Hyde was also encouraging them to take liberties with Irish, which would ultimately result in a new version of the language (see sections 8.6–8.7).

When we talk about maintaining a language, we normally mean maintaining it among native speakers. This had been the policy of the SPIL, and of Hyde himself, until the founding of the Gaelic League. Language learners, no matter how proficient, are not normally regarded as part of the community of speakers. When we talk about Spanish speakers, or French speakers, we mean people who are at least bilingual in these languages. The term 'Spanish speaker' does not include students of Spanish from Ireland, even though some of these may attain a very high level of proficiency in the language. However, the Gaelic League took a different approach to this question. For the League, all Irish people were potential Irish speakers; all that was preventing them from speaking their own language was their inhibitions and their spiritual enslavement by Britain. Language was not so much a question of competence as of willingness.

There was one serious obstacle to the course advocated by Hyde. In 1893 very few Irish people could speak Irish, and those who could had very little desire to do so. Certainly, only a minority of those who listened to his speeches and read his article could speak Irish. The Gaelic League set about trying to change this situation among the native speakers of Irish and among the wider community. Shortly after the League was founded, an article in the GJ described the way in which it was targeting the two communities. It begins by discussing the presence of the League in Dublin:

Addresses, readings, etc. in Irish may take place at the weekly meetings . . . to demonstrate to the public the actuality and existence at their doors of the *living* Irish language, and to show that there are, even in Dublin, men who speak Irish freely and masterfully, and who can exhibit the powers of the language as still alive and vigorous; and also that there is in Dublin a large number of people who understand Irish well enough to form an intelligent audience for a speaker of Irish.

(GJ, November 1893: 228; quoted in Ó Huallacháin 1994: 52–3, emphasis original)

The writer then goes on to state that the League is also conscious of the need to preach its gospel in the Irish-speaking districts:

They propose at the earliest opportunity to change the venue of their work from Dublin to the Irish-speaking districts; to appeal to Irish-speaking people—to teach, exhort and encourage them not to abandon this noble heritage of national speech . . . to eradicate finally that unworthy feeling of shame attached to the speaking of Irish which has been the worst enemy of the language—in this way both by principle and practice to secure that the Irish language will be handed down to ever increasing numbers of Irishmen.

(GJ, November 1893: 228; quoted in Ó Huallacháin 1994: 53)

Before the founding of the League, one of its leading members, Eoin Mac Neill, had suggested a way of appealing to the masses:

Our primary object should be to make the Gaelic language live in the homes of the people...We must directly appeal to the common people...Large numbers will not come far to hear us. We must therefore address small numbers, organizing our movement on, perhaps, a parochial basis...To supply men and funds an organization is necessary.

(GJ, March 1893: 179; quoted in Ó Huallacháin 1994: 52)

This suggestion was followed by the League. Branches were soon established all over the country, with a chairman, secretary, and treasurer for each branch. Members paid an annual fee to support the activities of the League. These included language classes and also cultural activities like concerts of Irish folk-music, dancing classes, and trips to the countryside. Very early on the League began to organize competitions on a local and national level which offered prizes in various categories for the contestants, which provided a further stimulus to the movement.

By 1904, eleven years after its foundation, the League had established itself as an important force in contemporary society, and had branches in London, New York, and even Buenos Aires. Part of its success was due to the fact that it appealed to the new urban middle classes. These shared many of the values of the British middle classes at the time. They believed in progress, in education, in the duty of the middle classes to act as guides and mentors for the working classes and peasants. However, the Gaelic Leaguers differed from other progressive organizations in Britain in that they saw their role not as empire-builders, but as nation-builders. The Gaelic League offered them an outlet for their energies.

It also provided them with a social life. The middle classes had money to spend on holidays and day-trips, and the League organized activities on a modest scale that they could participate in. Photographs taken at the turn of the twentieth century show us earnest-looking, moustachioed gentlemen dressed in heavy suits, and ladies in elaborate hats and long skirts, seated in front of open-air platforms where an exhibition of Irish dancing is taking place, or mounted on high bicycles with a picturesque view in the background. Apart from the Irish-language element of their activities, there is nothing that distinguishes them from English or Scottish members of a naturalists' society on a day-trip to the countryside.

The League offered its members an escape from the dreariness of urban life in the Victorian and Edwardian eras. There was a strong element of pageantry in its activities: people could get dressed up in kilts and cloaks in order to take part in the competitions it organized. They could also change their names from the

English language versions to the Irish equivalents, which provided them with almost a new identity. All of this added to the glamour of the new movement.

One of the principles accepted at the founding of the Gaelic League was that it should be non-political. In a statement issued in 1893, we read: 'Politics, in any form, do not enter into the objects of the Gaelic League, and are strictly excluded from its proceedings' (quoted in Ó Súilleabháin 1998: 245). In the early years this ensured it support from all shades of political opinion— moderate nationalist, separatist, and even unionist. Shane Leslie, a cousin of Winston Churchill's whose family had estates in Ulster, was a supporter of the nationalist cause and a member of the Gaelic League. James Hannay wrote in 1906:

I myself claim to be a loyalist, that is to say, I believe King Edward to be by right and in fact Sovereign of this Kingdom of Ireland... Quite possibly, though I do not know this, I am one of a minority in the League... But... my principles and my opinions have made no difference whatever to my position in the League... No man joining the League, no matter what his political or religious opinions may be, need fear persecution or ostracism so long as he is true to the great purpose of the League.

(quoted in Ó Huallacháin 1994: 61)

In the first ten years or so, this political neutrality gave the League a broad base among all sections of society. It was an organization where both Catholic and Protestant clergymen could take an active part without alienating their flocks. In its early stages, it could genuinely claim to be inclusive and pluralist.

I will now look at the various ways in which the Gaelic League left its mark on Irish life.

7.6 Education

As with the SPIL, education was a priority with the Gaelic League. It felt that the concessions that had been made in the period 1878–93 had not gone far enough, and immediately set about pressurizing the authorities to make greater provision for teaching Irish at all levels.

In 1900 legislation was passed which made it possible to teach Irish at primary level in all schools. This was an important step, and one which reflected the new perception of Irish as a national language, not just the language of an ever-dwindling minority. In 1904 a bilingual programme for Irish-speaking districts was introduced, which allowed for the use of Irish as the medium of instruction for other subjects. It would be a long time before this policy was implemented, but again the trend was clear: Irish was slowly but surely being granted the same official status as English.

At secondary level, concerns were expressed in the 1890s about the wisdom of Irish being on the list of exam subjects. A Vice-Regal Inquiry was established in 1899 to examine this issue, and its investigations soon became the object of controversy. A group of academics from Trinity College, led by the classicist John Pentland Mahaffy, suggested that Irish be removed from the secondary school curriculum altogether. The Gaelic League opposed this. Both Mahaffy and Hyde were called to give evidence before the commission. What added piquancy to this was the fact that both of them were Trinity graduates, and both were members of the establishment. Hyde had prepared well by canvassing the support of several Indo-European and Celtic scholars of note, including an Oxford don. Another Trinity scholar, Robert Atkinson, was also asked for his opinion by the Inquiry. Atkinson, a professor of Sanskrit and Comparative Philology, knew Old and Medieval Irish, but had no regard for the modern language. He described the set text for the Intermediate Examination, *Tóruigheacht Dhiarmada agus Ghráinne* [The pursuit of Diarmaid and Gráinne], as indecent, dismissing it with the oft-cited line: 'I would allow no daughter of mine of any age to see it' (quoted in Mathews 2003: 39). Hyde responded with a robust defence of Irish literature. In the end, the dispute ended with a victory for the Gaelic League. Irish was retained on the syllabus, and within three years the number of pupils studying Irish at secondary level had increased threefold.

Later commentators have seen this controversy as a pivotal moment in the development of nationalist culture. P. J. Mathews distinguishes a number of aspects of the controversy which were significant:

Firstly, it represents the coming of age of the Gaelic League as a significant force in Irish national life … Secondly, the language controversy was not merely a battle over the merits or demerits of the Irish language, it was also a battle for academic ascendancy between Trinity College and an emerging generation of nationalist intellectuals … Finally, and most significantly, the dismissal of the Irish language and its literature as inherently immoral by Atkinson and Mahaffy and the knee-jerk response of those who could only countenance an idealized Irishness, set the terms within which the major cultural debates of the coming decade, particularly those sparked off by the theatre movement, would take place.

(Mathews 2003: 44–5)

The last point made by Mathews above refers to the way in which the Gaelic League rushed to the defence of Hyde and attacked Atkinson in the weeks following the controversy. The Catholic primate, Cardinal Logue, defended the Irish language against the charges of indecency laid against it (Mathews

2003: 42). The Gaelic League weekly, *An Claidheamh Soluis* [The sword of light] (CS), wrote an editorial describing Atkinson's testimony to the Vice-Regal Inquiry as 'the worst attack ever made on the whole Irish race, on all Irish thought, on the genius of the people' (CS, 18 March 1899; quoted in Ní Chollatáin 2004: 65). Even W. B. Yeats joined in the chorus of voices condemning Atkinson: 'The academic class in Ireland, because the visible enthusiasm of the time threatened its interests or the interests of the classes among whom it dined or married, set its face against all Irish enthusiasms in the first place, and then, by perhaps slow degrees, against all the great intellectual passions' (quoted in Greene 1966: 11).

Atkinson was ridiculed on account of his ignorance of Irish. One of the most prolific writers of the Revival period, Peadar Ó Laoghaire, published a series of articles in the CS in which he dissected an edition Atkinson had published of a seventeenth-century text. Three years after the controversy, Ó Laoghaire still felt so indignant that he entitled an article on the Irish verb *be* 'An rud a chuir Atkinson amú' [What led Atkinson astray]. In this and in other articles of his on the Irish language, two fictitious characters, Tadhg and Doncha, discuss the ins and outs of Irish grammar in the form of a dialogue:

Tadhg: Táim ag machtnamh, a Dhoncha, ar an dearúd uafásach san a dhin Atkinson nuair a chuir sé síos 'na leabhar an tuathal san: 'Is [Subject] [Predicate]'.

[I'm thinking, Doncha, about that terrible mistake which Atkinson made when he put down that blunder in his book: 'Is [Subject] [Predicate]'.

Doncha: Is mairg duit a bheadh 'od bhodhra féin ag machtnamh ar thuathalaibh Atkinson. Dá mbeitheá ag machtnamh ortha go ceann bliadhna, ní bheadh macht-namh déanta agut ortha go léir.

[I pity you if you're bothering yourself thinking about Atkinson's blunders. If you were thinking of them for a whole year, you still wouldn't have thought of them all.]

(O'Rahilly, undated: 72)

Judging by the vehemence of the reactions, Atkinson had struck a raw nerve in the ranks of the Gaelic League.

It is over a hundred years since this controversy created such a stir, and it may seem strange that I have devoted so much time to it here. However, as Mathews remarks, there was much more at stake than a few questions of Irish grammar. I am not interested here in defending Atkinson, but there is one aspect to the matter which has been overlooked. Within the context of the Victorian morality of the day, Atkinson was completely right when he described the text-book used in schools, *The Pursuit of Diarmid and Gráinne*, as indecent. In the tale, Gráinne, a young girl, is betrothed to Fionn, a man old enough to be her father. At the wedding-feast, she sets her eye on one of Fionn's warriors, Diarmaid, and elopes with him. For a while Diarmaid resists her advances and they sleep separately, but finally he gives in to her and they become lovers.

For a modern reader, this is all pretty tame, but if the contents of the text had been more widely known in Ireland in 1899, not only Cardinal Logue, but virtually every member of the Gaelic League would have concurred with Atkinson's assessment. That they did not can only mean that none of them had read the text. They attacked Atkinson not because of his literary judgement, which was in keeping with the moral standards of the day, but because he was an Englishman from Trinity College who had dared to cast aspersions on the Irish people and their language. The unfortunate professor was punished for his nationality, not his morals.

The ridiculing of Atkinson's knowledge of Irish was also revelatory. Up to now, the academic interest in Irish had been philological, focused on the older language. Atkinson was very much a product of that system. Indeed, as Greene (1966) grudgingly admits in his article on the controversy, Atkinson's achievements in the study of the older language are quite substantial. But for the Gaelic League it was the living speech of the people which was paramount, not the older language. The argument over the place of Irish in secondary schools was the beginning of a split in academic circles between treating Irish as a dead language, like Greek or Latin, and treating it as one of the modern languages, like French or German. It also marked a victory for those who regarded the teaching of Irish as part of a larger project of national regeneration. After 1899, Irish was no longer just one more school subject; it had acquired a political dimension.

The fuss about the content of *The Pursuit of Diarmid and Gráinne* led both sides to overlook a far more serious issue, namely the level of difficulty the text presented for learners of Irish. I would agree with Atkinson that the book was unsuitable for his daughter, not because it would have corrupted her morals, but because it was written in EMI, and as such was inaccessible to the average secondary-school pupil, in the same way that Chaucer is inaccessible to modern learners of English. The controversy revealed much about the attitude of the Gaelic League towards the Irish language. What mattered was the symbolic victory of Irish rather than the practical consequences of that victory. Irish had been retained on the secondary-school syllabus—that was the important point for the Gaelic Leaguers. The fact that generations of unfortunate schoolchildren were unable to read the text which had figured in the controversy does not seem to have bothered anybody at the time.

With the position of Irish at secondary level secure, at least officially, it was time to engage with tertiary-level institutions. In 1908 the National University of Ireland (NUI) was established. This replaced the Queen's Colleges of Cork, Belfast and Galway, and the Royal University based in Dublin. The NUI now had three constituent colleges in Dublin, Cork, and Galway, with Maynooth linked to the university as a college. Queen's College Belfast became Queen's University Belfast, and Trinity remained independent.

The change in structure offered a chance to the Gaelic League to make demands for Irish in the NUI, and it called for Irish to be compulsory for all who wished to matriculate at one of the constituent colleges of the new university. This was highly controversial, given that there were still many secondary schools, including some of the more prestigious Catholic colleges, which did not teach Irish at all. The League in the period after 1900 had developed a confrontational style of presenting its case in public debate, and the campaign for Irish in the NUI was no exception. Nine years previously, the Intermediate Examination controversy had been fought out between three Protestants from Trinity College. The university battle was fought out between Catholic priests. Roughly speaking, the older generation of priests and bishops, and many teaching orders like the Jesuits which ran fee-paying schools, were opposed to Irish, or at best lukewarm about it. Younger priests, and the Christian Brothers' teaching order which catered for the children of the lower middle classes, favoured Irish. Their spokesman was Fr Michael O'Hickey, professor of Irish at Maynooth, while the conservative faction was represented by Fr Delany, president of the now defunct Catholic University College, and also a member of the Gaelic League. The argument was essentially between a pragmatic position, which regarded it as impractical to expect students to gain a sufficient knowledge of Irish in a short time, and an absolutist position, which held that the Irish-language requirement was a principle connected with the rights of the Irish nation, and as such non-negotiable. O'Hickey was uncompromising in his statements on the issue. Those who opposed the Gaelic League line were as culpable, in his view, as those who had voted for the parliamentary union with Britain a century earlier. Here is how he addressed the students of Maynooth at a meeting about the Irish-language requirement for matriculation:

Looking at the personnel of the Senate [of the NUI], I can entertain no hope that apart from pressure and an agitation of the most vigorous character, they will acquit themselves in a manner befitting Irishmen ... Even in the clerical Senators as a body, I can repose little or no trust. The Archbishop of Dublin has always taken the national side; as for the other clerical Senators I shall say nothing further than to recommend them to your earnest prayers ... Sir Jonah Barrington has preserved for us a blacklist of those who voted for the infamous Union [of 1800] ... A similar blacklist of the recreant Nationalist Senators must be preserved, that, in after times, all men may know who were the false and vile, in a supreme crisis of Ireland's fortune, and who the loyal and true.

(Ó Fiaich 1972: 73)

The debate was no longer about the educational merits of Irish, it was about who was and wasn't a patriot. O'Hickey's rhetoric may strike us as intemperate, but it was merely an example of the kind of argumentation that was commonly used by the Gaelic League. Since its foundation, it had acted as a pressure group, constantly lobbying public representatives, teachers, and the Irish people in general to support its cause. In the case of the Irish requirement for the NUI, the county councils had an important role to play, in that they awarded scholarships to university entrants. Pressure was put on the local authorities by publishing the names of the councils who supported the League's campaign. It was a crude method, but it worked: some of the councils threatened to withhold scholarships if Irish was not made obligatory for matriculation in the NUI. In 1909 a resolution to this effect was passed in the university senate by a narrow margin, and Irish became compulsory for entrance into the NUI colleges. This measure had a knock-on effect at secondary level. Whether they liked it or not, secondary schools had to introduce Irish into the curriculum if they wished their pupils to have a chance of progressing to tertiary-level education in the NUI.

7.7 Adult education

The Gaelic League was aware that nearly all of its members were adults, and that most of these had been denied the chance to learn Irish at school. Accordingly, it set up a system of voluntary Irish classes for adults at local level. Some of these were in districts where Irish was still spoken, and were aimed at teaching literacy to native speakers. The teachers employed to teach these classes were called *múinteoirí taistil* [travelling teachers]. Another group of teachers, called *timirí*, were appointed to various English-speaking districts, their job being to conduct classes for learners and to suggest ways in which the local community could promote Irish in its daily activities. A newspaper article from 1906 gives us an idea of the kind of person who would be suitable for the job of *múinteoir taistil*:

The type of teacher wanted is a man who can teach Irish independently of books, more especially in the initial stages. He must be an expert at *Modh Díreach* [direct method] and *clár dubh* [blackboard] work, and must have a competent knowledge both of Irish and English.

(CS, 1 December 1906; quoted in Ó Súilleabháin 1998: 117–18)

It is worth noting that the League adopted what at the time was a very advanced teaching method, namely the direct method, which implied not speaking English to the pupils, even at basic level, and also put a heavy emphasis on speaking rather than writing. After the dreary rote-learning of the primary and secondary school classroom, this must have been a breath of fresh air. By now a new text-book was available, Eugene O'Growney's *Simple Lessons in Irish* (O'Growney 1896). Compared to previous books of this sort, this represented a step forward as well.

However, being able to teach was only part of the role of a *múinteoir taistil*, as can be seen from another passage in the same newspaper article:

While sound teaching methods are essential, personality is more so. The *Múinteoir Taistil* should know his Ireland past and present; should have a thorough grasp of what Irish Ireland means; should be able to appeal to the sentiments of the people as well as to their intellectual side; should be a patriot and an enthusiast; good-humoured and optimistic; a knowledge of Irish songs, music, dances and games will help ... *Múinteoirí* [teachers] should feel that they are soldiers of Ireland and should talk to young and grown of Ireland's heroes and Ireland's glories, thus infusing the right spirit of nationality into all with whom they come into contact.

(CS, 1 December 1906; quoted in Ó Súilleabháin 1998: 118)

The second part of the job description is not one would normally expect of a language-teacher. The ideal candidate had to in some sense be a man of the people. He had to be able to play games, by which was meant Gaelic games. Music and dancing, by which were meant Irish music and dancing, had become an important component of the curriculum. Finally, there was a political element to the job. Teaching Irish was not just a question of helping pupils to master the sounds and grammar of the language, it served the higher purpose of creating patriots, of 'infusing a spirit of nationality'. The Gaelic League may still have been claiming to be non-political in 1906, but it is hard to see how a unionist or even a moderate nationalist could possibly have been accepted as a travelling teacher. Not surprisingly, many teachers later became involved in the armed struggle for independence.

Being a travelling teacher was a tough life, and the pay was modest. The main means of transport was by bicycle. The following advertisement appeared in the CS in 1907:

Tá beirt mhúinteoir Gaeilge ag teastáil uaim. Ní mór dóibh bheith ina nGaeilgeoirí cliste agus léann maith a bheith orthu i mBéarla. Tuarastal de réir £60 sa bhliain. Beidh sé riachtanach dóibh rothaíocht a dhéanamh.

[I'm looking for two Irish teachers. They must be resourceful Irish speakers and have a good written knowledge of English. Salary along the lines of £60 a year. It will be necessary for them to be able to ride a bicycle.]

(CS, 16 February 1907; quoted in Ó Súilleabháin 1998: 118)

Evidently, in 1907 the ability to cycle was the equivalent of a driver's licence nowadays.

The travelling teachers belonged to a different social class than the founders of the Gaelic League. Most of them were from Irish-speaking or bilingual districts, and their families would have not been wealthy. They tended to be young, and they had the zeal of revolutionaries. In the twenty-first century, we find it hard to imagine that anybody would devote their time to the promotion of a dying language for little or no pay. But the world of the early twentieth century was very different from our world. Idealism played a far larger part in society than it does nowadays. At the same time that the *múinteoirí taistil* were cycling through the wind and rain to spread the gospel of the revival of Irish, in Britain members of the Fabian society were trying to improve the minds of the workers, while in tsarist Russia left-wing intellectuals were sowing the seeds of revolution. The motivation in every case was similar—the desire to better society.

In order to provide training for the teachers, the League began to establish colleges in various Irish-speaking districts from 1904 onwards. The courses they provided were particularly popular during the summer months. The students stayed with local families, the idea being that the contact with the language outside the classroom would reinforce the knowledge that they had obtained during the formal classes. The colleges were a huge success, and many students learned Irish to a high standard as a result of the time they spent attending the courses.

7.8 Cultural activity

One initiative of the Gaelic League was the organization of cultural events at the local level. These included concerts, plays, and debates, as well as day trips to places of historical interest. A good example of the kind of local festival it organized is the *feis* [festival] held at Craughwell, County Galway, in 1902, to commemorate the blind folk-poet Raftery. On the poster advertising the *feis*, it stated that 'Prizes will be given for Irish Singing, Dancing, Story-telling, Flute-playing &c' (Mac Aonghusa 1993: plate XIV). The committee members included Lady Gregory, the patroness of Yeats and many other writers of the Anglo-Irish Revival, who lived nearby. If the weather permitted, events like these were held in the open air. In the early years, many of the proceedings were conducted in English, but the amount of Irish increased as time went by.

At the national level, an annual all-Ireland festival, the Oireachtas, was started in 1897. Various competitions were held at this festival, such as drama, dancing, singing, folklore, and poetry. The winners were rewarded with modest prizes. Most of the competitions contained a strong didactic element, in that their ultimate goal was to promote the speaking of Irish. In 1902 the following resolution was passed, recommending a new competition for the 1903 Oireachtas:

That a prize of 5 shillings (in books) be given to the pupil of each National School in an Irish-speaking district, who is adjudged by the votes of his or her fellow pupils to have spoken the most Irish during the year ending 31 March 1903. An Irish-speaking district shall be defined for the purpose of this competition to be a barony in which, according to the latest census available, 10% or upwards of the population is Irish-speaking.

(quoted in Ó Súilleabháin 1998: 240)

The League was keen on new songs that could be sung by its members at meetings and rallies. At the 1897 Oireachtas one Dermot Foley received a prize of £5 for his composition 'Go mairidh ár nGaeilge slán' [May our Irish language live]. The festival report describes it as 'a song of the Gaelic League Movement, with chorus suitable for singing at Gaelic League meetings' (Gaelic League 1897: 60).

One important feature of the Oireachtas was that it attracted not just the middle classes of Dublin and other urban centres, but also the communities of the Irish-speaking districts. As well as new literature and music, recognition was given to *sean-nós* [unaccompanied] singing, various kinds of folk-dancing, and folk-drama. This encouraged many native speakers to take part in this festival who would otherwise not have bothered with it, and convinced them that Irish had a value. It was the first time that anything of this sort had been witnessed in the districts in the west of Ireland where Irish was still spoken. This aspect of the activities of the Gaelic League was truly revolutionary. A hundred years ago, cultural events only took place in large urban centres. It was totally unheard of to bring them out to the countryside, particularly the west of the country, which was underdeveloped in terms of its infrastructure.

For the committed members of the Gaelic League, the Oireachtas was like a national rally. It was the custom for the president of the League to give an opening speech, in which he would exhort the faithful rank and file to keep up the good work in the coming year. Local dignitaries like members of the clergy and politicians were invited to attend the opening ceremony. The following extract from Douglas Hyde's address in 1897 gives the reader a flavour of the tenor of a typical president's speech:

A mhná uaisle agus a dhaoine uaisle,
Tá bród mór agus áthas mór orm agus ar gach uile dhuine bhaineas le Connradh na Gaedhilge, an cruinniughadh breágh éifeachtach so d'fheiscint anocht. Is maith an chomhartha é do chúis na Gaedhilge, agus is mór an brostughadh é do na daoinibh sin atá ag obair go teann agus go croidheamhail ar a son. Atá ann ár dtimchioll anocht

daoine maithe móra, daoine fíora fearamhla fóghlamtha, bailighthe le chéile as gach cearda i n-Éirinn agus iad ar aon intinn amháin, agus buidheachas le Dia is í an intinn sin teanga na tire do shábháil ón mbás. Tá píobaidhe na h-Éireann ag seinm go milis i n-ár gcluasaibh, tá caint na h-Éireann ag músgailt arís, an ar gcroidheachaibh, na smuainte do bhí le bliadhantaibh 'na gcodladh. Táimaoid ag bualadh buille láidir ar son Éireann anocht, buille níos láidre 'ná do shaoilfeá ar dtús, óir táimaoid ag taispeáint do'n domhan mór go bhfuil an tsean-Éire, Éire na Gaedhilge, beo ann go fóill, agus táimaoid ag dul 'n ár mbannaidhe go mbeidh sé beo ann go bráth.

[Ladies and gentlemen,
It is a source of great pride to myself and to everybody else belonging to the Gaelic League, to witness this fine, forceful assembly here tonight. It is a good sign for the cause of Irish, and it is a great incentive to those people who are working hard and whole-heartedly for this cause. Around us tonight are important members of society, genuine, brave, learned people, gathered together from every corner of Ireland with a single purpose, and thanks be to God that purpose is to save the national language from death. The pipes of Ireland are sounding pleasantly in our ears, the speech of Ireland is awakening again, in our hearts, the thoughts which were for many years asleep. We are striking a strong blow on behalf of Ireland tonight, a blow which is stronger than you would at first suppose, for we are showing the world that the old Ireland, the Ireland of the Irish language, is still alive, and we are promising that she will be live for ever.]

(Gaelic League 1897: 24–5)

In keeping with the tone of Hyde's speech, the 1897 Oireachtas witnessed the first airing of the aforementioned Dermot Foley's anthem 'Go mairidh ár nGaeilge slán' [May our Irish language live].

Patrick Pearse wrote in 1906 that '[The Oireachtas] is a Nation's Act of Faith in God and in itself' (CS, 4 August 1906; quoted in Ó Súilleabháin 1998: 244). Pearse was given to hyperbole, and perhaps this statement need not be taken at face-value. Presumably, for some of the attendees it was simply a social occasion. Nevertheless, for the hard-core Gaelic Leaguers the Oireachtas was the high point of the year, it was the occasion when all the hard work that they had put into the language movement bore fruit, and all their efforts seemed worthwhile.

7.9 Publishing

Two main areas of activity of the Gaelic League were propaganda and education. To cater for the needs of these activities, it had to make use of the main medium of communication at the beginning of the twentieth century, publishing. In the period 1893–1914 it published a variety of teaching aids, consisting mainly of text-books and collections of songs. It also encouraged people to compose new literature such as short stories and dramas. Many of the texts which it published were accompanied by glossaries and notes for learners of the language. This publishing activity encouraged new writers to put pen to paper.

In the early years, the League published a large number of pamphlets in English with a view to raising public awareness of the importance of Irish. The following extract contains some of the ideas put forward in the pamphlet *Irishwomen and the home language*:

> 1. Realize what it means to be an Irishwoman, and make others realize what that means by being Irish in fact as well as name.
> 2. Make the home atmosphere Irish.
> 3. Make the social atmosphere Irish.
> 8. Give Irish names to children.
> 10. Encourage Irish music and song.
> 12. Employ Irish-speaking servants whenever possible.
>
> (Butler undated; quoted in Crowley 2000: 196)

The pamphlet is clearly addressed to members of the middle class, who are to provide a good example for other classes:

> 9. Visit Irish-speaking districts. If Irish people who are students of the language go among their Irish-speaking fellow country-people in the right spirit, and instil the right principles into them, they will be conferring a benefit upon the people, and the people will in return confer a benefit on them by imparting their native knowledge of the spoken language to them.
>
> (Butler undated; quoted in Crowley 2000: 196)

The author of the pamphlet warns her readers to leave the public agitation and politics to the menfolk:

> Now, the women of our race are dignified and decorous; they shrink from mingling in a melee, and retiring into the inner courtyard, they leave the scene of strife in the outer world to the sterner sex. They may think, therefore, that in this language war they have no place. But they are mistaken, for it is warfare of an especial kind, warfare which can best be waged not by shrieking viragoes or aggressive amazons, but by gentle, low-voiced women who teach little children their first prayers, and, seated at the hearth-side, make those around them realize the difference between a home and a dwelling.
>
> (Butler undated; quoted in Crowley 195)

Some women did play a more active part in the Gaelic League than the author of the pamphlet recommends, but by and large it was dominated by men. It may have been revolutionary with respect to language, but otherwise it conformed to the mores of Victorian and Edwardian Ireland.

Another important innovation of the Gaelic League was the founding of a weekly newspaper in 1898, *Fáinne an Lae* [The break of day] (FL). In 1899, after a dispute with the owner, the League started its own weekly, the CS. The main aim of both publications was the 'dissemination of propagandist literature' (Nic Pháidín 1998: 54). Both of them were bilingual for the simple reason that there were not enough readers of Irish to support a weekly paper written entirely in this language. The two newspapers, especially the CS, played a central role in the various campaigns of the League aimed at raising the status of Irish.

In 1903 the League appointed a new editor to the CS, Patrick Pearse. Like Hyde, Pearse was something of an outsider in the Revival movement in terms of his background. He was born in Dublin in 1879 to an Irish mother and English father. At the age of 18 he joined the Gaelic League and soon became an active member of the committee. He also achieved an excellent command of Irish as a young adult.

Pearse was of a different stamp than the men who had founded the Gaelic league in 1893, who were older than him. Hyde, despite his nationalist rhetoric and the anti-British verse he wrote in his youth, was now in his forties, and becoming more conservative in his views. Pearse believed in a radical approach to the revival of Irish. He also had ideas about how the CS should be run. Shortly after taking over the job of editor, he wrote: 'Our ideal is to place in the hands of the Irish speaker in Glenties or Aran [districts in the west of Ireland] a newspaper giving him, in vivid idiomatic Irish, a consecutive and adequate record of the home and foreign history of the week' (CS, 14 March 1903; quoted in Ní Chollatáin 2004: 91). Unfortunately, this goal was never realized, for a number of reasons. The main one was the fact that the writers and readers were by and large learners of Irish, based in Dublin or some other town. The CS, like the League in general, never understood the needs of the Irish-speaking rural communities. The putative readers in 'Glenties or Aran' that Pearse refers to above, in so far as they existed at all, would have been literate in English only. What they wanted was local news—information about things like fairs, funerals, and prices in the county that they lived in. That information was already being supplied by local publications like the *Donegal News* and the *Derry Journal* in the case of Glenties, or the *Tuam Herald* in the case of Aran.

To answer the need for local news, the CS from 1907 onwards gave space to columnists based outside Dublin—one in the province of Munster, one in the province of Connaught, and one in the province of Ulster. It likewise gave a summary of events at home and abroad in the week that had passed. But no matter what the subject of a given article or column purported to be, the question of the Irish language was always to the fore. Thus, reports from the provinces focused on struggles by language activists to win recognition for

Irish in the courts or in business. International news was taken up by reports of what other small nations were doing to ensure parity for their language in relation to some larger language. As Pearse himself wrote when a reader complained that the CS was taking its foreign news from the British press: 'In point of fact, three quarters of our news matter is really original comment rather than a resumé of facts and the comment is always that of Gaels with the Gaelic viewpoint' (CS, 6 June 1903; quoted in Ní Chollatáin 2004: 93). The 'Gaelic viewpoint' he refers to is the question of the Irish language and related matters. In the sense that he managed to bring that question into virtually every single item published in the CS under his editorship, then he is certainly right in describing the news as 'original comment'. However, a publication which only supplies comment of this sort is unlikely to make a major impact on a general readership.

The articles and editorials which did have an impact of some kind were those written in English, usually by Patrick Pearse, dealing with events of the day in Dublin. Pearse took an uncompromising anti-British stance in his writings in the CS. In his philosophy, there was no room for moderate nationalists, or for writers who tried to create an Irish literature in English: 'Every piece of literature in Irish forms, in our view, part of the national literature, whereas no piece of English does, however it may glow with love of Ireland' (CS, 29 April 1905; quoted in Ní Chollatáin 2004: 103). In the same piece he remarks of Anglo-Irish writers: 'As literature, we rate their work high. We regret that it has not been done in Irish that it might be altogether ours. But we prefer that it should be done in English than that it should remain undone' (Ní Chollatáin 2004: 103). However, he excluded the dramatist John Millington Synge from the group of Anglo-Irish writers he approved of. In 1907 Synge's *Playboy of the western world* was premiered at the Abbey Theatre in Dublin, and provoked rioting among sections of the audience who felt that it was a slur on the Irish nation. Pearse and the Gaelic League came down firmly on the side of the protesters:

Mr Synge's play was indefensible . . . Whether deliberately or undeliberately, he is using the stage for the propagation of a monstrous gospel of animalism, of revolt against sane and sweet ideals, of bitter contempt for all that is fine and worthy, not merely in Christian morality, but in human nature itself.

(CS, 9 February 1907; quoted in Ní Chollatáin 2004: 103)

To be fair to Pearse, there was also a positive side to his character, which manifested itself in his active encouragement of new writing in Irish in the pages of the CS. Most of this new literature consisted either of short stories or poetry, of varying quality, but without this stimulus many writers would never have carried on with their work.

Summing up, perhaps the main achievement of the CS was to get people used to the idea that it was possible to discuss contemporary affairs in Irish. It also played a major role in the development of a literary standard language (see Chapter 8). Unfortunately, it never succeeded in breaking free of its obsession with the language question. Partly because of this, it failed to attract readers from the Irish-speaking districts.

7.10 The Gaeltacht

One of the most lasting legacies of the Gaelic League is an entity called the Gaeltacht. Nowadays, a Gaeltacht, plural Gaeltachtaí, is a district in which a number of people speak Irish as a first language. The word and the concept were bequeathed to us by the Gaelic League.

7.10.1 Galltacht and Gaeltacht

In a book about how the concept of the Gaeltacht arose and was developed, Ó Torna (2005) discusses the way in which the language revival coincided with a renewed interest in the west of Ireland and its landscape. Writers like Synge and W. B. Yeats, and painters like Jack B. Yeats, discovered in the rugged and unspoilt countryside a source of creativity which they were to exploit again and again in their work. At the same time, mass tourism was developing in Europe, and under the influence of Victorian Romanticism, a demand grew for wild and grand scenery, untouched by the forces of modern industrialization. In this way, 'the West came to stand for Ireland in general, to be representative of true Irishness' (Nash 1993: 86–7).

The Gaelic League, however, wanted something more than just scenery and a population living close to nature. It was vital that the local people should have retained the language which was the antithesis of English in terms of the values associated with it. The League needed a term for places where this language, Irish, was still spoken. For this they pressed into service the word Gaeltacht. McLeod (1999) and Ó Torna (2005) trace the history of this term; I elaborate their accounts in what follows.

As we saw in section 2.1.3, as far back as the Middle Ages the terms Gael and Gall were used to distinguish the pre-Norman inhabitants of Ireland from the newcomers. From these two nouns, adjectives were formed:

(1)   Noun   Adjective
     a. Gael   Gaelta
        Gael   Gaelic
     b. Gall   Gallta
        foreigner   foreign

To these adjectives, in turn, were added the suffix -(a)cht to form nouns:

(2)   Adjective   Noun
    a. Gaelta   Gaeltacht
    b. Gallta   Galltacht

-(a)cht as a suffix was primarily used to form abstract nouns, with the meaning 'state, condition of' (adjective). Thus in EMI we find pairs like:

(3)   tromdha   tromdhacht
      serious   seriousness

Originally, then, Gaeltacht would have meant 'state of being Gaelic', while Galltacht would have meant 'the state of being foreign'.

    McLeod (1999) notes that we find the word Galltacht appearing much earlier than Gaeltacht. The meaning was something like 'foreign ways', itself an extension of 'state of being foreign'. As early as EMI we also find Galltacht being used to denote 'the foreign community, the English settlers', as in this entry from the Annals of Ulster:

(4)   mac Uilliam Búrc...cenn...gaiscid na Galltachta
      [MacWilliam Burke...head...of the soldiers...of the English settlers]

                                    (DIL, under the entry *galldacht*)

This kind of extension is a common enough process in language in general. Compare English formations like *readership*, where the meaning denotes a group of people—'all the readers', although -**ship** usually means 'the state of being (noun)', e.g. *citizenship* 'the state of being a citizen'.

    Later still, Galltacht came to mean the place where the people who were Gallta dwelt, as in the following example from the Annals of the Four Masters, written in the seventeenth century:

(5)   O briain maol do écc don teidhm is in nGalldacht.
      [Ó Briain Maol died of the plague in the region inhabited by foreigners.]
                        (O'Donovan 1990 [1854]: 762; quoted in McLeod 1999: 2)

Once again, there is nothing unusual about this change in semantics. In English, for example, the suffix -**dom** can mean both 'a group of people', like *officialdom*, and 'a place', like *kingdom*.

    Ó Torna observes that we find the first use of the word Gaeltacht later than the first occurrences of Galltacht. The earliest usage seems to be in a Scottish text, Robert Kirk's translation of the New Testament (1690):

(6)   ar mhaithe choitchinn Ghaóidhealtacht Albann
      [for the common good of the Gaelic community of Scotland]

(Kirk 1690; quoted in McLeod 1999: 4)

Here, the meaning is 'people', not 'place'. In another Scottish text, written about 1700, the word *Gaoidhealtacht* (Gaeltacht) is used of a place as well, to denote the Highlands of Scotland. Ó Torna (2005: 41) suggests that the meaning of place may have spread from Scotland to Ireland sometime in the nineteenth century. In fact, we find the meaning of place in Irish as early as 1714, in the following phrase:

(7)   Mac Dhomhnaill agus dream eile da chairdibh i nGhaeltacht na hAlban
      [MacDonald and another group of his friends in the Gaelic region of Scotland]

(Carney 1950: 244)

The editor of the text in which the above phrase occurs translates *Gaeltacht na hAlban* as 'Scottish Highlands'. The fact that it was not used with reference to Ireland in this era is not surprising. By 1600, there was a definite geographical distinction in Scotland between the Lowlands, where Scots and English were spoken, and the Highlands, where Gaelic was spoken. No such boundary existed in Ireland until after 1850. Only then did it become clear that Irish had become confined to certain regions. By the same token, only then did it become possible, or necessary, to name those regions.

At any rate, in 1893 the word Gaeltacht turns up in the GJ, with the unambiguous meaning of place:

> Every member of the League whose calling allows him an annual vacation should endeavour to spend that vacation in the Irish-speaking country...It so happens that the districts to which the old tongue still cleaves are in almost every instance the most picturesque and the healthiest part of Ireland. That is to say, whether the object be to see beautiful scenery or to obtain a period of salutary rest, there are no places within reach better worth visiting than those which the Gaodhaltacht of Ireland abundantly provides.

(GJ, November 1893: 228)

By this time the Irish-speaking districts had shrunk to such an extent that they had to be sought out and identified, the way an explorer might try to locate an exotic tribe.

7.10.2 Conceptualizing the Gaeltacht

Caitríona Ó Torna makes the significant point that it was English-speaking Gaelic Leaguers, mainly from Dublin and other large towns, who first conceptualized the Gaeltacht as a distinct entity. In naming it, they also in a sense created it, endowing its population with special attributes which had not been associated with Irish speakers up to now. Before the language revival, the west of Ireland had been used as a setting in Anglo-Irish literature on many occasions. However, in this Anglo-Irish writing the inhabitants were portrayed as amiable, lazy, shiftless good-for-nothings, who would do anything for a laugh and a free drink. The Gaelic League saw things differently. For Leaguers, the people of the Gaeltacht, the Gaeil, were God's chosen people. Douglas Hyde characterized them in terms which we might find somewhat excessive nowadays: 'We along the west coast of Ireland are of pure blood, we have been unmixed with other nations, we have been longest left alone... we must have carried directly from our Aryan home a stock of more original folk lore than the Slavs, Teutons or Scandinavians' (Hyde 1986d [1889]: 99; quoted in Ó Torna 2005: 119).

The modern reader should bear in mind that this passage was written against the background of the exciting discoveries which scholars had been making about the various language groups within the Indo-European family, and their attempts to link the linguistic findings with archaeological and biological classifications. Every European nation seemed to be concerned with establishing that their language was closer to the original Indo-European than any other. One of the main concerns of the day was purity, with proving that one's ethnic group and language had not been contaminated by other influences. In the above passage, then, the writer is claiming that the inhabitants of the west of Ireland are purer, less contaminated than their countrymen who speak English. In so far as one can work out what the basis for this purity was, it seems to have been a combination of language (Irish) and location (the west coast of Ireland). I need hardly add that there is absolutely no scientific basis for such a claim. The idea is all the more curious for having been put forward by a native English-speaking member of the establishment, who includes himself in this special group ('We along the west coast').

Other writers at the turn of the century also described the Gaeil in ecstatic terms. Here we have the words of Fr Patrick Dinneen who, unlike Hyde, could genuinely claim to be a man of the people, but whose language is just as hyperbolic:

Is deacair cur síos i gceart ar thréithibh na bhfíor-Éireannach. I n-áiteachaibh ná baineann cónaí sna cathracha neart is brí astu, bíonn siad láidir teann... dathúil, cneasta, macánta.

[It is hard to describe the characteristics of the real-Irish. In places where city-dwelling does not deprive them of strength and vigour, they are strong, firm... handsome, kind, honest.]

(Dinneen 1903: 21; quoted in Ó Torna 2005: 113)

In another work, Dinneen focused on the spirituality of the Gaeil before they lost their language:

Daoine simplí, macánta, cneasta ab ea iad, gan eolas an oilc acu faoi mar atá le fáil i measc lucht na cathrach. Ní raibh taithí acu ar dhroch-leabhair ná ar dhroch-pháipéaraibh ... Bhí a gcreideamh chomh glan, chomh sealbhaithe, chomh dúthrachtach is a bhí le fáil riamh in Eaglais Dé.

[They were simple, honest, kind people, without the kind of knowledge of evil that is found among city-dwellers. They had no experience of bad books or bad newspapers. ... Their faith was as clean, as rooted, as fervent as was ever to be found in God's Church.]

(Dinneen 1905: 13; quoted in Ó Torna 2005: 133)

Dinneen's fellow priest, Peadar Ó Laoghaire, saw Irish as a means of protecting the Irish people from pernicious foreign influences:

An chéad rud atá againn le déanamh ná an falla cosanta a choimeád ina sheasamh: an Ghaeluinn a choimeád á labhairt i mbéalaibh ár ndaoine ... Is í an Ghaeluinn an falla cosanta chun díchreidimh agus gach drochrud a leanann é a choimeád as Éirinn.

[The first thing we have to do is to keep the rampart standing: to keep Irish in the mouths of our people ... Irish is the rampart which will keep irreligiousness and every other evil out of Ireland.]

(An Síoladóir, July 1921; quoted in Ó Torna 2005: 123)

Thus, as Ó Torna puts it, the Gaeltacht districts were a kind of sanctuary for the nation as a whole:

Samhlaítear ... na ceantair Ghaeltachta ina dtobar oidhreachta, gabhdán sheanchultúr an phobail sin a raibh ardchultúr na hÉireann fós ina seilbh acu.

[The Irish districts are imagined ... as a heritage source, a repository for the old culture of the community which still had possession of the high culture of Ireland.]

(Ó Torna 2005: 121)

In the writings of the language revivalists, there is a sharp contrast between the Gaeltacht and the rest of the country, which is now called the Galltacht. This last term was also reinterpreted by the Gaelic League ideologists. In the period 1600–1850, the terms Gall, Gallta, and Galltacht all had negative connotations. However, the ethnic, linguistic, and geographical group that they referred to were reasonably well defined: English speakers of non-Gaelic origin, living in the east of the country or in towns. By 1890, there was a complication associated with the term Galltacht which had not existed previously. If most of the territory of Ireland was English-speaking, did this mean that it was a Galltacht? The answer seems to have been in the affirmative. This in turn brought with it a whole string of negative connotations. As well as being the place where English is spoken, Galltacht came to signify the location of

everything that was most repugnant to the ideology of the Gaelic League. Here
is how an anonymous contributor to the CS in 1907 described the geographical and spiritual journey from Galltacht to Gaeltacht:

Behind me I was leaving anglicisation with all its hideousness and soulless materialism,
its big smoking chimneys and prison-like factories (called commercial prosperity)
where thousands of Irishmen and Irishwomen in their struggle for a sordid existence
forget that they have a soul. Before me lay the Gaeltacht where the spiritual passionate
Gael with his simple beautiful customs, speaking his own language and singing his own
sweet songs, lived as God intended that he should.

(CS, 15 June 1907; quoted in Ó Torna 2005: 145)

The scheme which opposed Gael to Gall, Gaeltacht to Galltacht, was clear and
well defined, but it created a problem for Irishmen who were not of the
Gaeltacht, which meant most of the population. If you lived in the Galltacht,
did that make you a Gall, a West Brit, a *shoneen* [pejorative name for
Anglicized Irishman], with all the negative connotations that implied? The
answer was yes, if you persisted in your iniquity. However, there was a path to
salvation available, namely membership of the Gaelic League. Every Irish
person could become a Gael if they learned Irish, and visited the Gaeltacht
as often as possible. The Galltacht was more like purgatory than hell: redemp-
tion was possible if you were prepared to repent of your sins. The reward for
those who chose the path of salvation was considerable. In the following
passage, Patrick Pearse views the Gael as the saviour not just of Ireland, but
of mankind in general:

The Gael is not like other men ... a destiny more glorious than that of Rome, more
glorious than that of Britain awaits him: to become the saviour of idealism in modern
intellectual and social life, the regenerator and rejuvenator of the literature of the
world, the instructor of nations, the preacher of the gospel of nature-worship, hero-
worship, God-worship.

(Pearse 1898: 49; quoted in Ó Torna 2005: 148)

Most of the pamphleteers and writers in the CS were more restrained in their
rhetoric than Pearse. Nevertheless, they saw it as their duty to visit the
Gaeltacht regularly. Happily, this duty could be combined with pleasure, by
engaging in what Ó Torna calls language tourism. By 1900, the Irish middle
classes were beginning to go on holidays in seaside-resorts like Bray, Youghal,
and Kilkee. One writer saw an opportunity here for the language movement:
'Moreover, owing to the patriotic affection of Irish people for such resorts as
the Isle of Man, Buxton, Harrogate, or Brighton, the districts we allude to [in
the Gaeltacht] in no way labour under the common disadvantage of being
"overdone" ... Hence we affirm that the spending of a holiday in these regions

is no sacrifice but a manifold benefit' (GJ, November 1893: 228). Readers of the GJ and the CS were reminded that visits to the Gaeltacht were not to be a pretext for frivolous holiday-making:

The visits of town Leaguers to the Gaedealtacht should always be made with a purpose. We go, of course, partly for relaxation and partly in search of the *blas* [correct accent]. But in addition to amusing ourselves and increasing our stock of Irish we can, during the summer sojourns with the Gael, do much to advance the movement, and that in more ways than one.

(CS, 22 July 1905; quoted in Ó Torna 2005: 83)

Members of the Gaelic League were like soldiers—they had a war to wage. Here is a notice in the CS, 1902:

Irish Speaking Galway. The West's Asleep! But if ever in this world the West is going to be roused up out of its slumbers, it will be when The Great Invasion of Galway comes off on Sunday, July 27th, next. Not from Dublin alone, but every Town and Village throughout the West will send its Representative, till from far and wide throughout Connaught the Clan-na-Gael shall gather to declare war on Anglicisation!

(CS, 19 July 1902; quoted in Ó Torna 2005: 82)

The military imagery of the above passage recurs again and again in the articles, notices, and editorials of the CS:

Then imagine a score of virile, ardent Gaelic Leaguers breaking in on that 'virgin soil', traversed by Pádraig Mac Piarais [Patrick Pearse] where the Gall is pushing the Gael so hard . . . The spectacle of young men, brought up entirely without Irish, making such heroic efforts to acquire it, would, by force of contrast, strongly appeal to those who know it, but will not speak it.

(CS, 14 February 1903; quoted in Ó Torna 2005: 84)

Like the Evangelical preachers of Victorian and Edwardian Britain, the Gaelic Leaguers had a mission to fulfil, namely to rouse the population of the Gaeltacht out of their torpor and apathy:

When they visit these places, it will be easy for members of the Gaelic League . . . to give a powerful stimulus to the movement by simply conversing with the people, removing prejudice, letting in light . . . teaching them that their native Gaelic is no inferior kind of speech, but a really noble and great language; and in this way breaking the ice of apathy, and giving an opening for the enthusiasm which, well we know, only waits to break forth and sweep all obstacles before it.

(GJ, November 1893: 228)

At times the tone the Gaelic Leaguers adopt towards the people of the Gaeltacht is unashamedly paternalistic:

We are not fearful of the response. There can be no doubt that the Irish-speaking population, which is the proper field for such labours, has hitherto been practically untouched by the movement; and we do not fear that when the honour of maintaining their national language and responsibility of deserting it are brought home to the people themselves, humble, illiterate, and poor though the Irish-speaking peasant may be, he will teach a striking lesson in patriotism to this complacent generation of respectable, educated, and highly-civilized lip Irishmen.

(GJ, November 1893: 227)

Like every missionary movement, there were a certain number of backsliders and lukewarm converts in the Gaelic League. Their presence did not go undetected, however. Here is an extract from a stern editorial by Patrick Pearse on the subject:

Care should be taken to include only serious students who will talk as little English as possible. Very many, who are only half Gaelic Leaguers, visit Irish-speaking districts, and do more harm than good. They speak English constantly in the hearing of the Irish speakers and frequently they sing English songs. We must take care that they do not spoil the Irish-speaking districts.

(CS, 6 June 1903; quoted in Ó Torna 2005: 87)

The attitude to the Gaeltacht was similar to the way in which nature reserves are viewed in our own time. Visitors could be supportive, but they could also pose a threat to the linguistic environment if they did not know how to behave, or if they did not have a good command of Irish:

Persons, with a limited knowledge of Irish, visiting Irish-speaking districts would do well to be careful that in Gaelicising themselves they do not Anglicise the people of the place. I have known visitors to such places who, with the best of intentions in the world, have taught more English than they have learned Irish. For goodness sake, if they cannot speak Irish let them remain silent or speak French, German, or anything, but not make *Béarlóirí* [English speakers] of the Gaels.

(CS, 19 October 1907; quoted in Ó Torna 2005: 87)

Summing up, language tourism was holidaying with a difference. It had a very serious purpose, and was attended by all kinds of prohibitions and shibboleths, the violation of which would bring shame and dishonour to the perpetrator and to the Gaelic League itself. Even allowing for the differences in mentality between our own society and that of Edwardian Ireland, it is hard to avoid the conclusion that holidaying in the Gaeltacht in the company of Patrick Pearse and his ilk might have brought with it a certain amount of stress and tension. But, as we have seen, Gaelic Leaguers were not there to have a good time, they were there to strengthen and revitalize the Irish nation.

7.10.3 The Gaeltacht: myth and reality

One of the non-linguistic aspects of the Gaeltacht areas which was attractive for city-dwellers was the pre-industrial way of life of the inhabitants. For the most part, they were engaged in small-time farming and fishing, using methods which had changed little over the centuries. They wore what seemed to be exotic costumes. Reading and writing were virtually unknown to them, but they practised oral arts like story-telling and folk-singing.

The study of folklore, and of folk-music, became an essential part of the Gaeltacht experience. For students attending summer colleges in the Irish-speaking districts, instruction was twofold. There were the formal language classes during the day. Side by side with these, there was the informal instruction to be absorbed from the inhabitants. Students lodged with local people. The expectation was that they would learn about the culture of the Gaeltacht in the setting of their lodgings: 'In addition to class work there be ample opportunity for all kinds of social gatherings, such as *Scoraíochta, Céilí* [gatherings involving story-telling and singing] ... Much might also be done in the way of collecting the songs and stories, proverbs and folklore current in the various localities' (CS, 15 June 1901; quoted in Ó Torna 2005:89). This emphasis on informal instruction occurs again and again in the writings of the time:

Not the least valuable part of the training...will be that which the students will unconsciously acquire after the formal classes are over, as they listen to the chatter of the *Bean Tighe* [housewife] over her carding or her spinning or the *Fiannaidheacht* [heroic story-telling] of some local *seanchaí* [story-teller] when the fireside group forms in the gloaming.

(CS, 7 January 1905; quoted in Ó Torna 2005: 93)

In the above passage, we encounter two figures—the *bean tí* and the *seanchaí*—who were to become stock-characters in the perception of the Gaeltacht by outsiders. Both of them are symbols of the primitive, frugal, but ultimately wholesome way of life that by 1900 had become inextricably bound up with the Irish language.

For at least some members of the Gaelic League, the more remote and economically deprived the region, the more authentically Irish/Gaelic it was. Here once again is Patrick Pearse waxing lyrical on the subject of the Gael and his environment:

Only on the lonelier mountain slopes...does one find the *ipsissimus* [real] Gael—the Gael as he was in the days when Grainne Mhaol's warships swept these seas, and the clans that garrisoned these mountains were wont periodically to swoop down on the burghers of Galway and Athenry. I met him last week beyond Cnoc Leitreach—met

strong men and women in the prime of life whose Irish organs of speech have never
been defiled by a word of English.

                                      (CS, 17 January 1903; quoted in Ó Torna 2005: 144)

As Ó Torna remarks, the above passage bears the imprint of the anthropologist. It is as if the Gael is a vanishing species that has to be tracked down in
the wilderness of the west of Ireland. She sees Pearse as a latter day Romantic:

Is i dtéarmaí tagartha an Rómánsachais atá an Gael á shainiú . . . ag an bPiarsach—cur
síos ar phobal gan truailliú a raibh saol ar an tseanslí á chaitheamh acu, a dteanga
dúchais á labhairt acu gan drochthionchar an Bhéarla.

[The Gael is being defined by Pearse . . . in the terms of reference of Romanticism—
describing an undefiled community living life in the old way, speaking their native
language without the bad influence of English.]

                                                                    (Ó Torna 2005: 144)

For those who subscribed to the above view of the Gaeltacht, it was necessary
to keep it unchanged for all time, to prevent it becoming like the rest of
Ireland:

Má ba iad na ceantair Ghaeltachta an pointe teagmhála a bhí ag muintir na hÉireann
lena ré stairiúil órga féin agus má bhíothas chun coincheap den náisiún a bhunú ar an
tuiscint go raibh nasc sna ceantair Ghaeltachta leis an seansaol, ansin b'éigean a
dhearbhú go gcaomhnófaí an tobar nó an fhoinse sin. Níor mhór é sin a dhéanamh
ar son an phobail féin, a raibh de rath orthu an cultúr neamhghalldaithe a bheith acu,
agus ar son phobal na Galltachta araon.

[If the Gaeltacht districts were the point of contact for the people of Ireland with their
own historical golden age, and if the concept of the nation was to be based on the
understanding that the Gaeltachts were connected to the old way of life, then it was
necessary to ensure that this source be preserved. This had to be done both on behalf of
the Gaeltacht community, which was fortunate enough to have an un-Anglicized form
of culture, and on behalf of the people of the Galltacht.]

                                                                    (Ó Torna 2005: 149)

Not everyone was as starry-eyed about the Gaeltacht areas as the writers of the
passages quoted above. One of the most striking facts about these districts was
their economic deprivation. As well as Gaelic Leaguers, various government
officials visited districts where Irish was spoken, and their reports make for
depressing reading. As late as 1925, we come across descriptions like the
following:

The holdings are uneconomic without exception, and the greater portion of the
population depend on migratory labour in Scotland and on the earnings of the younger
members of the family who are hired with the farmers of the Laggan district during

summer and autumn months ... The present industries in the district are not sufficient to support one-tenth of the population.

(Government of Ireland 1926; quoted in Walsh 2002: 54)

The official accounts tally with the reminiscences of inhabitants of the Gaeltachts. Here is a description of houses on the Blasket Islands, which would become an icon of the Gaeltacht in the twentieth century:

D'fhonn roinnt a dhéanamh sa tigh, bhíodh drosar trasna lár an tí ón bhfalla ar thaobh, agus síonáil ag freagairt do ón dtaobh eile. Do bhíodh dhá leabaidh laistíos díobh san; daoine iontu. Bhíodh dhá mhuic ag dul fé leabaidh acu, agus bhíodh prátaí fén gceann eile ... Insa taobh eile don síonáil, taobh na cisteanach, bhíodh na daoine i rith an lae, nó cuid den ló, deichniúr acu b'fhéidir. Do bhíodh cúib leis an síonáil; cearca inti. Cearc ar gor in aice léi i seanachorcán. Istoíche bhíodh bó agus dhá bhó, gamhain nó dhá ghamhain, asal, dhá mhadra ceangailte do thaobh an fhalla nó ar fuaid an tí.

[In order to divide the house up [into compartments], there would be a dresser across the middle of the house from the side wall, and a corresponding partition on the other side. There would be two beds below that for people to sleep in. There would be two pigs under one of the beds, and potatoes under the other one ... On the other side of the partition, the kitchen side, is where the people would be during the day, or part of the day, ten of them, perhaps. There would be a hen-coop against the partition, with hens in it. There would be a hen hatching beside it in an old saucepan. At night there would be one or two cows, one or two calves, a donkey, and two dogs tied to the side of the house or somewhere in the house.]

(Ó Coileáin 2002: 331)

The author of the above description, Tomás Ó Criomhthain, also refers casually and laconically to food shortages at the end of the nineteenth century: 'Bliain ghorta insan Oileán agus a lán áiteanna nárbh é dob ea í' [It was a year of hunger in the Island and many other places] (Ó Coileáin 2005: 263) There is no note of surprise or shock in this statement, which suggests that hunger was a commonplace in the lives of the inhabitants of this particular Gaeltacht.

Not all members of the Gaelic League were blind to the poverty of the Irish speakers, as the following extract from one of the travelling teachers shows:

I dtaobh na ndaoine, tá an Ghaedhilge go beo bríoghmhar ina measg; acht faraoir, tá an bhochtanas [sic] agus an ganntanas léithe. Níor leag mé súil ar aon áit ariamh chomh bocht le hIorrus; tá an ghorta dá theasbánadh féin ar 'chuile taobh; pé áit ar bith bhfuil talmhan [sic] mhaith ann tá sé faoi bhuláin, agus tá na daoine bochta ar mhóintibh nó ar thaobh-sléibhe.

[As for the people, Irish is well and alive in their midst; but alas, it is accompanied by poverty and scarcity. I never set eyes on a place as poor as Erris; hunger is displaying itself on every side; any good land is covered by boulders, and the poor people are on moors or the mountain-side.]

(Connradh na Gaedhilge 1906: 50; quoted in Ó Torna 2005: 71)

However, for the most part the writers of the League either didn't notice the want that surrounded them when they visited the Gaeltacht, or simply chose to ignore it. In any case, the Gaelic League was not an agency for economic reform. The only significant contribution that the language revival made to the material circumstances of the Gaeltacht inhabitants was that it created a new form of tourism, one based on language. A limited amount of employment was created by building the teacher-training colleges, and likewise the tradition of lodging with local people provided them with some income in the summer months. Needless to say, none of this addressed the real needs of the Irish-speaking regions. A report from 1926 reveals how little had changed more than thirty years after the founding of the League:

Without effectively dealing with the very congested Irish Speaking populations, all hope of relieving the congestion in those areas will have vanished, and no future can be open to the traditional Irish Speaker affected but one of continued poverty and degradation in his native surrounding, involving dependence on American money, old age pensions, migrating labour in Britain or elsewhere, and Government relief; or emigration, with the consequent loss to the living language position.

(Government of Ireland 1926; quoted in Walsh 2002: 99)

Despite the best efforts of the League, most of the inhabitants of the Gaeltachts remained hostile, or at best indifferent, to the language of their ancestors. For them, it was just a language, something they spoke from day to day. Furthermore, they were bewildered by the sudden change in status which Irish seemed to have undergone. In the following extract from the autobiography of a travelling-teacher, the author tells of an encounter with a man in the author's native district. His interlocutor describes his attitude to Irish:

'Ní fheadar,' ar seisean. 'Tá a lán daoine ag iarraidh an Ghaedhilg d'fhoghluim anois, agus bhí a lán ad iarraidh í chaitheamh uatha an uair sin. Bhíodh na sagairt agus na daoine móra i gcoinnibh Gaedhilge nuair a bhíos óg, agus tá cuid acu anois ar buile chun í thabhairt thar n-ais arís. Is deacair dom leithéid-se an scéal a thuisgint'.

['I don't know,' he said. 'A lot of people are trying to learn Irish now, and there were a lot trying to rid themselves of it then. The priests and the important people were against Irish when I was young, and now some of them are crazy about trying to bring it back. It's hard for the likes of me to understand what's going on.']

(Ó hAnnracháin 1937: 261–2; quoted in Nic Eoin 2012: 542)

A small number of native speakers were recruited as teachers and activists, in this way managing to escape from the life of drudgery to which they would otherwise have been condemned. Story-tellers and singers whose repertoire was recorded by members of the League must have experienced some gratification at being appreciated by a wider audience. But the gap remained wide between the middle-class intellectuals who chose Irish as an extension of their nationalist personae, and the illiterate peasant communities to whom they preached the gospel of cultural and linguistic renewal.

A commentator on the failure of the Revival to engage native speakers in the twentieth century, offers an interesting sociolinguistic comparison:

I sense that by 1922 (and probably by 1893) Irish had become the key distinguishing feature of a Gaeltacht subculture which was also the anti-culture of an underclass in relation to anglicized Irish middle-class society. In this it resembles broad Cockney in east London. Its speakers still do not regard it as 'respectable' but it shows their independence of middle-class values and 'high' culture, bringing a sense of integrity and collective privacy which 'Gaeltacht chauvinism' reflects . . . This is not incompatible with a sense of shame about it . . . but the language is their own possession, it is part of themselves, and there is a deep psychological 'class-war' element in their resentment of and resistance to its appropriation by (to them) 'upper-class' outsiders.

. . . What has happened in the course of the attempted revival is that a section of the anglicized upper class . . . has adopted the lower class *patois*. The lower-class reaction is exactly what would have been expected in London if the West End 'toffs' of the 1920s had presumed to combine with their 'slumming' improving lectures on the virtues and desirability of maintaining Cockney English, and then went on to try and talk it, finally offering instruction to the Cockneys on how they should talk it 'correctly'.

(Hindley 1990: 212)

As a description of the attitudes and practices of the Gaelic League with respect to the Irish-speaking regions, the above is accurate, perhaps painfully so. Of course, Hindley was writing from the perspective of 1990, with the benefit of knowledge and insights that were unavailable to the Gaelic Leaguers. Nevertheless, his analysis, I believe, goes a long way to explaining what at the time seemed incomprehensible, namely the reluctance of the native speakers to become engaged in the work of the Gaelic League.

7.11 The Gaelic League and politics

As we noted in section 7.5, the founders of the Gaelic League insisted that it remain non-political, and adhered to this stance for sometime after 1893. From about 1900 onwards, this policy was to be gradually eroded. The younger generation, under the leadership of Patrick Pearse, insisted more and more that there was a link between language and the nationalist cause, that one could not be separated from the other. Furthermore, nationalist politics was heading once more in the direction of independence from Britain. Arthur Griffith founded Sinn Féin in 1905 with the aim of restoring the Dublin parliament; one method suggested for achieving this was a boycott of the Westminster assembly. Many members of the Gaelic League joined this new political movement. At the same time, efforts were being made to resuscitate the near-moribund Irish Republican Brotherhood (IRB). Under the new leadership of Denis McCullough, Bulmer Hobson, and Sean MacDermott, the IRB began recruiting members from about 1905 onwards. This radical organization, which aimed at the armed overthrow of British rule, attracted many new members from the Gaelic League.

Nominally, the League was still non-political, but few people really believed this after 1910. The following quotation from the autobiography of Seán T. Ó Ceallaigh is revelatory in this regard:

Nuair a bhí mé ag obair ar an *Claíomh Solais* sna blianta tosaigh bhí caoi agam chomh maith ar a lán a dhéanamh ar son an I.R.B. Bhínn ag dul timpeall na tíre go dtí feiseanna ag iarraidh díol an pháipeir a mhéadu agus ar ndóigh chastaí a lán daoine óga de m'aois féin orm i mbailte éagsúla ... Is cuimhin liom gur mó cuairt a thug mé ar na bailte sin agus gur thug mé fir óga isteach san I.R.B. i ngach ceann acu. Ma bhí mé i mo thimire tuarastail ag an *Claíomh Solais* san am sin, bhí mé i mo thimire onóra don I.R.B. san am céanna.

[When working for *An Claidheamh Soluis* in the early years I had an opportunity to do a lot for the IRB. I used to go around the country to *feiseanna* [language festivals] trying to increase sales of the paper, and, of course I met many young people of my own age in the different towns ... and I recruited young men for the IRB in every one of them. If I was a paid agent for *An Claidheamh Soluis* at that period, I was an honorary agent for the IRB at the same time.]

(Ó Ceallaigh 1963: 59; trans. in Ó Huallacháin 1994: 62)

In the years leading up to the outbreak of World War I, Irish society became increasingly polarized, and many felt that the Gaelic League could no longer maintain its neutral position. An article in *Irish Freedom*, the paper of the separatist movement, put the matter plainly in 1913:

The work of the Gaelic League is to prevent the assimilation of the Irish nation by the English nation ... That work is as essentially anti-English as the work attempted by Fenianism or the Society of United Irishmen. The aim of the English is the direct contrary of this.

... The Irish language is a political weapon of the first importance against English encroachment; it can never be a political weapon in the hands of one Irish party against another ... The sooner the country and the Gaelic League know what they are at, the better.

(*Irish Freedom*, September 1913; quoted in Ó Huallacháin 1994: 67)

Patrick Pearse, in his article *The Coming Revolution*, delivered more or less the same message, albeit in more prophetic tones:

If we had not believed in the divinity of our people, we should in all probability not have gone into the Gaelic League at all. We should have made our peace with the devil, and perhaps have found him a very decent sort; for he liberally rewards with attorney-generalships, bank balances, villa residences, and so forth, the great and little who serve him well. Now we did not turn our backs on all these desirable things for the sake of *is* and *tá* [the verbs *to be* in Irish]. We did it for the sake of Ireland. In other words, we had one and all of us...an ulterior motive in joining the Gaelic League. We never meant to be Gaelic Leaguers and nothing more than Gaelic Leaguers.

(Pearse 1922: 92)

For him, the Gaelic league was only part of a total revitalization of Irish society: 'The deed of the generation that has now reached middle life was the Gaelic League: the beginning of the Irish Revolution' (Pearse 1922: 95). Despite the exalted language, Pearse probably hit the nail on the head in these passages: the rank and file of the Gaelic League did not join in order to learn a language. Some of them, including Pearse, did learn Irish, and learned it well. Others never got beyond the first primer, and contented themselves with Gaelicizing their names. The great majority learned to speak Irish reasonably well. But most of them were men of action rather than philologists, and the League was just a rung on the ladder of the struggle for independence.

Douglas Hyde, the president of the League, was left behind by all these events. Pressure was mounting on him to openly endorse the nationalist stance. He resisted, arguing that the strength of the League was its non-involvement in politics. This neutrality led to him being accused of being anti-nationalist. Here are the words of Earnán de Blaghd [Ernest Blythe], recalling the period 1913–16: 'Between 1913 and 1916 Dr. Douglas Hyde's influence as a leader of opinion underwent something like a complete eclipse' (de Blaghd 1972: 31). De Blaghd defends Hyde, but acknowledges that many others felt that he had sold out: 'The suggestion whispered around at the time, that Hyde was not really a Nationalist at all but was rather something like a mild Unionist-Imperialist, had no justification' (de Blaghd 1972: 31).

The problem was that Hyde, despite his protests to the contrary, was linked by class and background to the Anglo-Irish Ascendancy, who more or less unreservedly supported Britain in the war with Germany. By January 1915 the sons of his friends were being slaughtered on the battlefields of Flanders, as Hyde acknowledged in a letter to a friend: 'Nearly everyone I know in the army has been killed. Poor young Lord de Freyne and his brother were shot the same day and buried in one grave. The MacDermot of Coolavin, my nearest neighbour, has had his eldest son shot dead in the Dardanelles. All the gentry have suffered. *Noblesse oblige*. They have behaved magnificently' (Mac Aonghusa 1993: 146). In the heated atmosphere of Ireland during World War I there was no longer any room for dual loyalties: one was perceived either as a separatist or a unionist. There was no place any more for people like Hyde, who was neither one nor the other. There was certainly no place on the nationalist side for sentiments like those expressed in Hyde's letter.

Matters came to a head at the *Ard-Fheis* [AGM] of the League in 1915, when the somewhat disingenuous resolution was passed, stating that: 'The Gaelic League shall be strictly non-political and non-sectarian, and shall devote itself solely to realizing the dawn of a free Gaelic-speaking Ireland' (*Freeman's Journal*, 12 October 1915; quoted in Ó Huallacháin 1994: 69). After the resolution had been passed Hyde resigned his presidency, pleading ill-health. The word *free* in the above resolution was too political for him, and he felt that he could no longer continue to lead a movement whose basic philosophy had changed.

The following year, 1916, was the year of the Easter Rising. Six of the seven signatories of the Easter Proclamation which declared Ireland a republic, were members of the Gaelic League. Following the rising, the insurgents were interned, and fifteen of the leaders executed. The severity of the reprisals drove many Irishmen into supporting the struggle for a fully independent republic, and made it even more difficult to be a moderate. The League still claimed to be non-political, but this was evidently not true, as Hyde noted in a memoir written in 1918:

A number of Sinn Feiners make it a point to set up a horrible hullaballoo if anyone ventures to say the Gaelic League is political. This is part of that obliquity of vision, amounting almost to a disease, a kink in the mind, which I have observed in numerous representatives of that party. The fact, however, remains that they have left the Gaelic League a body to which no Redmondite [member of Home Rule party] and no Unionist can any longer subscribe.

(Ó Huallacháin 1994: 72–3)

Hyde accepted the new order of things, although he had reservations about it: 'On the whole, however, I am not at all sure that the turn things have taken may not be the best thing for the language movement. It has put an end to my dream of using the language as a unifying bond to join all Irishmen together, but it at least rendered the movement homogeneous' (Ó Huallacháin 1994: 73). His friend James Hannay had warned Hyde earlier about where the Gaelic League was headed: 'The movement you started will go on, whether you lead it or take the part of poor Frankenstein who created a monster he could not control' (Dunleavy and Dunleavy 1991: 314). As the War of Independence got under way in the early months of 1919, Hyde must have wondered whether he had not indeed been assigned the role of Frankenstein in the unfolding drama.

During the War of Independence, much of the material meant to be published in the CS was censored. The editor in this period was Piaras Béaslaí, an active member of the IRB in the guerrilla war being waged with the British forces. While he was in office, the CS openly supported the separatist cause, linking it to the language movement. In January 1919, the Sinn Féin deputies who had been elected in 1918 convened what they called the first *Dáil* [parliament] in Dublin, in defiance of British rule. Here is how the CS reported the meeting:

Táid siad chun teacht le chéile i n-éan Dáil mhór—Dáil Éireann a thabharfar uirthi agus cloisfar an Ghaedhilg dá spreagadh go binn i bPárliament na nGaedheal, murab ionann is Párliament na nGall go raibh súile na ndaoine dírithe air le dathad bliain anuas. Beidh cuid de na daoine is mó le rádh i gConnradh na Gaedhilge ar an nDáil sin...Is follus go bhfuil an lámh uachtair ag lucht na Gaedhilge sa tír seo fé dheoidh is fé dheireadh. Tá an buadh ag an 'Language Movement'. Is mithid dúinn feasta feuchaint chuige go mbeidh an buadh ag an dteangain féin.

[They are going to convene in one big Assembly—it will be called *Dáil Éireann* [Parliament of Ireland] and Irish will be heard being melodiously spoken in the parliament of the Gaels, unlike the Parliament of the Galls which has been before the eyes of the people for the last 40 years. Some of the most important people in the Gaelic League will be at that Assembly...It is clear that the supporters of Irish have finally got the upper hand in this country. The language movement has triumphed. Now we need to make sure that the language itself will triumph.]

(CS, 11 January 1919; quoted in Ní Chollatáin 2004: 158)

The League still persisted in claiming that it was non-political, but it was a claim that few believed. In the period 1900–20 the Irish language became yoked to a particular political standpoint, that of extreme nationalism, which manifested itself in anti-British rhetoric. This association with separatist republicanism was to persist long after the War of Independence had ended and Ireland had become independent.

The Sinn Féin deputies set up what was effectively an alternative government for Ireland, which operated illegally and in semi-secrecy for the period 1919–22. One innovation of this government was the appointment of a minister for Irish in 1920. The first holder of this position was the president of the Gaelic League. The new ministry made various recommendations about introducing Irish into areas of the public service in which it had never been present before. For example, it was urged that 'Public boards..., as far as feasible, should have persons with a working knowledge of Irish on their staffs "so that the public might transact their business through the medium of the vernacular"' (Ó Huallacháin 1994: 80).

In 1922 the Free State of Ireland was established as a political entity for twenty-six of the thirty-two counties of Ireland, with six of the Ulster counties remaining under British rule. The new constitution recognized

Irish as the 'national language', and provision was made for making the language compulsory in education, and to a lesser degree, in public administration. It looked as though the dream of the Gaelic League was finally to be fulfilled.

7.12 Conclusion—the substance and the shadow

I have already alluded to the meeting of the first Dáil in 1919, and to the fact that Irish was spoken during the sitting. This had tremendous significance for the language movement. The use of Irish must have caused some inconvenience, because not all the deputies spoke it, and, of those who had attended classes in the Gaelic League, not all spoke it well enough to take part in a debate. This is an instance of language being used more for symbolic purposes than as a genuine means of communication. Colmán Ó Huallacháin comments on this use of Irish:

Certain things done about Irish owe their importance to their use as a particular kind of outward sign, while the degree to which those involved are affected may be minimal from the point of view of actual understanding or use of the language for communication . . . In the case of Irish, it is helpful, for clarification of important aspects of its development in society during this century, to characterise as 'emblematic' its employment as a symbol having only minimal, if any, reference to communication in society though at the same time, conveying some kind of reference to ethnic distinctiveness.

(Ó Huallacháin 1994: 58)

Some people at the time understood the difference between symbolic use and communicative use quite well. As early as 1920 the short-story writer Pádraic Ó Conaire was to state:

An Phoblacht a bhuanú in Éirinn ar bhunchloch an Ghaelachais an obair atá le déanamh ag Sinn Féin, ach tá a lán daoine a thugas Sinn Féinithe orthu féin anois nach dtuigeann é sin. Deir siad gur cairde don teanga iad féin, ach más ea b'fhearrde an teanga na sean-naimhde. Na cairde seo nach cairde, cineál ornáide acu an teanga, nó an moladh a bheir siad don teanga, ar nós na gcultacha péacacha a bhíos ag an A[ncient] O[order of] H[Hibernians].
    . . . Teanga a bhí mar ornáid agus mar ornáid amháin ag cine, níor mhair an teanga sin ariamh agus ní mhairfidh choíche . . . An teanga nach bhfuil géarghá léi, an teanga nach labhraítear ach le daoine a bhfuil teanga eile seachas í acu, an bás atá i ndán don teanga sin.

[What Sinn Féin has to do today is establish the Republic in Ireland on the foundations of Gaeldom, but many of those who call themselves Sinn Féiners do not understand that. They say that they are friends of the language, but if so, then the language was better off with its old enemies. For these friends who are not friends, the language is a kind of ornament, or the praise they give the language, like the fancy costumes worn by the Ancient Order of Hibernians.

... Any language which was an ornament and nothing but an ornament for a race, that language never survived, and such a language never will survive... A language which is not an essential requirement, a language which is only spoken by people who have another language besides it, that language is doomed to extinction.]

(Denvir 1978: 171)

The writer of the above words captured succinctly the essence of the problem facing the new state and the Gaelic League in 1922. Most Irish people, even members of Sinn Féin, the nationalist party, were not really serious about replacing English with Irish. And yet if that were not to happen, then what was the point in learning Irish at all? As Ó Conaire points out, one normally learns another language in order to communicate with people who don't speak one's own. By this logic, English speakers should not really be speaking Irish to each other, except for symbolic purposes.

It is hard not to agree with Ó Conaire, but in a way his merciless logic works against him. Most of the members of the Gaelic League were second-language speakers, many of whom had not mastered Irish to a very high level. By Ó Conaire's reasoning, these people should not have been speaking Irish to each other. But in fact there were very few occasions when real-life circumstances demanded that they use Irish when dealing with a monoglot speaker who did not understand English. This in turn meant that Irish really was nothing more than an ornament, and it was somewhat irrational for Ó Conaire to castigate his countrymen for treating it in a purely symbolic fashion.

In terms of official status, Irish had never enjoyed such prestige as it did in 1922. It had, after all, been declared the national language. Unfortunately, reality cannot be changed by a mere declaration. In fact, the further the reality is from a declaration, the more hollow the latter sounds. Even a dyed-in-the-wool republican like Constance Markievicz could see that there would be problems with implementing the new policies with regard to Irish:

It is not possible to revive Irish by law. In the present state of the knowledge of Irish, we have not got enough Irish teachers to go round, compulsion is no good. It is very difficult to get every person to write his name in Irish; you would have a most extraordinary result. To fill up the correct name of every townland in Ireland is a matter of most alarming difficulty.

(Markievicz 1922; quoted in Ó Huallacháin 1994: 85)

Adrian Kelly draws attention to the fact that educators in 1922 were convinced that Irish could be revived solely within the school system:

However, economics was not recognized as an agent of linguistic change by the Free State government, and the idea that the schools alone had brought about the use of English as a vernacular was the central premise on which the whole revival effort of the independent Irish government was based. The philosophy of the revivalist movement was founded on the incorrect assumption that if English had replaced Irish as the language of the country primarily because of an anglicised education system, then the reverse could be brought about by a native government.

(Kelly 2002: 5)

Events after 1922 were to prove the correctness of Kelly's assessment of the situation in the above passage. Irish was made compulsory for all children, right through the educational system; in some cases it even became the sole language of instruction. But the language remained largely within the classroom. Education was one strand which could contribute to its revival, but it was not sufficient.

Paradoxically, the achievement of independence had taken much of the momentum out of the revival of Irish. As mentioned earlier, for many the language movement had been merely one of the ways in which they could work for independence. Now that independence had been achieved, there was not the same impetus to keep supporting Irish. Some people in the Gaelic League seem to have believed that once the status of Irish was changed, the rest would follow, with the Irish people spontaneously beginning to speak Irish in every walk of life. The actual implementation of the programme for revival had not been considered in any depth. Apart from education, the activities of the Gaelic League had been confined to the symbolic and cultural level. One could use the Irish form of one's name, or dance Irish jigs and reels, without having to speak a word of Irish in everyday life. One could even go to the Gaeltacht for one's holidays, and speak Irish while there, and then come back home and continue to live one's life through the medium of English. As long as British rule was maintained, there was no real danger that one would actually have to use Irish in the workplace, or in the public sphere. The achievement of independence meant that this suddenly became a real possibility; not only that, certain members of the new government were serious about implementing the policies which had been adopted for Irish.

For committed activists, the coming of independence was a huge anti-climax. Until 1921, the British could be blamed for all Ireland's woes, including the decline of Irish. Now the Irish nation was in control of its own destiny, and yet the revival of Irish seemed as distant as ever. Here is how one activist expressed his disappointment:

Tháinicc cainnt an Phiarsaigh an oidhche údan fíor ó shoin. Tá Gaedhilg ar stampaí, ach go dtéighidh sí i gcroidhthe na ndaoine, amhail mar chuaidh soisgéal Naomh Pádhraic ní bheidh an báire linn.

[Pearse's words of that night have come true since then. Irish is to be seen on stamps, but until it goes into the hearts of the people, like St Patrick's gospel, we will not win.]

(Ó Gaora 1943: 243; quoted in Nic Eoin 2012: 547)

As the years went by, people like the author of the above words were to become more and more disillusioned. Some of them persisted with their work and tried to enforce the state's provisions for the use of Irish, by speaking Irish at meetings of local councils, for example. These idealists soon found themselves being marginalized by their fellow-Irishmen, who were anxious to get on with the business of running the country efficiently, in the only language that was common to all, namely English.

Up to now, the revival of Irish had been a dream, an aspiration for the future. Now there was a real chance to turn that shadow into substance. In the years that followed the winning of independence, successive governments would have to deal with the implications of making Irish the official language, and giving it a special place in the constitution. Successive generations of Irish men, women, and children would experience the implementation of various programmes for making the revival of Irish a reality. For better or for worse, Irish was there to stay in the national consciousness and national identity.

Further reading

For Ireland 1870–1922, see Lee (1973).

For cultural nationalism in Ireland 1870–1920, and its interaction with the social, economic, and political movements of the day, see Hutchinson (1987: 114–96) and Mathews (2003).

For the Society for the Preservation of the Irish Language, see Ó hAilín (1969) and Ó Murchú (2001). The latter is a minute description of the day-to-day activities of the organization.

For Douglas Hyde, see Daly (1974) and Dunleavy and Dunleavy (1991). Daly contains extracts in Irish from the diary that Hyde kept from an early age. Hyde's memoir (de hÍde 1937) is mostly taken up with his public activity on behalf of the Gaelic League.

For the Gaelic League, see Ó hAilín (1969); Ó Tuama (1972); and Ó Huallacháin (1994: 38–72). Mac Aonghusa (1993) and Ó Súilleabháin (1998) are book-length studies by two former officers of the Gaelic League. Hutchinson (1987: 211–49) discusses the Revival in the context of popular rural culture on the one hand and the elitist Anglo-Irish tradition on the other.

For the Gaelic League and education, see Ó Fiaich (1972) and Kelly (2002: 1–13). Mathews (2003: 35–45) is a recent account of the Mahaffy-Hyde controversy over the syllabus for secondary schools.

For *An Claidheamh Soluis*, see Ní Chollatáin (2004). As well as a description of the main themes that appeared in the weekly, this contains an electronic appendix with long extracts from the publication. Nic Pháidín (1998) is a detailed study of *Fáinne an Lae*, the forerunner of CS.

For the conceptualization of the Gaeltacht, see Ó Torna (2005). This presents and discusses the various native and foreign ingredients that went into the construction of this entity. It also shows how the notion of the Gaeltacht connected with other cultural phenomena, including the visual-arts movement represented by figures like Jack B. Yeats. Hindley (1990) is mainly a study of the Gaeltacht in the twentieth century, but his remarks on why the Gaelic League failed to attract native speakers (Hindley 1990: 179–220) are applicable to the period 1890–1920 as well.

For the Gaelic League and politics, see de Blaghd (1972); Nowlan (1972); and Ó Huallacháin (1994: 56–75). Hutchinson (1987) looks closely at the political dimension of the cultural nationalism of 1870–1920.

For source documents relating to language 1870–1922, see Crowley (2000: 175–222).

8

The modernization of Irish (1870–1922)

8.1 Reshaping the language

The fifty-odd years from 1870 to 1922 witnessed a transformation not just of the status of Irish, but of its written form. One of the achievements of the Revival was the huge increase in the amount of material being published in Irish, and in the variety of subject matter compared to what had been available before. This publishing boom was fed to some extent by the large numbers of learners who were hungry for reading matter. Compared to native speakers of Irish, the people who attended the classes of the Gaelic League were well educated, and had a high level of literacy in English. They associated language-learning with the printed word. Many of them never mastered the intricacies of the spoken dialects, which were not always reflected in the written form of the language, but they did manage to achieve a fair competence in reading and writing.

Printing presented formidable challenges to the Gaelic League and to the growing body of scholars and academics who were studying and teaching Irish. One problem was that traditional Irish orthography was not adapted to the modern spoken dialects. Not surprisingly, then, much time was spent discussing the merits of various ways of representing the sounds of the language in writing, and weighing the pros and cons of spelling reforms.

8.2 Orthography

In Chapter 6, we saw that in the first half of the nineteenth century the traditional way of writing Irish had more or less died out. The few people who still wrote Irish between 1850 and 1870 tended to use an orthography based on English spelling. We noted in section 6.2.1 that in some respects this orthography was better able to reflect the sounds of contemporary Irish than the traditional one, which had evolved in the late Middle Ages and was very much out of date. However, there was the disadvantage that the new orthography was not fixed. Such a state of affairs is not satisfactory if one wishes to communicate on a large scale, and this was certainly what the writers and publicists of the Gaelic League wanted. Recall that they wanted Irish to be a truly national language, not a parochial one. They were writing not just for the local community, but for everybody who supported the cause of reviving Irish, whether they lived in Ireland or outside it.

There were two issues at stake. One was the question of the print itself. A special font had been devised for representing the language in print, the so-called Gaelic font (Figure 8.1). This was based on the way that Gaelic scribes wrote the letters of the Latin alphabet. The Gaelic font had been used for a number of publications in the period 1600-1850. It must be borne in mind, however, that in the period 1700-1850 the Roman font had been used as well. From a practical point of view, the Roman type was cheaper and more familiar to all Irish people, regardless of whether their first language was English or Irish. However, it was felt that the Gaelic font was more truly Irish than the Roman one. As early as 1883, a debate started in the pages of the GJ about which font better represented the real character of the Irish nation. A letter on the subject gives us a taste of the kind of arguments used in favour of the Gaelic font: 'A very pretty poem by a contributor signing himself "Leath Chuinn" follows the article on the Ossianic poems. But why print this poem in English letters? Of course the accents have to be left out, and the words are full of h's, giving them a most uncouth length and appearance' (GJ, February

Alphabet

ᴀ	b	c	ᴅ	e
a	b	c	d	e
ꜰ	ᵹ	h	ı	ʟ
f	g	h	i	l
m	n	o	p	ʀ
m	n	o	p	r
ꞃ	ꞇ	u		
s	t	u		

Lenited consonants

ḃ	ċ	ḋ	ḟ	ṡ
bh	ch	dh	fh	gh
ṁ	ṗ	ṙ	ṫ	
mh	ph	sh	th	

FIGURE 8.1 The Gaelic font

1883: 134; quoted in Ó Conchubhair 2009: 155). Another letter in the GJ stated the case for this typeface even more forcefully:

Those Irishmen who cry out for Irish books in Roman type would not study or read them if they had them; for, if a man will not take the slight trouble of learning the Irish alphabet, it is not likely he will go to the heavier labour of learning the language itself. To attempt to please such persons by abandoning our ancient and beautiful characters would, therefore, be a useless endeavour, and without any tangible results. We have used our own characters for fourteen hundred years, and it is too late now for well-meaning but mistaken friends over the water, or the lazy and unpatriotic or thoughtless fellow-country men at home, to try to persuade us to change our ways, and abandon another portion of our nationality, another link with the noble past of our saints and scholars.

(GJ, January 1883: 103–4)

The debate about the type-font is yet another case where the symbolic function of language overshadowed the communicative purpose. For many people at the time, the question was not whether the font was efficient, but whether it was Irish. Few of the contributions on either side of the debate managed to maintain a tone of sobriety and reason. One exception was Osborn Bergin, the professor of Irish in University College Dublin, who delivered a lecture on Irish spelling in 1910. In it, he pointed out that alphabets are merely conventions, and that the so-called Gaelic alphabet was not really Irish at all:

What is commonly called the Irish alphabet is not of Irish invention. Our ancestors never laid claim to the honour which some of their descendants covet on their behalf. Their own name for the form of writing in Irish manuscripts and in most Irish printed books was *in aibigtir latinda*—'the Latin alphabet'. We have simply been more conservative in Ireland than in the rest of Europe, so that an Irish manuscript of the sixteenth century looks, at a glance, like a continental Latin manuscript of the eighth.

(Bergin 1911: 14)

Bergin goes on to draw attention to the impracticality of teaching school-children to read the old script:

Now the best Irish or Gaelic type is beautiful to look upon, more beautiful than the ordinary modern Roman, just as a good manuscript ranks higher artistically than the printed transcript. But those who ought to know best will confess that the older form of the alphabet is more trying to the eyes. You may not notice this in skimming a page or two, but in hard reading, where close attention is needed, where the meaning of the sentence may depend on the presence or absence of an aspiration mark [superscript dot to represent <h>]...then the inconvenience of the Gaelic lettering is only too evident. Any of you who have had much to do with proof-reading know well the constant worry caused by the confusion between ɼ and ɲ, ç and ʈ, ꝉ and ļ, above all by those terrible dots breaking off or going astray.

(Bergin 1911: 17)

Unfortunately, Bergin's appeal to sanity fell on deaf ears, and for many years after his lecture was delivered, most books continued to be printed in the Gaelic font.

More important than the question of type-font was the actual spelling of Irish. This had never been standardized in the way that the spelling of other languages had. The traditional orthography which had been inherited by the last scribes of the nineteenth century was a corrupt version of the spelling used to represent the language of Early Modern Irish. But even the EMI orthography was not consistent. Bergin adverts to the fact that for a long word like *scéalaigheacht* 'story-telling', there were 1,152 possible spellings in EMI. Another complication was that scribes in the period 1650–1850 often introduced spellings which were historically incorrect, as when they wrote the personal name *Seán* 'John' as *Seághan*, introducing a <gh> which had never been present in the word. Finally, many words were in use in 1900 which did not exist 300 years previously, and for which there were no guidelines as to how they should be spelled.

This situation had been more or less remedied by 1904, when the first comprehensive modern Irish–English dictionary (D) was published, compiled by Patrick Dinneen (Dinneen 1904). Strangely enough, this dictionary largely followed the spelling devised by the much-maligned Robert Atkinson we encountered in section 7.6. In his edition of a text by the seventeenth-century writer Geoffrey Keating, Atkinson (1890) had devised a new way of representing Irish in print. What he did was to standardize the variant spellings for EMI found in the manuscripts, so that the spelling of words like *scéalaigheacht* 'story-telling' was now fixed and there was no longer the same possibility of variation. Dinneen adopted this approach for his dictionary, and because the latter proved so popular, it to some extent provided a spelling standard for the new written form of Irish.

This illustrates one of the ways that standards develop across languages. For some reason, certain texts acquire an authority that leads writers to imitate the spelling and grammar of their authors. For example, Luther's translation of the Bible into German during the Reformation had an enormous influence on subsequent generations of writers of this language. As a result, standard written German contains many traces of the language of Luther's Bible. While Dinneen did not have quite the same authority as the Bible, his standardized spelling did have the support of the Gaelic League and many influential scholars, and this undoubtedly ensured its acceptance by most sections of the Irish-speaking world.

Nevertheless, there were numerous objections to D's system on the grounds that it was outmoded, and the spelling dispute continued long after this dictionary first appeared. One of the most vociferous opponents of the EMI standard was Peadar Ó Laoghaire, who we encountered in Chapter 7. His catch-cry was fidelity to the 'speech of the people':

The same cries are ringing in our ears. 'Avoid provincialisms!' Not I! I am determined to write down most carefully every provincialism I can get hold of. Then I shall be sure to have the *people's* language, at least in that province. 'Spell your Irish according to Keating's standard'. Not I! Even Keating's books never caught any real grip upon the minds of the people. I shall use the Irish alphabet as an instrument for the purpose of representing on paper the exact speech of the people, using my ear for that purpose. 'But your ear can answer only for one province'. Exactly so. But it can answer for that one. Let some other ear answer in the same manner for each of the other provinces, and then we shall know where we are.

(O'Rahilly undated : 139; emphasis original)

In keeping with his principles, Ó Laoghaire devised his own system of spelling. Bergin in his 1910 lecture juxtaposes Ó Laoghaire's versions of certain words with those of EMI:

(1) amú'   for amudha, amugha 'lost'
     anso   for annso   'here'
     ainim   for ainm   'name'
     bia   for biadh   'food'
     bliain   for bliadhain   'year'
     ceárta   for ceardcha   'forge'
     dothal   for doicheall   'inhospitality'

(based on Bergin 1911: 38)

The guiding principle in the above is clear enough, namely to make the spelling approximate as closely as possible to the pronunciation of the author. Thus consonants are not written unless they represent some sound. In the first example the word for 'lost' is spelled *amú'* precisely because it is pronounced /amoo/. Likewise, vowels are inserted into the traditional spellings if necessary: *ainm* 'name' has two syllables, hence the revised form *ainim*. Length marks are employed to represent long vowels (*ceárta* 'forge'). The digraph <ch> is dispensed with if it does not actually represent the final sound in the Scottish pronunciation of *loch* or the German name *Bach*: thus *ceardcha* 'forge' is replaced with *ceárta*, and *doicheall* 'inhospitality' with *dothal*.

The shortcomings of such an approach are obvious enough as well, and Ó Laoghaire acknowledges them in the passage quoted above: where there are differences in pronunciation of the same word, the spelling can only reflect the language of the people of one region. This was anathema to some Gaelic

Leaguers. After all, the whole point of the Revival was to make Irish a language for the whole nation, not just a single region. As early as 1897 a writer in the GJ wrote:

On this point we hope that there is nobody so bogburied as to imagine that the interests of Irish will be best served by everyone writing the *comhradh cailleach* [old wives' tales] that he has known from infancy. A common standard must be aimed at … By no other means is it possible to create a literature that will grasp and draw together the now random elements of an Irish-reading public.

(GJ, June 1897: 26)

The same writer advises readers to follow the spelling found in Atkinson (1890): 'We recommend all who intend to write Irish to get Keating's "Three Shafts of Death" and to follow its correct and consistent spelling of Irish' (GJ, June 1897: 26).

The problem of spelling is a universal one, and is by no means confined to Irish. In 1879 the British Spelling Reform Association had been founded to revise English orthography. This was followed in the early 1900s by the British Simplified Spelling Society, and a number of proposals have been made since then about reforming the system; to date, none of them have been accepted. Indeed, few linguistic subjects provoke such an emotional response among the general populace as attempts to change spelling conventions, which is strange when one considers that most of them have only been fixed in the last 200 years. However, leaving aside the reaction of the person on the street, there is a serious linguistic issue at stake here, namely the tension between the sounds of a language and its grammatical structure. I can illustrate this with a single example from Irish. In this language, adjectives are formed from nouns by the addition of a suffix -**mhar**, pronounced /vor/:

(2) Noun   Adjective
     ceol 'music' ceolmhar 'musical'
     grá 'love'   grámhar 'loving'

In Irish, when the sound /v/ comes into contact with the sound /h/, it undergoes a process called devoicing, whereby /v/ changes to /f/. Thus, when the suffix -**mhar** was added to the word *lúth*, pronounced /looh/, /vor/ became /for/, the whole word being pronounced /loofor/. This meant that there was a discrepancy between the spelling and pronunciation in the case of this item:

(3) Noun   Adjective   Pronunciation
     lúth 'vigour'   lúthmhar 'vigorous'   [loofor]

The digraph <mh> normally stands for /v/ in Irish, so there is no way of knowing that it represents the sound /f/ in the above word. Because of anomalies like this, it was decided to reform the spelling of Irish in the 1940s. The old form *lúthmhar* was duly changed to *lúfar*, which reflects the pronunciation very closely. The problem with the new spelling is that it masks the two components which make up the word: neither the root *lúth* nor the suffix **-mhar** are visible. Part of language learning consists in making connections between one word and another, e.g. between *ceol* 'music' and *ceolmhar* 'musical'. With the pair *lúth–lúfar* the connection is lost, which is one reason why one might want to retain the traditional orthography.

Considerations like these were very much in the air at the time that Bergin and a few like-minded colleagues set up the Society for the Simplification of the Spelling of Irish in 1910. The approach of this society was a common-sense one, and its system would have made the learning of reading and writing in Irish easier, as many of its conventions were closer to English than to traditional Irish spelling. For example, the Society advocated the graph <v> for the sound /v/, where Irish has <mh> and <bh>:

(4) Sound   Traditional spelling   Reformed spelling   Meaning
     /v/   bhean   van   'woman'
     /v/   mhargadh   varaga   'market'

On the other hand, as Ó Conchubhair (2009: 188) points out, the reformers failed to take into account the symbolic importance of Irish having an orthography which was distinct from that of English: the spelling of *bhean* 'woman' as *van* was seen as a deplorable Anglicism. Furthermore, opponents of change felt that it would cut Irish readers off from the body of Irish literature written in the old spelling. Finally, the proponents of the new spelling were all speakers of one dialect, which limited its application to the speech of other regions.

In Bergin (1911), the author deals with each of these issues and rebuts them by means of scholarly arguments. Despite this, and the publication of a small number of texts in the new spelling, by and large the proposals of the Society for the Simplification of the Spelling of Irish met with indifference or downright hostility, and Dinneen's dictionary remained the unofficial orthographical standard until the reforms of the 1940s. At the same time it was recognized that individual authors like Peadar Ó Laoghaire had the right to modify the traditional spelling for the sake of authenticity in representing the language of native speakers. Orthographical standardization for Irish was never as thorough or universal as for English and more widely spoken languages.

Bergin, like many another academic before and since, could not understand that people's view of language tends to be emotional, not rational, and this was even truer of Irish than of other languages. As we shall see in the next section, emotions were to the fore as well in the discussion of another thorny subject, namely the dialects of Irish.

8.3 The dialects and standardization

One of the greatest problems facing the Gaelic League was the fact that Irish was spoken in remote districts separated from each other by large wedges of English-speaking territory. This, and the lack of literacy, meant that instead of a single language as understood nowadays, what one had in 1890 were a number of local dialects, confined to a very small area. Speakers of these dialects were not accustomed to using Irish with strangers, and thus regarded any deviation from what they took to be the norm with suspicion, refusing to make any effort to understand what was being said to them. This situation was complicated further when learners began to visit the Irish-speaking districts in the hope of practising their Irish. By and large, the Irish of the Gaelic Leaguers tended to be bookish, and their pronunciation left a lot to be desired; native speakers generally lacked the patience and flexibility that would have enabled them to speak in such a way that the learners might have understood. This meant that one of the ideological planks of the Revival, namely that the Gaeltacht was to function as a source for the reinstatement of Irish as the national tongue, presented considerable practical challenges to all but the most linguistically talented.

The question of the dialects has become one of the many language-myths surrounding Irish. There is a widespread view that Ireland is unique among the nations of the earth by virtue of Irish having dialects, and that the existence of these dialects is a source of untold difficulty and misery for the language learner. Like all language-myths, there are elements of both truth and wild exaggeration in this belief. First of all, all living languages, no matter how widely or narrowly spoken, have dialects. In many cases, the differences between the dialects are much greater than in the case of Ireland. A hundred years ago, illiterate speakers in northern and southern Italy would have experienced considerable difficulty in communicating with each other. And even in a small country like Ireland, there is a huge variety in the range of dialects of English.

However, what Irish lacked (and still lacks) is a standard language which is accepted and used by the majority of the population in public and formal communication. For standard varieties to spread throughout communities, certain conditions have to be met. Usually, some kind of authority must be capable of imposing its version of language on others. This authority may be connected with a centralized state, which in turn ensures that this version of a language is used in education, the media, publishing, and like domains. In times past other institutions, like the church, played a similar role. As we have seen in previous chapters, institutions of this sort were totally lacking for Irish in the period 1600–1900. Even nowadays, more than a hundred years after the founding of the Gaelic League, when a written standard exists for Irish, the guidelines it recommends are seldom adhered to. The situation was infinitely worse in 1900, when Irish lacked any real government support, and had no presence, official or unofficial, in public life.

Even a language like Scots Gaelic, which was also in a weak position around 1900, was more standardized than Irish. There were two reasons for this. First, the Presbyterian churches in the Gaelic-speaking districts were quite happy to use Gaelic in their services and, more importantly, in teaching the people to read the Bible. As a result, there was a more or less accepted standard for reading and writing, based on the spelling and grammatical structure of the Bible. Furthermore, the number of people who could read and write Gaelic was much higher than in the case of Irish. The presence of a written language helped to bind the spoken dialects together. It also provided speakers with a higher register than that of everyday life, in contrast to Irish, where only the low register survived.

The lack of an accepted standard makes the teaching of a language to non-native speakers very difficult. Language courses tend to be based on standard varieties, which are characterized by uniformity of spelling, grammar, and pronunciation. Even though English is spoken in Ireland, Scotland, and Wales with a different accent than in England, language courses usually do not recommend regional pronunciations. Text-books and courses are based on the English spoken in the south-east of England, what is often called Received Pronunciation. Likewise, the vocabulary of the text-books is spelled in the same way as in the main dictionaries used for English. Later on, a learner will be confronted with regional dialects, and this can be something of a shock, as one realizes that living speech is not the same as the idealized form of language that one has been exposed to in the classroom. Nevertheless, it is felt, probably rightly, that it is better not to emphasize the differences between different kinds of English in the initial stages of language learning.

Returning to Irish, the Gaelic League of the 1890s was faced with a formid-able task. The only written form of Irish, even when the spelling had been standardized, reflected the language as spoken 300 years earlier. As such, it would have been virtually impossible to impose it on native speakers, as it would have obliged them to learn new grammatical forms and new voca-bulary, and to master a complicated orthography. Nevertheless, there were those who advocated precisely this course. In the writings of the period, one can distinguish two objections to the living dialects. One might be described as linguistic/pedagogical, with arguments being advanced similar to the ones I have just mentioned concerning register, intelligibility, and status:

We would advise students of Irish, who are natives of Munster or Ulster, to abandon the latter, and to accustom themselves to the standard sounds just as the English and other nations do not use their respective dialects in society or literature. Not but that the study of dialects is useful in its way, nor that we should desire them to be neglected or despised; but if a language is to have a literature, and to be revived as a general medium of communication, it must adopt one uniform standard. There is as yet too much sectional and provincial feeling among Irish scholars to permit us to hope much from our appeal to their nationality as Irishmen yet, but we think that commonsense in this respect is fast gaining in the minds of the rising generation, and that the necessity of unity and some degree of uniformity is presenting itself to them daily in a clearer light.

(GJ, February 1883: 115–16)

It is not clear what the writer had in mind with 'the standard sounds'. To this day there is no standard pronunciation of Irish, still less so was there one in 1893, when the above passage was written. The comparison with English was not very helpful either, in that the sociolinguistic position of the two languages could not have been more different. Thus, while the writer may have been correct in his diagnosis of the problem, his solution to it was simplistic in the extreme.

The other objection to the dialects might best be described as social or ideological. Ó Conchubhair (2009: 194–6) draws attention to the nineteenth-century view that dialects represented a decline from what was perceived as the perfection of classical languages like Latin. It was generally believed that Latin, with a complicated system of cases for its nouns, and a whole range of endings for its verbs, was superior to a Romance language like French that only had one common case, and which had lost many of the verbal endings of Latin. In the same way, then, EMI was perceived as superior to the dialects which succeeded it: 'The Irish tongue ... has been corrupting and breaking up; many words are rapidly becoming obsolete and being lost; English barbarisms are creeping into it; it is losing some of the cases of its nouns and terminations of its verbs' (*Irishman and United Ireland,* 13 January 1883; quoted in Ó Conchubhair 2009: 196). A further argument was that standardization was a prerequisite for a national language, a language which would be a means of communication between different classes and regions. Standardization had acquired a new importance during the Romantic period. It is no accident that German and Italian were standardized in the nineteenth century when the two

nation states of Germany and Italy were coming into being. For Irish nationalists, a standardized language would be preferable to unwritten dialects,
spoken by small communities: it would give the language a cohesion which
it had lacked until then.

The conservative faction advocated a return to the language of EMI, which
was still the written norm as late as 1650. One writer in particular was singled
out as worthy of imitation: Seathrún Céitinn [Geoffrey Keating]. The reason for
this was that one of the first books to be published during the Revival was a work
I mentioned in the previous section, Keating's *Trí bhior-ghaoithe an bháis* [The
three shafts of death] (Atkinson 1890). As we saw, this work had a profound
effect on the development of Irish orthography, but it also provided a written
standard that had been lacking until then. Keating's name thus acquired a kind
of talismanic charm for advocates of a revival of the EMI style. Time and time
again in the writings of the period 1890–1920 we come across the adjective
'classical' in conjunction with his name and style. We have already encountered
this adjective in section 2.2.3, where it was used with reference to EMI. The
implication of describing a style as classical was that it represented a high point
in the history of a language, one to be imitated by later generations.

For many of the early Revivalists, especially the more scholarly ones, anything that happened after the death of Keating was a kind of decay. Thomas
O'Neill Russell published a provocative article in 1883 in the GJ entitled 'Cá
h-ait a labhairthear an Ghaedhilg is fearr?' [Where is the best Irish spoken?]:

Is follus do gach aon smuaineas air an g-cuis so, agus thuigeas aon nidh timcheall
na Gaedhilge, go bh-fuil an teanga ag dul i m-blodhaibh go luath i m-beulaibh na
n-daoineadh neamhmhuinte le n-a labhairthear an chuid is mo dhi.

[It's clear to everyone who thinks about this matter, and who understands anything
about Irish, that the language is quickly going to pieces in the mouths of the uneducated people by whom it is spoken for the most part.]

(GJ, June 1883: 255)

Russell lamented the failure of contemporary speakers to pronounce silent
letters like the <f> found in the suffix that marked the future tense. The future
of the verb *mol* 'praise' was written as *molfaidh*, which was pronounced as
[molhi] in most of the dialects; in other words, the <f> of the suffix -**faidh** was
pronounced as /h/. Russel objected to this pronunciation on the grounds that
there were still a few districts where an /f/ was to be heard in the future ending;
for him the f-less pronunciation was simply sloppy. He likewise deplored the
fact that the old dative case of EMI was no longer present in Irish. For Russell,
and many others at the time, change was not acceptable; it was a sign of
decadence.

Another proponent of a return to the classical standard was Richard Henebry, who felt that it would be easy to get native speakers to master the style of Keating:

Our native Irish speakers, of whatever province soever, can easily by training correct their vernacular to the normal of the last classic writers, subsidizing insensibly by the way much of the splendid spirit of recent philological study, whereby voice would be given once more to a stored-up wealth of words that have long lain silent. The head-waters are abundant to over-flowing; we have but to make a staunch in the broken conduit, and the flow will go on copious and sparking like long ago.

(GJ, June 1892: 142–3)

In a series of articles published in *The Leader* Henebry gave a full exposé of how he believed Irish should be written, contrasting this ideal with the corrupt speech of his day. The list of his recommendations found in Ó Háinle (1994: 760) contains most of the features by which EMI differs from MI. In other words, he also advocated turning back the clock and regaining the elegance and classical purity which, it was believed, was present in the prose writings of EMI.

Not everybody accepted that there should be a return to the style of Keating and other writers of the early seventeenth century. Peadar Ó Laoghaire was very much against the use of the old spelling. This was part of his general advocacy of the speech of the plain people of Ireland, or rather, the part of Ireland that he came from, west Cork: 'In order to preserve Irish as a *spoken* tongue, we must preserve our *spoken* Irish. That is to say, we must preserve it exactly as the people speak it. That is to say, we must write and print exactly what the people speak' (O'Rahilly undated: 138; emphasis original). This reliance on the native speaker is to be found again and again in his writings: 'The best model for Irish prose composition is to be found…in the mouth of the native Irish speaker' (O'Leary 1902: 12–13; quoted in Ó Háinle 1994: 761). By and large, the younger generation of Gaelic Leaguers supported Ó Laoghaire. In an essay in the CS in 1908, Patrick Pearse attacked the conservatism of Henebry: 'He [Henebry] is animated by a passionate hatred of change of any sort. In other words, he will not allow growth in the language…He takes his stand (quite arbitrarily) at the year 1600 or thereabouts and calls every change that has come into the language since then a "corruption", and "unIrish", and "base"' (CS, 24 November 1908; quoted in Ó Háinle 1994: 763).

Other commentators drew attention to the impracticability of returning to the past:

We should lay ourselves open to fatal criticism if we adopted as our literary medium a non-existent artificial form of Irish, which would fail to interest the mass of the

Irish-speaking population...The power of man could never again popularize in Ireland the diction of Keating and other writers in the seventeenth century.

(GJ, December 1897; quoted in Ó Conchubhair 2009: 211)

The anonymous author of the above passage grasped very well the challenges that literacy posed for native speakers, and the very real danger of discouraging them from learning to read Irish:

It is a commonplace that no language can hope to live now-a-days that has not a contemporary literature. In other words, if people cannot read and write a language, they will willingly abandon it for a language they can read and write. This means that our standard of written Irish, to be effective and to aid in preserving the language, must be within easy reach of the mass of the people who speak it. Our literature, then, must be in close relation with the usage of the people...It will be seen that I plead for a quite modern standard in close accord with popular usage.

(GJ, December 1897; quoted in Ó Conchubhair 2009: 211)

In the end, the language of the people was to win out, and after 1910 very few writers on the subject seriously considered a return to the older written version of Irish. On the whole, this has to be seen as a positive and beneficial step. If it was difficult to convince native speakers of the advantages of learning to read a form of Irish which was familiar to them, it would have been ten times more difficult to persuade them to learn to read a totally unfamiliar version of the language. However, the adoption of the living speech of the people created another problem, namely which dialect was to form the basis for the new form of Irish that the Gaelic League was trying to codify?

8.4 Which dialect?

No sooner had it been more or less generally accepted that the living speech should form the basis for a new kind of Irish, than the debate began about which dialect had the greater claim to precedence over the others. From the very beginning of the Revival, different dialects were being put forward as the most suitable for the learner. At the same time, no region in particular had the prestige to impose its dialect as a standard on the other parts of the country. The situation was aggravated by the prevalent provincialism not only of the native speakers, but also of the learners. In general, learners favoured the region that was closest to them geographically. Belfast Gaelic Leaguers went to Donegal in west Ulster to learn Irish, while inhabitants of southern Ireland (Munster) went to Irish-speaking regions in Cork, Kerry, and Waterford. For people living in Galway, in the western province of Connaught, the choice of Gaeltacht was obvious, as they had Irish speakers on their doorstep, in the region called Connemara. Only in the case of Dublin did learners go to different regions, although there was a tendency for them to favour Connemara, as it was easier for them to get there by train.

A book called *Modern Irish grammar* (Craig 1899) may serve as an example of the kind of problem that arose. The author, J. P. Craig, was a native speaker of Irish from Donegal, and in his book he consistently extols the virtues of his own dialect at the expense of other regions. His enthusiasm for his own version of Irish led him to dismiss as outmoded many grammatical features which were actually attested for other dialects at the time: 'We may now contrast the modern forms of the present tense with those of the classic [EMI]. The parts in brackets are dead to most Irish speakers' (Craig 1899: 74). In fact, many of the verbal endings he claims to be 'dead', like the first-person plural ending -**maoid**, were alive and well, and are still to be heard in some regions where Irish is spoken.

One reason why Craig may have felt obliged to defend Ulster Irish was that there was a certain bias towards Munster Irish (Cork, Waterford, Kerry) among learners. This was probably due to the strong influence of Peadar Ó Laoghaire and Patrick Dinneen, the man whose 1904 dictionary fixed the spelling of Irish; both of them were speakers of Munster dialects. Academics in particular were drawn to the Irish-speaking regions of the south. Osborn Bergin, professor of Irish in University College Dublin, described Ó Laoghaire as 'the greatest living writer of Irish' (Bergin 1911: 38); his judgement was probably influenced more by the author's dialect than by the content of his works. The writing system advocated by the Society for the Simplification of the Spelling of Irish was based on the dialect of Ó Laoghaire, even though it was by no means the strongest variety in terms of numbers. Furthermore, the erroneous belief was widespread that Munster Irish was closer to the classical Irish of Keating than the speech of other regions. This belief has persisted to the present day, as shown by the following extract from one of the websites offering information on Irish: 'Munster is in many ways the most "archaic" dialect, retaining spellings and pronunciations from pre-reform Irish' (Gaeilge website). Opinions like this were first voiced in the period 1880–1914, and their frequency provoked Craig to write that:

It is a noticeable fact, however, that every localism below the Eisgir Border [middle of Ireland] gets classical recognition while those above it are usually ridiculed. 'dá ngoradh fein = warming themselves'. Another example of a Southernism getting classical recognition.

(GJ, November 1897: 122)

Even though the EMI standard had been rejected in favour of the speech of the people, its influence continued to be felt in that people were still trying to prove that certain dialects were closer than others to the older language. In fact, all dialects contain archaisms and innovations, and there is absolutely no linguistic justification for claiming that Munster Irish is older than the dialects of Connaught or Ulster.

The editor of the GJ and a minority of scholars tried to maintain a balanced stance on the superiority or inferiority of the various dialects, but they were outnumbered by the advocates of regional kinds of Irish. This meant that the victory of the speech of the people was both a blessing and a curse. On the positive side, it gave a new status to the living language, breaking with the obsolete literary style. On the negative side, it meant that both learners and native speakers were encouraged to speak and write in dialect, even if this hindered communication. The speakers of local varieties became the ultimate authority regarding pronunciation, grammar, and vocabulary, and students were told to imitate them blindly, no matter what they did. While it was pedagogically sound to urge learners to follow the example of native speakers, it was unwise to limit students to exposure to one dialect only. This became common practice out of fear that learners would mix dialects and produce an inauthentic kind of Irish, thereby violating what was felt to be the special character of the language.

Despite the centralized authority of the Gaelic League, and later of the new Irish state, the independence of the dialects has continued to bedevil Irish to the present day. It is understandable that native speakers should resent having to yield to unfamiliar conventions, but it is less comprehensible that learners should have felt loyalty to what was, after all, something that they had learned rather than heard from the mouth of their mother. But the main culprits were the Irish departments of tertiary-level institutions, who had the means to establish a standard dialect and impose it on their students; in a small country with a handful of universities, this would have been a straightforward task. Instead, individual departments of Irish opted for one particular dialect and insisted on a rigid adherence to its features; other dialects were regarded as a corrupting influence.

The text-books available for learning Irish tended to be based on a more neutral form of the language, and as mentioned earlier, the spelling adopted by Dinneen in his dictionary was that of EMI. There was, then, a considerable discrepancy between the written language which the students were exposed to, and the local dialects they were expected to master by listening to elderly members of the community telling folk-tales. Only the most gifted students can learn dialects, whether in their native language or in a foreign one, if only because they are not codified in written form, and there are no text-books based entirely on regional versions of a language. Not surprisingly, many learners managed to learn the written forms of Irish, but their command of the spoken language was far less satisfactory. To this day, there is no agreed standard pronunciation of Irish, and no modern, unambiguous guidelines are provided for students regarding the relation between sound and speech.

The dialect controversy was only one of many debates at the time concerning how Irish should develop. Another major concern was the existence of external influences which seemed to threaten the language. This is the subject of the next section.

8.5 Perceived threats to Irish

When one reads through the writings of the period in the GJ and CS, one is struck by the recurrence of certain metaphors used in referring to Irish. It is described as 'an ancient tongue', it is 'pure', 'clear', 'vigorous', and 'idiomatic'. However, readers are warned about the danger of it being 'corrupted', 'polluted', and 'enfeebled' by 'barbarisms', and turned into a 'mongrel', 'patois', or 'jargon'. In the mouths of native speakers it is 'healthy' and 'organic', but there is the ever-present risk of it being 'infected' and succumbing to 'decay'.

Watts (2011) explores some of the myths that have informed the discourse about English in the last 200 years. Among those he identifies are two which seem relevant in the present context. One is the myth of the pure language (Watts 2011: 127), the other the myth of contamination through contact. Ó Conchubhair (2009) deals with similar themes in relation to Irish. His main thesis is that anxieties in Ireland during the Revival about the language were part of a more general European concern about the decline of civilization. Perceived threats to the national culture and language led Gaelic Leaguers to formulate a myth of the pure language and a myth of contamination for Irish.

The myth of the pure language was connected to another one, namely the myth of longevity (Watts 2011: 30). Applied to Irish, the gist of these two beliefs was that once upon a time, before the Anglo-Norman invasion, Irish existed in splendid and unsullied isolation from the rest of the world, and was the only language spoken by the Gaels, the original inhabitants of Ireland. This language was still in existence at the end of the nineteenth century, but it was under threat. Those Irishmen who wished to get in touch with their true nature, and commune with their ancestors, could still do so by learning a modern dialect. As so often in this chapter and the previous one, a quotation from Peadar Ó Laoghaire may serve to represent this line of thought:

It is a language which, on account of its almost unchanging character, enables us who use it now to think the thought, and feel the feelings, and live, as it were, in the same time with our forefathers who trod the earth and breathed the air of this country twenty–thirty centuries back. The articulations of its syllables; the sounds of its words; the modes of thought which it expresses, are for us bits of antiquity—young in their usefulness, but really more venerable in their age than round towers or pyramids or hieroglyphics. Just imagine it! While we read over *Fáinne an Lae*, the Irish saints of the Christian period of our country's history, or the heroes of the previous periods, could if they were to re-visit this world, recognize the language with but little difficulty! They would find it the same as what they were accustomed to. The differences which they would find are really no more—sometimes not so much—as living people find now between one province and another. That is a vast, a sublime thought—I should have said a sublime *fact*.

(FL, 5 February 1898; quoted in Ó Conchbuair 2009:
190, emphasis original)

Sublime nonsense would better describe the tenor of the above passage than 'sublime fact'. Contrary to what Ó Laoghaire claims, the gulf separating Medieval Irish from the modern dialects is enormous. I can illustrate this with a single example, with what is called the verbal complex in Old Irish. Unlike MI, the verb in Old Irish had two sets of forms which often differed considerably from each other. Furthermore, other parts of speech could be inserted into the verb. For example, *imm-dích* means '(s)he protects'. Observe now what happens when there is an object with the verb:

(5) Imm-a-n-dích.
     imm-him-NAS-dích
     'He protects him.'

The object pronoun *a* 'him' is inserted into the verb, between the prefix **imm-** and the root **-dích**, and this *a* causes the following consonant to be nasalized (<n> appears before the following <d>). To make matters worse, we get a different result when the same sentence is negated:

(6) Ní-n-imm-dích.
     NEG-NAS-imm-dích
     'He does not protect him.'

The object is now in front of the prefix **imm-**, but *a* 'him' is not visible because the negative marker *ní* 'not' ends in a vowel, which as it were absorbs the *a*. The only indication of the presence of *a* 'him' is the <n> inserted before *imm-dích*.

I do not wish to burden the reader with too much technical detail, but I have probably made my point: the Old Irish verbal system was highly complex. In contradistinction to this, in MI the system resembles much more the one we are familiar with in English and other languages, where verbs, subjects, and objects are discrete elements:

(7) Cosnaíonn   sé   é
     protects   he   him
     'He protects him.'

Apart from the position of the verb at the beginning of the sentence, the structure in (7) is very similar to that of English: the subject and object are separate words, rather than being incorporated into the verb as in Old Irish. Note also that we have a different lexical item for the verb to protect: *cosain* (MI) versus *imm-dích* (Old Irish). There is arguably more continuity between Latin and Modern French than between Old Irish and MI.

I have only dealt with two examples of the differences between Irish as spoken in the year 900 compared to the year 1900, connected with grammatical forms and vocabulary. If one adds to that the huge differences in pronunciation and word order, the absurdity of Ó Laoghaire's claims about the continuity between the old and contemporary languages becomes patent. But linguistic facts played little part in the debates about purity at the time. What mattered most to the participants was that they should establish a pedigree for Irish that stretched back into the mists of time, thus making it a suitable national language for present, past, and future generations.

The main perceived threat to the purity of Irish was contamination by English. Once again, this reflects a common view at the time that degeneracy in language is symptomatic of a lack of moral fibre in its speakers. As Watts remarks: 'Hence, any corruption of the language through language contact situations entails that the speakers have been corrupted' (Watts 2011: 127). In the writings of the Gaelic Leaguers, we come across the term 'barbarism' to refer to English influence. Ó Conchubhair (2009) observes that there was a dislike in the language movement of any kind of imitation of English, even of the most subtle kind, as this quotation from another article by Peadar Ó Laoghaire shows:

To write Irish, using English literary usages, is to produce written matter in which there is neither life nor strength nor sweetness. It is Irish in form. The syntax is correct. No person can find fault with the grammar. But, when a person has read one or two sentences he turns away to something else. The stuff is mawkish, tasteless, unreadable...The living Irish speech which, thank God, we still possess, is a real, good, sound, true acorn. It has within itself, in full perfection, the elements and the forces which are capable of producing a mighty oak. An attempt to infuse foreign elements into it will only have the effect of destroying it.

(O'Rahilly undated: 137–8; quoted in Ó Conchubhair 2009: 87)

There were two sources of Anglicization in Irish. One was the existence of large numbers of borrowings, assimilated and unassimilated, in the spoken Irish of the Gaeltacht. The other pertained to the influence of English on grammar and syntax.

8.6 Borrowings

Loan-words in a language often offend the ears of learners. Native speakers tend to be unaware of the provenance of a particular word, and not to care whether it is a borrowing or not. On the other hand, learners are slightly put out when they discover an item from their own language comfortably ensconced in the vocabulary of another tongue; they feel that they have been duped, that there must be another more authentic way of expressing the idea than through a borrowing. This sensitivity to a foreign presence was heightened in the case of the Gaelic League because of the history of Irish and English. Time and time again we come across articles and letters expressing the dismay of Leaguers at the level of borrowed vocabulary in the speech of the Gaeltacht:

Is adhbhal mhór an oiread sin focal Sacs-bheurla sgéithid amach na daoine, go mór-mhór i gConnachta, agus is measa ná sin, ní féidir a d-teagasg gur Beurla iad . . . Ann-so dhuit focla éigin do chualas féin—Bit (of a bridle), *spoka, nave, doubt* or '*doot*', *makreil*, *pota, liosta* (list), *stuff* (etc.). Agus ní fhuil acu focal, Gaedhilge no Beurla, ar son *felloe, tyre*, etc. Do badh ceart do'n mhuintir sgriobhas gan focal truaillighthe do chur síos, acht amháin na focla fíor-Ghaedhilge do chur, lé n-a n-aith-bheodhadh.

[The amount of Anglo-Saxon words which the people spew forth is great, especially in Connaught, and worse than that, it is impossible to teach them that they are English . . . Here are some words which I heard myself—Bit (of a bridle), *spoka, nave, doubt* or '*doot*', *makreil, pota, liosta* (list), *stuff* (etc.). And they have no word, Irish or English, for *felloe, tyre*, etc. Those who write ought not to put down corrupted words, but only use real Irish words, in order to revive them.]

(GJ, March 1893, 186–7; quoted in Ó Conchubhair 2009: 98)

As we saw in Chapter 6, such borrowings were extremely common from the beginning of the nineteenth century onwards, but it was only with the Revival and the pressure to clean up the language that they became a serious issue. The writer of the following letter to the FL regarded all borrowings, no matter how old they were, as a sign of a lack of patriotism:

But there are many real grievances which you as an editor of all the compositions sent in for publication in FL should try to prevent if we want to preserve our ancient tongue from becoming a mongrel jargon. I allude to the nonsensical copying of English words which some writers by disguising the original in the Irish character, would have us believe are real Irish words. The objectionable words are: *náisiún* = nation, *séipéal* = chapel, *parróiste* = parish, *Lunndain* = London, *prógar* = poker, etc., etc. Surely no real Irishman with any love for his pure native Irish would allow such trash to be published.

(FL, 27 August 1898; quoted in Ó Conchubhair 2009: 100)

The small number of native speakers who became League activists were divided on the subject of Anglicisms. One of them, Tomás Bán Ó Concheanainn, reacted strongly against what he perceived as the corruption of his native dialect of Aran by borrowings:

Níl mé in Árainn ach trí lá ach chuala mé mórán Béarlachais ar feadh na haimsire sin. Chuala mé na ráite seo. 'Níl aon *chance* aige'. 'Tá sé *all right*'. Tá sé *sure*áilte de.' 'Tá sé an-*smart*áilte'. 'Tá sí *upset*áilte'. 'Cén chaoi a bhfuil tú, a *Visther* O'Callaghan?'

[I'm only three days in Aran but I have heard a lot of Anglicisms during that period. I heard the following expressions. 'He has no *chance*'. 'He is *alright*'. 'He is *sure* of it'. 'He is very *smart*'. 'She is *upset*'. 'How are you, *Mister* O'Callaghan'?]

(FL, 27 December 1898; quoted in Ó Conchubhair 2009: 99)

One of the most prolific writers among the native speakers, Peadar Ó Laoghaire, was highly critical of English influences but, surprisingly, he took a more nuanced approach to borrowings than did Ó Concheanainn. In the following dialogue, Ó Laoghaire's imaginary folk-linguists, Tadhg and Doncha, who we already encountered in section 7.6, discuss the subject of borrowings from English. At the beginning Doncha, the less sophisticated member of the pair, is disturbed by what he regards as 'bad Irish':

Doncha: Dhe mhuise, a Thaidhg, tá drabhaíol cainte ná beadh aon mhath d'aenne bheith dhá cur síos. Cad é an saghas Gaelge bheidh agut má chuirean tú síos *manage*-áil, agus *leech*áil, agus *grumble*áil, agus a léithéidí!

[Oh my goodness, Tadhg, there's a kind of trashy talk that would not be worth recording. What kind of Irish will you have if you were to record *manage*áil, and *leech*áil, and *grumble*áil, and the like!]

(O'Rahilly undated: 136)

Tadhg, with his customary *savoir-vivre*, assures his friend that such usages are permitted if one wishes to capture the full flavour of certain registers:

Tadhg: Ní cheapfainn uaim féin a leithéidí sin. Ach má bhím ag innsint sgéil duine eile, agus go ndéanfaig an duine sin úsáid de na foclaibh sin, ní fuláir dómhsa iad do chur síos 'na chaint don duine sin nó bréag do chur air. An airíon tú leat mé, a Dhoncha? Níor mhair aon teanga riamh fós gan an uile shaghas cainte inti, uasal agus íseal, garbh agus cneasta, sleamhain agus anacair.

[I wouldn't say that kind of thing myself. But if I'm telling a story about somebody else, and that person uses those words, I have to put them into the speech of that person or else misrepresent him. Do you get my drift, Doncha? No language ever existed without having every kind of speech, high and low, harsh and mild, smooth and rugged.]

(O'Rahilly undated: 136)

However, as Ó Conchubhair (2009) points out, the author of the above words was virtually alone among the Revivalists in his relaxed attitude to borrowings—most Leaguers were very much against them.

Ó Laoghaire may have been prepared to put up with borrowings, but he was far from tolerant when it came to grammar. I now turn to this issue.

8.7 'Irish forms of thought are not the same as those of other nations'

The second source of contamination from English, and one which was far less easy to identify and eradicate than vocabulary borrowing, was related to grammar and syntax (word order). In modern studies of language learning, it has become customary to talk of interlanguage, which shares characteristics of both the learners' native language and the target language they are trying to learn, but also has features of its own which are not found in either of the two other languages. A typical feature of interlanguage is transferral from the native language of a certain feature not found in the target language, or the over-generalization of a feature. Thus learners of Irish usually bring with them the intonation patterns of English, or they may generalize the use of one of the verbs to be, tá, failing to use the other verb is, or under-using it. They may also produce forms which are alien to Irish, but are not directly ascribable to English either. Ó Curnáin (2012) gives an example from present-day Irish of a change produced by contact with English:

(8)   Traditional Irish   Interlanguage
      mo cheann-sa   ceann mi-se
      my one-EMP PRT   one me-EMP PRT
      'MY one'   'MY one'
                (based on Ó Curnáin 2012: 310)

Speakers of the interlanguage produce the new *ceann mise*, which is not equivalent to Irish *mo cheann-sa* (with *mo…sa* corresponding to English *MY*). Nor is it equivalent to English *MY one*, with the possessive *MY* heavily stressed in speech.

   It is reasonable to assume that the learners who began to speak Irish in the period 1890–1914 must have spoken an interlanguage, and that the grammar of this interlanguage must have been heavily influenced by their native English. Not surprisingly, this led to a sudden and radical change in the kind of Irish being spoken, and also in the kind of Irish that was being written, as the vast majority of writers were learners. Not only that, but many of the new text-books, grammars, and dictionaries were produced by learners. Predictably enough, this more subtle kind of contamination by English did not escape the beady eye of Peadar Ó Laoghaire. He was particularly exercised by syntax: 'If the syntax be good, we have good Irish, even if half the words were foreign. If the syntax be bad, the language is not Irish at all, even though each separate word may be the purest Irish' (O'Rahilly undated: 85). At times Ó Laoghaire could be slightly obsessive on the subject of syntax, but the point he was making was important: it is not enough to use Irish words in writing or speaking, one must also be aware of the underlying structures of the language.

One error in particular provoked Ó Laoghaire's ire. The mistake in question was caused by the existence of two verbs *to be*, *is* and *tá*, which resembles the *ser-estar* distinction of Spanish. The technical name for *is* is the copula. The use of the copula is one of the greatest difficulties facing a learner of Irish, and it is only fair to say that few students ever fully master it. For Ó Laoghaire, the copula was at the very heart of the Irish language:

In the Irish mind the verb *is* is the expression of the mental act which introduces some piece of information and asserts the truth of it. That is the very essence of *is*. It is impossible for *is*, from its very nature and essence, to do anything else but express the mental act which introduces the information given and asserts the truth of that information. This is not a grammatical rule. It is an essential truth. To make any other use of *is* is not to violate Irish grammar. It is to violate the essence of the Irish language.

(O'Rahilly undated: 68)

Ó Laoghaire firmly believed that the reason that the verb *to be* was so different in Irish and English was that what he called 'the Irish mind' was different from that of other nations. Later on in the same essay on the copula he writes:

These fundamental principles of Irish thought were built and shaped long centuries before the principles which have fashioned English thought and speech were dreamt of...Some people seem to imagine that thought is essentially the same in the minds of all human beings, and that difference of language is only a mere accidental difference in the mode of expressing the thought. That is a most egregious mistake. There are extensive fields of thought, constantly formed in the Irish mind, and as constantly expressed in Irish speech, which cannot be formed at all in English minds, nor, as a consequence, expressed in English speech. The English mind is not only ignorant of those fields of thought, but utterly incapable of reaching them.

(O'Rahilly undated: 71)

This notion of the uniqueness of Irish was one that was widely held at the time:

The exclusively English speaker has no idea of the nice distinctions drawn by the Irish mind...It is enough to say that the language is full of evidences that Irish forms of thought are not the same as those of other nations, and perhaps differ from English forms more than from any other. They are clearer, more delicate, more subtle in distinction, more exact in definition, and thoroughly individual in expression.

(FL, 12 March 1898; quoted in Ó Conchubhair 2009: 123)

An anonymous contributor to the GJ saw 'an Irish mode of thought' as the key to attaining 'Irish idiomatic purity':

Verbal purism has perhaps been overdone by some Irish scholars. Idiomatic purism has been largely neglected. A foreign idiom is always a solecism and a blot. To attain to Irish idiomatic purity, it is necessary to cultivate an Irish mode of thought. As Father O'Leary justly says in last month's *Gaelic Journal*, 'it is *never* safe to translate from English into Irish, following the English mode of thought'.

(GJ, June 1895: 48; emphasis original)

Abstracting away from the claims about the Irish mind and the English mind being essentially different, there is an important methodological point at stake here. Teachers of foreign languages are constantly faced with the problem of on the one hand encouraging their pupils to speak without constraint, and at the same time guiding them into native modes of expression. When there are large numbers of native speakers of a language, they will act as a corrective to the mistakes of the learners. However, in the case of Irish it was very much a case of the blind leading the blind. Apart from a few stalwarts like Peadar Ó Laoghaire, there were no native speakers with the linguistic education necessary to correct the learners, who were largely left to their own devices. Douglas Hyde may have been concerned about idiomatic purity, but there were times when his own grasp of idiom left a lot to be desired. Contamination from English in the area of grammar and syntax has continued unabated since the Revival began, being an inevitable consequence of the philosophy of the Gaelic League. The only way of ensuring that Irish retained its purity of idiom was to prevent learners from speaking it, rather than encouraging them to do so. But this in turn would have meant abandoning the whole Revival project.

8.8 The codification of Irish

In the previous sections various schemes and ideas concerning the shape that Irish was to take have been outlined and discussed. In many instances, I have been rather harsh in my criticism of the approaches taken, and particularly of the non-linguistic ideologies underpinning much of the argumentation. However, these shortcomings should not blind present-day readers to the real achievements made in the period 1880–1920 with respect to the codification of Irish as a modern, written language.

The Revivalists encountered a language without any fixed orthography or grammar, spoken in remote parts of the country, with the individual dialects widely separated from each other by long distances. Because of the sociolinguistic situation, Irish was totally excluded from formal domains like education, publishing, and administration. To bring such a language into the modern world was a mammoth task in any circumstances.

Within forty years, a system of spelling had been more or less established, which was to be retained until the orthographical reforms of the 1940s. In 1880, there were two kinds of Irish—the spoken language of the people, and the written language based on seventeenth-century authors like Keating. After 1900, there was a consensus that the language of the people should form the basis of the variety to be used in the Revival. The biggest drawback was that no dialect in particular was given precedence. This was certainly more democratic than the situation obtaining in more centralized societies at the time, but it meant that neither the grammar nor the pronunciation could be completely standardized. Nevertheless, there was a core of common elements to be found cross-dialectically; if learners mastered one regional variety, and were prepared to make an effort, there was nothing to prevent them from acquiring a passive understanding of the others.

8.9 Vocabulary

Perhaps the area in which the Gaelic League made most progress was in the domain of vocabulary. In many respects, the words used by a typical native speaker in 1880 were not significantly different from those used 100 or even 200 years earlier. The scientific and cultural developments of the preceding centuries which had transformed the word-stock of English and other mainstream European languages had left Irish virtually untouched.

New words enter a language as need arises, and through various channels. We already noted the large number of borrowings, assimilated and unassimilated, in nineteenth-century Irish (see section 6.2.3). Another way of creating new vocabulary items is to use the existing resources of the language, in a process called word-formation. In eighteenth-century Britain, the need frequently arose to denote the female equivalent of a male person or animal, as in *lion*: *lioness*. As a result, the feminizing suffix -**ess** is attested in a relatively high number of words for this period (Tieken-Boon van Ostade 2006: 266). English also borrowed words freely from other languages. This, combined with word-formation, ensured that its vocabulary was enriched considerably in the period 1700–1900, and there were few subjects which one could not discuss in this language for lack of suitable words.

Up to 1700, word-formation had been extensively used in Irish. In fact, if we take the Irish equivalent of English -**ess**, the feminizing prefix **ban-/bain-/ben-**, we find that it is extremely productive in the period 800–1600; DIL has three whole pages of words formed in this way. The prefix was still being widely used in the seventeenth century to create new words. The following derivatives are attested for the first time in the period 1600–1700:

(9) Base   Derivative
     cliamhuin 'son-in-law'   ban-chliamhuin 'daughter-in-law'
     seomradóir 'chamberlain'   bain-tseomradóir 'female chamberlain'
     maighistir 'master'   ban-mhaighistir 'mistress'
     prócadóir 'procurator'   ban-phrócadóir 'female procurator'
     cléireach 'clerk'   bain-chléireach 'female clerk'
     pátrún 'patron saint'   ban-phátrún 'female patron saint'

The sources for the above examples are translations. Translating is a common motivation for word-formation: the translator comes across a term or expression not found in the native language, and is forced to find an equivalent for it, using the resources available to him.

After 1700, as we have seen, there was much less writing in Irish in the learned register than before, and those who wrote in this register were more concerned with preserving traditional lore than in breaking new ground. Hence there was little need for new vocabulary. The prefix **ban-/bain-/ben-** seems to have become obsolete, being found in existing vocabulary, but not being used to make new words. Thus the two texts I examined in section 6.2.1 with respect to their vocabulary, PF and HM, contain not a single example of a new formation with the prefix. However, PF exploits an alternative way of feminizing a masculine noun. The method in question is to take the genitive of *bean* 'woman', *mná* 'of woman', and use it as an adjective:

(10) fíodóir 'weaver'   fíodóir mná
                          weaver of.woman
                          'female weaver'

This is the method of forming feminizing nouns that survived into twentieth-century dialects. According to de Bhaldraithe (1953: 4) **ban-/bain-/ben-** is no longer a living prefix. The present-day feminization of the word *doctor* is *dochtúir mná*, literally 'doctor of woman', i.e. 'female doctor', which is exactly the innovative pattern we find in PF. De Bhaldraithe offers no recently coined examples with **ban-/bain-/ben-**.

Due to developments like that exemplified with the feminizing prefix, the resources of word-formation were considerably impoverished by the time the Gaelic League set about modernizing Irish. At the same time, there was a pressing need to provide all kinds of new vocabulary for the urban environment in which many Irish learners lived. Traditional Irish had a rich vocabulary for describing the primitive way of life on the west coast, as well as many pithy folk-proverbs. But these were of little use in the city, or in trying to draft legislation, or in teaching tertiary-level students.

Other languages had drawn on Latin and Greek when faced with new concepts and inventions. English *telephone* and *microscope* were formed by taking roots (**tele-**, **-phone**, **micro-**, **-scope**) from Greek and combining them to make new words. The same technique has been exploited by many other European and non-European languages. This kind of word-formation become popular in Europe during the Renaissance, but was never adopted in Ireland. For this reason, Irish vocabulary often seems very unfamiliar to learners.

8.9.1 Expanding the vocabulary

The writers of GJ and CS were aware of the need to modernize the language, and from the 1890s collections of new terms began to appear in these journals. In 1907 the Gaelic League set up a terminological committee to try to introduce some kind of consensus into the process of expanding the vocabulary of Irish. As things stood, there were at least four ways of providing new terms for Irish:

8.9.1.1 Borrowing

As we saw earlier, there was a strong reluctance to borrow words from English. However, the process could be made more palatable if the word was nativized. An example of this is the word *eleictreach* 'electrical', found in a dictionary published in the early 1900s (O'Neill Lane 1904). The native ending **-each**, typical of adjectives, has been added to the English source *electric* to make the word look Irish.

Here are some other items borrowed from English at this time:

(11) English   Irish
        cigarette   siogairéad
        mechanics   mecanuigheacht
        drama   dráma
        literature   litridheacht

Unlike the authors of the period 1800–70, the Gaelic League writers were careful to provide Irish spelling and also, if necessary, an Irish suffix for the borrowing, to the extent that it is at times difficult to recognize a word in its new guise. Nevertheless, it was still felt by many that borrowing of any kind was to be frowned on. This led them to resort to a different kind of loan-word, one referred to in the literature as calquing.

8.9.1.2 Calquing

This consists of replicating the internal structure of an item in the source language into the borrowing language. We can see an example of this in the passage below:

(12) Teanga na nGaedheal is eadh an Ghaedhilg dar linne, agus is mithid dúinn a admháil gur mó go mór...í ná aon chúigeachas ná aon pharóisteachas dá fheabhus.

[Irish is the language of [all] Irish people in our opinion, and we must admit that it is greater...than any provincialism or parochialism however excellent it may be.]

(FL, 16 July 1898; quoted in Nic Pháidín 1998: 106)

I focus on the word *cúigeachas* 'provincialism' from the above excerpt. The writer who introduced this term into Irish first broke English *provincialism* up into its constituent parts:

(13) Root   Suffix 1   Suffix 2
     province -ial   -ism

He then took Irish *cúige* 'province', and applied the same process to it, adding suffixes in two stages:

(14) Root   Suffix 1   Suffix 2
     cúigea   -ach   -as

The result, *cúigeachas*, is a piece-by-piece equivalent of English *provincialism*.

The following were coined around this time by means of various suffixes, as the result of the need to provide equivalents for English words:

(15) Base   Suffix   New word
     Conradh   -theoir Conraitheoir
     '[Gaelic] League'   '(Gaelic) Leaguer'
     cuntas   -óir   cuntasóir
     'account'   'accountant'
     riaghail   -tas   riaghaltas
     'to govern'   'government'
     aer   -aigh   aeraigh
     'air'   'to dry (food for preservation)'

Prefixes were likewise called into service to translate common English prefixes like **un-, re-, co-, semi-, trans-**:

(16) | Base | Prefix | New word |
|---|---|---|
| cumasach | neamh- | neamhchumasach |
| 'able' | | 'unable' |
| taithigheach | neamh | neamhthaithigheach |
| 'accustomed' | | 'unaccustomed' |
| siolla | trí- | trí-shiolla |
| 'syllable' | | 'tri-syllable' |
| cuir | ath- | athchuir |
| 'plant' | | 'transplant' |
| stad | leath- | leathstad |
| 'stop' | | 'semicolon' |
| léigh | aith- | aithléigh |
| 'read' | | 'revise' |
| éifeachtach | coimh- | coimh-éifeachtach |
| 'efficient' | | 'co-efficient' (in maths) |

Calquing can involve word-internal elements, as in the above examples, or it can operate with multi-word idioms. Learners of a language are particularly prone to this kind of calquing, mainly because it is less obvious than when a new word is actually brought into being, and so takes place subconsciously. Nic Pháidín (1998) points out an example of an idiom being translated word for word:

(17) eastát   Mucrois   ag dul   fá'n   gcasúr
      estate   of.Muckross   going   under.the   hammer
      'Muckross estate was auctioned'

   (FL, 19 May 1900; quoted in Nic Pháidín 1998: 103)

To an English speaker, there is nothing strange about this idiom, but supposing that a monoglot Irish speaker had encountered this expression at the end of the nineteenth century, they would have been perplexed as to what it meant. In Irish, 'going under the hammer' meant literally 'walking under a hammer', until learners started reshaping the language.

8.9.1.3 Extending the meaning of a word

In English, some words acquired a range of meanings with time, in addition to their original semantics. In Irish, however, the same words had a more limited range. Thus, English *company* originally had the meaning of 'a social gathering, companionship'. This more or less corresponds to Irish *cuideachta*. Later, the English word acquired the new meaning of 'a commercial firm'. In 1898, in a piece in the FL the meaning of Irish *cuideachta* was extended to encompass the modern concept of 'firm'. In the following passage, the writer is referring to a newly formed tram company:

(18)   Soláthróidh an chuideachta chéadna an solas electreach ar na sráidibh i n-ionad an ghalsholais comh luath is beidh gach nídh réidh aca.

[The same company will provide the electric light on the streets in place of the gaslight as soon as they have everything ready.]

(FL, 31 December 1898; quoted in Nic Pháidín 1998: 107)

Here are some more examples of meaning extensions:

(19) Word   Old meaning   New meaning
     cumhacht   'power, force'   '(electric) energy'
     rúnaidhe   'confidant'   'secretary'
     cléireach   'cleric, scribe'   'clerk'
     stáitse   'platform'   'stage (of theatre)'
     foilsigh   'show, reveal'   'publish'
     coiste   'jury, gathering'   'committee'
     buidhean   'band, troop'   'battalion'

8.9.1.4 Substituting a descriptive phrase for a single word

This is a device often resorted to by speakers when confronted with a word in a foreign language for which they can find no equivalent in their own—they simply describe what is involved. Thus one writer, trying to convey the notion of *(electric) tram*, used a descriptive phrase consisting of a noun followed by a qualifier:

(20) Noun   Qualifier   New word
     trucail tintreach   trucail tintreach
     truck   of.lightning   '(electric) tram'

These descriptive phrases are common in the writings of the period:

(21) English   Irish
     railroad   bóthar iarainn
                          road of.iron
     strike (of workers) obadh saothair
                          refusing of.work
     homespun (clothes)   éadach tíre
                          clothes of.country
     sedan (chair)   cathaoir iompair
                          chair of.carrying

All four methods of creating new words were harnessed by the writers of the time in order to extend the vocabulary of Irish, and many of the words coined have stayed in the language ever since.

8.9.2 The older language as a source of vocabulary

Even with these four ways of expanding the lexicon at their disposal, the writers of the Gaelic League still found themselves limited in their means of expression. Furthermore, the last device mentioned, namely the use of descriptive phrases, while much favoured by native speakers in conversation, did not lend itself to journalism or more scientific discourse. If there was a precise term in English, writers wanted a precise term in Irish. If English had a single word for something, it was felt that Irish should have just such a word as well. This led to two further developments in the realm of vocabulary expansion.

8.9.2.1 Reviving obsolete words, sometimes giving them a new meaning

If we compare the lexicon of the medieval period with that of the nineteenth century before 1870, we get the impression that the range of Irish vocabulary had contracted markedly by the latter era. The writers of the Revival drew on earlier stages in the history of Irish, from Old Irish to Late Modern Irish, in search of words which were suitable for modern concepts. Below I give some examples with the old meaning on the left, and the proposed new meaning on the right:

(22) Earlier language

Earlier language	New usage
ailtire 'builder'	'architect'
dáil 'assembly'	dáil Éireann 'parliament of Ireland'
feis 'feast, entertainment'	'cultural festival'
foirgneamh 'building'	'building'
marc 'horse, mare'	'pony'
teachta 'messenger'	teachta dála 'deputy, member of parliament'
toghairm 'invoking, calling'	toghairm 'appeal'

8.9.2.2 Reviving obsolete kinds of word-formation

Like vocabulary itself, word-formation is not constant in a language over time. Just as words come and go, so do ways of forming new words. If we look at the history of Irish, we can observe a striking change with respect to the process called compounding. This entails putting two or more words together to form a single new word. Until the end of EMI, this was very common in Irish. Here are some examples from the period 1200–1600:

(23) Word1   Word2   Compound
      long   rámh   long-rámh
      'ship'   'oar'   'ship's oar'
      brághaid geal   brághaid-gheal
      'throat' 'white' 'white-throated'
      fíon   caor   fíon-chaor
      'wine'   'berry' 'grape'

After 1700 compounding disappeared from the living language, being retained only in poetry, in such expressions as *barra-chas* 'curly-haired', formed from *barra* 'head' and *cas* 'curly'. Like the prefix **ban-**, while some compounds are to be found in twentieth-century Irish, it has been observed that 'this is not a productive mechanism' (de Bhaldraithe 1953: 254). Instead, where English has compounds, Irish employs a phrase consisting of a noun + qualifier: de Bhaldraithe cites the example of *bean tí*, literally 'woman of house', i.e. 'housewife'.However, because of the influence of English, and because of the unwieldiness of phrases as opposed to single words, compounding was reintroduced into Irish as a means of word-formation. The writers of the Revival were often more at home in EMI than in the spoken dialects, and thus would have been widely exposed to compounds. To what extent they were conscious that this mechanism had long been dead is not clear. While they tended to be ultra-sensitive to the presence of non-native words, they were less nuanced when it came to non-native patterns of word-formation. At any rate, judging by the number of new compounds from the period 1890–1920, compounding was very popular. In the examples below, the motivation for the compound is fairly obvious:

(24) Word 1   Word 2   Compound
      dún   seomra   dúin-seomra
      'fort'   'room'   'strong-room'
      gal   solas   gal-sholas
      'gas'   'light'   'gaslight'
      féin   riaghail Féin-riaghail
      'self'   'rule'   'Home Rule'
      cois   liathróid cois-liathróid
      'foot'   'ball'   'football'

Compounding was even resorted to when the word in English was not a compound, as in the following examples:

(25) | Word 1 | Word 2 | Compound |
| --- | --- | --- |
| ard | scoil | ard-scoil |
| 'high' | 'school' | 'university' |
| Gall | oideachas | Gall-oideachas |
| 'English (pejorative)' | 'education' | 'English education' |
| cruinne | tómhas | cruinne-thómhas |
| 'world, earth' | 'measure' | 'geometry' |
| clár | dealbh | clár-dhealbh |
| 'flat surface' | 'figure' | 'plane figure' (math) |
| gluais | míniughadh | gluais-mhíniughadh |
| 'gloss' (explanatory note) | 'explanation' | 'glossing' (explaining) |
| iris | leabhar | iris-leabhar |
| 'record' | 'book' | 'journal, magazine' |

The revival of old words with new meanings, and the renewed use of compounding, led to the forging of a link between earlier stages of the language and the contemporary version of Irish. The language was being used once more to express more abstract and sophisticated concepts than those found in everyday peasant life.

8.9.3 The reception of the new words

In any language, the fate of a new word is never certain. Of the thousands of new words which appear in English every year, some became part of everyday discourse. Others become part of various kinds of specialized jargons, like those used in science, or linguistics. Still others sink without a trace.

It has to be borne in mind that there was no centralized state department responsible for the coining of new terms in Irish at the time of which that I am writing. Not surprisingly, there was a certain amount of duplication among authors with respect to new terms. As a result, the English word *telephone* was rendered in no fewer than three ways:

1. Borrowing—telefón
2. Word-formation

(26) | Root | Suffix | New word |
| --- | --- | --- |
| guth | -án | guthán |
| 'voice' | | 'telephone' |

-**án** was originally a dimunitivizing suffix, used to express the idea of a smaller version of the original word. It had become obsolete, but was revived in this period, sometimes functioning as an ending for names of machines or appliances, which seems to be the case also with *guthán* above.

3. Descriptive phrase

(27) Noun   Qualifier   New word
      feadán   cainte   feadán cainte
      pipe   of.talk   'telephone'

In the end, the first two words for *telephone* became accepted and have remained in common use until the present day. Their acceptance was undoubtedly facilitated by the fact that after 1922 the state became responsible for the coining and dissemination of new words, which provided an official stamp of approval hitherto lacking.

However, as I have stressed several times in this chapter and the previous one, there was a yawning chasm between the new written Irish of learners and the traditional Irish of native speakers. Not surprisingly, there was a great reluctance on the part of the latter to accept the new terms. There were two reasons for this resistance. One might be described as sociolinguistic. For the most part, native speakers did not participate in the reshaping of the written language. Learners who tried to use the new words were met with suspicion and incomprehension. This can be illustrated with the new word for *bicycle*, *rothar*. The manner in which this word came into being is obscure. The first part *roth* means 'wheel', but the apparent suffix -**ar** is not attested after the Old Irish period. However, as an Irish word, there is nothing objectionable about the structure of *rothar*, in that there are many other native words of similar shape: *othar* 'sick person', *fothar* 'steep cliff'. Lots of everyday English words in English originate as trade-names, but as long as they sound English, speakers will adopt them without thinking twice. In principle, there was no reason why native speakers of Irish could not have accepted *rothar* in the same spirit.

The problem was that if they had actually encountered a real bicycle, and asked what it was called, they would have been told that it was called *bicycle*. There would not have been a friendly Gaelic Leaguer on hand to tell them that it should be called *rothar*, and native speakers were not given to reading the GJ or the CS. Not surprisingly, then, they simply borrowed the word as *bicycle*, plural *bicycles*.

Another difficulty concerned the pronunciation of revived words. Some of these, like *dáil* 'parliament', already existed in LMI, but with a completely different meaning. These presented no problems of pronunciation to the native speaker or the learner. Others were not so easily integrated into the contemporary language. The writers who advocated the use of words from Medieval Irish seemed to forget that the orthographic system and pronunciation had changed considerably since the words were first used. Consider the word *toghairm*, which was proposed as a modern translation for *court appeal*. In Old Irish, it would have been pronounced as it was written, with the digraph <gh> representing a voiced version of /ch/. In LMI, <gh> was lost between vowels, and the preceding vowel altered, so that words like *rogha* 'choice' came to be pronounced as /rou/ or /roe/. This means that a literate speaker of Irish would have pronounced the first part of *toghairm*, *togha*, as [tou] or [toe]. Furthermore, an extra vowel developed in speech between the <r> and <m> at the end of words like *gairm*. So somebody who was literate in LMI would probably have pronounced *toghairm* as [tourim], which would have made it sound as if related to the word *togha* 'choice', whereas it is a different word entirely. One way or another, the written form would have presented tremendous difficulties, simply because it came from Medieval Irish, which was a different language from LMI. In the same way, if we were to write English *home* using the Old English spelling *hām*, most readers would be at a loss as to the meaning and pronunciation, even though the two words have the same source.

Even borrowings could bring pronunciation troubles with them. Consider the word *electreach*, which was proposed as an Irish adaptation of English *electric*. Even though the spelling and the ending **-ach** make the word look Irish on paper, it does not sound Irish. This is because of a constraint which prevents certain consonants from occurring together in this language. One of these forbidden groups of consonants is /kt/, which we get in *electreach*. Earlier borrowings from English replaced the sequence <ct> with <cht>, so that *act* becomes *acht* in Irish. By the time of the Gaelic League, the people guiding the whole borrowing process were either English speakers or totally bilingual, so that a non-native sequence no longer grated on the ear as it would have done if a robust Irish-speaking community had existed. As a result, despite the best efforts of the Gaelic League to filter out foreign influences, alien elements made their way into the language surreptitiously.

At the level of grammar, the new compounds were also disruptive. As we saw, the spoken Irish of the 1890s did not allow for the creation of compounds, preferring instead phrases like *bean tí* 'housewife'. Note that the order of elements is reversed in the Irish phrase as opposed to the English compound: *bean* 'woman, wife' comes first, then *tí* 'house'. In other words, the main noun comes first, and is then followed by a qualifier. The same is true of many other common expressions:

(28) Noun   Qualifier
    fear   oibre
    man   of.work   'worker'
    cailín   aimsire
    girl   of.service   'servant-girl'
    cos   adhmaid
    leg   of.wood   'wooden leg'

The new compounds reversed this order, by placing the qualifier first, before the main noun:

(29) Qualifier   Noun   Compound
    cois   liathróid   coisliathróid
    foot   ball   'football'
    iris   leabhar   irisleabhar
    record   book   'journal, magazine'

This meant that for a native speaker of Irish, it was extremely difficult to process the meaning of the new words. A comparable situation in English would be if instead of words like *blackboard*, *housewife*, we had *boardblack, *wife of house. There was no point in telling an illiterate speaker of Irish from the Aran Islands that words like *coisliathróid* 'football' existed in Old Irish: from the point of view of the language in the 1890s, compounds were simply ungrammatical. In the same way, Old English had a compound *lār-hūs*, literally 'lore-house', which meant 'school', but a proposal to substitute *lore-house* for modern *school* (borrowed from medieval Latin *schola*), would probably not be taken very seriously nowadays.

    Planned innovations can, with time, find acceptance among the general populace, but one condition for this is a high level of literacy and also the actual use of the new items in everyday speech. Literacy in Irish, unfortunately, remained the preserve of language-learners for the most part. Because their first language was English, they had no objection to compounds or other non-native patterns of speech. The net result was that the new vocabulary rarely got beyond the printed page. Modern dictionaries like OD are teeming with scientific terms like *heitreadocsach* 'heterodox' or *hidreafóbach* 'hydrophobic'. The unusual form of these terms in itself is not problematic. After all, many speakers of English never encounter the word *hydrophobic*, and we more or less expect it to be confined to the register of scientific discourse. In the case of Irish, though, such words are rarely used even in writing, apart from translations of some elementary science text-books which nobody reads.

8.9.4 Censoring vocabulary

In Mac Mathúna (2007: 236), the author discusses a practice common among editors of texts at the time of the Revival. This involved excising words or expressions which they considered un-Irish and replacing them with what they considered to be truly Irish equivalents. One of the books that Mac Mathúna discusses in detail is the 1911 edition of *O'Gallagher's Sermons*, an eighteenth-century work mentioned in section 5.2.2. The 1911 editor, Pól Breathnach, substituted Irish words for what he considered to be unacceptable borrowings. The scholar T. F. O'Rahilly in turn subjected Breathnach's edition to a rather scathing review, which it is worth quoting from. O'Rahilly begins by adverting to the change from Roman to Gaelic font in Breathach's edition, and then adds, 'And once liberty in matters of spelling is conceded to the editor of a text, the temptation is, no doubt, a strong one to go a step further and improve his author's grammar or vocabulary wherever he sees fit' (O'Rahilly 1912: 67). He then goes on to criticize Breathnach's decisions with respect to vocabulary:

On the last page of his edition Fr. Walsh [Breathnach] gives a list (which is, however, far from complete) of the words occurring in the original which he has replaced by words of his own. Some of these substitutions are not very happy. Thus, *seód* [jewel] is hardly a synonym of *preasánta* [gift], a word which, moreover, has the authority of O Maolchonaire (1616)...*Dathadóir* which is made to replace Gallagher's *peintéir*, means only, so far as I know, 'a dyer'. The only authoritative word in modern Irish for 'painter' is *pinnteoir*, a word which has a history of five centuries behind it.

(O'Rahilly 1912: 68)

In the first case discussed above, the substitution of *seód* for *preasánta*, the editor tried to extend the meaning of the native word to encompass the idea of English *gift*. With the second substitution, *dathadóir*, on the other hand, we seem to be dealing with a calque. The word *painter* consists of the root *paint* and the suffix -**er**. The Irish verb *dathaigh* means 'to colour', while the suffix -**adóir** is used to form agents, the 'doer of the action denoted by the verb'. In other cases of substitution, the editor replaced the original borrowings with words which had long been obsolete: '*Teistimhin*, inserted by the editor in place of *tēxt*, is merely a twentieth-century resurrection of the Old-Irish borrowing of the Lat. *testimonium*; the modern Irish word is *téx(t)*, *téacs*' (O'Rahilly 1912: 68).

O'Rahilly's remarks echo some of the points I have been making in the previous section concerning the reception of new words. An individual does not have the authority to suddenly change the meaning of words, just because he doesn't like their origin: 'If a number of the words employed by Gallagher displeased his editor, the farthest he should in reason have gone would have been to suggest his own alternatives in footnotes. To attempt to decide by one's own prejudices what words are to form part of the language and what are not, is, to say the least, unsatisfactory' (O'Rahilly 1912: 69).

It was not just the writings of the past that were subjected to purification, but also the living speech of the Gaeltachts. As we saw in section 8.5, recent borrowings from English in particular were frowned upon by the Gaelic League. This had implications for the recording of the vocabulary of Irish in dictionaries, both before and after 1922. Compilers of dictionaries simply omitted words which did not meet their criteria of Irishness. For example, the initial consonant in the English word *joke* was not part of the traditional list of Irish sounds. Early borrowings from English substituted the sound /sh/ for /j/, e.g. *Geoffrey* became *Séafraidh* /shayfree/ in Irish. As we saw in Chapter 6, widespread bilingualism in the nineteenth century meant that it was no longer necessary to make this substitution. As a result, /j/ began to make its way, albeit marginally, into the repertoire of Irish consonants. By the time that the Gaelic League began its reforming work, words like *jar* and *jug* were common in spoken Irish. Two dictionaries were compiled in the period under scrutiny, an English–Irish one (Lane 1904) and an Irish–English one (D). Neither of them contain the words *jar* or *jug*. Even a later work like OD (1977), although it allows words like *jab* 'job' and *jib* 'jib', does not acknowledge the existence of *jar* and *jug*. This absence cannot be an oversight, but must be ascribed to censorship.

In many languages, it is not unusual for there to be some disparity between officially recommended dictionaries, which tend to be conservative, and the spoken language which is to be heard in a community at a particular point in time. However, if the language is one used in a wide range of registers, both formal and informal, we can be sure that the learned words will at least be found in official writing or in literature. Likewise, dictionaries intended for non-experts tend to contain a fair sample of informal speech, even if purists and academics frown upon new expressions and usages. In other words, there is representation of all registers, not just the more formal ones.

With Irish, from about 1890 onwards we witness a growing gap between the sanitized, written vocabulary mainly favoured by second-language speakers, and the spoken lexicon of native speakers, with the latter only partially represented in official dictionaries. Not surprisingly, this led to much confusion and misunderstanding when learners, armed with their official terminology, tried to communicate with the inhabitants of the Gaeltachts, and were met with blank incomprehension. The latter, in their turn, saw the alien words and expressions as yet another example of the usurpation by city-dwellers of their language.

8.10 New kinds of writing

Whatever the merits or faults of the new vocabulary, it had one important effect. It enabled the Revivalists to cultivate new styles of writing that had never existed in Irish before. We can divide these styles into various categories according to subject matter.

8.10.1 Literature

As we saw in Chapter 6, the literature that existed in Irish in the period 1800–70 was a far cry from what we would regard as literature nowadays. Genres like the novel and drama were almost totally unknown in Irish at the time. The Gaelic League set about trying to change this state of affairs. We can identify two strands in the new writing, strands which more or less correspond to the native-/non-native speaker divide.

When the Gaelic League started, it was hoped that native speakers would learn to read and write and begin producing stories, plays, and poetry of their own. The adherents of this approach have been described as 'nativists' (O'Leary 1994: 14–16). With time, a small percentage of native speakers did begin to write. The work they produced was heavily influenced by the folklore tradition which was still very strong in the Gaeltacht areas. So, for example, what were published under the title of short stories are often just written versions of folk-tales, with unsophisticated story-lines and stereotypical characters. A good example of this kind of writing is the book *Séadna*, by Peadar Ó Laoghaire. This is an Irish version of the Faust legend, in which a poor cobbler, Séadna, sells his soul to the devil in return for three gifts. The tale is presented within the framework of an actual oral telling of it, and each chapter begins with a running commentary on the action by the audience listening to the narrator. Ó Laoghaire justified this expedient in a letter of 1900: 'It is easier to write Irish dialogue than continuous Irish prose ... Irish has lived for the past two or three centuries, only in the people's mouths and in the utterances of the poets ... It is speech addressed by a speaker to a listener, not by a writer to a general public' (O'Leary 1994: 13). Peadar Ó Laoghaire here puts his finger on the advantages and disadvantages of the nativist approach. His *Séadna* was eminently suitable to be read aloud to illiterate Irish speakers of his dialect, but as a narrative it is rambling and prolix. The flow of action is severely retarded by the insertion of the dialogues of the imaginary listeners. Thus at the beginning of Chapter 3 in the book, there is a whole two pages devoted to a description of the newly born nephew of one of the group assembled to listen to the next episode of the story. While such additions provide a rich mine of linguistic information for the scholar, they are hardly likely to appeal to the modern reader.

One of the main genres to develop as a result of the Revival was the autobiography. Encouraged by scholars and language enthusiasts, men and women from the Gaeltachts wrote or dictated their life-story; in some cases, the narrative was edited and touched up by somebody else before publication. The problem with such works is that the kind of linear narrative that modern readers expect, rightly or wrongly, is totally absent. We can observe this lack of coherence in a work called *An tOileánach* [The islandman]. This is probably the best-known of the Gaeltacht autobiographies. In it, an elderly fisherman from the Blasket Island, in south-west Ireland, looks back on his life. The trouble is that his reminiscences are unordered. For instance, in Chapter 1 of the book we start off with his earliest memories, followed by a description of his parents. Then, without word or warning, we are treated to an account of the sinking of a ship near the Blasket Islands and of how the islanders salvaged a cargo of putty from it. Whether this happened before or after the author was born is not clear, and its relevance to his life-story is debatable, to put it mildly. The rest of the 300-odd pages of the book are taken up with anecdotes of this sort, in some of which the author figures, in some of which he doesn't.

A work like this is an invaluable document for the anthropologist, the folklorist, the social historian, and the linguist. But it is not innovative. Nativist writing maintained the oral style of story-telling, simply transferring it to a different medium. Editors tended to maintain the spellings and dialect-features of the narrators *in toto* out of respect for the folk-tradition that these works represented. This in turn increased the difficulties of learners in reading them. Not only was the style alien, but also the medium itself.

In response to this, what O'Leary (1994: 14) calls a 'progressive' strand developed among those who wished to cultivate writing in Irish. The progressives tended to be learners, and of an urban background. Their most prolific and vociferous representative was Patrick Pearse. On the pages of the CS, he attacked what he perceived as the shortcomings of the folk tradition:

The Language movement has not yet produced a drama...A drama is a picture of human life intended and suitable for representation by means of action...We have the same 'Bean-tighe' [housewife], the same 'Sean-fhear' [old man], the same 'Fear Óg' [young man], the same 'Buachaill Aimsire' [servant-boy], the same 'Cailín Comhursan' [neighbouring girl] in a dozen plays: and these worthy folk foregather in the kitchen; and dance the same dances and chat in the same way about the same topics, no matter what part of Ireland they hail from, what period they are supposed to be living in, what events—grave or gay—they are taking part in.

(CS, 16 June 1906; quoted in Ní Chollatáin 2004: Appendices, 59)

He was also troubled by the fact that Irish-language literature was so divorced from the realities of life in Ireland in the 1900s:

This is the twentieth century and no literature can take root in the twentieth century which is not of the twentieth century...We would love the problems of today fearlessly dealt with in Irish: the loves and hates and desires and doubts of modern men and women. The drama of the land war, the tragedy of the emigration-mania; the stress and poetry and comedy of the language movement; the pathos and vulgarity of Anglo-Ireland; the abounding interest of Irish politics, the relations of priest and people; the perplexing education riddle; the drink evil; the increase in lunacy; such social problems as (say) the loveless marriage; these are matters which loom large in our daily lives; which bulk considerably in our daily consideration but we find not the faintest echoes of them in the Irish books that are being written.

(CS, 26 May 1906; quoted in Ní Chollatáin 2004: Appendices, 39)

Pearse learned Irish remarkably well, so well that it is difficult to detect the influence of English on his creative writing. Furthermore, his short stories are all set in a traditional Irish-speaking district in Connemara. The characters in them speak to some extent like the characters in *Séadna*, in dialect. What distinguishes Pearse's work is the presence of a narrative structure that is lacking in the nativist literature. His short stories have a beginning, a middle, and an end. Furthermore, the narrative style he employs is totally new in the context of Irish literature. Take this opening paragraph in one of his stories:

(30)   Bhí sean-Mhaitias ina shuí le hais a dhorais. An té a ghabhfadh an bóthar, shílfeadh sé gur dealbh cloiche nó marmair a bhí ann—sin nó duine marbh—mar ní chreidfeadh sé go bhféadfadh fear beo fanacht chomh ciúin, chomh socair sin. Bhí a cheann cromtha aige agus cluas air ag éisteacht. Is iomaí sin fuaim cheolmhar a bhí le cloisteáil, an té a mbeadh aird aige orthu. Chuala sé scréach na coirre éisc ón duirling, agus géimneach na mbó ón mbuaile, agus gealgháire na bpáistí ón bhfaiche. Ach ní le ceachtar acu seo a bhí sé ag éisteacht chomh haireach sin—cé go mba bhinn leis iad go léir—ach le glór glé glinn chlog an Aifrinn a bhí ag teacht chuige le gaoth i gciúineadas na maidne.

[Old Matthew was sitting by the door. Anybody who passed would think that it was a statue of stone or marble—or a dead person—that was there, for it was impossible to believe that a living man could stay so quiet and still. His head was bent and he was listening intently. There were many musical sounds to be heard, for those who were prepared to listen. He heard the screech of the heron from the shore, and the lowing of the cattle from the milking-yard, and the cheerful laughter of the children from the green. But it wasn't to any of these he was listening so carefully—though he found them all sweet—but to the clear sound of the Mass bell which came to him on the wind in the quiet of the morning.]

(Ó Buachalla 1979: 65)

This may not be the most original or striking piece of prose ever composed, but it is written competently and clearly. It provides a setting for the story, and introduces the main character. In other words, it conforms to the aesthetic norms of late-Victorian English literature, the literature that Pearse was reared on. Now compare this passage with the opening of *Séadna*:

(31) Bhí fear ann fadó agus is é ainm a bhí air ná Séadna. Gréasaí ab ea é. Bhí tigh beag deas cluthar aige ag bun cnoic, ar thaobh na fothana. Bhí cathaoir shúgáin aige do dhein sé féin dó féin, agus ba ghnáth leis suí inti um thráthnóna, nuair a bhíodh obair an lae críochnaithe, agus nuair a shuíodh sé inti bhíodh sé ar a shástacht.

[Once upon a time there was a man whose name was Séadna. He was a shoemaker. He had a nice snug house at the butt of a hill, on the leeward side. He had a chair made of rope which he had made himself, and he used to sit in it in the evening, when the work of the day was done, and when he sat in it he was at his ease.]

(Ua Laoghaire 2011: 2)

The opening phrase 'once upon a time' places us immediately in the world of the folk-tale. Like Pearse, Ó Laoghaire also introduces us to the setting and main character of his tale in the opening paragraph. However, the picture we get of Séadna is more general, less individual, than that of old Matthew in the previous passage. Séadna could be any shoemaker in any house at any time. Describing his daily routine in the third sentence, Ó Laoghaire uses the past habitual, for the simple reason that every day was the same as the next. In Pearse's story, on the other hand, Matthew is distinguished from other old men by the way that he sits—like 'a statue of stone or marble'. This is a way of describing things not found in folk-tales.

The purpose of this discussion is not to decide who was the better writer, Pearse or Ó Laoghaire; that is a matter for literary critics. What I am trying to illustrate is how the progressive writers, under the influence of English literature, were slowly changing the nature of Irish writing in this period. Another writer, Pádraic Ó Conaire, went a step further than Pearse, introducing totally new subject matter and styles into Irish. In one of his short stories, for example, the narrator is Herod, the king of Judea. The story of Salome and John the Baptist is told not in the third person, but as a monologue in the mouth of the dying king. Here is the opening of the story:

(32) Breá liom thú ag teacht ar cuairt chugam sa bpóithrín beag brocach seo atá agam sa bhfásach, a Réisín, a mhic altrama. Ach fan amach uaim roinnt nó beidh tromualach crumh agus piast agat ag filleadh uait go hIarúsalem!

[I'm glad to have you visiting me in this little rotten hovel of mine in the desert, Réisín, my foster-son. But keep away from me or you'll have a heavy load of maggots and worms when you return to Jerusalem.]

(Ó Conaire 1977: 11)

There is no introductory paragraph, no formula along the lines of 'Once upon a time' to lead us into the story. We are dropped into the middle of the narrator's monologue without a word of warning. In the story, Ó Conaire takes the readers out of the familiar world of the Gaeltacht and transports them to the exotic world of the Middle East. The description of this exotic world demands exotic vocabulary. The expression *mac altrama* 'foster-son' is an example of a word common in Medieval Irish being revived. Other neologisms include *banrinceoirí* 'dancing-girls' (with the obsolete feminizing prefix **ban-**), and the compound *cruinnchíochach* 'round-breasted'.

Ó Conaire's dialogues are a far cry from the formulaic exchanges of the characters in *Séadna*, or even the more straightforward narratives of Pearse's stories. In the following conversation, Herod's wife Herodias has caught him ogling her stepdaughter Salome:

(33) 'Níor cheapas gur tú a bhí ann,' arsa mise, ciotach go leor.
      'Agus ní aithneofá mo lámhsa thar láimh mná ar bith eile!' ar sise.
      'Más ag éirí tuirseach díom atáir…'

      ['I didn't realize that it was you', said I, awkwardly enough.
      'And you wouldn't recognize my hand from the hand of any other
      woman!' said she. 'If you're getting tired of me…']

(Ó Conaire 1977: 12)

The language of the above passage is grammatically correct. In the context of Irish as it had existed up to 1900, though, the exchange is pragmatically odd. Pragmatics is a linguistic term that refers to how we interpret utterances in a particular context. Thus it is concerned with the actual use of language as distinct from pure grammatical form. For this reason, it is more difficult for learners to acquire pragmatic competence in a foreign language as distinct from grammatical competence.

Ó Conaire was bilingual, but most of his reading had been in English, and this shows in his stories in terms of the pragmatics. The above exchange between Herod and Herodias is comprehensible to an English speaker who is familiar with the conventions of prose and drama of the nineteenth and twentieth century. Even without knowing exactly who Herod and Herodias are, we can surmise that he is a wayward husband, and she a jealous wife. Herodias' exclamation 'And you wouldn't recognize my hand from the hand of any other woman!', is interpreted as ironic by a modern Anglophone reader.

Supposing, however, that Ó Conaire's story had been read aloud to a group of Gaeltacht people gathered by the fireside of a cottage in the west of Ireland, it is doubtful whether the effect would have been the same. The pragmatics of traditional Irish is quite different from the pragmatics of English. I can try to illustrate this by taking another extract from the autobiography *An tOileánach* [The islandman]. The context is a visit to the author's house on Christmas Eve by his uncle, who sits down by the fire and starts drinking. After a while, the author goes outside and finds the uncle's young son outside, crying for his father. The author brings him and addresses the father:

(34)   'An leat an garsún so?' arsa mise leis an réic.
       D'fhéach sé air.
       'Is liom agus ní liom,' ar seisean.
       'Táimid chomh dall agus do bhíomair riamh,' arsa mise arís leis.
       'Dhera, a dhuine ná ficeann tú nách liomsa do chuaigh sé—ní hí
       an tseithe ramhar bhuí sin do bheadh air dá bar liomsa do
       raghadh sé,' ar seisean—'ach leis an amalóig bhuí do mháthair
       do.'
       'Is dóigh liom,' arsa mo mháthair leis, 'nár chuaigh aon duine acu
       leat féin, ach leis an máthair iad uile,' ar sise.
          'Ná an diabhal duine acu, dá bar liom a bhfuil sa bhaile acu!'
       arsa Diarmuid an tseóigh.
       ['Is this boy yours?' said I to the rake.
       He looked at him.
       'He is and he isn't', said he.
       'We're as wise as before', said I to him in reply.
       'Ah, man, don't you see that he didn't take after me—he wouldn't
       have that thick sallow hide if he had taken after me', said he—'but
       after that sallow, ungainly mother of his.'
       'I suppose', said my mother to him, 'that none of them took after
       you, but they all took after the mother', said she.
       'Not a damned one of them, if every one of them in the village was
       mine!' said the droll Diarmuid.]

                                                        (Ó Coileáin 2002: 151)

Fortunately for the modern reader, we are told on the next page that this is a humorous exchange between members of an extended family, rather than the prelude to a quarrel. To the middle-class Gaelic Leaguers from Dublin and other cities, this kind of dialogue must have seemed bizarre. In a small community where everybody knew everybody else all their lives, such apparent liberties were acceptable, but not in the more anonymous and refined society that the Gaelic Leaguers were familiar with. In the same way, learners of Irish could never get used to the idea that native speakers did not use polite formulae like *please, thank you*, or *excuse me*. Such formulaic expressions are only necessary in modern urban communities, where one comes across strangers in daily life, and needs neutral and indirect ways of addressing them.

Ó Conaire was the first writer to fully embrace the conventions and style of English literature, but he started a trend which was to accelerate after 1920. More and more literature was written for learners of Irish, who had more or less the same expectations as they would have had for English literature. Like with vocabulary, the gap between the traditional nativist writers and the modern progressive ones was to widen as the years went by.

8.10.2 Journalism

As we have just seen, it was possible to produce literature in Irish without coming to grips with the reality of modern urban living, and many writers continued to exercise this option long after the Revival period. However, because of the subject matter, this possibility was not open to journalists— they had to engage with the here and now. As we saw in section 7.9, there were certain restrictions on the range of subjects covered in the GJ and CS, with the emphasis being on matters pertaining to the Irish language. Nevertheless, the medium itself necessitated a new style regardless of the subject matter.

One area where the existence of weekly and monthly journals made a lasting difference was in establishing a terminology for public writing itself. The following terms became established in the period 1890–1920:

(35) Irish   English
      foilsigh   'publish'
      cuir i gcló/ clóbhuail   'print'
      clódóireacht   'printing'
      columhain   'column'
      páipéar nuaidheachta   'newspaper'
      sgéala na seachtmhaine   'story of the week'
      comhfhreagras   'correspondence'
      fear eagair   'editor'
      eagarfhocal   'editorial'

More important than the vocabulary, though, was the change in style and register that journalism brought with it. In general, we can say that writing intended for the public tends to be much more impersonal than dialogue or even narration. In Irish the conversational tone had traditionally dominated. In the new journalism, we find an increased use of the impersonal form of the verb, as in the following report from a courtroom:

(36)   'Cuireadh leath-bhliadhain príosúin ar ghréasuidhe agus ar a mhnaoi i
        mBaile Átha Cliath i dtaobh gur leigeadar do leanbh mic dóibh bás
        d'fhagháil le h-ocras.
        [A cobbler and his wife were given a six-month prison sentence in
        Dublin for allowing their male child to die of hunger.]

                (CS, 22 July 1899; quoted in Ní Chollatáin 2004: Appendices, 43)

The verb—*cuireadh*—is in the so-called impersonal form. In speech, one is
more likely to use a personal form, e.g. *The court imposed a six-month
sentence*, where we are told who the subject is. In another issue of the CS,
we find an editorial entitled *Leanfar den obair* 'The work will be continued',
where once again the verb is impersonal. Even though this sentence is entirely
grammatical, it is hard to imagine it being spoken by somebody from the
Gaeltacht, where people tended to be more direct in their approach. Other
strategies employed to make statements impersonal include the use of *duine*
'person' as an equivalent for English *one*, as in:

(37)   Ba dhóich le duine ar imtheachtaibh 'Fáinne an Lae' go raibh pláinéid
        mí-ádhmharach éigin dlúithe dhe.
        [One would think from the events in 'Fáinne an Lae' that some unlucky
        planet was attached to it.]

                (CS, 1 June 1918; quoted in Ní Chollatáin 2004: Appendices, 69)

Language often offers us alternative ways of saying the same thing. One
concept which can often be expressed by two different means is number.
Thus one can talk about *judges*, or simply use the term *judiciary* to refer to a
group of judges; likewise, one can talk about *clients* or *a clientele*. We refer to
nouns like *judiciary* and *clientele* as collectives. Generally speaking, we are
more likely to meet collectives in journalism than in ordinary speech. In the
journals and newspapers of the Gaelic League, we also find such collectives
instead of the plural of ordinary speech:

(38) Plural   Collective
     longa   loingeas
     'ships'   'shipping'
     mná   bantracht
     'women'   'women-folk'

Another way that language can vary is by using a single word instead of a whole
phrase. Thus, instead of saying *They cleaned the windows*, we can say *the cleaning
of windows by them*, where the noun *cleaning* conveys the meaning of the verb
clean. Such verbal nouns tend to be more economical than their corresponding
verbs, and thus it is no surprise that they occur in texts like advertisements or in
the titles of newspaper articles. In spoken Irish, verbal nouns are rarely used on

their own. The following sentence is grammatically correct, but one cannot imagine a native speaker uttering it in conversation:

(39) Chuir glanadh   na   bhfuinneog áthas   orthu.
     put   cleaning   of.the   windows   joy   on.them
     'The cleaning of the windows made them happy.'

However, we find verbal nouns frequently used as nouns in journalistic prose, as in the following:

(40) Tá   labhairt   na Gaedhilge   agus   gabháil
     is   speaking   of.Irish   and   singing
     amhrán   Gaedhilge   dá   chosc.
     of.songs Irish   AGR 3PL   prohibit.INF
     'The speaking of Irish and singing of Irish songs is being prohibited.'
                (CS, 20 July 1918; quoted in Ní Chollatáin 2004: Appendices, 70)

We also come across short titles like *cur na gcrann* 'planting of the trees', which was probably a translation of English *tree-planting*. In yet another case, the verbal noun is used to refer to a whole trade or industry:

(41) iasgaireacht   na   hÉireann
     fishing   of.the   Ireland
     'the Irish fishing industry'

I have only discussed a small sample of the kind of stylistic advances which were made in the sphere of journalism in the years 1890–1920. By themselves, the individual changes may seem insignificant. However, combined with the enormous increase in modern vocabulary, the result of these changes was that by the 1920s it was possible for a journalist to report in Irish on the current affairs of urban Ireland in language that was clear and accessible to the new cohort of language learners:

(42) Atá coigcrigh eile ag teacht i dtír agus ag glanadh le coraí móra. Francaigh atá le sráideanna Átha Cliath a ghlanadh feasta. Danmarcaigh atá le monarchain fheola a chur le chéile i bPortláirge. Beilgigh atá le ceann i gcóir siúcra a dhéanamh i gCeatharloch. Ma's de réir meastachán páighe a dtíortha féin a cheapas siad an obair a dhéanamh i bhfus, béidh sé in a chíortuaifeal aca amhail mar atá sé i Luimneach fá láthair. Atá costas maireachtála chó hard sin i nÉirinn nach féidir le fear oibre é féin is a mhuirín a thógáil ar an dá thuistiún tairgitear i n-aghaidh na huaire a oibrigheas sé…Atá biadh ró-dhaor amach is amach sa tír seo…Is ró-mhithid do'n Rialtas luach bídh a laghdú. Cá bhfuil toradh an Choimi-siúin úd a bhí ag éisteacht fianaise in a thaobh tamall ó shin?'

[Other foreigners are arriving here and using big containers for cleaning. The streets of Dublin are to be cleaned by Frenchmen from now on. Danes are to construct meat factories in Waterford. Belgians are to build one for sugar in Carlow. If they expect to do the work here according to the estimates of pay in their own countries, there will be the same kind of uproar as there is in Limerick at present. The cost of living is so high in Ireland that a worker cannot support himself and his family on the eight pence an hour which is being offered to him for his work... Food is much too expensive in this country... It is high time for the Government to reduce the price of food. Where is the effect of that Commission that was hearing evidence about that a while ago?]

(CS, 10 October 1925; quoted in Ní Chollatáin 2004: Appendices, 50)

In the newly founded Free State, Irish was to be used much more in the public domain than hitherto. Thanks to the pioneering work of the editors and writers of GJ and CS, a new high register was available in which matters like education, administration, and legislation could be discussed.

8.11 Conclusion

In this chapter I have surveyed the details of the transformation that Irish underwent in the period of the Revival. As we noted time and time again, the disadvantages facing those who undertook the task of modernizing the language were formidable. There was no fixed orthography or grammar, most native speakers were illiterate in Irish, and the language was totally unadapted to the needs of urban life at the beginning of the twentieth century. Within the space of thirty years the spelling had been more or less fixed, and agreement had been reached that the new Irish would be based on current speech. Admittedly, this last point created its own problems as it gave the same rights to all the dialects, a situation which was to prove a stumbling-block for learners for years to come.

It was in the area of vocabulary and style that the most striking advances were made. Little had changed in these areas in the previous 300 years. Thanks to the work of the writers of the newly founded journals, and also the efforts of a few scholars and lexicographers, many of the existing deficiencies were made up for. Likewise, the colloquial, earthy style of Gaeltacht speech was supplemented by a more standardized, learned mode of discourse.

On the negative side, the single great failing of the Revival was that it did not manage to involve the native speakers, who were increasingly alienated and excluded from the decisions being made concerning their language. This was a fatal flaw. The life of a language depends on its being spoken as a mother-tongue by a community of speakers. If it is written as well, so much the better, but if it is written and spoken only by learners, then ultimately it will become a dead language.

In 1870, Irish was still spoken by thousands of people, but hardly written at all. By 1920, it was being written with various degrees of proficiency by hundreds, or perhaps thousands of people, but the number of native speakers had dropped significantly. The status of the language was infinitely higher than two generations previously: it had official support and recognition, and there was nothing to prevent it becoming a medium for creative literature, academic discourse, journalism, and for all those areas of life from which it had been excluded until then. But a written language without a spoken language behind it is like stage scenery as opposed to the real thing, pretty enough in its own way, but lacking in substance.

Further reading

For the spelling conventions of modern Irish, see Bergin (1911); Ó Murchú (1977); Ó Háinle (1994); and Ó Conchubhair (2009: 145–92). Of these, Ó Murchú is the most accessible for readers who do not know Irish, but it assumes a familiarity with phonetic transcription. Ó Murchú maps clearly the evolution from the spelling of EMI to that found in present-day Irish, in the course of which he refers to the debates on the subject of orthography which took place during the Revival.

For the dialects of modern Irish, see O'Rahilly (1932); Ó Siadhail (1989); and Ó Conchubhair (2009: 193–214). O'Rahilly is intended for students of Irish with a good knowledge of traditional grammatical terminology, while Ó Siadhail is targeted at a readership with a background in modern linguistics. Ó Conchubhair concentrates more on attitudes during the Revival towards dialects and standard languages, and presents no difficulties for the general reader.

For the standardization of Irish, see Ó Háinle (1994). This is less technical than such works tend to be, and includes information on the personalities involved in the process as well as describing the form the standardization took.

For negative attitudes towards the influence of English, see Ó Conchubhair (2009: 97–119).

For the new vocabulary of Irish, see Ó Háinle (1994: 765–74).

For new literature in Irish, see O'Leary (1994) and, O'Leary (2006). The former provides a clear exposé of the nativist versus traditionalist debate during the Revival, and of the relation between the new prose and the folktale. The latter is a more general survey.

For the use of dialect in literature, see Ó Háinle (1994: 754–64).

For the development of a journalistic style in Irish, see Nic Pháidín (1998) and Ní Chollatáin (2004).

9

Conclusion

Since 2012, Irish society both north and south has been busy commemorating the centenaries of various historical events, and there are still more to come. Probably the most significant of these anniversaries will be marked in 2016, when the Rising of 1916 will be commemorated. This insurrection was to lead to the establishment of the new Free State in 1922, with Northern Ireland remaining part of the United Kingdom. It is thus of paramount importance for the history of modern Ireland.

No commemoration of 1916 would be complete without a mention of Patrick Pearse, the main character behind the Easter Rising, and one who has figured much in this book. In an essay published recently in the online *Dublin Review of Books*, Bryan Fanning discusses an article of Pearse's written for the CS in 1906 (CS, 4 August 1906). In the article, Pearse imagines what Ireland might be like in a hundred years' time, presenting his forecast in the form of an imaginary edition of the CS from 2006. The new Ireland he envisages has regained independence, and undergone various other changes in terms of the economic, social, and cultural environment. One prediction that seems to have come (partly) true concerned the climate: 'as a result of the draining of the bogs and the re-forestation of the country—the temperature of Ireland has risen several degrees within the last century' (Fanning 2013). However, with respect to the linguistic climate of Ireland in the twenty-first century, Pearse's hopes were not realized. In his imaginary Ireland of 2006, Irish has replaced English as the main medium of communication in Ireland, and English is no longer a world language, due to the decline of British power. Even in the educational system, it has been replaced as a second language by various other tongues, including Japanese. Needless to say, the exact opposite has happened—the author of the article could not have been more wrong.

Pearse rightly predicted the break-up of the British Empire, but erroneously assumed that its language would disappear along with political control. He completely failed to foresee the rise of the United States as a world power, and the concomitant spread of American English even to the Old World. In the twenty-first century, not only do Irish teenagers speak English, but they speak a variety of this language which is moving closer and closer to that spoken in the United States. Irish society and culture have likewise become Americanized in the last fifty years. Pearse's animosity to Anglophone culture was directed against Britain, but we can probably assume that the present-day situation would not have delighted him.

Finally, and this would probably have been the cruellest blow of all for Pearse, the English malaise has spread to his beloved Connemara, the place where he learned Irish, and whose inhabitants he idealized in his CS editorials and short stories. The present-day teenagers of Ros Muc, where Pearse's cottage has been preserved as a national heritage site, look and speak more or less like their counterparts in cities like Dublin, Cork, Galway, and Limerick. Much of their communication takes place through electronic media like the Internet and Facebook, and their language is identical to that of teenagers all over the Anglophone world.

Ought one, then, to dismiss the Gaelic League as an organization of well-meaning but benighted idealists, as an interesting but insignificant footnote in the history of modern Ireland? The answer to that question depends on how rigorously one judges the legacy of the League. If the touchstone of its success is whether 100 per cent of the population of Ireland is speaking Irish, then we have to say that it was a spectacular failure. However, there is another way of looking at this question. After all, anybody who sets himself an impossible task is bound to fail. My contention in this book is that by the time the Gaelic League was founded, it was too late to reverse the language shift. If this is correct, then there was never a real possibility of Irish becoming a majority language in Ireland again. In that sense, the Gaelic Leaguers had unreasonable hopes, and their endeavours could only have ended in failure. But that does not mean that they did not succeed partially, even in ways that they themselves never envisaged.

As we saw in Chapters 7 and 8, there were two aspects to the activities of the Gaelic League. One aim was to arrest the decline of Irish as a first language. Even the most optimistic commentator would have to admit that this aim has not been achieved. It is even debatable whether the activities of the Gaelic League contributed to slowing down the attrition of the Irish-speaking districts. But nothing short of a miracle could have prevented the disappearance of Irish as a first language given the circumstances I described in previous chapters. In fact, Irish does not compare so unfavourably to other endangered languages. If we look at Scots Gaelic in 1890, we see that in some respects it was more robust than Irish. While the absolute number of speakers was lower, they were all concentrated in one geographical area, the Highlands and Western Isles. Furthermore, literacy was higher among the Scots Gaelic community and the language possessed a wider range of registers. Nevertheless, the net result has been the same in both countries—inexorable decline in the face of emigration, globalization, mass communication, and the breakdown of traditional ways of life.

However, a different way of assessing the legacy of the Revival movement is to look at its concrete achievements. Even as Irish was dying out in the Gaeltacht areas of Ireland, the Gaelic League and its successors were encouraging learners of Irish to visit these districts and to record the language of the last native speakers. Linguists collected and described the remaining dialects of Irish, while folklorists collected stories and songs. Some of the local inhabitants were induced to write or dictate their life stories, in which they described customs and practices which were rapidly disappearing. In this way, a valuable part of the Irish heritage was preserved. Admittedly, there is a certain lifelessness about folk-tales that are no longer to be heard, and the Gaeltacht areas have to some extent become glorified theme-parks, but few would argue that the work of collecting and recording was in vain.

Outside the Gaeltachts, the legacy of the Revival is perhaps more controversial. Without the Gaelic League, Irish would never have been placed on the curriculum of all schools in the new independent Ireland. For many schoolchildren, compulsory Irish has proved more of a curse than a blessing, but regardless of how individuals may feel about it, there is no doubt that since the 1890s it has had a presence in Irish life that it never enjoyed before. A very small percentage of the population managed to learn the language well. Most other learners mastered the elements of the language, but never had the inclination to progress beyond this. Many, if not a majority, of Irish people have negative attitudes towards Irish and its place on the school curriculum. Once again, one might be inclined to assess this result as a failure, in terms of what the Gaelic League set out to do.

One commentator takes a different line in his account of the contemporary situation. He sees grounds for hope in the fact that Irish people are still willing to take the trouble to learn Irish and to speak it, even if this is limited to certain occasions: 'This is very different from the Irish situation. What is remarkable about that situation, and what is unique as far as I know, has been the creation of a community of people who have learned Irish as a second language, who speak and write with a degree of fluency, and who use the language regularly and seriously' (McCloskey 2001: 46). The author goes on to compare this with the goals of the Gaelic League:

All of this seems like a very modest achievement indeed, if we measure it against the hopes of those who founded the original language movement Conradh na Gaeilge [Gaelic League] in the late nineteenth century. Measured against what we now understand of the difficulty of what was attempted and is being attempted, it is a very substantial and very unusual achievement indeed (unique, in fact, as far as I know).

(McCloskey 2001: 47)

McCloskey is aware that the Irish spoken by this new community is different from traditional Irish:

It is impossible to know at this point what (if anything) will ultimately emerge from this froth of linguistic experimentation and creativity.

   We can be reasonably sure that it will not much resemble anything that early revivalists such as An tAthair Peadar Ó Laoghaire would have recognized or approved of.

(McCloskey 2001: 48)

The point he is making here is that this is a language which has been shaped by learners for other learners. With the passage of time, the new Irish is diverging further and further from the traditional Irish spoken until recently in Gaeltacht areas. This may not have been the original goal of the Gaelic League, but it does nevertheless represent a tangible result. Irish is part of Irish life.

   McCloskey does not say it, but the situation he describes is one in which the language has more of a symbolic function than a communicative one. For example, in the last twenty years many businesses, aided by government grants, have begun to use Irish in advertising and even to some extent in their transactions. Some bank ATM machines offer customers the option of conducting transactions through the medium of Irish. The practical problem with the banks' initiative is that even advanced learners lack the technical terminology for conducting financial transactions in Irish. Likewise, on trains in the Republic of Ireland, stations are announced in Irish and English. The phonetics of the voice recordings are heavily influenced by English, and place-names in Irish are unfamiliar to most Irish people. Consequently, a hypothetical Irish speaker who wished to disembark at a particular station would still have to check the English announcement to ensure that he was getting out at the right stop.

   There has been much criticism of initiatives such as these for being wasteful and inefficient. But that is surely to miss the point of the Irish versions, which is not to convey information but to signal the symbolic significance of the language as part of the cultural heritage of the Irish people. And this is where Irish plays a part in the lives even of those who resent having to learn it at school.

   As stated earlier, young people in Ireland look and sound very much like their American counterparts. A foreign visitor to a shopping mall in the suburbs of south Dublin might be forgiven for thinking at first that they were in a suburb of New York or Los Angeles. However, after a while they would begin to notice subtle differences. Some of the teenagers lounging on the seats or skateboarding in the car-park would have distinctly un-American names like Cian or Aisling. Some of the shops would have advertisements in an indecipherable script. And one or two of the teenagers might occasionally throw a phrase or sentence of Irish into their conversation, if they happened to be attending an Irish-language school.

In Northern Ireland, Irish has an even more visible presence, as there it has become a sign of belonging to the nationalist community. In another essay written more than a hundred years ago, *The Murder Machine*, Patrick Pearse had humorously considered the possibility of Irish being spoken not just by nationalists, but also by the unionist community of Ulster: 'The prospect of the children of Sandy Row [a unionist enclave in Belfast] being taught to curse the Pope in Irish was rich and soul-satisfying' (Ó Buachalla 1980: 375). This prediction has not come true, any more than his other predictions, but there have been some surprising developments since the Good Friday peace agreement of 1998, with respect to the presence of Irish in public life in Northern Ireland. Twenty years ago nobody, least of all the author of this book, would have foreseen that in 2013 the BBC Northern Ireland television channel would be broadcasting programmes in Irish on a daily basis. Admittedly, most of the viewers of these programmes are nationalists, but some members of the unionist community have openly embraced the learning of Irish in recent years. The hope of the founders of the Gaelic League was that Irish would be for people of every political and religious option, and something of this spirit has survived.

One factor which facilitated the appearance of Irish in the public domain in Northern Ireland was a concession made to the unionist community, namely, the recognition of Ulster Scots as a language in its own right. This proliferation of languages in what was formerly a monolingual entity is symptomatic of modern Ireland as a whole. Since about 1990, Ireland has become a destination for immigrants from various parts of the world. With many of these making a permanent home in the country, the ethnic composition of the population is changing rapidly. This raises important questions regarding national identity, including linguistic identity, in the years to come. As we have seen, the Irish language was harnessed by the nationalist movement in the late nineteenth century, and throughout the twentieth century it was perceived as a bulwark against foreign influences, as a touchstone of what it meant to be Irish. Not surprisingly, supporters of the language movement stressed its role in providing a link with previous generations, and with the Gaelic culture of the past. Despite the best efforts of people like Douglas Hyde, non-Catholics and unionists were excluded from participation in this heritage in the years after 1922, a situation which persisted until very recently.

If Ireland really is to be become a multicultural society, then the Irish language can no longer function as a badge of identity for just one section of the community, those who claim descent from putative Gaelic ancestors. Officially, government agencies for promoting the Irish language are at pains to stress their openness to all ethnicities, both those with deep roots in the country and those who have recently arrived. At the same time, what one might call the exclusivist baggage inherited from the past is something of a problem for advocates of an open, multicultural society that embraces all kinds of nationalities and religions. If one insists on associating a language with a particular people and a particular place, then other peoples from other places, speaking other languages, are automatically excluded. As we saw in Chapter 7, this Romantic philosophy was at the heart of the Revival, and it has maintained a position in language movements and attitudes until the present day.

As an illustration, I need do no more than quote from a poem by Seán Ó Ríordáin, one of the best-known modern poets who wrote in Irish in the twentieth century. In it, the poet urges the reader to go to one of the Irish-speaking regions, Dún Chaoin in Kerry:

FILL ARÍS

> Fág Gleann na nGealt thoir,
> is a bhfuil d'aois seo ár dTiarna i d'fhuil,
> dún d'intinn ar ar tharla
> ó buaileadh Cath Chionn tSáile,
> is ón uair go bhfuil an t-ualach trom
> is an bóthar fada, bain ded mheabhair
> srathar shibhilatacht an Bhéarla,
> Shelley, Keats is Shakespeare:
> fill arís ar do chuid,
> nigh d'intinn is nigh
> do theanga a chuaigh ceangailte i gcomhréiribh
> 'bhí bunoscionn le d'éirim:
> dein d'fhaoistin is dein
> síocháin led ghiniúin féinig
> is led thigh-se is ná tréig iad,
> ní dual do neach a thigh ná a threabh a thréigean.

[RETURN AGAIN

> Leave *Gleann na nGealt* behind you
> and all that there is in your blood of this year of the Lord,
> close your mind to what has happened
> since the Battle of Kinsale was fought,
> and since the load is heavy
> and the way long, from your intellect cast off
> the saddle of English civilization,
> Shelley, Keats and Shakespeare:
> return again to what is yours,
> wash your mind and wash
> your tongue which got tangled up in syntax
> that was contrary to your instinct:

make your confession and make
peace with your own kind
and with your own house and don't leave them,
it is unnatural for anybody to leave their house or their people.]

(Ó Ríordáin 2011: 152)

The message of the poem is pretty clear. English language and culture are alien, imposed, non-organic. The metaphors of the poem reinforce this message. English is a *srathar* 'saddle-pack', i.e. something burdensome. Before returning, the reader is told to 'wash' his tongue, which, by implication, has been sullied by the other language.

Ó Ríordáin's philosophy with respect to language and culture is similar to that of Herder, the German Romantic we met in section 6.1.2: there is an organic connection between a certain *treabh* 'people, race' and a certain language, and if that link is broken, then one cannot be completely oneself. For adherents of this ideology, it is almost as if the Irish language were in the DNA of the Irish people. The embracing of Irish will ensure a connection with one's inner being:

Sin é do dhoras,
Dún Chaoin fé sholas an tráthnóna,
buail is osclófar
d'intinn féin is do chló ceart.

[That is your door,
Dún Chaoin in the light of evening,
knock and there will be opened
your own mind and your true self.]

(Ó Ríordáin 2011: 152)

Given that the poem represents a commonly held view concerning Irish, and that the author was a highly influential figure, one has to ask what this language, and the culture it represents, offers to newly arrived immigrants and their children, who might find themselves studying this poem at school or university? If you are the bilingual child of non-Irish parents, one of whose languages is English, how is it possible to find a place for oneself in a culture which is presented in unashamedly ethnic terms? Since the time of the Gaelic League, Irish has been described as the heritage of a distinct ethnic group, those who can claim some kind of Gaelic ancestry. That being so, it seems that there is no room in it for people of other cultures.

Ó Ríordáin wrote the poem in the 1950s, when there was mass emigration from Ireland, and even in Dublin there were few foreigners to be found. Like Patrick Pearse and others before him, his rhetoric was anti-English rather than being directed against all foreigners. I am not claiming that he was xenophobic, but a linguistic philosophy which links a particular language exclusively to a particular nation, by definition cannot be inclusive of other nations or ethnicities. A policy which is anti-British and resents the English language, but which welcomes other languages and nations, is not a coherent policy for the kind of multicultural society that Ireland officially claims to be trying to build.

Just how absurd it is to insist on a link between a language and a particular nation or ethnic group can be illustrated by some evidence from the nineteenth century. The source of the evidence is Amhlaoibh Ó Súilleabháin, the diarist we encountered in section 6.2.3:

> Is clos dom gurb í an teanga Ghaelach is teanga mháthartha i Monstserrat san India Thiar ó aimsir Oilibher Cromaill, noch do dhíbir cuid de chlanna Gael ó Éirinn gusan Oileán sin Montserrat. Labhartar an Ghaeilge ann go coiteann le daoine dubha agus bána. Maise mo ghrá croí na díbearthaigh bhochta Ghaelacha. Cia dubh bán iad is ionúin liomsa clanna Gael.

> [I hear that the Irish language is the mother-tongue in Montserrat in the West Indies since the time of Oliver Cromwell, who banished many Gaels from Ireland to that island of Montserrat. Irish is commonly spoken there by both blacks and whites. Ah, God help the poor Irish exiles. Whether black or white the Gaels are dear to me.]

> (de Bhaldraithe 1970: 84–5)

The editor of Ó Súilleabháin's diaries, Tomás de Bhaldraithe, includes in his book a letter written in 1905, containing yet another reference to the presence of Irish in Montserrat:

> None indeed of those I knew intimately were ever in Montserrat save *one*, John Donovan, lately in charge of Parnell Bridge (Cork), who died about eighteen months ago. He was a native of Ring, near Clonakilty, and spoke Irish very fluently. He frequently told me that in the year 1852, when mate of the brig Kaloolah, he went ashore on the island of Montserrat which was then out of the usual track of shipping. He said he was much surprised to hear the negroes actually talking Irish among themselves, and that he joined in the conversation . . . He said the blacks were much astonished when he spoke to them.

> (de Bhaldraithe 1970: 84–5; emphasis original)

There is thus fairly reliable evidence that Irish was spoken by black inhabitants of Monserrat as late as the nineteenth century. Since then, Irish has died out in the West Indies, just as it has done in most of Ireland. Nevertheless, present-day inhabitants of Montserrat could claim it as part of their linguistic and cultural heritage if they so wished. Seán Ó Ríordáin's poem could just as well have been addressed to twentieth-century black inhabitants of Montserrat who were out of touch with their real self because they were now speaking English rather than Irish, the language of their ancestors.

Some readers may feel that at this point that I am exaggerating somewhat the importance of the Montserrat connection. The fact that a few sailors or stevedores on a tiny Caribbean island spoke some Irish for a few hundred years, is hardly a strong counter-argument to the claim that Irish has for most of its history been spoken by members of a particular ethnic group on the island of Ireland. And yet the two passages quoted above prove that Irish could have been transplanted to a different environment and ethnic group. There is nothing in the bogs and mountains of Ireland, nothing in the DNA of its people, that predisposes them to speaking Irish rather than English or any other language. The Romantic connection between language and nation is nothing more than a nineteenth-century construct. Like all such constructs, it served its purpose in the building of the Irish nation in the twentieth century:

The Irish national identity which was constructed in the late nineteenth and early twentieth centuries was a base on which the argument or project of political independence was constructed... The Irish language was a component in the argument of that project. The Irish national identity (including the Irish language and particular cultural forms), which was constructed in that era, was a product of the time.

(Watson 2008: 68)

The author of the above passage, Iarfhlaith Watson, argues that there has been an ideological shift in the attitude of the state and society towards the Irish language in the last fifty to sixty years. According to him this has led to a toning down of the more strident nationalist demands regarding the revival of Irish, and their replacement by a view of Irish as the language of choice for certain minorities or individuals. One could imagine that this more individualistic approach to the language question would allow for the possibility of multiple identities. This in turn might enable recent immigrants and their children to learn and speak Irish without giving up their own particular culture and language. In other words, speaking Irish would be seen as a right open to all inhabitants of Ireland.

Watson is at pains to emphasize that national identity is still central to the presence of Irish in Irish society:

Efforts to revive the Irish language reflect wider ideological processes. Although there have been ideological shifts, and identity has changed (because it is always under construction), national identity has remained at the heart of justifications for reviving the Irish language. People learn Irish and support its promotion because of this sense of identity.

(Watson 2008: 74)

Because of the far-reaching changes to the composition of the Irish population in recent years, it could be argued that the question of national identity is one of the most pressing issues facing Irish society at the present time. My hope is that the perspective on the history of Irish and English offered by this book will contribute to and enrich this ongoing debate. It is by no means the final word on this subject, but if it succeeds in stimulating or even provoking discussion on one aspect of Irish identity in the twenty-first century, it will have achieved its purpose.

Further reading

For Ireland since 1922, see Murphy (1975).

For a general survey of literature in Irish from 1922 to 1940, see O'Leary (2006). Nic Eoin (2006) deals with prose and drama from 1940 to 2000, while de Paor (2006) covers poetry in the same period. Nic Dhiarmada (2006) takes stock of Irish literature at the time of writing, pointing to the challenges and opportunities facing it in the new millennium.

For an overview of the role of Irish in modern Ireland, see Nic Pháidín and Ó Cearnaigh (2008). This contains articles on a wide range of subjects, including census data on Irish, literature in Irish, Irish in education, and Irish speakers outside of Ireland.

For essays on different aspects of the Gaeltacht at the end of the twentieth century, see Mac Mathúna et al. (2000). Ó Tuathaigh et al. (2000) has a different emphasis. It contains a large number of short sketches of individual Gaeltacht communities, written either by local inhabitants or by visitors with an intimate acquaintance with the places in question.

Hindley (1990) is a study of the Gaeltacht as a social phenomenon in twentieth-century Ireland. Because of its hard-headed stance about the weakness of Irish in the Gaeltacht, this work has provoked much criticism; for a different assessment, see Ó Ciosáin (1991).

For the symbolic function of Irish, see Ó Huallacháin (1994: 58–60) and Watson (2008: 71–2).

For an in-depth, recent study of Irish in Northern Ireland, see Mac Giolla Chríost (2005: 134–71). This explores such issues as language attitude, language use, and language rights.

For the role of Irish in society and national identity, see Cronin (2005) and Watson (2008).

For the future of Irish, see Mac Giolla Chríost (2005: 199–233). This emphasizes the role of planning and legislation in both jurisdictions of the island of Ireland, north and south. It proposes a new model of language planning, one based on community networks. The author also responds to the changing cultural and ethnic make-up of Irish society, and concludes his discussion with some comments on the place of Irish in the urban landscapes of present-day Ireland.

Ó hIfearnáin and Ní Neachtain (2012) deals with the sociolinguistics of Irish in the twenty-first century. Topics covered include code-switching, language death, and the use of Irish in the media.

McCloskey (2001) places Irish in the context of world languages. This work is forward-looking and optimistic; as such, it offers a welcome alternative to the predominantly pessimistic opinions in circulation on the future of Irish.

Walsh (2011) is a vigorous challenge to the orthodox opinion that the cultivation of Irish and economic development are incompatible. It also presents a comprehensive account of Irish and its speakers in the twenty-first century.

Finally, Flynn (2012) questions the validity of the whole Revival enterprise in independent Ireland.

Glossary of linguistic terms

agreement—matching of number (gender, person) between the grammatical forms of different words, e.g. between the singular form of a verb and of a singular pronoun.

analytic verbs—verbs which require a pronoun to tell us which person is involved; English has analytic inflection, as the form of the verb itself does not give us this information.

bilingualism—proficiency in two languages.

calque (loan translation)—a kind of borrowed item which replicates or imitates the semantic structure of the original. An example is Old Irish *leth-inis* 'peninsula', from **leth-** 'half' and *inis* 'island', which is a calque of Latin *paen-insula*, from *paene* 'almost' and *insula* 'island'.

code-switching—the mixing of two languages within a single utterance or text.

collective—a noun which refers to a group of individuals as a single entity, e.g. *judiciary* for a group of judges.

compound—a word consisting of two or more other words, e.g. *redbreast, bookcase*.

copula—a verb-like element used to equate two nouns, e.g. in the sentence *Catherine is a teacher*, *is* is a copula.

devoicing—a process whereby certain consonants lose voice, which is the vibration of the vocal cords. An example would be the change from /b/ to /p/, or /z/ to /s/.

dialect—non-standard variety of language, spoken in a particular region or by a particular class.

diglossia—the coexistence of two languages, or two versions of a single language, in a linguistic community.

digraph—a combination of two graphs to represent a single sound, e.g. <ch> in the word *church*.

diplomatic version—an edition of a manuscript which preserves the spelling and word-division of the original.

diphthong—a sound which consists of two vowels, but which is perceived as a single entity; an example is the vowel /au/ in English *how* or Irish *gabha* 'smith'.

Early Modern Irish—*c.*1200–*c.*1600.

eclipsis—a process in Irish whereby the first consonant of a word is altered following certain short grammatical words; the new sound is written in front of the eclipsed consonant. In the phrase *an bpógann sí*? 'does she kiss?', <bp> represents the sound /b/; the original /p/ of *pógann* has been eclipsed by /b/.

external history—account of changes affecting the community which speaks a language.

graph—an individual element of a writing system. In the case of English and Irish, graphs correspond to letters of the alphabet.

impersonal form—form of verb without any person or number marking; in the Irish sentence *Léitear na litreacha gach lá* 'The letters are read every day', the verb *léitear* is impersonal, because we are not told who is doing the reading.

infinitive—the form of the verb that is not marked for tense or person; in English, it can occur by itself or it may be preceded by *to*. Thus, *go* in the following examples is an infinitive *I must go, I want to go*.

inflection—the process whereby a single lexical item takes on different forms to express different grammatical meanings, e.g. *run, running,* and *ran* are inflected forms of the verb *run.*

initial mutations—the changes to consonants in Irish caused by lenition and eclipsis collectively.

interlanguage—variety of speech that consists of features of the language being learned and the first language of the learner.

internal history—account of concrete changes in a language, e.g. sound changes, the loss of verbal endings.

Late Modern Irish—*c.*1600 onwards.

lenition—a process in Irish whereby the first consonant of a word is altered following certain short grammatical words; in spelling, it is marked by the presence of <h> after the consonant. In the phrase *an bhean* 'the woman' /on van/, the first sound /b/ of *bean* /ban/ has been lenited to /v/, represented in spelling as <bh>.

Middle Irish—*c.*900–*c.*1200.

normalized version—an edition of a manuscript which brings the spelling and word-divisions into line with current conventions.

noun—a word which describes some entity, e.g. *woman, fear, ability.*

number—a grammatical distinction between one entity (singular) and more than one entity (plural); this manifests itself in the forms that nouns and verbs take, e.g. *cat—cats.*

object—the entity affected by the verb in a sentence, e.g. the noun *man* in *The woman kisses the man.*

Old Irish—*c.*600–*c.*900.

particles—(usually short) words whose form does not change, e.g. in Irish, *ní* marking negation, *an* marking a question.

pragmatics—the study of how language is used in various communicative situations.

prefix—an element added at the beginning of a word to modify its meaning, e.g. **re-** in the word *redo* is a prefix.

person—this refers to the participants in an action or state; we normally refer to first person (*I*), second person (*you*), and third person (*he, she, the girl*).

preposition—a word which precedes a noun to express some kind of relation of time or space, e.g. *at Christmas, in the shop.*

Primitive Irish—*c.*400–*c.*600.

pronoun—a word which stands for a noun, e.g. *you, it, she, they.*

register—a variety of language used in particular situations, e.g. a formal register used in official documents.

sociolinguistics—the social aspects of language use.

standard language—version of language used for official purposes.

subject—the entity initiating the action or state denoted by the verb, e.g. the noun *woman* in the sentence *The woman kisses the man.*

suffix—an element added at the end of a word to modify its meaning or give it a new grammatical form. The ending **-ness** in *greatness* and the ending **-ed** in *shouted* are suffixes.

syllable—a unit of speech that corresponds to a single beat; minimally it contains a vowel. The word *syllable* can be divided into three syllables /sy-la-bel/.

synthetic verbs—verbs where person and number are part of the verb itself; in Italian *amo* 'I love', the **-o** at the end expresses first-person singular.

verb—a word which denotes an action or state.

verbal noun—a noun formed from a verb; e.g. in the phrase *the founding of the city*, *founding* is the verbal noun of *found.*

word-formation—the creation of new words.

References

Ahlqvist, Anders (1994). 'Litriú na Gaeilge [The spelling of Irish]'. In Kim McCone *et al.* (eds.). *Stair na Gaeilge* [The history of Irish]. Maigh Nuad: Coláiste Phádraig, 23–59.

Atkinson, Robert (1890). *Trí bior-ghaoithe an bháis* [The three shafts of death of Rev. Geoffrey Keating]. Dublin: Royal Irish Academy.

Bergin, Osborn (1911). *Irish spelling*. Dublin: Browne and Nolan.

Bergin, Osborn (1916–55). *Irish grammatical tracts*. Supplement to *Ériu*, 8–10, 14, 17.

Bergin, Osborn (1938). 'The native Irish grammarian'. *Proceedings of the British Academy* 24, 205–35.

Bergin, Osborn (1970). *Irish Bardic poetry*. Dublin: Dublin Institute for Advanced Studies.

Bhaldraithe, Tomás de (1953). *Gaeilge Chois Fhairrge: an deilbhíocht* [The Irish of Cois Fhairrge: morphology]. Báile Átha Cliath: Insitiúid Ard-léinn Bhaile Átha Cliath.

Bhaldraithe, Tomás de (1970). *Cín lae Amhlaoibh* [Humphrey's diary]. Baile Átha Cliath: An Clóchomhar.

Bhaldraithe, Tomás de (2004). 'Irish dictionaries'. In Royal Irish Academy. *Corpas na Gaeilge* [The Irish language corpus] *1600–1882*. Dublin: Royal Irish Academy, 72–88.

Blaghd, Earnán de (1972). 'Hyde in conflict'. In Seán Ó Tuama (ed.). *The Gaelic League idea*. Cork: The Mercier Press, 31–40.

Blaney, Roger (1996). *Presbyterians and the Irish language*. Belfast: Institute of Irish Studies, Queen's University Belfast.

Bolg an tSolair: or, Gaelic magazine (1795). Belfast: Northern-Star Office.

Boorde, Andrew (1870 [1547]). *The first book of the introduction of knowledge*. Ed. F. J. Furnivall. London: N. Trübner.

Breatnach, Liam (1994). 'An Mheán-Ghaeilge [Middle Irish]'. In Kim McCone *et al.* (eds.). *Stair na Gaeilge* [The history of Irish]. Maigh Nuad: Coláiste Phádraig, 221–333.

Breatnach, Pádraig A. (1978). 'Metamorphosis 1603: dán le hEochaidh Ó hEodhasa [Metamorphosis 1603: a poem by Eochaidh Ó hEodhasa]'. *Éigse* 17: 169–80.

Brennan, Martin (1969). 'Language, personality and the nation'. In Brian Ó Cuív (ed.). *A view of the Irish language*. Dublin: The Stationery Office, 70–80.

Brewer, J. S. and William Bullen (eds.) (1867–73). *Calendar of the Carew manuscripts: preserved in the Archiepiscopal library at Lambeth*. London: Longman, Green, Reader, and Dyer.

Brún, Pádraig de (2009). *Scriptural instruction in the vernacular: the Irish Society and its teachers, 1818–1827*. Dublin: Dublin Institute for Advanced Studies.

Brún, Pádraig de *et al.* (1971). *Nua-dhuanaire I* [New anthology I]. Baile Átha Cliath: Institiúid Ardléinn Bhaile Átha Cliath.

Burca, Seán de (1958). *The Irish of Tourmakeady, Co. Mayo*. Dublin: Dublin Institute for Advanced Studies.

Butler, Mary E. L. (undated). *Irishwomen and the home language*. Dublin: Gaelic League.

Buttimer, Neil (2006). 'Literature in Irish, 1690–1800: from the Williamite wars to the Act of Union'. In Margaret Kelleher and Philip O'Leary (eds.). *The Cambridge history of Irish literature*, vol. 1. Cambridge: Cambridge University Press, 320–71.

Buttimer, Neil (2012). 'The Great Famine in Gaelic manuscripts'. In John Crowley *et al.* (eds.). *Atlas of the Great Irish Famine*. Cork: Cork University Press, 460–72.

Caball, Marc (1993). 'Parliement Chloinne Tomáis I: a reassessment'. *Éigse* 27: 47–57.

Caball, Marc (2012). ' "Solid divine and worthy scholar": William Bedell, Venice and Gaelic culture'. In James Kelly and Ciarán Mac Murchaidh (eds.). *Irish and English: essays on the Irish linguistic and cultural frontier, 1600–1900*. Dublin: Four Courts, 43–57.

Caball, Marc and Kaarina Hollo (2006). 'The literature of the later medieval period, 1200–1600: from the Normans to the Tudors'. In Margaret Kelleher and Philip O'Leary (eds.). *The Cambridge history of Irish literature*, vol. 1. Cambridge: Cambridge University Press, 74–139.

Calendar of state papers relating to Ireland (1860–1912). London: Longman, Green, Longman, and Roberts.

Callahan, Joseph (1994). 'The Irish language in Pennsylvania'. In Thomas W. Ihde (ed.). *The Irish language in the United States: a historical, sociolinguistic, and applied linguistic survey*. Westport, CT: Bergin and Garvey, 18–26.

Campion, Edmund (1970 [1571]). *A historie of Ireland written in the yeare 1571*. Port Washington, NY and London: Kennikat Press.

Carleton, William (1990 [1830]). *Traits and stories of the Irish peasantry*. Gerrards Cross: Colin Smythe.

Carney, James (1950). 'A tract on the O'Rourkes'. *Celtica* 1: 238–79.

Catholic Miscellany (1828). 'Review of Anderson's *Historical sketches*', 203–12.

Chambers, J. K. (2003). *Sociolinguistic theory*. Oxford: Blackwell.

Clyne, Michael (1997). 'Multilingualism'. In Florian Coulmas (ed.). *The handbook of sociolinguistics*. Oxford: Blackwell, 301–14.

Comyn, David and Patrick S. Dinneen (eds.) (1902–14). *Foras feasa ar Éirinn* [History of Ireland]. London: Irish Texts Society.

Conellan, Thaddeus (1815). *An Irish English primer, intended for the use of schools; containing about four thousand Irish monosyllables with their explanation in English: together with a few of Aesop's Fables in Irish and in English, by T. Conellan*. Dublin: Graisberry and Campbell.

Connradh na Gaedhilge (1906). *Tuarasgabháil na bliadhna, 1904–5* [Yearly report, 1904–5]. Baile Átha Cliath: Connradh na Gaedhilge.

Corkery, Daniel (1924). *The hidden Ireland*. Dublin: Gill and MacMillan.

Craig, J. P. (1899). *Modern Irish grammar*. Dublin: Sealy, Bryan and Walker.

Croker, Thomas Crofton (1998 [1825]). *Fairy legends and traditions of the south of Ireland*. Cork: Collins Press.

Cronin, Michael (1996). *Translating Ireland*. Cork: Cork University Press.

Cronin, Michael (2005). *Irish in the new century*. Dublin: Cois Life.

Cronin, Seán (1980). *Irish nationalism: a history of its roots and ideology*. Dublin: Academy Press.

Crowley, John *et al.* (eds.) (2012). *Atlas of the Great Irish Famine.* Cork: Cork University Press.

Crowley, Tony (2000). *The politics of language in Ireland, 1366–1922.* London/New York: Routledge.

Crystal, David (2008). *A dictionary of linguistics and phonetics.* Oxford: Wiley Blackwell.

Cullen, Louis (1969). 'The hidden Ireland: the re-assessment of a concept'. *Studia Hibernica* 9: 7–48.

Cullen, Louis (1990). 'Patrons, teachers and literacy in Irish: 1700–1850'. In Mary Daly and David Dickson (eds.). *The origins of popular literacy in Ireland: changes and educational development 1700–1920.* Dublin: Department of Modern History, T.C. D, Department of Modern History, U.C.D., 15–44.

Cunningham, Bernadette (2000). *The world of Geoffrey Keating.* Dublin: Four Courts.

Cunningham, Bernadette and Raymond Gillespie (2012). 'Cultural frontiers and the circulation of manuscripts in Ireland, 1625–1725'. In James Kelly and Ciarán Mac Murchaidh (eds.). *Irish and English: essays on the Irish linguistic and cultural frontier, 1600–1900.* Dublin: Four Courts, 58–95.

Curtis, Edmund and R. B. McDowell (eds.) (1943). *Irish historical documents 1172–1922.* London: Methuen.

Daly, Dominic (1974). *The young Douglas Hyde.* Dublin: Irish University Press.

Daunt, William J. Neill (1848). *Personal recollections of the late Daniel O'Connell, M.P.* London: Chapman and Hall.

Davis, Herbert and Louis Landa (eds.) (1964). *The prose writings of Jonathan Swift,* vol. 4. Oxford: Blackwell.

Davis, Thomas (undated). 'Our national language'. In *Thomas Davis: selections from his prose and poetry.* Dublin: The Talbot Press, 172–9.

Denvir, Gearóid (1978). *Aistí Phádraic Uí Chonaire* [The essays of Pádraic Ó Conaire]. Gaillimh: Cló Chois Fharraige.

Denvir, Gearóid (1997). 'Decolonizing the mind: language and literature in Ireland'. *New Hibernian Review* 1: 44–68.

Denvir, Gearóid (2006). 'Literature in Irish, 1800–1890: from the Act of Union to the Gaelic League'. In Margaret Kelleher and Philip O'Leary (eds.). *The Cambridge history of Irish literature,* vol. 1. Cambridge: Cambridge University Press, 544–98.

Dinneen, Patrick (1903). *Saoghal i nÉirinn* [Life in Ireland]. Baile Átha Cliath: M. H.Gill.

Dinneen, Patrick (1904). *Irish–English dictionary.* Dublin: Irish Texts Society.

Dinneen, Patrick (1905). *Muintir Chiarraidhe roimh an Droch-shaoghal* [The people of Ireland before the Famine]. Baile Átha Cliath: M. H. Gill.

Dinneen, Patrick and Tadhg O'Donoghue (1911). *Dánta Aodhagáin Uí Rathaille* [The poems of Aodhagán Ó Rathaille]. London: Irish Texts Society.

Dobrée, Bonamy (1932). *The letters of Philip Dormer Stanhope, 4th Earl of Chesterfield.* London: Eyre and Spottiswoode.

Dolley, Michael (1972). *Anglo-Norman Ireland, c.1100–1318.* Dublin: Gill and MacMillan.

Donlevy, Andrew (1742). *The catechism or Christian doctrine, by way of question and answer.* Paris: James Guerin.

Doyle, Aidan (1996). 'Nominal borrowings and word-formation in Irish'. In Henryk Kardela and Bogdan Szymanek (eds.). *A festschrift for Edmund Gussmann.* Lublin: Wydawnictwo KUL, 99–113.

Dunleavy, Gareth W. (1974). *Douglas Hyde*. Lewisburg: Bucknell University Press.

Dunleavy, Janet Egleson and Gareth W. Dunleavy (1991). *Douglas Hyde*. Berkeley: University of California Press.

Durkacz, Victor Edward (1983). *The decline of the Celtic languages*. Edinburgh: John Donald Publishers.

Edgeworth, Maria (1833). *Maith agus dearmad agus Rosanna* [Forgive and forget and Rosanna]. Belfast and Dublin: Ulster Gaelic Society.

Fanning, Bryan (2013). 'Patrick Pearse predicts the future'. *Dublin Review of Books* 35. http://www.drb.ie/essays/patrick-pearse-predicts-the-future

Fenning, Hugh (ed.) (1965). 'The journey of James Lyons from Rome to Sligo, 1763–1765'. *Collectanea Hibernica* 11: 91–110.

Fishman, Joshua A. (1967). 'Bilingualism with and without diglossia; diglossia with and without bilingualism'. *Journal of social issues* XXIII, 2: 29–37.

Fishman, Joshua A. (1972). *Language in sociocultural change*. Stanford: Stanford University Press.

Fitzgerald, Garret (1984). 'Estimates for baronies of minimum level of Irish-speaking amongst successive decennial cohorts: 1771–1781 to 1861–1871'. *Proceedings of the Royal Irish Academy* C: 117–55.

Flynn, Donal (2012). *The revival of Irish: failed project of a political elite*. Dublin: Original Writing.

Fréine, Seán de (1965). *The great silence*. Dublin: Foilseacháin Náisiúnta Teoranta.

Fromkin, Victoria *et al.* (2007). *An introduction to language*. Boston: Thomson Wadsworth.

Gaeilge website. http://www.gaeilge.org/irish.html

Gaelic League (1897). *The Oireachtas proceedings 1897*. Dublin: The Gaelic League.

Gallagher, James (1736). *Sixteen Irish sermons in an easy and familiar style, on useful and necessary subjects*. Dublin: Henry Babe.

Geoghegan, Patrick M. (2008). *King Dan: the rise of Daniel O'Connell, 1775–1829*. Dublin: Gill and Macmillan.

Goodwin, M. (1837). *An Irish and English spelling-book. For the use of schools, and persons in the Irish parts of the country*. Dublin: M. Goodwin.

Government of Ireland (1926). *Gaeltacht commission: report*. Dublin: Stationery Office.

Greene, David (1966). 'Robert Atkinson and Irish studies'. *Hermathena* CII: 6–15.

Greene, David (1969). 'Irish as a vernacular before the Norman invasion'. In Brian Ó Cuív (ed.). *A view of the Irish language*. Dublin: The Stationery Office, 11–21.

Greene, David (1972). 'The founding of the Gaelic League'. In Seán Ó Tuama (ed.). *The Gaelic League idea*. Cork: The Mercier Press, 9–19.

Hardiman, James (1971 [1831]). *Irish minstrelsy, or Bardic remains of Ireland*. Shannon: Irish University Press.

Harris, Jason and Keith Sidwell (eds.) (2009). *Making Ireland Roman*. Cork: Cork University Press.

Harrison, Alan (1999). *The Dean's friend. Anthony Raymond 1675–1726, Jonathan Swift and the Irish language*. Dublin: Caisleán an Bhúrcaigh.

Hickey, Raymond (2007). *Irish English*. Cambridge: Cambridge University Press.

híde, Dubhghlas de (1937). *Mise agus an Connradh* [Myself and the League]. Baile Átha Cliath: Oifig an tSoláthair.

Hindley, Reg (1990). *The death of the Irish language: a qualified obituary*. London/New York: Routledge.

Holmer, Nils (1942). *The Irish language in Rathlin Island, Co. Antrim*. Dublin: Hodges and Figgis.

Hutchinson, John (1987). *The dynamics of cultural nationalism: the Gaelic Revival and the creation of the Irish nation state*. London: Allen and Unwin.

Hyde, Douglas (1889). *Leabhar sgéulaigheachta* [A book of story-telling]. Baile Átha Cliath: Gill.

Hyde, Douglas (1971 [1893]). *Love songs of Connacht*. Shannon: Irish Academic Press.

Hyde, Douglas (1986a [1885]). 'The unpublished songs of Ireland'. In Breandán Ó Conaire (ed.). *Language, lore and lyrics*. Dublin: Irish Academic Press, 66–73.

Hyde, Douglas (1986b [1886]). 'A plea for the Irish language'. In Breandán Ó Conaire (ed.). *Language, lore and lyrics*. Dublin: Irish Academic Press, 74–80.

Hyde, Douglas (1986c [1888]). 'Some words about unpublished literature (1986)'. In Breandán Ó Conaire (ed.). *Language, lore and lyrics*. Dublin: Irish Academic Press, 81–92.

Hyde, Douglas (1986d [1889]). 'Irish folk-lore'. In Breandán Ó Conaire (ed.). *Language, lore and lyrics*. Dublin: Irish Academic Press, 93–103.

Hyde, Douglas (1986e [1894]). 'The necessity for de-Anglicising Ireland'. In Breandán Ó Conaire (ed.). *Language, lore and lyrics*. Dublin: Irish Academic Press, 153–70.

Ihde, Thomas W. (ed.) (1994). *The Irish language in the United States: a historical, sociolinguistic, and applied linguistic survey*. Westport, CT: Bergin and Garvey.

Jackson, Donald (1973). 'The Irish language and Tudor government', *Éire-Ireland* 8: 21–8.

Jackson, Kenneth (1990). *Aisling Meic Con Glinne* [The vision of Mac Con Glinne]. Dublin: Dublin Institute for Advanced Studies.

Jennings, Brendan (2008). *Mícheál Ó Cléirigh, his associates, and St Anthony's College, Louvain*. Dublin: Four Courts Press.

Johnston, Edith Mary (1974). *Ireland in the eighteenth century*. Dublin: Gill and MacMillan.

Joyce, P. W. (1882). *Ancient Irish Music: Comprising one hundred airs hitherto unpublished, many of the old popular songs, and several new songs*. Dublin: M.H. Gill.

Kallen, Jeffrey (1994). 'Irish as an American ethnic language'. In Thomas W. Ihde (ed.). *The Irish language in the United States: a historical, sociolinguistic, and applied linguistic survey*. Westport, CT: Bergin and Garvey, 27–40.

Kavanagh, Stanislaus (1932). *Commentarius Rinuccinianus* [Rinuccini commentary]. Dublin: Irish Maunscripts Commission.

Kelleher, Margaret and Philip O'Leary (eds.) (2006a). *The Cambridge history of Irish literature*, vol. 1. Cambridge: Cambridge University Press.

Kelleher, Margaret and Philip O'Leary (eds.) (2006b). *The Cambridge history of Irish literature*, vol. 2. Cambridge: Cambridge University Press.

Kelly, Adrian (2002). *Compulsory Irish: language and education in Ireland 1870s–1970s*. Dublin: Irish Academic Press.

Kelly, James (2012). 'Irish Protestants and the Irish language'. In James Kelly and Ciarán Mac Murchaidh (eds.). *Irish and English: essays on the Irish linguistic and cultural frontier, 1600–1900*. Dublin: Four Courts, 189–217.

Kelly, James and Ciarán Mac Murchaidh (2012a). 'Introduction'. In James Kelly and Ciarán Mac Murchaidh (eds.). *Irish and English: essays on the Irish linguistic and cultural frontier, 1600–1900*. Dublin: Four Courts, 15–42.

Kelly, James and Ciarán Mac Murchaidh (eds.) (2012b). *Irish and English: essays on the Irish linguistic and cultural frontier, 1600–1900*. Dublin: Four Courts.

Kew, Graham (ed.) (1998). *The Irish sections of Fynes Moryson's unpublished itinerary*. Dublin: Irish Manuscripts Commission.

Kirk, Robert (1690). *Tiomna Nuadh ár dtighearna agus ár slanuigheora Josa Criosd, ar na tharruing go fírinneach as Greigis go Gaoidheilg* [The New Testament of our lord and saviour Jesus Christ, translated faithfully from Greek to Gaelic]. London: R. Ebheringtham.

Knott, Eleanor (1957). *An introduction to Irish syllabic poetry of the period 1200–1600*. Dublin: Dublin Institute for Advanced Studies.

Lane, Thomas O'Neill (1904). *English–Irish dictionary*. Dublin: Sealy, Bryars, and Walker.

Lee, Joseph (1973). *The modernisation of Irish society, 1848–1918*. Dublin: Gill and Macmillan.

Leersen, Joep (1996a). *Mere Irish and fíor-Ghael*. Cork: Cork University Press.

Leersen, Joep (1996b). *Remembrance and imagination: patterns in the historical and literary representation of Ireland in the nineteenth century*. Cork: Cork University Press.

Lenoach, Ciarán (2012). 'An Ghaeilge iarthraidisiúnta agus a dioscúrsa [Post-traditional Irish and its discourse]'. In Ciarán Lenoach *et al.* (eds.). *An chonair chaoch* [The blind path]. Gaillimh: Leabhar Breac, 19–109.

Lenoach, Ciarán *et al.* (eds.) (2012). *An chonair chaoch* [The blind path]. Gaillimh: Leabhar Breac.

Mac Aogáin, Parthalán (1968). *Graiméir Ghaeilge na mBráthar Mionúr*. [The Irish Grammars of the Brothers Minor]. Dublin: Dublin Institute of Advanced Studies.

Mac Aonghusa, Proinsias (1993). *Ar son na Gaeilge* [For the sake of Irish]. Baile Átha Cliath: Conradh na Gaeilge.

Mac Cionnaith, Láimhbheartach (1938). *Díoghluim dána* [Collection of poems]. Baile Átha Cliath: Oifig an tSoláthair.

Mac Cóil, Liam (2008). 'Stíl na nIarlaí [The style of the Earls]'. In Tracey Ní Mhaonaigh and Tadhg Ó Dúshláine (eds.). *Éire agus an Eoraip sa 17ú haois* [Ireland and Europe in the seventeenth century]. Maigh Nuad: An Sagart, 172–213.

Mac Craith, Mícheál (2006). 'Literature in Irish, 1550–1690: from the Elizabethan settlement to the Battle of the Boyne'. In Margaret Kelleher and Philip O'Leary (eds.). *The Cambridge history of Irish literature*, vol. 1. Cambridge: Cambridge University Press, 191–231.

Mac Erlean, John (1910). *Duanaire Dháibhidh Uí Bhruadair I* [The poems of David Ó Bruadair I]. London: Irish Texts Society.

Mac Giolla Chríost, Diarmait (2005). *The Irish language in Ireland*. London/New York: Routledge.

Mac Hale, John (1871). *A selection of Moore's melodies*. Dublin: Duffy.

Mac Héil, Seán (1981 [1844]). *Íliad Hóiméar, leabhair I–VIII*. Gaillimh: Officina Typographica.

Mac Mathúna, Liam (2007). *Béarla sa Ghaeilge* [English in Irish]. Baile Átha Cliath: An Clóchomhar.

Mac Mathúna, Liam (2012). 'English and Irish in selected warrants and macaronic verse'. In James Kelly and Ciarán Mac Murchaidh (eds.). *Irish and English: essays on the Irish linguistic and cultural frontier, 1600–1900*. Dublin: Four Courts, 116–40.

Mac Mathúna, Liam *et al.* (eds.) (2000). *Teanga, pobal agus réigiún: aistí ar chultúr na Gaeltachta inniu* [Language, community and region: essays on the culture of the Gaeltacht today]. Baile Átha Cliath: Coiscéim.

Mac Murchaidh, Ciarán (2008). 'Current attitudes to Irish'. In Caoilfhionn Nic Pháidín and Seán Ó Cearnaigh (eds.). *A new view of the Irish language*. Dublin: Cois Life, 212–23.

Mac Murchaidh, Ciarán (2012). 'The Catholic church and the Irish language'. In James Kelly and Ciarán Mac Murchaidh (eds.). *Irish and English: essays on the Irish linguistic and cultural frontier, 1600–1900*. Dublin: Four Courts, 162–88.

MacCurtain, Margaret (1972). *Tudor and Stuart Ireland*. Dublin: Gill and MacMillan.

MacDonagh, Oliver (1988). *The hereditary bondsman: Daniel O'Connell 1775–1829*. London: Weidenfeld and Nicholson.

Markievicz, Constance (1922). 'Registration of births, deaths, and marriages'. http://historical-debates.oireachtas.ie/D/DT/D.S.192203010007.html

Marstrander, Carl J. S. (1915). *Bidrag til norske sprogs historie i Irland*. Kristiania: J. Dybwad.

Mathews, P. J. (2003). *Revival*. Cork: Cork University Press.

McCaughey, Terence (2001). *Dr Bedell and Mr King: the making of the Irish Bible*. Dublin: Dublin Institute for Advanced Studies.

McCloskey, James (2001). *Voices silenced: has Irish a future?* Dublin: Cois Life.

McCone, Kim *et al.* (eds.) (1994). *Stair na Gaeilge* [The history of Irish]. Maigh Nuad: Coláiste Phádraig.

McGowan, Lynn (1994). 'The Irish language in America'. In Thomas W. Ihde (ed.). *The Irish language in the United States: a historical, sociolinguistic, and applied linguistic survey*. Westport, CT: Bergin and Garvey, 1–8.

McKenna, Lambert (1944). *Bardic syntactical tracts*. Dublin: Dublin Institute for Advanced Studies.

McLaughlin, Gráinne (2009). 'Latin invective verse in the Commentarius Rinuccinianus'. In Jason Harris and Keith Sidwell (eds.). *Making Ireland Roman*. Cork: Cork University Press, 154–69.

McLeod, Wilson (1999). 'Galldachd, Gàidhealtachd, Garbhchrìochan [Galldachd, Gàidhealtachd, Highlands]'. *Scottish Gaelic Studies* 19: 1–20.

McManus, Damian (1994a). 'An Nua-Ghaeilge Chlasaiceach [Classical Modern Irish]'. In Kim McCone *et al.* (eds.). *Stair na Gaeilge* [The history of Irish]. Maigh Nuad: Coláiste Phádraig, 335–445.

McManus, Damian (1994b). 'Teanga an dána agus teanga an phróis [The language of poetry and the language of prose]'. In Pádraig Ó Fiannachta (ed.). *An dán díreach* [Bardic poetry]. Maigh Nuad: An Sagart, 114–35.

McManus, Damian (1996). 'Classical Modern Irish'. In Kim McCone and Katharine Sims (eds.). *Progress in medieval Irish studies*. Maynooth: St Patrick's College, 165–87.

Meyer, Kuno (1886). *Merugud Uilix maicc Leirtis: the Irish Odyssey* [The wanderings of Ulysses son of Laertes: the Irish Odyssey]. London: David Nutt.

Miller, Arthur W.-K. (1879–80). 'O'Clery's Irish glossary'. *Revue Celtique* 4: 349–428.

Miller, Arthur W.-K. (1881–83). 'O'Clery's Irish glossary'. *Revue Celtique* 5: 1–69.

Millett, Benignus (1976). 'Irish literature in Latin, 1550–1700'. In T. W. Moody *et al.* (eds.). *A new history of Ireland*, vol. III. Oxford: Clarendon Press, 561–86.

Moffitt, Miriam (2008). *Soupers and Jumpers*. Dublin: Nonsuch Publishing.

Montague, John (1995). *Collected poems*. Dublin: Gallery Press.

Moody, T. W. *et al.* (eds.) (1976). *A new history of Ireland*, vol. III. Oxford: Clarendon Press.

Mooney, Canice (1944). 'The beginnings of the Irish language revival'. *Irish Ecclesiastical Record* 64: 10–18.

Morley, Vincent (2011). *Ó Chéitinn go Raiftearaí: mar a cumadh stair na hÉireann* [From Keating to Raftery: how the history of Ireland was composed]. Baile Átha Cliath: Coiscéim.

Mugglestone, Lynda (ed.) (2006). *The Oxford history of English*. Oxford: Oxford University Press.

Murphy, Denis (ed.) (1993 [1896]). *The Annals of Clonmacnoise . . . translated into English, AD 1627*. Llanerch: Felinfarch.

Murphy, John A. (1975). *Ireland in the twentieth century*. Dublin: Gill and Macmillan.

Murphy, John A. (1984). 'O'Connell and the Gaelic world'. In Kevin B. Nolan and Maurice R. O'Connell (eds.). *Daniel O'Connell: portrait of a radical*. Belfast: Appletree Press, 32–52.

Murray, Damien (2000). *Romanticism, nationalism and Irish antiquarian societies, 1840–80*. Maynooth: Department of Old and Middle Irish, NUI Maynooth.

Nash, Catherine (1993). '"Embodying the nation": the west of Ireland landscape and Irish identity'. In Barbara O'Connor and Michael Cronin (eds.) *Tourism in Ireland: a critical analysis*. Cork: Cork University Press, 86–114.

Neilson, William (1990 [1808]). *An introduction to the Irish language*. Belfast: Ultach Trust.

Ní Chinnéide, Síle (1954). 'Dhá leabhar nótaí [Two notebooks]'. *Galvia* 1: 32–41.

Ní Chinnéide, Síle (1957). 'Dialann Í Chonchúir [O'Conor's diary]'. *Galvia* 4: 4–17.

Ní Chollatáin, Regina (2004). *An Claidheamh Soluis agus Fáinne an Lae 1899–1932* [The Claidheamh Soluis and Fáinne an Lae 1899–1932]. Baile Átha Cliath: Cois Life.

Ní Dhomhnaill, Cáit (1975). *Duanaireacht* [Bardic poetry]. Baile Átha Cliath: Oifig an tSoláthair.

Ní Mhaonaigh, Máire (2006). 'The literature of medieval Ireland, 800–1200: from the Vikings to the Normans'. In Margaret Kelleher and Philip O'Leary (eds.). *The Cambridge history of Irish literature*, vol. 1. Cambridge: Cambridge University Press, 32–73.

Ní Mhóráin, Brighid (1997). *Thiar sa Mhainistir atá an Ghaoluinn bhreá: meath na Gaeilge in Uíbh Rathach* [Over in Mainistir they speak lovely Irish: the decline of Irish in Ivereagh]. An Daingean: An Sagart.

Ní Mhunghaile, Lesa (2009). *Charlotte Brooke's Reliques of Irish poetry*. Dublin: Irish Manuscripts Commission.

Ní Mhunghaile, Lesa (2012). 'Bilingualism, print culture in Irish and the public sphere'. In James Kelly and Ciarán Mac Murchaidh (eds.). *Irish and English: essays on the Irish linguistic and cultural frontier, 1600–1900*. Dublin: Four Courts, 218–42.

Ní Shúilleabháin, Máire (1985). *Amhráin Thomáis Rua Uí Shúilleabháin* [The songs of Tomás Rua Ó Súilleabháin]. Má Nuad: An Sagart.

Ní Uallacháin, Pádraigín (2005). *A hidden Ulster: people, songs and traditions of Oriel*. Dublin: Four Courts Press.

Ní Urdail, Meidhbhín (2000). *The scribe in eighteenth and nineteenth-century Ireland*. Münster: Nodus.

Nic Craith, Máiréad (1993). *Malartú teanga: an Ghaeilge i gCorcaigh sa naoú haois déag* [Changing language: Irish in Cork in the nineteenth century]. Bremen: Cumann Eorpach Léann na hÉireann.

Nic Craith, Máiréad (2012). 'Legacy and loss; the Great Silence and its aftermath'. In John Crowley *et al.* (eds.). *Atlas of the Great Irish Famine*. Cork: Cork University Press, 580–8.

Nic Dhiarmada, Máirín (2006). 'Afterword: Irish-language literature in the new millennium'. In Margaret Kelleher and Philip O'Leary (eds.). *The Cambridge history of Irish literature*, vol. 2. Cambridge: Cambridge University Press, 600–27.

Nic Eoin, Máirín (2006). 'Contemporary prose and drama in Irish: 1940–2000'. In Margaret Kelleher and Philip O'Leary (eds.). *The Cambridge history of Irish literature*, vol. 2. Cambridge: Cambridge University Press, 270–316.

Nic Eoin, Máirín (2012). 'An dírbheathaisnéis gluaiseachta [The language-movement autobiography]'. In Eoghan Mac Cárthaigh and Jürgen Uhlich (eds.). *Féilscríbhinn do Chathal Ó Háinle* [A festschrift for Cathal Ó Háinle]. Gaillimh: An Clóchomhar, 523–53.

Nic Pháidín, Caoilfhionn (1998). *Fáinne an Lae agus an Athbheochan (1898–1900)* [Fáinne an Lae and the Revival (1898–1900)]. Baile Átha Cliath: Cois Life.

Nic Pháidín, Caoilfhionn and Seán Ó Cearnaigh (eds.) (2008). *A new view of the Irish language*. Dublin: Cois Life.

Nowlan, Kevin B. (1972). 'The Gaelic league and other national movements'. In Seán Ó Tuama (ed.). *The Gaelic League idea*. Cork: The Mercier Press, 41–51.

Ó Buachalla, Breandán (1968). *I mBéal Feirste cois cuain* [In Belfast by the sea]. Baile Átha Cliath: An Clóchomhar.

Ó Buachalla, Breandán (1979). 'Ó Corcora agus an Hidden Ireland'. *Scríobh* 4: 109–37.

Ó Buachalla, Breandán (1983). 'Na Stíobhartaigh agus an t-aos léinn: Cing Séamas [The Stuarts and the learned class: King James]'. *Proceedings of the Royal Irish Academy* C: 81–134.

Ó Buachalla, Breandán (1996). *Aisling ghéar* [A sharp vision]. Baile Átha Cliath: An Clóchomhar.

Ó Buachalla, Séamas (1979). *Na scríbhinní liteartha le Pádraig Mac Piarais* [The literary writings of Patrick Pearse]. Baile Átha Cliath agus Corcaigh: Cló Mercier.

Ó Buachalla, Breandán (1980). *A significant Irish educationalist: the educational writings of P. H. Pearse*. Dublin and Cork: Mercier Press.

Ó Catháin, Seán (1933). 'Some studies in the development from Middle to Modern Irish, based on the Annals of Ulster'. *Zeitschrift für Celtische Philologie* 19: 1–47.

Ó Ceallaigh, Seán T. (1963). *Seán T.: scéal a bheatha á insint ag Seán T. Ó Ceallaigh* [Seán T.: the story of his life as told by Seán T. Ó Ceallaigh]. Baile Átha Cliath: Foilseacháin Náisiúnta Teoranta.

Ó Ciardha, Éamonn (2002). *Ireland and the Jacobite cause, 1685–1766*. Dublin: Four Courts Press.

Ó Ciosáin, Éamon (1991). *Buried alive: a reply to Reg Hindley's 'The death of the Irish language'*. Dublin: Dáil Uí Chadhain.

Ó Ciosáin, Niall (1997). *Print and popular culture in Ireland, 1750–1850*. Dublin: Lilliput Press.

Ó Ciosáin, Niall (2005). 'Gaelic culture and language shift'. In Laurence M. Geary and Margaret Kelleher (eds.). *Nineteenth-century Ireland: a guide to recent research*. Dublin: University College Dublin Press, 136–52.

Ó Ciosáin, Niall (2012). 'Pious miscellanies and spiritual songs: devotional publishing and reading in Irish and Scottish Gaelic, 1760–1900'. In James Kelly and Ciarán Mac Murchaidh (eds.). *Irish and English: essays on the Irish linguistic and cultural frontier, 1600–1900*. Dublin: Four Courts, 267–82.

Ó Coileáin, Seán (2002). *An t-oileánach* [The islandman]. Baile Átha Cliath: Cló Talbóid.

Ó Conaire, Breandán (ed.) (1986). *Language, lore and lyrics*. Dublin: Irish Academic Press.

Ó Conaire, Pádraic (1977). *Scothscéalta*. Baile Átha Cliath. Sáirseal agus Dill.

Ó Conchubhair, Brian (2009). *Fin de siècle na Gaeilge: Darwin, an Athbheochan agus smaointeoireacht na hEorpa* [The *fin de siècle* of Irish: Darwin, the Revival and European thinking]. Gaillimh: An Clóchomhar.

Ó Conchúir, Breandán (1982). *Scríobhaithe Chorcaí* [The scribes of Cork]. Baile Átha Cliath: An Clóchomhar.

Ó Cuív, Brian (1951). *Irish dialects and Irish-speaking districts*. Dublin: Dublin Institute for Advanced Studies.

Ó Cuív, Brian (1969). 'The changing form of the Irish language'. In Brian Ó Cuív (ed.). *A view of the Irish language*. Dublin: The Stationery Office.

Ó Cuív, Brian (1973). 'The linguistic training of the medieval Irish poet'. *Celtica* 10: 114–40.

Ó Cuív, Brian (1975). *The impact of the Scandinavian invasions on the Celtic-speaking peoples c.800–1100 AD*. Baile Átha Cliath: Institiúid Ard-léinn Bhaile Átha Cliath.

Ó Cuív, Brian (1976). 'The Irish language in the early modern period'. In T. W. Moody *et al.* (eds.). *A new history of Ireland*, vol. III. Oxford: Clarendon Press, 509–45.

Ó Cuív, Brian (1977). *Párliament na mban* [The parliament of women]. Dublin: Dublin Institute for Advanced Studies.

Ó Cuív, Brian (1986a). 'Irish language and literature, 1691–1845'. In T. W. Moody and William Edward Vaughan (eds.). *A new history of Ireland*, vol. IV. Oxford: Clarendon Press, 374–435.

Ó Cuív, Brian (1986b). *Aspects of Irish personal names*. Dublin: Dublin Institute of Advanced Studies.

Ó Cuív, Brian (1994). *Aibidil Gaoidheilge agus caiticiosma* [Irish alphabet and catechism]. Dublin: Dublin Institute for Advanced Studies.

Ó Cuív, Brian (ed.) (1969). *A view of the Irish language*. Dublin: The Stationery Office.

Ó Curnáin, Brian (2012). 'An Ghaeilge Iarthraidisiúnta agus an phragmataic chódmheasctha thiar agus theas [Post-traditional Irish and the pragmatics of code-switching in the west and south]'. In Ciarán Lenoach *et al.* (eds.). *An chonair chaoch* [The blind path]. Gaillimh: Leabhar Breac, 284–364.

Ó Dochartaigh, Cathaoir (1976). 'The Rathlin catechism'. *Zeitschrift für Celtische Philologie* 35: 175–233.

Ó Doibhlin, Breandán (2003). *Manuail de litríocht na Gaeilge* I [Manual of Irish literature I]. Baile Átha Cliath: Coiscéim.

Ó Doibhlin, Breandán (2006). *Manuail de litríocht na Gaeilge* II [Manual of Irish literature II]. Baile Átha Cliath: Coiscéim.

Ó Doibhlin, Breandán (2007). *Manuail de litríocht na Gaeilge* III [Manual of Irish literature III]. Baile Átha Cliath: Coiscéim.

Ó Doibhlin, Breandán (2008). *Manuail de litríocht na Gaeilge* IV [Manual of Irish literature IV]. Baile Átha Cliath: Coiscéim.

Ó Doibhlin, Breandán (2009). *Manuail de litríocht na Gaeilge* V [Manual of Irish literature V]. Baile Átha Cliath: Coiscéim.

Ó Doibhlin, Breandán (2011). *Manuail de litríocht na Gaeilge* VI [Manual of Irish literature VI]. Baile Átha Cliath: Coiscéim.

Ó Domhnuill, Uilliam (1602). *Tiomna Nuadh* [New Testament]. Dublin: Seón Francke.

Ó Domhnuill, Uilliam (1608). *Leabhar na nUrnaightheadh gComhchoidchiond* [Book of Common Prayer]. Dublin: Seón Francke.

Ó Dónaill, Niall (1977). *Foclóir Gaeilge-Béarla.* [Irish–English dictionary]. Baile Átha Cliath: Oifig an tSoláthair.

Ó Duinnshléibhe, Seán (2011). *Párliment na bhfíodóirí* [The parliament of weavers]. Gaillimh: An Clóchomhar.

Ó Dúshláine, Tadhg (1996). 'Gealán dúluachra: seanmóireacht na Gaeilge c.1600–1850 [A bright spell in midwinter: sermons in Irish c.1600–1850]'. In Ruairí Ó hUiginn (ed.). *Léann na Gaeilge: súil siar, súil chun cinn* [The study of Irish: a glance backwards, a glance forwards]. Má Nuad: An Sagart, 83–122.

Ó Fiaich, Tomás (1970). 'Richard Weston agus "Beir mo bheannacht go Dundalk" [Richard Weston and Take my blessing to Dundalk]'. *Seanchas Ard Mhacha* 5: 269–88.

Ó Fiaich, Tomás (1972). 'The great controversy'. In Seán Ó Tuama (ed.). *The Gaelic League idea*. Cork: The Mercier Press, 63–75.

Ó Fiannachta, Pádraig (1978). *An barántas* [The warrant]. Má Nuad: An Sagart.

Ó Gaora, Colm (1943). *Mise* [Myself]. Baile Átha Cliath: Oifig an tSoláthair.

Ó Gráda, Cormac (1994). *An Drochshaol: béaloideas agus amhráin* [The Famine: folklore and songs]. Baile Átha Cliath: Coiscéim.

Ó Gráda, Cormac (2012). 'Cé fada le fán [Though long astray]'—review of Kelly and Mac Murchaidh (2012). *Dublin Review of Books* 23. http://www.drb.ie/essays/cé-fada-le-fán

Ó hAilín, Tomás (1969). 'Irish revival movements'. In Brian Ó Cuív (ed.). *A view of the Irish language*. Dublin: The Stationery Office, 91–100.

Ó hAilín, Tomás (1971). 'Seanchas ar léamh agus scríobh na Gaeilge i gCorca Dhuibhne'. *Journal of the Kerry Archaeological and Historical Society* 4: 127–38.

Ó Háinle, Cathal (1978). 'An t-úrscéal nár tháinig [The novel that never happened]'. In Cathal Ó Háinle (ed.). *Promhadh pinn* [Testing the pen]. Baile Átha Cliath: An Clóchomhar, 74–98.

Ó Háinle, Cathal (1994). 'Ó chaint na ndaoine go dtí an Caighdeán Oifigiúil [From the speech of the people to the Official Standard]'. In Kim McCone *et al.* (eds.). *Stair na Gaeilge* [The history of Irish]. Maigh Nuad: Coláiste Phádraig, 745–93.

Ó hAnnracháin, Peadar (1937). *Mar chonnac-sa Éire* [As I saw Ireland]. Baile Átha Cliath: Oifig an tSoláthair.

Ó hAnnracháin, Stiofán (1979). *Go Meiriceá siar* [West to America]. Baile Átha Cliath: An Clóchomhar.

Ó hIfearnáin, Tadhg and Máire Ní Neachtain (eds.) (2012). *An tsochtheangeolaíocht: feidhm agus tuairisc* [Sociolinguistics: function and description]. Baile Átha Cliath: Cois Life.

Ó Huallacháin, Colmán (1994). *The Irish and Irish*. Dublin: Assisi Press.

Ó hUiginn, Ruairí (2008). 'The Irish language'. In Caoilfhionn Nic Pháidín and Seán Ó Cearnaigh (eds.). *A new view of the Irish language*. Dublin: Cois Life, 1–10.

Ó Laoghaire, Peadar (1920). *Séadna*. Baile Átha Cliath: Brún agus Ó Nualláin.

Ó Lochlainn, Colm (1939). *Tobar fíorghlan Gaedhilge* [The truly pure well of Irish]. Baile Átha Cliath: Faoi chomhartha na dtrí gcoinneal.

Ó Madagáin, Breandán (1974). *Teagasc ar an Sean-Tiomna.* [Teachings on the Old Testament]. Baile Átha Cliath: An Clóchomhar.

Ó Maonaigh, Cainneach (1944). *Smaointe beatha Chríost* [Meditations on the life of Christ]. Dublin: Dublin Institute for Advanced Studies.

Ó Maonaigh, Cainneach (1952). *Scathán shacramuinte na haithridhe* [Reflection of the sacrament of penance]. Dublin: Dublin Institute for Advanced Studies.

Ó Muirithe, Diarmuid (1980). *An t-amhrán macarónach* [The macaronic song]. Baile Átha Cliath: An Clóchomhar.

Ó Murchú, Máirtín (1977). 'Successes and failures in the modernization of Irish spelling'. In Joshua A. Fishman (ed.). *Advances in the creation and revision of writing systems*. The Hague: Mouton, 267–89.

Ó Murchú, Máirtín (1985). *The Irish language*. Dublin: Department of Foreign Affairs/ Bord na Gaeilge.

Ó Murchú, Máirtín (1998). 'Language and society in nineteenth-century Ireland'. In Geraint Jenkins (ed.). *Language and community in the nineteenth century*. Cardiff: University of Wales Press, 341–68.

Ó Murchú, Máirtín (2001). *Cumann Buan-Choimeádta na Gaeilge* [The Society for the preservation of the Irish language]. Baile Átha Cliath: Cois Life.

Ó Ríordáin, Seán (2011). *Na dánta* [Collected poems]. Gaillimh: Cló Iar-Chonnachta.

Ó Siadhail, Mícheál (1989). *Modern Irish*. Cambridge: Cambridge University Press.

Ó Súilleabháin, Donncha (1998). *Athbheochan na Gaeilge* [The revival of Irish]. Baile Átha Cliath: Conradh na Gaeilge.

Ó Torna, Caitríona (2005). *Cruthú na Gaeltachta 1893–1922* [The creation of the Gaeltacht, 1893–1922]. Baile Átha Cliath: Cois Life.

Ó Tuama, Seán (ed.) (1972). *The Gaelic League idea*. Cork: The Mercier Press.

Ó Tuathaigh, Gearóid (1972). *Ireland before the Famine, 1798–1848*. Dublin: Gill and MacMillan.

Ó Tuathaigh, Gearóid (1974). 'Gaelic Ireland, popular politics and Daniel O'Connell'. *Journal of the Galway Archaeological and Historical Society* 34: 21–34.

Ó Tuathaigh, Gearóid (1986). 'An chléir Chaitliceach, an léann dúchais agus an cultúr in Éirinn, 1750–1850 [The Catholic clergy, folklore and culture in Ireland, 1750–1850].' In Pádraig Ó Fiannachta (ed.). *Léann na cléire*. Maigh Nuad: An Sagart, 110–39.

Ó Tuathaigh, Gearóid *et al.* (eds.) (2000). *Pobal na Gaeltachta: a scéal agus a dhán* [The Gaeltacht community: its history and future]. Gaillimh: Cló Iar-Chonnachta.

O'Curry, Eugene (1995 [1861]). *Lectures on the manuscript materials of ancient Irish history*. Dublin: Four Courts Press.

O'Donovan, John (1845). *A grammar of the Irish language*. Dublin: Hodges and Smith.

O'Donovan, John (1990 [1854]). *Annala Rioghachta Eireann; Annals of the Kingdom of Ireland by the Four Masters*. Dublin: de Búrca Rare Books.

O'Growney, Eugene (1896). *Simple lessons in Irish*. Dublin: M. H.Gill.

O'Leary, Peter (1902). *Irish prose composition*. Dublin: Irish Book Company.

O'Leary, Philip (1994). *The prose literature of the Gaelic Revival, 1881–1921*. Pennsylvania: Pennsylvania State University Press.

O'Leary, Philip (2006). 'The Irish Renaissance, 1890–1940'. In Margaret Kelleher and Philip O'Leary (eds.). *The Cambridge history of Irish literature*, vol. 2. Cambridge: Cambridge University Press, 502–92.

O'Rahilly, Cecile (1952). *Five seventeenth-century political poems*. Dublin: Dublin Institute for Advanced Studies.

O'Rahilly, Thomas (1912). 'Review of Pól Breathnach (ed.). *Gallagher's Sermons*'. *Gadelica* 1: 66–72.

O'Rahilly, Thomas (1932). *Irish dialects past and present*. Dublin: Browne and Nolan.

O'Rahilly, Thomas (1941). *Desiderius*. Dublin: Dublin Institute for Advanced Studies.

O'Rahilly, Thomas (ed.) (undated). *Papers on Irish idiom*. Dublin: Browne and Nolan.

O'Riordan, Michelle (1990). *The Gaelic mind and the collapse of the Gaelic world*. Cork: Cork University Press.

O'Riordan, Michelle (2007). *Irish Bardic poetry and rhetorical reality*. Cork: Cork University Press.

Paor, Louis de (2006). 'Contemporary poetry in Irish: 1940–2000'. In Margaret Kelleher and Philip O'Leary (eds.). *The Cambridge history of Irish literature*, vol. 2. Cambridge: Cambridge University Press, 317–56.

Pearse, Patrick (1898). *Three lectures on Gaelic topics*. Dublin: M. H. Gill.

Pearse, Patrick (1922). *Political writings and speeches*. Dublin: Maunsel and Roberts.

Picard, Jean-Michel (2003). 'The French language in medieval Ireland'. In Michael Cronin and Cormac Ó Cuilleanáin (eds.). *The languages of Ireland*. Dublin: Four Courts Press, 57–77.

Reily, Hugh (1720). *Ireland's case briefly stated; or, a summary account. Of the most remarkable transactions in that Kingdom since the Reformation*. London.

Risk, Henry (1968–71). 'French loan-words in Irish, I–II'. *Études Celtiques* 12: 585–655.

Risk, Henry (1974). 'French loan-words in Irish, III'. *Études Celtiques* 14: 67–98.

Roosevelt, Theodore (1926). *Works*, XXIV. New York: Charles Scribner.

Royal Irish Academy (1983). *Dictionary of the Irish language*. Dublin: Royal Irish Academy.

Royal Irish Academy (2004). *Corpas na Gaeilge* [The Irish language corpus] *1600–1882*. Dublin: Royal Irish Academy.

Russell, Paul (1995). *An introduction to the Celtic languages*. London/New York: Routledge.

Seintiomna [The Old Testament] (1685). London.

Sidwell, Keith and David Edwards (2009). 'The Tipperary hero'. In Jason Harris and Keith Sidwell (eds.). *Making Ireland Roman*. Cork: Cork University Press, 59–85.

Smyth, Thomas. (1858 [1561]). 'Information for Ireland'. *Ulster Journal of Archaeology* 6: 165–7.

Smyth, William J. (2006). *Map-making, landscapes and memory*. Cork: Cork University Press.

Society for the Preservation of the Irish Language (1878). *An chead leabhar Gaedhilge. First Irish book.* Dublin: M. H. Gill.

Spenser, Edmund (1997 [1633]). *A view of the state of Ireland.* Ed. Andrew Hadfield and Willy Maley. Oxford: Blackwell.

Stanihurst, James (1970 [1633]). *Ancient Irish histories: the works of Spencer, Campion, Hammer and Marleburrough in two volumes; Vol. I, containing Spencer's View of the state of Ireland, and Campion's Historie of Ireland.* Port Washington, NY, and London: Kennikat Press.

Stanihurst, Richard (1979 [1577]). 'A treatise containing a plain and perfect description of Ireland'. In Liam Miller and Eileen Power (eds.). *Holinshed's Irish chronicle. The histories of Irelande from the first habitation thereof, unto the yeare 1509. Collected by Raphaell Holinshed, and continued until the yeare 1547 by Richarde Stanyhurst.* Dublin: Dolmen Press.

Stenson, Nancy (1993). 'Variation in phonological assimilation of Irish loanwords'. In Mushira Eid and Gregory K. Iverson (eds.). *Principles and predictions: the analysis of natural language.* Amsterdam: Benjamins, 151–66.

Stenson, Nancy (2003). *An Haicléara Mánas* [Manus the hackler]. Dublin: Dublin Institute for Advanced Studies.

Suleiman, Yasir (2008). 'Egypt'. In Andrew Simpson (ed.). *Language and national identity in Africa.* Oxford: Oxford University Press, 26–43.

Tieken-Boon van Ostade, Ingrid (2006). 'English at the onset of the normative tradition'. In Lynda Mugglestone (ed.). *The Oxford history of English.* Oxford: Oxford University Press, 240–73.

Titley, Alan (2000). 'An náisiúnacht Ghaelach agus náisiúnachas na hÉireann [Gaelic nationality and Irish nationalism]'. In Micheál Ó Cearúil (ed.). *Aimsir Óg II.* Baile Átha Cliath: Coiscéim, 34–49.

Trudgill, Peter (2001). *Sociolinguistics.* London: Penguin Books.

Ua Duinnín, Pádraig (1901). *Amhráin Eoghain Ruaidh Uí Shúilleabháin* [The poems of Eoghan Rua Ó Súilleabháin]. Baile Átha Cliath: Conradh na Gaedhilge.

Ua Laoghaire, Peadar (2011 [1907]). *Séadna.* Baile Átha Cliath: Cois Life.

Uí Ógáin, Ríonach (1985). *An rí gan choróin* [The uncrowned king]. Baile Átha Cliath: An Clóchomhar.

Uí Ógáin, Ríonach (1995). *Immortal Dan: Daniel O'Connell in Irish folk tradition.* Dublin: Geography Publications.

Wall, Maureen (1969). 'The decline of the Irish language'. In Brian Ó Cuív (ed.). *A view of the Irish language.* Dublin: The Stationery Office, 81–90.

Walsh, John (2002). *Díchoimisiúnú teanga* [The decommissioning of a language]. Baile Átha Cliath: Cois Life.

Walsh, John (2011). *Contests and contexts: the Irish language and Ireland's socio-economic development.* Oxford: Peter Lang.

Walsh, Micheline (1962). 'The last years of Hugh O'Neill: Rome, 1608–1616'. *The Irish Sword* 5: 223–35.

Watson, Iarfhlaith (2008). 'The Irish language and identity'. In Caoilfhionn Nic Pháidín and Seán Ó Cearnaigh (eds.). *A new view of the Irish language.* Dublin: Cois Life, 66–75.

Watts, Richard J. (2011). *Language myths and the history of English.* Oxford: Oxford University Press.

Wigger, Arndt (2000). 'Language contact, language awareness, and the history of Hiberno-English'. In Hildegard L. C. Tristram (ed.). *The Celtic Englishes*, vol. II. Heidelberg: Carl Winter, 159–87.

Wilde, W. R. (1979 [1852]). *Irish popular superstitions*. Dublin: Irish Academic Press.

Williams, Kevin (1989). 'Reason and rhetoric in curriculum policy: an appraisal of the case for the inclusion of Irish in the school curriculum'. *Studies* 1989: 191–203.

Williams, J. E. Caerwyn and Máirín Ní Mhuiríosa (1979). *Traidisiún liteartha na nGael* [The Irish literary tradition]. Baile Átha Cliath: An Clóchomhar.

Williams, J. E. Caerwyn and Patrick K. Ford (1992). *The Irish literary tradition*. Cardiff: University of Wales Press.

Williams, Nicholas (1981). *Pairlement Chloinne Tomáis* [The parliament of the Clan Thomas]. Dublin: Dublin Institute for Advanced Studies.

Williams, Nicholas (1986). *I bprionta i leabhar* [In print in a book]. Baile Átha Cliath: An Clóchomhar.

Williams, Nicholas (1994). 'Na canúintí a theacht chun solais [The dialects coming to light]'. In Kim McCone *et al.* (eds.). *Stair na Gaeilge* [The history of Irish]. Maigh Nuad: Coláiste Phádraig, 446–78.

Williams, Nicholas (2010). 'Gaelic texts and English script'. In Marc Caball and Andrew Carpenter (eds.). *Oral and print cultures in Ireland, 1600–1900*. Dublin: Four Courts Press, 85–101.

Zeuss, Johann Kasper (1853). *Grammatic Celtica*. Leipzig: Weidmann.

Name index

Atkinson, Robert 181–3, 218, 220

Barra, Dáibhí de 144–7
Barron, Philip 140
Béaslaí, Piaras 208–9
Bedell, William 73, 120, 121
Bergin, Osborn 26, 49, 56–7, 154, 217–18, 219, 221–2, 228
Bhaldraithe, Tomás de 101, 102, 156, 239, 245, 270
Bismarck, Otto von 118
Blaghd, Earnán de 207
Blythe, Ernest, *see* Blaghd, Earnán de
Boorde, Andrew 52–3
Boyle, Robert 73
Breathnach, Father Pól 250
Breatnach, Liam 55
Breatnach, Pádraig A. 62
Brennan, Martin 132
Brewer, J. S. 45–6
Brooke, Charlotte 89
Brún, Pádraig de 121, 123
Brún, Pádraig de *et al.* 69, 75
Buitléir, Tomás Dubh, *see* Butler, Thomas, 10th Earl of Ormond
Bullen, William 45–6
Búrca, Seán de 103
Butler, Thomas, 10th Earl of Ormond 50, 190
Butt, Isaac 161

Caball, Marc 70, 71
Callahan, Joseph 128
Campion, Edmund 56
Carleton, William 140
Carney, James 195
Céitinn, Seathrún, *see* Keating, Geoffrey
Chambers, J. K. 114
Charles I, King of Great Britain and Ireland 63–4
Charles II, King of Great Britain and Ireland 64
Chesterfield, Lord, *see* Stanhope, Philip
Clare, Richard de 15
Clyne, Michael 127
Comyn, David 73, 169

Conellan, Thaddeus 153
Connolly, James 163
Corkery, Daniel 83, 85, 96, 111
Craig, J. P. 228
Croker, T. Crofton 140
Cromwell, Oliver 63–4
Cromwell, Richard 64
Cronin, Seán 114
Crosbie, Patrick 71
Crowley, Tony 10, 17, 35, 43, 45–6, 53, 56, 88, 110–11, 116, 133, 190
Cullen, Louis 96–7, 143
Cunningham, Bernadette 72–3
Curtis, Edmund 17
Cusack, Michael 163

Daly, Dominic 171, 174–5
Daunt, William J. Neill 110
Davis, Herbert 88
Davis, Thomas 115–17
Davitt, Michael 161
Denvir, Gearóid 137, 210–11
Dinneen, Patrick S. 73, 84–5, 196–7, 218–19, 221, 228, 229
Dobrée, Bonamy 82
Donlevy, Andrew 92
Dunleavy, Gareth W. 172, 208
Dunleavy, Janet Egelson 208

Edgeworth, Maria 139–40
Edward VI, King of England and Ireland 39
Edward VII, King of Great Britain and Ireland 180
Edwards, David 74
Elizabeth I, Queen of England and Ireland 39, 46–7, 50, 62

Fanning, Bryan 263
Fishman, Joshua A. 95, 126, 127
Fitzgerald, Garret 97
Fitzgerald, Gerald Fitzmaurice, 3rd Earl of Desmond 16
Fitzgerald, James Fitzmaurice 39
Foley, Dermot 188, 189
Ford, Patrick K. 128–9

Subject index